R00433 99430

CHICAGO PUBLIC LIBRARY
WOODSON REGIONAL

R0043399430

WOODSON

The
Chicago Public Library

Call No. _cop./_
Branch _Woodson Regional Library Center_

Form 178

Male-Female Comedy Teams in American Vaudeville
1865–1932

Theater and Dramatic Studies, No. 16

Bernard Beckerman, Series Editor
Brander Matthews Professor of Dramatic Literature
Columbia University in the City of New York

Other Titles in This Series

No. 14 *Stanislavski's Encounter with Shakespeare: The Evolution of a Method* Joyce Vining Morgan

No. 15 *The Art of the Actor-Manager: Wilson Barrett and the Victorian Theatre* James Thomas

No. 17 *Distance in the Theatre: The Aesthetics of Audience Response* Daphna Ben Chaim

No. 18 *French Theatre Experiment Since 1968* Lenora Champagne

No. 19 *Evreinov: The Theatre of Paradox and Transformation* Spencer Golub

No. 20 *William Poel's Hamlets: The Director as Critic* Rinda F. Lundstrom

No. 21 *Gertrude Stein's Theatre of the Absolute* Betsy Alayne Ryan

No. 22 *Boulevard Theater and Revolution in Eighteenth-Century Paris* Michèle Root-Bernstein

No. 23 *A Critical Examination of Theatrical Designs of Charles Ricketts* Eric Binnie

Male-Female Comedy Teams in American Vaudeville 1865–1932

by
Shirley Staples

UMI RESEARCH PRESS
Ann Arbor, Michigan

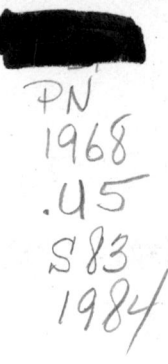

Copyright © 1984, 1981
Shirley Louise Staples
All rights reserved

Produced and distributed by
UMI Research Press
an imprint of
University Microfilms International
Ann Arbor, Michigan 48106

Library of Congress Cataloging in Publication Data

Staples, Shirley.
  Male-female comedy teams in American vaudeville,
1865-1932.

  (Theater and dramatic studies ; no. 16)
  "A revision of the author's thesis, Tufts University,
1981."
  Bibliography: p.
  Includes index.
  1. Vaudeville–United States–History. 2. Comedians–
United States. I. Title. II. Series.

PN1968.U5S83 1984   792.7'0973   83-24253
ISBN 0-8357-1520-5

To my parents

Contents

Introduction *1*

1 The Background in Europe and America *7*

2 The Earliest Male-Female Teams, 1865–1876 *17*

3 Male-Female Teams in the Family Variety Hall, 1876–1893 *39*

4 Male-Female Sketch Teams and Polite Vaudeville, 1893–1905 *75*

5 Male-Female Teams on the Big Time, 1905–1912 *117*

6 The Standard Male-Female Teams, 1912–1925 *157*

7 Male-Female Teams and the Decline of Vaudeville, 1925–1932 *189*

8 George Burns and Gracie Allen *205*

Conclusion *237*

Notes *249*

Bibliography *311*

Introduction

Emma and Mickey Shannon were a male-female team in vaudeville—not in real life, but in a 1927 play, *The Shannons of Broadway*. In Act One, Emma and Mickey argue about how they should redo their act. She wants a new plush drop, while he wants just an aniline drop. "You gotta carry a stage hand to set up a plush drop!" complains Mickey.

    Emma: Well, suppose you do. Don't that add class to the act? Ought to have a piano-player, too. That's what adds the real class.
    Mickey: Yeah, and a musical director and six chorus gals, and a maid for you and a valet for me, and a secretary for us both, and a dog leader for the blight [Emma's pooch] there—ah—!
    Emma: Now, you listen to me, Mickey Shannon! Will you ever get it through that thick Irish head of yours that class is everything? Class is what counts for more than anything in all this world. Now, you can kid yourself that we've made good with our old act and saved money and all, but you can't tell me that if we didn't class up our new one we couldn't get as much as the big ones and more—'cause we got the material.[1]

The conversation of this fictional team reveals an important trend, not only in the entertainment offered by male-female teams, but in all of vaudeville. From a rowdy saloon entertainment for all-male audiences, vaudeville eventually became a respectable, middle-class amusement with pretensions to glamour and sophistication, and a nationwide business enterprise. There were few male-female comedy teams in the earliest variety shows, but they flourished along with vaudeville, and many male-female teams attained star status in the competitive, carefully engineered shows known as "big-time" vaudeville—an entertainment defined by the credo that "class is everything."

Many male-female teams who got their start on the Bowery lived to perform in the fabled Palace, thus in their own lifetimes seeing vaudeville transformed by the standards espoused by Emma Shannon. Charles Ross, for example, of the successful team Ross and Fenton, began his career in the eighties at Miner's Bowery Theatre. He drifted westward, and his description of an engagement in Deadwood, Dakota, reveals something about the variety entertainment of the early days. The theatre was "just an annex to a dance hall and gambling hall," recalled Charles Ross, and in the haphazardly mounted shows, a single performer was called on for many different stage stunts:

> I used to figure in the black-face first part, do a specialty, joining in a rough and tumble song and dance with three or four others, play a part in a new play every night, do German, Irish, Italian, negro and other dialects, give a monologue, appear in the afterpiece in three or four different characters and then do odd things to chink in....[2]

The show continued late into the night, and then the miners and the girls would dance until morning.[3]

It was while playing here that Ross met "the prettiest girl I had ever seen. Tall, slender, a perfect blonde. I fell in love with her at first sight." Her stage name was Mabel Fenton. She burst into tears when she saw the Deadwood theatre; she had been lured there on the pretense that it was a legitimate theatre and that she would play dramatic leads. Ross arranged for the dismayed girl to leave on the next stage out, and conducted a rapid courtship in the intervening days. After Ross pummelled the manager and threatened him with a gun to get the salary he was due, the two left Deadwood as husband and wife.[4] Henceforth, Ross and Fenton would perform as a team, offering travesties of popular and classical plays such as *Hamlet, The Lady of Lyons,* and *The Heart of Maryland.* They had only modest success at first; in 1888 they were playing in out-of-the-way theatres and making only $40.75 a week.[5]

But they came to New York by 1894, worked in the family theatres beginning to prosper there, and eventually earned spots in the Weber and Fields company. When that company disbanded, Ross and Fenton returned to a career as a two-act, alternating vaudeville engagements with musical comedy appearances. By 1907 they were making in a single night in vaudeville more than twice what they had made in an entire week in 1888.[6] Following standards which Emma Shannon would have approved, Ross and Fenton now mounted their acts with spectacular scenery, several supporting players, and Mabel Fenton "made up like a peacock" with an abundance of "frills and feathers." Considered "one of the handsomest men in America," Ross had become a matinee idol, and the team's comic acting on the vaudeville stage was reviewed with the respect accorded legitimate theatre performers.[7]

By then vaudeville was a very different sort of entertainment from that which had given Ross and Fenton their start. Ross observed in 1911 that the vaudeville artist's status had changed:

> He owns his own home...and he is no longer looked down upon as low variety. His position is assured. The social distinction between the variety and the legitimate stage is gone forever....[8]

The team retired with a small fortune—still one of the happiest marriages in show business, it was said—and ran the Ross-Fenton Farm, a hotel in New Jersey;[9] Emma and Mickey Shannon also ended up as hotel proprietors in *The Shannons of Broadway*. The rising status of the male-female team and the increasing refinement of their acts, and the significance of these changes, are important concerns of this work.

It is worth recalling, however, that although vaudeville brought Ross and Fenton security and status, their variety tenure also had its rewards. Ross and Fenton's apprenticeship before the boisterous, demanding audiences in the early variety houses taught them invaluable stage lore. Ross pointed out that it was in variety that he received "a thorough schooling in a wide range of his art, all the way from 'nigger' acts to glove fights."[10] Watching the team in 1913, *Variety* reviewer "Jolo" (Joshua Lowe) was moved to comment that

> After all is said and done, it still is the old-time variety performer who "makes good" in vaudeville, whether it be "pop," "advanced," "supreme," or of any other calibre.[11]

But the intimacy and vitality of variety would be lost in the huge theatres and shows packaged for mass consumption of latter-day vaudeville. Later male-female teams too often lacked the experience and expertise of the old-timers, and the emphasis on "class" and profit would eventually cause comedy to suffer.

The careers of Ross and Fenton, and others like them, illustrate the important changes which took place in vaudeville from its beginnings in the 1860s to the end of its creative era in the late 1920s. The fortunes of the male-female act rose and fell with American vaudeville, and this study of the conditions which brought the male-female act into being, of the forces which shaped its development, and the ways in which the male-female act changed over the decades, provides, it is hoped, a useful perspective on vaudeville's history. The subject of the male-female team is not merely a glass for viewing vaudeville, however; one aim of this study is to demonstrate that the male-female act was an important influence on the evolution of twentieth-century vaudeville.

In *The Shannons of Broadway*, it is perhaps not coincidental that the female partner is the spokesman for "class," because vaudeville's transformation from the gun-toting, dance-hall milieu Charles Ross started in to the status-conscious, star-studded shows symbolized by the Palace was largely effected by the presence of women in the audience—and on the stage. Turn-of-the-century male-female teams, with their polite, drawing-room humor, their romantic plots and lyrics, and their sophisticated, stylishly dressed female partners, catered deliberately to the growing number of women coming to vaudeville in the late nineties and afterwards. It was both a cause and effect of the increase in female patronage that male-female teams turned more and more to domestic humor. After Ross and Fenton left the Weber and Fields company, for example, they augmented their travesty repertory with a different kind of sketch for them, a domestic comedy called "Just Like a Woman." Ross played an intoxicated husband who came home after a night on the town to an irate wife; after the "usual family quarrel," the husband saw his mistake and asked forgiveness, and the act ended happily. Not only was the act praised as "wholesome" and "quite a temperance lesson," but it was thought to have "a world of witty lines and just enough of a touch of pathos at the end to bring the whole to the level of real life."[12]

Such acts, with their "wholesome" domestic concerns, must have been perfectly suited to the middle-class family audience, and especially to the women, who came to vaudeville in the twentieth century. A central figure in this study is the audience itself, the nineteenth-century immigrants and farmers and housewives who became the urban middle class in the twentieth century and were ultimately responsible for the format and themes of vaudeville. This constituency determined the kinds of roles played by male-female teams, and it is an underlying assumption of this study that the characters and jokes and manners offered by the men and women onstage were an engaging mirror of the values and ideas of the men and women across the footlights. Evoking a certain "level of real life" was one way male-female routines held the attention of their viewers.

It is my belief that the most effective source of diversion in the male-female act was the comic treatment of relations between the sexes; more than any other stage tactic, this accounted for the male-female team's popularity and uniqueness. No theatrical act revealed more about the social scripts for the sexes in America, especially the changes in the woman's role during these years, an era bounded at one end by the early feminist meetings and by the flapper revolution at the other. Perhaps not by chance, the rise in popularity of the male-female act coincided with growing interest in—and anxiety over—the Woman's Rights Movement, and routines such as "Just Like a Woman" tapped this public preoccupation. Just what was a woman like; or what *should* she be like? The "New" women in the real world were caricatured by their onstage counterparts in male-female routines: as would-be reformers turned happy, stay-at-home wives in turn-of-the-century domestic sketches; as clownish suffragettes in the early teens; as the laughably hardboiled "dames" seen onstage in the teens and twenties; and as dizzy "dumbbells" such as the one played by Gracie Allen in the late twenties. Throughout vaudeville, these comic characters and plots reaffirmed offstage views of proper relations between the sexes. But as the debate over the New Woman intensified, as women in society asserted new rights, and as female partners assumed new responsibility in routines, male-female acts sometimes took an ambivalent or even provocative stance towards traditional male-female roles. Offstage tensions infected the stage work, and could be an effective theatrical tool for evoking a response from audiences.

It is perhaps a comment on twentieth-century audiences that Burns and Allen have become identified as the quintessential male-female vaudeville team. Gracie Allen's lovable laugh and inimitable way of looking at the world, and George Burn's dry rejoinders and silent absorption in his cigar captured the imagination of the mass audience. Their career as a team spanned thirty-five years: vaudeville headliners and radio's best-loved comedy team in the thirties (they were voted the number one radio team in 1934, over Amos and Andy, Olsen and Johnson, and Stoopnagle and Budd),[13] in 1950 Burns and Allen made a bold move into a totally new medium, television, and successfully held their loyal fans until Gracie Allen's retirement in 1958 finally ended the partnership. Today, the names Burns and Allen awake recognition in almost everyone, along with appreciation of their comic artistry; reruns of their movies and television shows can still be seen today, and recordings of their radio routines still sell. Their patter may have been hammered out for a vaudeville audience, but it has continued to entertain audiences into the 1980s. If vaudeville had produced no other male-female team but Burns and Allen, this achievement alone would tell almost every American, from vaudeville's demise until the present day, what was meant by a male-female comedy team. Reasons for Burns and Allen's long-lived attraction are explored in this study, and I have attempted a more in-depth analysis than is usually offered of the appeals and workings of their act. Burns and Allen simultaneously exploited and transcended twentieth-century attitudes about gender, and I believe this largely accounts for their extraordinary success.

In fact, Burns and Allen are the only vaudeville male-female team still remembered today, even by nostalgia buffs. As valuable as Burns and Allen's contribution might be, it is to be regretted that their predecessors and contemporaries have been forgotten. The fact is, that by the time Burns and Allen had made a name for themselves, big-time vaudeville was essentially dead. A team such as Ross and Fenton, totally unknown today, was much more representative of vaudeville at its height and their career more revealing of vaudeville's history. It is especially misleading that today the "dumbbell" character is almost exclusively associated with Gracie

Allen, and many people assume Burns and Allen can be credited with the character's invention. To be sure, Gracie Allen made the role her own, but it was the product of a long-established tradition, and vaudeville audiences were long familiar with the type when Gracie Allen came along. Besides, even the first "dumbbell" acts came fairly late in vaudeville's history, and that was only one of many kinds of entertaining routines offered by male-female teams.

But it is hard now even to imagine those days when live shows on vaudeville stages were followed as faithfully as television and movies are today. From the late nineteenth century almost until the depression, every night in thousands of vaudeville houses across the nation, audiences gathered to watch coon singers and ballroom dancers, cyclists and jugglers, monologuists and performing dogs, and male-female teams. Hundreds of professional male and female partners made their living performing a self-contained act which featured only two characters: he and she. Humor featuring a man and a woman was also found in legitimate plays, of course, but for the mass audience, the male-female team was *the* vehicle for this primordial source of laughs. Vaudeville accounted for one-half of the nation's theatregoers,[14] and virtually every vaudeville bill featured a male-female comedy act: it was a very well-liked piece of theatre.

To chronicle the stories of these forgotten male-female teams, to learn why they were so popular with audiences and what they tell us about American vaudeville, and to trace the developments in male-female team humor which culminated in the artistry of Burns and Allen, are the broad goals of this study. By documenting and examining what is known of the most popular male-female acts, I have tried to recapture something of the talent and impact of the best teams. Given its popularity and importance in the entertainment world of its own day, and its heritage for the present day, the vaudeville male-female comedy team deserves to be more than a footnote in theatre history.

1
The Background in Europe and America

Not only is the conspicuous success of male-female teams in American between 1870 and 1930 unique in theatre history, but American vaudeville may well have been the setting which fostered the first professional male-female comedy teams. Comical male-female interaction on the stage was nothing new, of course, but the earliest "female partners" were impersonators. Whoever their unrecorded predecessors might be, the *Ur*-male-female team was the first *commedia* actor and actress to hold the stage alone. In fact, early *commedia* scenarios invariably featured at least two pairs of lovers: the courtly flirtations of the *inamorati* had a robust counterpart in the more earthy lovemaking of the *zanni* and the *fantesca*. In the seventeenth century, Paris's *Comédie-Italienne* would give center stage to the latter male-female pair; if Domenico Biancolelli was creator of the modern Harlequin, it was his daughter Caterina who made Colombine the most important female role in *commedia*.[1] When the era of the *commedia* troupe had passed, Colombine and Harlequin remained central figures in the continuing Western popular theatre tradition.

By the time of eighteenth-century English pantomime, for example, the elegant lovers of *commedia* had virtually disappeared, along with many of the traditional *commedia* masks. Comic scenes between a Colombine and a Harlequin were a principal attraction in such pantomimes as "The Loves of Harlequin and Colombine," "Arlequin Cru Colombine & Colombine Cru Arlequin," "Colombine; or, Harlequin Turn'd Judge," and "Cupid & Psyche; or, Colombine Courtezan," which typically featured well-known performers like Richard Yates and Kitty Clive. On several occasions a King's Theatre pantomime was preceded by "A New Prologue between Harlequin and Colombine." In the economically staged fairground pantomimes, it was common for a Colombine and Harlequin and a Pierrot, or a Colombine and a Harlequin, to be the only "Italian" characters; some fairground pantomimes featured only two or three characters altogether. English performer Mr. Phillips was said to be sensational in a Harlequin-

Colombine scene played opposite his wife at the St. Laurent Fair in 1737.[2] Given the popularity of these male-female comic bits, it seems a likely possibility that some enterprising actor and actress might have tried to make a living as a twosome, staging two-character entertainments based on popular pantomimes. Nonetheless, before the mid-nineteenth century, any such "teams" either went unrecorded or else never existed.

The existence of professionally-independent teams with self-contained routines depended on established venues for individual acts, and before the nineteenth century, these opportunities simply did not exist; towns and populations were too small to support a thriving "variety" stage in addition to a dramatic theatre. The quips and pranks of the popular theatre tradition survived either as an ingredient in drama itself (as in Shakespeare's plays, which could accommodate slapstick and tragic poetry in a single plot), as an entr'acte interruption in a legitimate theatre program, or as an imitation of legitimate play structure—as a *commedia* scenario or a pantomime, both revealed on close analysis to be a string of self-contained *jeux*. Banding together in companies and performing ersatz plays had offered the *commedia* players greater security, and several hundred years later, both the French and English fairground performers still travelled together in small companies. There were hints that men and women in these companies teamed up for an entr'acte scene or a musical number, but no such combinations have been proved to be anything other than occasional.

There simply was not sufficient market for a professional to make a living with a single specialty act. Even with fairs and festivals sprinkled throughout England and the continent, it was not practical for a specialty performer to tour so extensively. Until the advent of the railroad and macadamized roads in the nineteenth century, travel was an arduous and dangerous adventure, making it an unattractive alternative for a single player or pair. In contemporary writings, the most reiterated fact about even the itinerant eighteenth-century *dramatic* performers is their poverty. Strolling player William Templeton declared that the touring players' attire was often little better than a beggar's, and that they were often hungry. Although some travelled by wagon or horseback, the poorer sort tramped, with their personal belongings and a portion of the scenery or wardrobe on their backs. The adventuresome actress Charlotte Charke testified that

> going a Strolling is engaging in a little, dirty kind of war.... And to say Truth, I am not only sick, but heartily ashamed of it, as I have had nine Years Experience of its being a very contemptible Life....[3]

Certainly these conditions did not attract female performers, a necessary component of the male-female act. Life on the road was hardly a fit existence for a man and still less suitable for women. Whereas women, by definition, were expected to be submissive, dutiful, motherly, retiring, and imbued with religious virtues, actors were exhibitionist, vulgar, immoral, bohemian, anti-family, and anti-society. Thus, women were at a premium in the legitimate theatre, and an attractive woman, even of meager talent, could usually avoid descending in status to the rank of entr'acte or street entertainer.[4]

Ironically, the new importance of popular entertainment forms in England and France in the eighteenth and nineteenth centuries, although it furnished opportunities for specialty performers, was initially a hindrance to the development of the male-female team. The success of the fair theatres, and later on, the music halls in England and the boulevard theatres in France, meant that these entertainments were jealously watched over by the legitimate theatre operators, who lobbied fiercely to make certain their exclusive, licensed privilege for performing spoken drama was not encroached upon. As a result, very early on, comic songs, novelty acts, and dance became the traditional fare in the halls and on the boulevards.

In the British music hall, for example, the Christy Minstrels introduced the sketch in 1857, but subsequent attempts in the early sixties to infringe upon the law resulted in prosecutions and fines. Such strict legislation tended to discourage the experimentation which might have fostered the development of a male-female comedy act. No doubt the impulse was present; according to one student of the music hall, performer William Randall "and his wife used to appear together until the Sketch trouble blew up, when they separated (so far as the stage went) and did single turns." In this conservative environment, even the legal innovation of lady serio-comics did not become fully accepted until the end of the sixties.[5] The early prejudice in favor of comic song had far-reaching effects; the male-female act was never an important draw for the British music-hall audience.[6]

It therefore seems likely that it was not in Europe, but in America, that the male-female team first became established professionally. Whereas in the late sixties French *cafés chantants* and English music halls were largely given over to songs by single performers, and in England women had only just fully established themselves as serio-comics, by 1870 at the very latest, professional male-female teams were making a living touring the American variety halls.

Itinerant performers specializing in singing and dancing, acrobatics, and clowning were coming to America by the eighteenth century, and these performers must have been familiar with the characters of Harlequin and Colombine so popular in the Old World. Whether or not he had seen Italian "Mimick Scenes" before he came to America in 1702, Anthony Aston, the first known professional player in America, certainly knew this tradition after appearing in the fair booths back in England in 1706; in the 1724-25 season Aston was in the troupe which presented the first recorded pantomime at Bartholomew Fair, "The Loves of Harlequin and Colombine."[7] As early as 1738, American performers were concocting their own "Pantomime Entertainment,"[8] and the Hallam troupe—America's first prominent company—was well-practiced in these pieces in which a male and a female were featured so prominently. Members of the Hallam family had played in and produced pantomime entertainment in the English fairs,[9] and during their long tenure as the American theatre's Royal Family, pantomime would regularly grace their bills.[10] Low comedy made by a man and a woman was thus a part of the American popular stage from the beginning.

Just as in Europe, American variety performers banded together for travel security and to increase the attractiveness of their offerings; occasional man-and-woman combinations undoubtedly formed. For example, around 1849, A. B. French—then a would-be performer, later king of the showboat world—joined forces with a Mr. Church and his daughter Celeste, to perform magic tricks, banjo numbers, and song and dance acts at landings from their shanty boat *Quickstep*. One of their offerings was a dance act by Celeste and French.[11] When Spaulding and Rogers's "Floating Circus Palace" was launched in 1851, the museum show featured an invisible lady act by a Professor and Madame Lowe.[12] There must have been other such combinations as variety entertainments became more popular, although no permanent male-female acts are yet known to have existed before the very end of the 1860s.

The distinguishing factor in America was that, unlike England or France, here anything was possible. There were no established theatre traditions in America; constant experimentation and making-do were necessary merely to keep theatre alive. The only arbiters of what passed as theatre in America were play-going people, and for this rag-tag crowd, the more popular, the more democratic—the better. European visitors to America in the 1820s and 1830s, such as Fanny Kemble and Frances Trollope, described American audiences as boisterous and uncouth.[13] These vociferous theatregoers actually determined much of what they saw onstage, by hissing, booing, and stamping their feet when disappointed, or by enthusiastic cheering when they were pleased. Most theatre managers found it expedient to cater to the growing taste for cannons, patriotic speeches, striking scenic effects, and grandiose acting.[14] "Democracy is too new a comer upon the earth," wrote one foreign observer of America in 1833, "to have been able as yet to organize its pleasures and amusements. In Europe, our pleasures are essentially exclusive, they are aristocratic like Europe itself. In this matter, then, as in politics, the American democracy has yet to create everything fresh."[15]

Perhaps by 1833 the fragmentation of the American audience into elite and popular components was not yet obvious, but by the 1840s Americans were indeed developing "everything fresh," new stage entertainments which were popular in form itself. Changes in American culture made the need for more popularized amusements greater than ever. Between 1830 and 1860, the American population doubled. Of the twenty-million-plus increase in population, two and one-half million were immigrants, one-half of which had arrived between 1845 and 1850.[16] By 1850 there were already eighty-five cities with populations exceeding 8000, eight cities with over 100,000; New York City had already exceeded 900,000 by 1860, an increase of over twice its population in 1840.[17]

The rise of the city meant that both rural migrants and foreign immigrants found themselves in a bewildering new world in which old folkways provided little guidance, a world far from kin and community, usually with a slum backdrop, reverberating with noisy machines and foreign accents. Struggling new city dwellers had neither time nor place for the outdoor games, the tall tales, the corn-husking parties and quilting bees of rural life; they needed low-priced entertainments which provided quick thrills while demanding little time or active participation.[18] Immigrants were particularly alienated from established stage entertainments by the language barrier, making simplicity another necessity.[19] It was the olio format, which neglected character development and plot for a fast succession of simple stage skills, that best satisfied the new needs.

P. T. Barnum was probably the first entertainment entrepreneur to realize the potential rewards of catering to the restless urban audience. He offered at low prices the curios, deformity, and miscellaneous entertainments previously available as entr'acte fare in regular theatres; the innovation was so successful that by the 1840s the "dime museum" was fast becoming a national institution.[20] These theatrical "varieties" were taken to the frontier audience by the showboat. The first deliberately planned showboat had been launched in 1831, and during the 1840s and 1850s there were dozens of small showboats with companies more inclined to song-joke-dance-and-lecture entertainment than to full-length plays.[21] Equestrian shows were also well-liked by the growing popular audience; by 1824, an embryonic circus show had appeared, and circus experienced an impressive growth beginning in the 1830s. Acrobatics were especially popular after the successful Ravel family's tours began—the first was in 1832; regular tours continued until 1858—and their balancing, tumbling, pantomime, and Herculean features were widely copied.[22]

But the first fully developed olio entertainment was the minstrel show. The vogue had started in New York City, when four unemployed blackface circus performers banded together in 1842 to double their chances of success. Until the Civil War most troupes stayed in the Northeastern cities, where the urban masses were mad for minstrelsy. There were no conventions at first; minstrelsy's well-defined format and content were hammered out as audiences responded enthusiastically to favorite characters and stage styles, and came to expect them.[23] The three-part structure which evolved was ideally suited to the popular audience: spurning complications of plot and character development, each turn was self-contained and provided instant amusement; the earthy "niggers'" jokes and eccentric dancing matched the exuberance and raucousness of the audience.[24]

These were essentially the same attractions of other popular stage shows. Just as blackface entertainment was important to the museum and circus show, minstrelsy frequently featured Barnum-like attractions, routines "in the style of the Ravels," and travesties of stage-competitors like Jennie "Leatherlungs" Lind. Slavery was their most conspicuous subject, but minstrels also joked about contemporary fads and movements such as Millerites, Shakers, Phrenology, and Woman's Rights, especially the right to wear bloomers. And as early as 1843, minstrels had depicted "Paddy" as "de biggest fool dat eber walk," the same gleeful, heavy-drinking Irish brawler who would monopolize the variety show for decades to come.[25] In other words, there were more and more kinds of popular theatre to choose from, and although format or setting varied from showboat to medicine wagon, appeals were the same in each: short, self-contained acts featuring a diversity of skills and subjects, all infused with sentiment, patriotism, low comedy, and theatricalism.

One setting for this kind of olio entertainment that was new to America was the beer garden and saloon. By the mid-fifties the growing German population was teaching the country a taste for lager beer, and as in Germany an evening in the beer garden was accompanied by entertainment.[26] Likewise, by the early fifties, the kind of amusement known as the "concert saloon" had already appeared in American cities, offering its patrons the opportunity to enjoy a good smoke and a drink along with a show—which was simply an inducement to keep customers in a happy, drink-buying mood.[27] It has been suggested that the American concert saloon took its cue from the English music hall, a tavern-annex arrangement gaining popularity in the late 1840s;[28] perhaps the beer gardens were an equally important influence. The point is that all these new venues for theatre developed in response to the vast urban population's need for entertainment: just as Barnum had catered to the upper segment of the middling folk, so others saw the profits to be gained from amusing the lower elements.

Moreover, segregated "stag" amusements were a natural taste for a society becoming increasingly prudish. The concert saloon was a haunt for "the man-about-town." Although in the highest-class concert saloons men were "generally sober, well-dressed, and tolerably well-behaved," in the lowest, they would "swear and talk obscenely in loud voices; drink to excess, leer, and roar, and stagger, and bestow rude caresses on the women...."[29] The devotees of this sort of carousing were "men from every grade of life," the "laborer and mechanic, the salesman and accountant, the bank-clerk and merchant."[30] Even reputable gentlemen could be found "slumming" in these downtown watering holes: one writer of the day testified to finding "plenty of the youths of the 'best society'," quiet Germans, lawyers, city officers, and aldermen in the concert saloons.[31] A seedy bachelor culture was perhaps inevitable in the strait-laced drawing-room society of Victorian America. Still another influence was the panic of 1857, which brought more poverty to the cities and an increase in the riff-raff element of society — and along with these, crime and the lowest sort of amusement. Saloons and dingy dance halls seemed to spring up overnight; prostitution flourished around Broadway and on the Bowery.[32]

At its worst the concert saloon was a haven for prostitutes, and even the best openly utilized female charms to attract male patrons with its "waiter girls." These women sat with the customers and drank and flirted with them, and were paid a percentage of the sales they promoted, twenty per cent on wine, less on beer.[33] The girls were often a bigger draw than the stage show, according to a newspaper reporter in 1860: "Too many [concert saloons] neglect nearly altogether their performances, relying upon the 'prettiest waiter girls in the city' for a full house and the sale of liquors and cigars."[34] Although some male visitors complained that "pretty is the term set down on the 'bills' — its application literally is a 'whopper,' for the better part of these Hebes and female Ganymedes are coarse, fat and prodigiously ugly,"[35] perhaps closest to the truth was a writer's explanation (1869) that in the best places, the girls "have some pretensions to comeliness and propriety of conduct," but that in the worst, the women were "coarse and sensual in form and feature, lascivious in conduct, rude and harsh of speech, degraded in feeling, outcast in society."[36] On one point, all contemporary observers of the waiter-girls agreed, that, prostitutes or not, "there are no virtuous girls in the concert saloons."[37]

It was this association with prostitution and vice that aroused public opinion against the concert saloons in the 1860s. No doubt the influx of pleasure-seeking soldiers and the frenzied wartime atmosphere played a part too in the concert saloon's growing notoriety. The *New York Evening Post* damned the conduct in concert saloons as a "truly diabolic form of shameless and avowed Bacchus and Phallus worship."[38] Other attacks were even more graphic. However truthful such descriptions, public outrage was sufficiently strong that in April 1862 the New York State Legislature passed "An Act to Regulate places of public amusement in the cities and incorporated villages of this State," making it law that all concert saloons had to be licensed, that no wine or beer could be sold in them, and no females could be employed to furnish refreshments in them.[39] In effect, henceforth the offending downtown resorts had either to do away with their entertainments and girls and become "decent" saloons, or else stop selling lager and become theatrical establishments. For several months, there was a general compliance in one way or another, but by the fall 1863 season most of the concert saloons were operating in the old way.[40]

Nonetheless, from 1863 on, the name "concert saloon" had loathsome connotations; more respectable places were coming to be referred to as "variety halls," "music halls," or "variety theatres."[41] In every big town managers were opening these new variety theatres, which, although they served alcoholic beverages and were patronized almost entirely by men,[42] were intended as places of decent entertainment, not saloons. M. B. Leavitt recalled that by the late sixties there were variety houses in every principal city. He listed among the better class such theatres as Fox's American Theatre and Frank Rivers's Melodeon in Philadelphia, the Canterbury in Washington, D.C., Trimble's Varieties in Pittsburgh, the Howard Athenaeum in Boston, the Front Street Theatre in Baltimore, and Montpelier's Theatre Comique in Cleveland.[43]

Perhaps the best-known fledgling variety theatre was the "444" in New York, owned by Robert Butler, with Tony Pastor somehow associated as early as 1861. The anonymous author of *The Night Side of New York* classed 444 not with the concert saloons, but in the category of "The Cheap Theatre." It had a fifteen-cent gallery "groaning with young bootblacks, unfledged rowdies, shiftless loafers," a twenty-five-cent parquette for young men-about-town, sailors, soldiers, and old men "with the odor of the car stables," and an orchestra packed by drygoods drummers, members of the bar, clerks, butchers, naval officers, and gentlemen with large quantities of money. The boxes were generally empty except on a Saturday matinee, when some women of the "semi-demi monde" might be found there.[44] To this observer it was just a "foul, tobacco-reeking hall," but he admitted it was popular with men of all classes, who enjoyed the "sly double jokes related at Butler's" and "lolling in one's seat, puffing at ease, gazing through the smoke at the graceful limbs of large-eyed dancing girls."[45]

Although it was probably as "low" and "vulgar" as claimed, the 444 was apparently a step up from the concert saloons. It was praised by the press, and a twentieth-century writer who recalled visiting "The Fours" insisted that the performances "were rather rough at times but there was no profanity or out-of-the-way speeches."[46] The 444 variety performers were obviously able to attract an audience on their own merits, for beginning in 1863, Tony Pastor carried them out on tour each summer. The troupe visited the respectable Boston Museum in the summers of 1863 and 1864 (which was, confessed Pastor, "a change for us, I can assure you"), and huge crowds came every night.[47]

The entertainment offered by Pastor and similar troupes was inherited from minstrelsy, circus, and dime museums: comic and sentimental songs, eccentric dancing and acrobatics, banjo and bone solos, and farcical afterpieces. A typical show was presented at Morris Brothers and Trowbridge's Opera House in 1866: selections by the orchestra to open the program, followed by thirteen acts—numerous ballads and dances by both male and female singles, a banjo solo, comic songs by Pastor, two short sketches, three double-male blackface acts, "Shamrock Sonnets" by William Carleton, plus a number by the chorus line, with the evening concluded with a sketch by the company.[48] A visitor to 444 in 1866 saw a five-hour bill of fourteen acts, and summed up its appeal as "restless activity": "nothing lags; the singer rushes through his song, the darkey jumps at his jokes, the legs of the ballet-girls are always twinkling."[49]

To most observers, it was still a lowly entertainment. On any evening on the Bowery, when the theatres were drawing in the crowds, newsboys and mechanics could be heard, in the words of one writer, "discussing the dramatic horrors they expect to witness, and laughing in anticipation of the dreary drolleries of Tony Pastor's opera house, where the mob is tickled and good taste disgusted for soiled postal currency in small amounts." The humor was "frequently indelicate," and the Bowery audience showed their appreciation with elbow-punching and uproarious laughter.[50]

But even if these theatres were offensive to uptown sensibilities, and were still akin to the concert saloon in atmosphere, "variety" was emerging as an entertainment appeal in its own right, distinct from the saloon pleasures of smoke and drink, gaming, and whoring. By the mid-sixties variety entertainment had long escaped its confinement to "entr'acte." With minstrelsy, circus, and variety halls flourishing in every good-sized city, hundreds of specialty performers were needed to fill the demand for variety entertainment. And unlike minstrelsy, the growing variety theatre circuit offered increased opportunities not only for male professionals, but women as well—a necessary prelude to the emergence of male-female comedy teams.

2

The Earliest Male-Female Teams, 1865–1876

The concert saloon was the springboard that catapulted women, through the back door as it were, to their first real foothold in the expanding popular entertainment business. By the late 1850s, the larger concert saloons featured a corps de ballet, of from six to twelve pretty "dancers" who performed pastoral numbers with veils, maneuvers in abbreviated military dress, and of course the infamous can-can.[1] The first saloon chorus lines were probably recruited from the waiter girls; given the increasing popularity of saloon entertainments—and the crucial drawing power of the girls themselves—it was both an obvious and economical business decision to have soubrette-dressed waiter girls open the show with a song and dance. The men threw coins on stage for their favorites,[2] and ever larger numbers of saloon soubrettes aspired to this more profitable, less demeaning work.[3] The process was given a tremendous boost in the early sixties, when waiter girls were outlawed by the New York State Legislature,[4] and saloon women had to make their living on the stage, not in the boxes.

One habitué of 444 claimed that most of the dancers were clumsy and heavy and not very good; but he revealed that many of the dancers had performed in the respectable theatres before ending up in this low haunt, and admitted that there were one or two exceptions who were not bad.[5] As variety emerged as an entertainment business separate from the saloon milieu, it was becoming an alternative for those women who, although on the farthest fringes of the theatre, considered themselves professionals and scorned the waiter-girl trade. Time and new recruits must have upped the ante in talent.

By the second half of the sixties, many women were well established as variety specialists, although even these still had to serve in the chorus-line. There were no "one act people" then, recalled a graduate of variety; anyone of any success had a wide range of capabilities.[6] It was not always easy to fill a bill: variety houses had limited budgets; the booking profession was nonexistent; transportation was unreliable, as performers often were themselves. Since the supply of performers available to a single house at any one time was small, performers were expected to contribute three or four specialties in a single show. Even the most talented woman performed several numbers with the corps de ballet and acted in the afterpiece, as well as performing her own specialty—invariably song or dance—at least once. Understandably, managers hung on to successful performers, and most managers employed a number of regulars to furnish the bulk of the bill, with the "guest stars" furnishing the highlights.

But although long runs and resident troupes kept bills safely filled, they could also create boredom. As olio entertainment became more common, presumably audiences grew more demanding, competition increased between the houses in a single city, and the success of well-known acts palled. The obvious, financially feasible strategy was for managers to utilize their resources to the fullest by experimenting with new and interesting combinations of the players available, providing audiences with the greatest amount of variety with the least number of personnel. No doubt a performer's success was measured by the degree of novelty he added to a troupe, and performers must have been forever pondering new ways to market themselves. In response to these insistent demands, men and women who travelled and lived and performed on the same bills together eventually came up with the notion of combining their skills onstage.

The first suggestions of what may have been double numbers are found on bills around 1865. In the summer of 1865, for instance, Tony Pastor hired minstrel John Wild and his wife Blanche Stanley for his summer tour for $50 a week for the two of them.[7] In some advertisements for the tour Johnny Wild and Blanche Stanley were listed only as singles, but in others as performing "The Nerves" together in addition to their single specialties.[8] They may have had a supporting cast, but it sounds like a two-act, and was presumably popular, for in September well-known pantomime clown Frank Lacy and Florence Reynolds offered "The Nerves" at 444.[9] Another apparent two-person combination was Josh Hart and wife Laura Leclaire, who appeared in January 1866 with "their original drama, The Victim," gave "Two Fathers," and also "acted The Stage-Struck Chambermaid."[10] But this teaming up, if it was that—there may have been a supporting cast—was either not repeated or else not mentioned again, although Hart and his wife continued to perform at the same houses in a variety of capacities.[11]

These couples and others like them could not have been blind to certain theatrical successes taking place at the time. News travelled slowly on the far-flung variety circuit of the sixties, but eventually they must have witnessed performances by the male two-acts currently winning popularity.

Male combinations of various types could be seen in a minstrel show. In the sixties many minstrel pairs struck out on their own to try their endmen dialogue in variety, the new field. There were Collins and Oakes, Quilter and Goodrich, Parkhurst and Collins, Ashcroft and Morton. Sheridan and Mack, and Delehenty and Hengler, in particular, were enjoying conspicuous favor doing "double acts" — or "two-acts" — in the late sixties.[12]

A short story which appeared in the *New York Clipper* in 1870 implied the male two-act had been new in recent memory and now had a hold on audiences' imaginations. Titled "Two Song-and-Dance Men," the story told the life of fictional team Knight and Cottle (Tom and Charley), relating that "as they went on, they began to do double songs mixed into their dances, which is now very common, but they was about the first ones at it, sir." The narrator enthusiastically describes their performance of "Courting 'Neath the Moon":

> Knight would come dancing in and sing:—
> 'Why am I always singing,
> I'm such a happy coon;
> My love I'm always bringing
> To court beneath the moon.
> My heart is just now swelling—
> Then he'd give two or three steps to the right—
> Since I expect her soon—
> Then the same to the left, you see, sir—
> Sweet things to her I'm telling,
> When courting 'neath the moon.
> Then Cottle would come in, and they'd dance the interlude together; then Cottle would have his verse; then they'd have a verse together as a duet, winding up with
> And when we both are married
> We'll court beneath the moon.'
> If you never saw it, sir, it don't sound like much, perhaps, but if you were to see 'em, with every step they took coming in click, click, in just such time, you see, and the one a finishing out the other's ideas in steps, you'd have acknowledged, Sir, that it was just sublime, and that's the only word for it.[13]

Actual teamwork by the fictional pair was not much in evidence, and this was apparently true of real-life male teams of the day. Sheridan and Mack's two-act consisted of a song by Sheridan, followed by one by Mack, another by Sheridan and then another by Mack, with a double song and dance number not found until the end.[14] But these early double acts were a sensation in their time, and more than one husband and wife in variety also must have wondered if one act together might be better than two acts as singles.

A man and woman seeking new means of stage success could also look to other models, men and women who were male-female "teams" of a sort.

In the late sixties there were a few well known male-female partners supported by their own small stock companies, doing playlets that served entirely as vehicles for the star duo. Mr. and Mrs. Barney Williams and Mr. and Mrs. W. J. Florence were the best-known such players. Barney Williams had been doing Irish songs and stories at the museums and popular houses when he met and married an actress named Maria Pray in 1849; henceforth they performed the starring roles in dozens and dozens of short Irish plays such as "Crossing the Atlantic," "The Emerald Ring," "Ireland As It Is," and "Ireland and America."[15] These were farces tailored to suit the tastes of the masses, which probably could be done by the principals alone if necessary; in fact, according to Mrs. Williams, they also did "sketches."[16] Variety performers knew these acts, for the Williamses played in popular houses such as the Bowery Theatre—on occasion, Tony Pastor's—and in the late sixties were still in great demand.[17] When W. J. Florence married Mrs. Williams's sister Malvina Pray in 1853, the newlywed Florences decided to imitate their successful relatives. They quickly became a success on their own.[18] The Florences did some legitimate drama—they became assoiated with *The Ticket-of-Leave Man* and *The Mighty Dollar*[19]—but they also performed short Irish skits in the popular houses.[20]

    The careers of these barnstormers demonstrate the widening gulf between the legitimate stage and the new popular entertainments: their repertoires furnished a model more easily adaptable than legitimate plays for the needy variety performer, who was forced almost daily to seek new material. No doubt variety house farces such as "Young American in Ireland," "The Bill Poster's Dream," or "Lancashire Lass" were copies of short plays like "The Irish Emigrant," "The Young Actress," or "The Yankee Housekeeper" (from the Florences' repertoire in this instance);[21] many of these farces featured male and female leads. During the Lauri pantomime troupe's run in Providence, Rhode Island, for instance, "each evening's performance was preceded by an Irish sketch, in which Hugh Fay and Miss Kate Emmet were quite successful, and were received with much favor."[22]

    A man and woman were also featured performers in pantomime, which like its English source still featured the adventures of Colombine and Harlequin, and also in another English import, extravaganza. In a small collection of extant Lauri family handbills, every pantomime features a boy-girl scene of some type; in the two-character first scene of the pantomime "Mother Hubbard," for example, Bo-Peep laments the uneven current of her love in song, Boy Blue tries to make peace, and the scene ends with their marriage. Such scenes must have called attention to the potential of comical male-female interaction.[23]

When circumstances dictated it, any of these non-plot-oriented entertainments could be boiled down to a two-person version. Between about 1868 and 1872, a troupe called the Nellie Maskell Burlesque Company was frequently seen in New York, with the principals Nellie Maskell and her husband Valentine Love. In the 1868-69 season the whole troupe did "After Dusk," a burlesque of Boucicault's *After Dark,* currently playing its first American engagement at Niblo's Garden. But when the new variety show at Tammany Hall commenced in January the bill included "After Dusk" by Mr. and Mrs. Valentine Love, apparently without the company, as on several other occasions.[24] Similarly, whereas in August 1869 a new pantomime called "The Salamander, or Baked Alive," was done by a troupe in Philadelphia, in 1870 at the lowly St. Louis Varieties a Sig. Constantine and Mlle. Evelina were said to "have another of their laughable pantomimes on this week called "'Salamandrix, or Baked Alive'."[25] Clearly, as the seventies approached, men and women were more often teaming up on occasion, a process which would culminate in the emergence of permanent teams.

But perhaps the most important stimulus for the formation of male-female variety teams was any perceptive male performer's inevitable realization that, in addition to any theatrical skills she had, an attractive female partner gave his act two automatic appeals: novelty, and the attraction of female sex appeal. For decades olio entertainment had been monopolized by men, and female performers were a welcome novelty, especially for an entertainment with a male audience. The very presence of women onstage had brought customers into American theatres from the beginning; "Give me de prette vimin and I will fill my house," claimed Alexander Placide, theatre manager in Charleston between 1795 and 1812.[26]

"Prette vimin" were not in abundance on the early popular stage, however, but their potential box-office power was demonstrated by ersatz lookalikes, the impersonators of pretty plantation "yaller gals" featured in minstrel skits. The "wench" impersonators were experts—usually younger men with soprano voices, beardless faces, and tiny hands and feet—who recreated sweet, graceful Negro women with the light skin and facial features of desirable white women. The impersonations did not furnish comedy, but used serious sentimental language to portray coquettish flirtations, happy romances, and sad untimely deaths of virgins, popular themes in minstrel songs and sketches.[27]

Meanwhile, real women were the draw in a homegrown, popularized version of European ballet flourishing in the forties; it was largely the view of women's limbs, not their dancing ability, that attracted, for contemporaries testified that "the more outré the dancing, the more applause."[28] Prominent New York minister Charles B. Smythe indignantly declared that "the attitudes were exceedingly indelicate...ladies dancing so as to make their undergarments spring up exposing the figure beneath from the waist to the toe...when a danseuse is assisted by a danseur, the attitudes assumed by both in conjunction suggest to the imagination scenes which one may read of in descriptions of ancient heathen orgies."[29]

The demand for scantily clad women onstage culminated in 1866 with *The Black Crook,* one of the first spectacles to abandon the pretense of being art and to exploit female sex appeal unabashedly. "This was more than an event; it was an epoch," wrote theatrical entrepreneur M. B. Leavitt; it ran for sixteen months and grossed one million dollars, dramatically demonstrating the potential of the female form as a theatrical commodity;[30] the timely arrival of Lydia Thompson and her British Blondes provided a sensation which drove home the lesson. *White Crooks, White Fawns, Black Fawns,* and a host of still more full-blooded imitators followed in quick succession. Mark Twain suggested even Edwin Booth would have to "make a little change and peel some women" if he were to please popular taste.[31]

On any day in the late sixties and seventies, somewhere a racy spectacle featuring buxom beauties would be playing. One ingenious brand of burlesque was the "female minstrels," female casts in snug-fitting tights, dancing, singing, and embellishing minstrelsy as only women could. M. B. Leavitt claimed his company, Madame Rentz's Female Minstrels, created in 1870, was the very first;[32] at any rate, it caused an uproar:

> "In San Francisco, we had advertised that we were going to put on the can-can," recalled John E. Henshaw, who began his acting career as a prop boy with the troupe. "Mabel Santley did this number and when the music came to dum-de-dum, she raised her foot just about twelve inches; whereupon the entire audience hollored 'Whooooo!' It set them crazy."[33]

Variety sketches were deliberately contrived to create an opportunity for the corps de ballet to preen and kick, such as the "Female Sharpshooters" at Baltimore's Front Street Theatre in 1870; or "The Female Clerks of Washington," seen at Tony Pastor's in the 1870-71 season; or "The Female Brokers of Broad Street" at the Waverly variety house in the 1869-70 season.[34] One downtown reporter pointed out that the ballet, with its "scantily-robed females" and "very loose flinging about of flesh-colored tights," was "the heavy trump card of the cheap theatre."[35] The Canterbury Variety Theatre in New York straightforwardly advertised its fare as the can-can, female minstrels, and forty young ladies; another New York house boasted with word play of the "Twin Blondes,"

> in the costume of the lights of the harem, surrounded by their beautiful satellites — Clara, Frank, Minnie, and the far-famed six Annies and six Fannies — forming the most

beautiful dozen in the world, each clad in the gorgeous apparel of the Sultanic favorites....[36]

Given the sure success on variety stages of an attractive woman doing what came naturally, it was a timely expedient for a man to put a well-endowed wife in his act; given also the conspicuous success of male two-acts and sketch artists like the Williamses, it was not surprising that around 1870 a number of male-female combinations appeared in variety houses here and there around the country. Almost all of them were husband and wife performers already travelling around the country together and appearing at the same houses, previously billed as singles, but now performing together.

For example, Fred McAvoy was frequently found on variety hall bills in the late sixties, sometimes alone, other times with Annie McAvoy appearing separately on the same bill. Then, in 1870, the Indianapolis Opera House featured "Fred and Annie McAvoy," billing which suggests they performed as a team. Without a doubt, by fall, 1871, they were appearing as a two-act, in "their original musical sketch called 'The Emmigrants'," and in their Irish opera, "Pat's Frolic."[37] Similarly, Dan Morris and Josie Morris (or Miss Josie Shelby) were performing on the same bills in the 1867-68 season. Josie performed in the corps de ballet, with Dan the better known. He was an Irish and Dutch comedian often engaged alone; at the Theatre Comique in New York, he played the lead in a farcical Dutch "Richard III."[38] Nevertheless, Dan Morris thought it worthwhile to combine his comedy and Josie's dancing; by December 1870, the two had teamed up in Irish specialties and a double Irish jig.[39]

Husband and wife Harry Watson and Lizzie Sherman were seen at the same houses from spring, 1869, through winter, 1870. On one occasion Harry Watson was seen in an Ethiopian act with a male partner, with Lizzie Sherman giving her singing number on the same bill. Perhaps performing as a twosome prompted Harry Watson to consider teaming up with his songstress-dancer wife; at any rate, when next heard of in March 1870 Watson and Sherman were praised because they did "double acts" well.[40]

But the most popular of these early teams seems to have been Martha Wren and James Collins. Martha Wren was from a family supposedly descended from Christopher Wren and well acquainted with President Lincoln's family; she numbered a doctor and a judge among her brothers.[41] One newspaper claimed:

> She has played under nearly all the old managers and in nearly every first-class theatre in America. She plays several instruments, sings and dances; has written poems, edi-

torials, biographies, theatrical anecdotes, etc., etc., for many widely circulated daily and weekly papers. She has been associated with literary, political, artistic, scientific and dramatic people all her life.[42]

As a child Martha Wren played children's roles on the legitimate stage; in 1859, young enough to be called "little Martha Wren," she performed with Laura Keene at Laura Keene's Theatre. In 1867 she played Oliver Twist to E. L. Davenport's Bill, Lucille Western's Nancy, and J. W. Wallack's Fagin.[43]

Thus, when she appeared with James Collins at the Globe and at Tony Pastor's in fall, 1870, she was probably not more than eighteen. Perhaps she had already determined she was never to achieve renown in adult roles on the legitimate stage, or she may have married into the variety profession. Husband or not, James Collins's previous experience was in the popular theatre; he had appeared in minor roles in burlesques by a company of "Blondes" (once as an owl), and then as a comic singer in variety.[44]

There is no evidence the two had previously travelled together; Wren and Collins burst upon the scene as a team in fall, 1870, exhibiting "double acts in whiteface." Perhaps they formed a two-act in imitation of the Williamses, for their first-known sketch, presumably Irish, was called "Barney's Courtship." It is the earliest title known without doubt to be a male-female double routine. Like the Williamses' short skits, it was a protean act, with James Collins playing both an elderly lady and Barney; Martha Wren presumably played a young girl. She was thought to sing well and look good.[45] After appearing with the sketch at the Globe for at least a month, they were still encored nightly, and popular enough to remain around New York City for most of that winter, at either Tony Pastor's or the Theatre Comique.[46] By spring Wren and Collins were touring in the far West, but their contribution was not forgotten; "Barney's Courtship" was staged by at least three other male-female combinations in their absence.[47]

By early 1871 the team had already enlarged their repertoire considerably. That winter and spring Wren and Collins were playing "All Over the World" and "The Arrival of Kneelson" in addition to "Barney's Courtship"; fall, 1871, brought "Beautiful Snow" and "Happy Policeman," with "Delicate Ground," "Crossing the Line," "Out on a Spree," and "Nan the Good for Nothing" all added by summer, 1872.[48] These offerings were far from new;[49] nonetheless, at the time few male and female duos staged anything even known by title, and Wren and Collins were mentioned more frequently in variety news columns than any mixed act before 1873. At that point they were probably performing together more regularly than any other male-female team and in the best — or most publicized — variety halls.

In contrast, most male-female acts mentioned in the opening years of the seventies were merely occasional combinations, often only for the run of a certain bill of players.⁵⁰ Altogether there were only a handful of men and women appearing together regularly in the early seventies, in teams scattered all over the country. Very rarely were there two male-female combinations at a house or in the same city at any one time—and in the majority of houses a male-female combination was probably not seen for months at a time. Even in New York, the city with the most variety entertainment to offer, male-female acts were infrequent. In the 1870–71 season, Tony Pastor's audience saw Wren and Collins in January, and Frank and Alford in April; only one other mixed routine, Charles and Carrie Austin's musical drill, was seen in the city during the entire season; no house had more than two teams visit during the season. Only Tony Pastor's featured male-female numbers in the 1871–72 season, with Mr. and Mrs. Fred McAvoy appearing in September, Wren and Collins in mid-January, the Siegels in mid-February, and Wren and Collins back in late June.⁵¹

Even the permanent male-female combinations of the early seventies were teams in only a loose sense. A couple was still engaged primarily as utility performers: when the Moore and Henderson team appeared at Tony Pastor's in spring, 1873, Kitty Henderson performed a single dance number, and then "later in the evening" she and Moore gave their double act, "The Happy Irish Couple." Likewise, at Tony Pastor's in February 1871, Martha Wren performed not only with her partner, but was required as well to dance with the "female minstrels" in "The Female Highwayman."⁵² Even if a man and woman had two-act material, it might not be needed, or a variety management might need only one of the team to round out the evening.⁵³

Nonetheless, as time passed, some of these husband-wife combinations came to consider themselves—and to be judged by others—a more valuable commodity as a two-act than as singles. As the profession became more stable, managers were able to engage larger companies and more often featured performers only in their most popular specialty. For example, after 1873, Josie and Dan Morris were always listed on bills as a team.⁵⁴ Also, the established teams continued to invent new two-acts, evidence that they found them successful. Staging a "double song and dance" called "The Apple of My Eye" in fall, 1871, Moore and Henderson had added "Dutch Skirmishers" by December 1872, "The Happy Irish Couple" by April 1873, and "The Two Deitchers" by May 1873.⁵⁵ Wren and Collins had dropped the old favorite "Barney's Courtship" by 1873 for two new sketches which seemed just as popular, "A Terrible Fix" and "Late Hours."⁵⁶ Watson and Sherman's 1874 act, "Love and Jealousy in Germany," was advertised as written by Harry Wharf, a suggestion that teams were soliciting and willing to pay for good double act material.⁵⁷

But the continued success of the mixed two-act was best demonstrated by the increasing numbers of performers specializing in it. By the 1875-76 season there were at least twice the number of teams as in the 1871-72 season. Now a single city saw more teams: whereas only four mixed teams appeared in New York in the 1871-72 and 1872-73 seasons, eight different male-female teams appeared there in the 1875-76 season.[58]

The most successful new team of the mid-seventies was John and Maggie Fielding. Both were experienced singles before becoming a double act. Maggie Fielding had made her first appearance when only six years old, at the Old Bowery Theatre under G. L. Fox; when she was ten years old her parents moved west, and she joined the stock company at Wood's Museum in Chicago, playing there until her thirteenth year. She then went on the road for two years with Edwin Forrest, playing boy parts, after which she joined Tony Pastor's company. John Fielding was a minstrel, billed as "the inimitable Ethiopian comedian" when he appeared at Tony Pastor's in April 1869.[59] There is no proof they were husband and wife, but perhaps John and Maggie Fielding met at Pastor's and married. Beginning in 1870 the Fieldings were invariably engaged at the same house, although apparently as singles; by the end of 1872 the Fieldings were exhibiting an Irish two-act called "Blarney"; henceforth they were to win success as a team.[60]

In early 1873 they entertained audiences with "The Emerald Isle" and "O'Connor's Child, or the Harp of Tara." In April they departed with Tony Pastor's travelling company, featured in "Blarney," "their original Irish character sketch." The Fieldings returned to New York in the fall to appear again and again at Tony Pastor's that season with "their own original Hibernian sketches," among them "The Tipperary Couple," "Blarney," "The Irish Domestics," and "Sports of the Emerald Isle." Spring, 1874, found "The Funny Irish Couple" once more engaged to tour with Tony Pastor's travelling company, an honor they would have yet again the following season. Indeed, from the 1872-73 season on, the Fieldings spent more weeks in New York City than any other team, and by the 1875-76 season, if not before, they had surely replaced Wren and Collins as the favorites of the city.[61] Perhaps the Fieldings' success can be attributed to the fact that each had been so popular independently (with Maggie receiving the better notices);[62] that two established singles chose to form a team suggests the male-female act was becoming a recognized opportunity for success.

But few teams were as equally experienced as the Fieldings. The majority of teams were formed because it was so practical for a married couple. Seemingly every team, old or new, mentioned in variety news columns in the mid-seventies was married: the male-female act was clearly a convenient way for a man and woman necessarily travelling together from one variety house to another to make a living. An unemployed wife was a burden, what vaudevillian Joe Laurie, Jr. later called "excess baggage," whereas a double act was paid more than a single, thus enabling a wife to contribute to her keep.[63] Thomas Winnett, for example, began working in the theatre in 1865, but never worked with a woman until his marriage. For a while he toured the country with Charles Holly as Winnett and Holly, "The Keystone Boys," performing songs and dances and clog-dancing; later Winnett had an act with Dave Oaks called "The Golden Shower." In 1869 he was a minstrel with Hooley's. In 1870 he could be found in a gymnastic single. He married Lottie, a non-professional, sometime before 1873, and suddenly "the Winnetts" began to appear on variety bills in "double acts and songs-and-dances"; by January 1876 they were veteran performers of "Teutonic Specialties."[64]

But even for the established female performer, travelling with a man and appearing onstage with him had its advantages: it provided safety from the rowdy male patrons out front. According to performer Sam Morton, teamed with his wife Kitty Morton, "A man with wife had his troubles." The female performers were still expected to mingle with the wine-buyers and aid the bar receipts, and each week when Morton objected, a long battle with the manager ensued. "A man was kept pretty busy protecting his wife or anyone he was fond of," Sam recalled; "The women were looked upon as legitimate prey for anyone."[65] Sam Morton was speaking of Western houses in 1888, but in the early seventies this honky-tonk atmosphere prevailed East or West.

Whereas for performers the mixed act was a practical choice, probably much of its appeal for mid-seventies audiences was still the novelty: the number of mixed acts in New York variety houses in the 1875-76 season was much lower than the number of double male acts seen.[66] But if the combination itself was still relatively new, the actual routines offered by male-female teams were anything but fresh. Just as Wren and Collins offered popular extravaganzas and farces of bygone days in two-act form, Jennie Kimball's and J. K. Stewart's "Mr. and Mrs. White" must have been a condensed version of the farcical afterpiece of the same title, a trusty applause-getter since the late 1830s. Watson and Sherman, the Loves, and others did burlesques of successful pantomimes like "Baked Alive," thereby capitalizing on the popularity of the Ravels and the Lauris. Minstrelsy was another source of material—familiar material—for the first male-female acts, unsurprisingly, since most male entertainers of the day had served some time in minstrelsy. "The Nerves," offered in 1865 by John Wild and Blanche Stanley, was a minstrel sketch actually seen at Wood's Minstrel House that same season;[67] perhaps it was even a "wench act"—an obvious choice from the minstrelsy repertoire for male-female teams, it would seem.

Indeed, in careful imitation of current trends, by the mid-seventies most male-female teams had turned to dialect comedy—either blackface or immigrant—as the way to make their living. With only a few exceptions, almost every mixed team, old or new, was working in a dialect act between 1872 and 1876, with Irish and "Dutch" (i.e., German) the most popular choices.[68] The significant fact about the surviving male-female Irish and Dutch acts is that they are virtually identical to the dialect routines done by male two-acts—even their costumes were identical[69]—with the difference that they were done by a man and woman.

Routines like the Fieldings' "The Tipperary Couple" and "Sports of the Emerald Isle," or Moore and Henderson's act, "The Happy Irish Couple," no doubt featured some breath-taking jigging and a spirited duet—such as this song and dance number from an 1875 *New York Clipper,* dedicated to Andy and Annie Hughes and titled "The Limerick Pair":

>We are a happy Irish pair,
>From the ould green sod we kem;
>In Limbrick we were bred and born,
>And Hughes it is our name.
>For singing and for dancing
>Our likes could not be found;
>We can bate thim all, both big and small,
>This grate big counthry round.
>
>Chorus: Oh, watch the movement of our feet. (Break.)
>In execution we're so neat. (Break.)
>We'll thry to plase yees one and all—
>The collywobbles we can cure—
>Kape your eyes upon us now,
>Ane watch us welt the flure. (Dance.)
>
>We are going to settle down for life
>On Columbia's glorious shore,
>That land of pace and happiness
>That thrue Irish hearts adore;
>But we must lave yees now, kind friends,
>We've tried yees to amuse—
>So don't forget the Limbrick pair—
>Annie and Andy Hughes.
>Chorus and dance, as at
>end of first verse.[70]

But, of course, lyrics boasting about a pair's dancing prowess were already standard with male song and dance teams. The braggadocio intended to describe the Hugheses—"For singing and dancing / Our likes could not be found"—is virtually identical to lines written for male teams; compare the lyrics in "Two Flowers from Paddy's Land," dedicated to Harrigan and Hart: "For singing and for dancing, too, / Just bate us if you can."[71] The Hugheses' act was hardly unusual, just as sentimental mock-Irish ballads like "Norah McGill," possibly performed by the Fieldings in 1875, were an abundant staple of the variety theatre of the day.[72]

For a man and woman putting together a two-act in the mid-seventies—as for all other variety performers—routines featuring Irish or German characters were an obvious choice, for the tidal wave of Irish and German immigration rivalled the Civil War in importance as a social phenomenon of nineteenth-century America. By the Civil War, 1,700,000 Irish immigrants had entered America, 1,250,000 Germans. After the hiatus of the war years, immigration rose again year by year, with 460,000 immigrants arriving in 1873 alone.[73] The profound effects of rising immigration on city and countryside, on both newcomer and native, were dealt with in hysterical and philosophical fashion in thousands of newspaper articles, sermons, and social tracts, on soapboxes, in novels, and on theatre stages.[74] For the variety audience, the commotion was anything but academic.

The native Americans who came to variety must have rubbed shoulders every day with Paddy and Hans. Variety patrons, with the exception of the high-bred slummers and the riff-raff at either extreme, were largely working men; the gallery of the Metropolitan Theatre in 1874, for instance, was jammed with boot-blacks and errand boys, with the parquet full of clerks, shopmen, and gamblers. The variety theatres catered to the people who flocked to the Bowery, and the Bowery was "the Cheapside of New York, the place of the People, the resort of mechanics and the laboring classes; the home and the haunt of a great social democracy."[75] This was the class who served immigrants in their own businesses, visited shops and saloons run by immigrants, and often competed with immigrants for jobs—exasperating dealings that made ideal material for comedy. The immigrant was only one of many popular figures on the legitimate stage, but was seen nightly on the variety stage.

But just as the native increase in population does not sufficiently explain the exploding growth of popular theatre and amusements, so native fascination with the immigrant is not sufficient explanation for the ascendancy of immigrant humor in variety by the mid-seventies. It was immigration that accounted for the mushrooming population of urban areas, and the multiplying variety houses were also in the cities—in precisely those neighborhoods overrun with Irish and German immigrants. In New York City, for example, there were already more than 370,000 Irish and Germans by the sixties, most of them crowded into downtown Manhattan. Contemporary writers noted that the great mass of traders on the Bowery were "foreigners" — "men from all quarters of the globe, nearly all retaining their native manner and habits, all very little Americanized." Standing at a certain point on the Bowery, the passer-by could see the Bowery Theatre below Canal Street, the flashy sign of Tony Pastor's up towards Prince Street, the German Stadt Theater, and the Atlantic Garten, all in a single glance. In this same spot, "the 'rich Irish brogue' is well represented," although "the 'sweet German accent' predominates."[76]

The cheap, easily appreciated, and nearby variety shows were the logical entertainment for the immigrant working people who lived on the Lower East Side. In fact, in 1872, a writer claimed that although Germans patronized the cheap Bowery theatres, "there is an unmistakenly Irish stamp on most of the faces present."[77] This may have been true at first, since Germans had a number of German theatres and beer gardens to choose from. But as the seventies wore on, the beer gardens offering variety featured English-speaking performers, and the intimate tone of much German humor in the variety house shows the Germans did not stay away.[78] The link between the audience and the entertainment is well illustrated by the practice of two male-female teams, the Morrises and Henderson and Moore, both of whom had Irish and Dutch acts in their repertoire. Presumably they supplied the appropriate act on the spot, depending on a certain night's audience.[79] The mix of natives, Germans, and Irish was fluid.

No doubt there were occasions, in particular cities (Boston for example) or on specific holidays, when a variety hall was filled with, say, Irish patrons. On such an occasion the Fieldings might pull out a partisan number like "When You and I Were Green":

> In thought I wander back, my love
> O'er thirty years or more,
> When you and I, with heavy hearts,
> Took leave of Erin's shore.
> What anguish when the moment came
> To bid a last adieu;
> How many bitter tears were shed
> When home was lost to view!
> ....
> We both were young and hearty then,
> The world we did defy,
> Although we had to battle with
> "No Irish need apply!"
> We felt no shame for motherland,
> But looked to her with pride;
> Let come what would, our hearts were true—
> Our land we ne'er denied.
> Chorus: We love her still, our dear old isle, etc.[80]

Such a song, evoking the "anguish when the moment came.... When home was lost to view," with its vow "We love her still, our dear old isle,"[81] and its curt reminder of the days when "No Irish need apply," must have been directed to a largely Irish audience. Just so, when Frank McAvoy's New Hibernicon, a diorama of Irish scenes accompanied by singing and dancing, was in New York city in spring, 1873, its audiences were

> largely composed of natives of the soil represented who have found a home in America, and their little ones, who possibly gazed for the first time upon the scenes where the youthful days of their ancestors had been passed. To such these views have an uncommon interest. Continued exhibitions are announced.[82]

But native Americans could appreciate most immigrant routines. "Deutschland Band," for instance, written by the "Dutch" Winnetts, was clearly intended to be enjoyed by a native audience:

> Ven we go do de bicknicks,
> Ve hafe a gay ould dime;
> Ve dance und sing, sweet moosic make,
> Dhrink lager beer und vine.
>   (Sym — with bass drum.)
> Den saurkraut ve dackle,
> Dot makes us "oh so phat,"
>   (Sym — with trombone)
> Ouf Boloney sausage ve dhake a try
> Und got de best of dot.[83]

The habits described were the most outwardly noticeable traits of the German immigrants, the very ones that were foreign, thus laughable, habits to natives — as to a typical American visitor to a German beer garden, who reported the menu as those "snake-looking" Bolognas and "salads that the devil and Dr. Faustus only know the ingredients of."[84] The humor was not necessarily harsh, and even served to teach native Americans something about being German. On the other hand, references to waltzing, drinking beer and Rhine wine, and eating pretzels and cheese must have also been enjoyed by Germans in the audience; in fact, "Deutschland Band" was dedicated to "All the 'German Emigrants' and 'German Star Comiques'."

Whenever possible, enterprising performers would no doubt have it both ways. Irish and German patrons enjoyed hearing familiar accents and loving references to "the ould green sod" or "Vaterland"; simultaneously, native patrons could laugh with superiority at the tortured English and funny un-American clothes. And although these airs frequently mentioned ills and complaints about the immigrant's treatment in America, such songs almost always expressed the immigrant's realization that America was now his home and his desire to be accepted;[85] the Limerick Pair was careful to praise "Columbia's glorious shore." Such sentiments were not objectionable, and probably even engaged the feelings and interest of a native population that was more accepting of its Irish and German citizenry, thanks to a new unity forged on the battlefields of the 1860s.

German routines in particular tended to be less nostalgic for the past than Irish routines, and also betrayed more self-consciousness about German immigrant status; for example, a song for male and female called "The German Emigrants" vividly and comically described the uncomical plight of the recent immigrant:

> He: We ust come from de old country
> My Katarene unt me—
> She: But den we get so oful sick
> Ven we did cross dot see.
> He: A man he stolt avay my trunk,
> In dot was my new pants
> She: Unt ven we asked him how dot was,
> He called us emigrants.
> Both: No matter vere dot vas we go,
> Sure, mine friends, I tolt you so,
> Everybody seems to know
> Dot we was emigrants.
> He: We go of Cincinnati town,
> We settle rite down dare—
> She: We ust eat plenty switzer kase,
> Unt drink dot lager beer,
> He: Unt den ve have a bully times,
> We board round at my aunt's.
> She: Pooty soon ve get civilized,
> Unt don't been emigrants.
> Both: Chorus.[86]

Such a routine was probably funny to both native audiences and first generation immigrants, although for different reasons. The second generation may have laughed the loudest; a German writer of 1865 complained that the children of immigrants were the worst "natives" and could exhibit the height of cruelty to "an old Dutchman."[87] Certainly both natives and assimilated immigrants could enjoy routines that mocked the greenhorn's social aspirations. The plans of the man and woman in a routine called "Because You Vos So Dutch"—to go to "Tarasoga" and "Branch Long" and to "live on big red herrings / Und some bully sourkroud"—are ridiculous, because it is not at all what one does "to be der belle" in the States.[88] Such routines provided those who dreamed of running with "der swell" with someone to feel superior to—and also an example of how not to act. These routines also suggest the German immigrant's real-life desire to be "civilized" and to "get long fus rate."[89] Whereas Irish immigrants were largely impoverished, unskilled peasants, the majority of German immigrants were artisans, tradesmen, or enterprising farmers, with a reputation for hard work, perseverance, and thrift which earned them respect, however begrudged.[90]

But whatever the social reasons for the subtleties of response to immigrant routines, they were never the whole story. The real attraction of acts such as the Hugheses' would surely have been the singing and dancing skill of the performers; one thing audiences of any ethnic background waited for must have been the moment when performers began to "welt the flure."

The remaining theme in male-female Irish and Dutch acts was romance, which figured in routines by several popular seventies teams—Wren and Collins's "Barney's Courtship," Watson and Sherman's "Love and Jealousy in Germany," probably Moore and Henderson's "The Apple of My Eye." Some of the male-female double numbers published in the *Clipper* from 1873 to 1875 involved romance; they provide some hints about routines like those just mentioned. There were, for instance, songs about parting, in which invariably lovers agreed either to stay in the homeland or else to emigrate together, as in the Irish "Don't Go Away, Mollie Darling" (from ould Ireland"), or in the Dutch number "Goot-pye, Katrina," in which Fritzie vows to take Katrina with him "To dot shweed lant, America."[91] Such routines were actually more concerned with the impact of immigration than with love itself.

More comical courtship numbers usually depicted infatuated lovers, a type well-illustrated by "Dere's Somedings de Matter mit Me":

> I'm youst a young Chermans vot likes lager beer,
> As all of dose peebles can see,
> But dere's somedings aboutd me dot feels mighdy queer.
> Und dere's somedings de matter mit me;
> As I walk of der streed ven der efening bell chimes,
> Und dot sweet Katarina I see.
> My heart chust chumps roundt like a song out of times,
> Oh, dere's somedings de matter mit me.

The girl has the same response when she sees her "Chaky," and at the end the two come together on stage for this exchange:

> He: Katarina, you know dot I lofe you so vell,
> Und I like for to hafe you to be
> My sveed little frau. Now quickly do tell,
> For dere's somedings de matter mit me.
> Kat: Now, Chaky, you know dot I can't help but say
> Dot your own little vife I will be,
> Und I'll lofe you so vell—for dere's no other vay,
> Und dat's vot's de matter mit me.

> Chorus (both): Through sunshine or foul weather,
> As one, we two shall be,
> And sweetly we'll live together,
> For dere's nothing de matter mit me.⁹²

For natives in the audience, the biggest laugh-getter must have been the naiveté of attempting to make love in broken English! And it was surely amusing in itself that such outlandish foreigners found in each other fit objects for love; the "Dutch" boy in "I Vonder Vat's Her Name" must have earned laughs when he sang:

> As I vas walk me oud last nide,
> I look me oph a Deitcher gel;
> She vas a awful lofely sighd—
> I tink she vas a belle.⁹³

The couples' infatuation was also funny in the way that young lovers of any ethnic background are universally funny to those who are not infatuated. Native and German alike would smile at "Chaky's" confession, that when he sees Katarina, "My heart chust chumps roundt like a song out of times."⁹⁴

Besides, at a time when newspapers like the Irish-Catholic *Boston Pilot* emphatically denounced "mixed marriages,"⁹⁵ everyone in a variety audience would no doubt be pleased to see stage lovers so charmed by their own nationality. In a routine like "Because You Vos So Dutch," it was precisely the fact that two lovers were of the appropriate nationality that explained "Der reason vy I love you."⁹⁶ While it is unlikely that variety acts were composed with serious views on intermarriage and miscegenation in mind, their instinctual support of the status quo was one reason such songs could safely appeal to everyone.

Finally, romance would seem to be a natural choice for a team composed of a man and woman; nonetheless, there was no real theatrical tension created between male and female in most mixed double routines. Stag audiences were naturally little interested in realistic relationships, for the rules and confinements of family life were what men on the town were out to escape; routines therefore revealed little about the status and roles of women outside the variety house. Onstage or off, women in the variety house were there to please men, and the degree of comicality or sensuality could run the gamut, according to the act or the actress (at either extreme, both the prostitute and the greenhorn can inspire the smirk). But whereas the danseuse was routinely observed to play the role of sex object, the female sketch artist primarily assisted male performers in creating comedy of the asexual concerns of men.

In a postwar society gripped by economic and racial tensions, immigration and the continuing Negro question were the matters more pressing to the male audience than domestic relations. Thus, the important appeal in male-female Irish and Dutch routines is the immigrant humor—the comical dialects and costumes, the laughter created by depicting the new immigrant's experiences and social aspirations. Even courtship songs were lacking any male-female dynamic. In the surviving songs, boy sees girl and almost instantly proposes, she agrees on the spot, and the number ends with a verse such as the one quoted above from "Dere's Somedings de Matter Mit Me." Such routines could have been done just as effectively by two males, and in fact were probably based on routines already done by popular male teams, for whom female impersonation was a well-established tradition.

"Hans and Lena," printed in the *Clipper* in early 1874 and dedicated to Sheridan and Mack, probably the male team most famous in this line, was typical:

(Enter Hans): Vile sthanding in der doorvay
Of dot Schneider's beer saloon,
I saw a leedle Dutch gal valking py.
Her dress sthood ouat behind her
Yust like a big baloon.
Und as I look she vink me mit her eye.

Spoken: Yaw, dot's soa! She vinked, und den she shmole [*sic*] more as elefen inches across from both sides—dot's a fact. Und den her dress—dot vas so nead—dey call 'em a ridin' goat—mit big bleck buttons all ofer, vich look like leedle turtles vas grawling up her beck. But den

Chorus: Sh's der neadest leedle Dutch gal
I hafe seen in all my life,
Und if I yust can find her ouat
I'll take her for my vife. (exit.)

"Lena" enters and echoes his sentiments, and the two come together at the end for a duet:

Now ve hafe met by chances,
Und ve make up righd avay;
Ve're der habbiest leedle couble in dis town.
Now soon ve vill got married,
Und togedder ve vill sthay;
Vile life's habby hill togedder ve'll glimb down.[97]

The humor is broader than in the known male-female acts, which was likely a general distinction between male-female routines and male two-acts using female impersonation. Otherwise, if the surviving routines are representative, the male-female immigration act was highly imitative of double male acts, little utilizing the distinguishing aspect of the partnership—its sexual make-up.

This was particularly true of male-female blackface acts of the mid-seventies. Though not as numerous as teams impersonating immigrants, they were fairly common. Two of the earliest mixed blackface acts were Billy and Maggie Ray, advertised in 1875 as "Playing a highly-successful engagement at Tony Pastor's Opera-House New York, in their Celebrated Plantation Sketches," and May and Nic Hughes, also billed in "plantation sketches," one of which was named "Uncle Joe's Return."[98] The title "Uncle Joe's Return" suggests it depicted that beloved figure, the old slave who returns to the plantation to mourn the passing of the happy days spent there before the war, the stock treatment also found in a surviving 1875 sketch for a man and woman called "Uncle William."[99]

These pictures of child-like Negroes happier as slaves than free clearly appealed to the generally racially prejudiced immigrants, who, as the newest and least secure members of society, were not generous in extending sympathy to a minority group. The Irish-Americans, for example, had been unanimously opposed to abolition: they did not want black migrants in their cities, and feared the free Negroes' effect on their job market.[100] The typical blackface routine, depicting stage blacks who did not want to live in the North but longed to return to the pre-war life on the plantation, was understandably consoling to working-class variety audiences in growing Northeastern and Midwestern cities.

But these themes had been established by minstrels and male variety performers long before the early seventies. A double male act from the same season as "Uncle William" featured an almost identical slave uncle and auntie—with the difference that the woman was impersonated.[101] Of course, the real social problems of blacks—and Northern obligations to ex-slaves—were ignored in all the routines, with their aging Uncles near to departing for the Promised Land (wish-fulfilling, perhaps, for many in the audience). The stage Negroes were not only played by whites, but were not in any way true to the characters represented. Thus removed from reality, it made little difference whether the Negro Auntie was played by male or female.

The absence of genuine male-female involvement in these routines is probably also explained by the shortage of capable character actresses for partners. Responsibility for making comedy was generally shouldered by the male teammates, with the women entertaining with their singing and/or dancing, or in some cases, by just looking pretty. One variety manager advertised in 1869 for a "First-Rate End Man" who could do "a good song and dance," but for a female vocalist, who "must be good looking, have a good figure, and have good wardrobe."[102] The comic mantle fell naturally on the man's shoulders, for most male variety performers had been schooled in the comedy-talking bits of tambo and bones; in contrast, the soubrette had made her entrance in the chorus-line, so that in the midseventies few women had ever had the opportunity to develop comic skills. Accomplished comediennes rarely shared the limelight with male partners, but were "stars" like Adah Richmond or Jennie Kimball.

Given this heritage, when a husband and wife joined a company in early variety days, invariably the man was hired as Ethiopian or immigrant comedian, the woman as vocalist and/or danseuse.[103] When these same couples teamed up for a double act, the concocted numbers gave each the opportunity to exhibit the skills known best already: William Carleton was "the ever popular Irish comedian and vocalist," his partner Jennie Gilmer "the charming songstress"; James contributed an Irish stump speech in the Emmersons' two-act, Dollie a song and dance.[104] Probably most teams did a double song much like those printed above, with the man handling the interspersed comic dialogue, and with a solo song or dance introduced at some point by the woman.

Nonetheless, it cannot be assumed that in the early seventies every female team partner was a wife thrown into the act merely as window dressing. Whereas striking female looks may have been the attraction which made one act go over, complex dancing done by a homely woman may have been another team's bread and butter; also, as more and more women entered variety, and as existing teams accumulated experience, the number of talented women must have been increasing. Kitty Henderson's clog dancing was "characterized by difficult movements and correctness of time"; Lizzie Sherman's singing was thought improved when she appeared at Trimble's in Philadelphia from what it had been before, and by 1874 the dancing of Emily Siegel, once a minor dancer in the corps de ballet, could "fairly take the house by storm."[105]

The important thing was that more men and women were working as teams, laying the groundwork for a tradition that would someday produce headliners equal to any male team. It was gradually becoming economically feasible for a man and woman to secure employment as a team, with only incidental utility work, and by spring, 1874, two-acts were actively advertising in newspapers. By 1876, the New York publisher of *The Variety Stage,* a collection of skits, included several one-acts labelled for "1 (M), 1 (F)."[106]

The rise in male-female teams was both a cause and effect of the fact that variety was changing. In the mid-seventies some variety houses still featured the can-can, and even Tony Pastor's theatre was occupied by Mme.

Rentz's Female Minstrels and Mme. Delacour's Can Can Troupe for the summer of 1874, while Pastor left on his annual summer tour. Not until 1882 would Blondes and Female Minstrels no longer hold sway at Pastor's in the summers.[107] But even though a pretty chorus-line was still a necessary ingredient for success, Tony Pastor had envisioned the formula of the future; perhaps his troupe's warm reception at regular theatres during summer tours had set him thinking. As Pastor himself later told the story, during his years at 444 Broadway he "studied the situation closely, and determined that if the women could also be induced to attend, the patronage could be materially extended."[108]

Thus, in July 1865 he opened Tony Pastor's Opera House at 199-201 Bowery, with a capacity of over 800. This "beautiful Temple of Amusement" had a "Family Circle," and Pastor announced that it was a place "which he designs making the Great Family Resort of the City, — where heads of families can bring their Ladies and children, and witness an exceptional entertainment — one that will please the most fastidious."[109] Pastor began by offering a matinee every Saturday "where ladies and children can safely attend without escort,"[110] and some women came; one writer testified in 1872 that "the Rough and servant-girl element predominate in the audiences" of the Bowery variety houses.[111] But at first the "Great Family Resort" was just a design in Pastor's head. Pastor himself later admitted that initially, "the charm did not allure"; in fact, eight years later variety was so unappealing to women that Pastor was still admitting ladies free at the Saturday matinee.[112]

The concept of a family audience at a variety house, Pastor explained in retrospect, "was a long time developing...one had to tone down a show that pleased the men to one that pleased the women."[113] So long as the audience was male, performers would naturally cater to their likings; but so long as the shows had the atmosphere of a stag entertainment, respectable women of any class would not attend. It would take more than a handful of women in the audience for the performers to risk a new style of playing. In this gradual transition the male-female routine was to play a part, for with its growing use of romantic and domestic themes, it was an act which appealed especially to women. Male-female acts were to increase in number in direct proportion to the women in the audience, and must have helped draw the first "ladies" who led the way.

3

Male-Female Teams in the Family Variety Hall, 1876–1893

Although unheard of little more than ten years before, the male-female team was a standard variety act by the late seventies, and one of the more popular drawing cards of the eighties. In the 1885–86 season, for example, Harry Miner usually had two or three mixed acts on the bill at each of his two theatres, sometimes as many as five.[1] Their names are forgotten now, but many male-female teams had their moments in the spotlight then—as on the evening when Farrell and Leland "took Immensely," or when Morosco and Gardner were "the hit of the entire bill." On those past occasions when Stanley and Conway "kept the house in roars of laughter," when the Nelsons were "heartily cheered," or the Peasleys "kept the house in a continuous round of applause," these performers and their audience must have known that magic felt when good theatre is at work.[2]

The faded descriptions tell us that male-female teams were enjoying a rare period of prosperity, and they were not alone in their good fortune; the late seventies and the eighties were palmy days for the entire variety profession. The performer with talent was probably never out of work, for there was a long string of variety houses across the nation, all seeking entertainers to occupy their boards; each major city had at least one house, usually five or six. For the unfastidious player, New York City alone reportedly had over six hundred concert saloons. The urban population of America increased sixty-one per cent between 1880 and 1890, and the variety profession expanded accordingly.[3]

Most managers began tailoring their offerings to attract the potential mass audience of respectable men and women and their families. As early as 1871, the Globe Theatre in New York claimed to offer "fun, wit, and humor without vulgarity"; at the Theatre Comique in 1872, supposedly "obscenity, vulgarity and profanity" were "carefully expurgated from the performances."[4] However true the claims, managers were trying to establish a different sort of reputation. Throughout the spring and summer of

1878, when Harry Miner's new London Theatre was being readied for the fall season, he chose one descriptive phrase to advertise it—"NO WINE-ROOM!"[5]

By the mid-seventies, presumably Pastor was at last succeeding in attracting some semblance of a family audience to his matinees, for he had set his cap on establishing an evening family patronage. On a Wednesday evening in December 1874 Pastor gave away sixty turkeys to female patrons, and each child who attended the special New Year's Day matinee received a "handsome toy."[6] In spring, 1875, he would bribe "ladies" with hams every Monday evening, ten barrels of flour every Wednesday evening, dress patterns on Friday, and ten tons of coal every Saturday evening; that same year Pastor moved a bit farther uptown.[7]

By the late seventies Pastor was routinely earning approving blurbs in newspapers, such as this notice in the *New York Figaro:*

> The veteran manager who presides over the fortunes of the neat little theatre down Broadway is untiring in his efforts to please the public. In addition to own [sic] presence on the stage, he has gathered about him a company of competent people. Variety without vulgarity is his motto, and he has adhered to this principal til his house has, in reality, become a popular family resort, where people may take it comfortable, always find something good, and go home pleased with Tony Pastor, Gus Williams and the company.[8]

Whether or not these were initially puffs, by 1881 Pastor had dispensed with the lavish door-prizes, and felt secure enough in his patronage to move to a new theatre still farther uptown, on 14th Street off Union Square, a respectable and busy shopping district near the somewhat more northward heart of the legitimate theatre world.[9] Any still reticent patrons were assured that

> Tony Pastor's theatre is recognized as the best and most respectable place in the city where variety performances are given, and a refined and genteel audience is always to be found within its doors,

and were duly informed when Pastor had been forced to hold an additional matinee—"by special request of hundreds of ladies who could not secure seats last Friday."[10]

Presumably this assurance was needed. If the glowing accounts of the multitudes of "ladies and children" present at Pastor's matinees had been truly accurate, the gimmicks and persuasive journalism would not have been necessary. The number of female patrons continued to grow, but they must have been outnumbered by men for many years—and certainly the women who attended variety would not have been described by the upper classes as "ladies."[11] Presumably decent women with children, from whatever class, had to be discriminating; in the eighties some houses were still condemned by the popular press for their dissolute atmosphere;[12] the frequent reprimands for offensive acts suggest that variety could be smutty on occasion.[13]

In like fashion, male-female teams did not always practice what they publicized. Many teams, following Pastor's tutelage, settled on the epithet "refined" as the most salable image for the times. McAvoy and Rogers dubbed themselves "Ideal Society Artists"; at the opening of the 1885 season, every issue of the *New York Dramatic News* contained Hallen and Hart's advertisement for their "company of ladies and gentlemen."[14] But that same year, Joe Hart, one of the "gentlemen" in Fred Hallen and Enid Hart's company, was chided in the *New York Dramatic News* because his stories were "bordering on the smutty." As for McAvoy and Roger's sketch, it somewhat contradicted its billing as "refined" by utilizing the low comedy prop of a dozen pounds of herring per season. Similar contradictions abounded.[15]

It was a period of transition; the tension between what variety had been and what it was trying to be contributed to its vitality. The injection of "refinement" into stage shows which had previously been merely low was a therapeutic shot in the arm, for performers unable to fall back on blue were forced to polish and repolish their acts, to entertain with genuinely funny comedy and more skillful singing and dancing—not just leers or vulgar noises. But although variety patrons were demanding the inoffensive, this audience was not overly fastidious. They still knew how to laugh, at themselves, too; comedy could have a sharp, sometimes almost sadistic bite. Stage business could still be rowdy and rambunctious, but had to be well thought-out to entertain the diverse, capricious audiences of an amorphous market. Variety had, as one modern writer put it, "the precisely correct blood count for that day's vaudeville—low comedy not yet touched by Keith's anemia."[16]

For the time being, supply and demand were at equilibrium. On the one hand, there was more demand for variety entertainment; thus the number of performers had increased—and this plentiful supply of acts encouraged an echelon of real talent. However, audiences were still sufficiently limited for competition between houses to be fierce.[17] Variety houses were small enough for an intimate relationship to exist between audience and performer; a performer could see his audience, knew its reaction exactly, and could play on it by the second. Neither performers nor managers could afford to ignore the play of features out front; lower-class audiences had a limited income, and demanded good entertainment for their money. And they came hesitantly at first, unconvinced this entertainment was for them, so performers had to see to the audience's pleasure to seduce them. The period from the late seventies to the early nineties was the era of this dynamic courtship. Variety had never been better.

As variety expanded, the number of male-female teams also increased. Whereas in the 1875-76 season only eight mixed teams had appeared in New York City's variety houses, at least seventy-two mixed teams were seen there in the 1879-80 season. The number remained high throughout the eighties, with at least eighty-three mixed teams visiting New York City in the 1884-85 season. Put a different way, whereas only sixteen or so mixed teams visited New York City between 1870 and 1875, over 138 male-female teams came during the first five years of the eighties.[18] Variety performers were naturally attracted to New York, in 1880 already the biggest city in America.[19] Led by the innovative Tony Pastor, New York City variety was no doubt the best to be seen in the country; those male-female teams who captivated New Yorkers were probably the most talented in the profession.

Beane and Gilday, Henshaw and Ten Broeck, Hallen and Hart, and the Whites appeared in New York City at least seven weeks of the year—sometimes for as many as fifteen weeks—for at least seven consecutive seasons; these teams were the "stars" among male-female acts. In what might be called the "extremely popular" category—those teams having four to six one-week bookings a year in New York, for at least seven consecutive years—were the Hugheses, Adams and Linton, Rogers and Vickers, Watson and Hutchings, Ellis and Moore, the Davises, the Peasleys, Richmond and Glenroy, the Jeromes, the Healeys, Wills and Adams, McAvoy and Rogers, Huber and Allyne, the Murphys, Bryant and Richmond, Morosco and Gardner, and Jones and Montague.

"Regulars"—teams appearing an average of two or three times in New York every year for at least seven consecutive seasons—were the Fieldings, Bennett and Gardner, Roach and Castleton, the Whitings, the Burgesses, the Conways, Redmond and Blake, Woodson and Bennett, Farrell and Leland, Hume and Lindsay, McCarthy and Coleman, the Smiths, the Maxwells, the Nelsons, the Vidocqs, Forman and Meredith, Carter and Anderson, the Allens, Hines and Remington, the Delanos, John Byrne and Miss Helene, the Grinnells, and the Daytons. Of course, all these teams toured; the performers who came to New York also went to Boston, Cincinnati, St. Louis, San Francisco, and the towns along the way. The type of acts staged by these teams provides a sampling of the entertainment offered by male-female teams in major variety houses across America.

The inheritance of these performers was the tradition of immigrant humor; twenty-two of the forty-five male-female teams appearing in New York City for the 1877-78 season can be identified as playing immigrant characters.[20] Fifteen of the forty-five teams most successful throughout the era (those named above) impersonated immigrants onstage, and the number was probably higher; teams were not always identified by type in bills or reviews—their fans knew their work. The Fieldings, Bennett and Gardner, Redmond and Blake, McCarthy and Coleman, the Peasleys, the Davises, the Murphys, and the Hugheses were Irish acts; Rogers and Vickers, Watson and Hutchings, Wills and Adams, Morosco and Gardner, and the Smiths were German acts; Ellis and Moore's act consisted of a stage German and an Irish woman.

The ongoing careers of early teams like the Fieldings, the Hugheses, and Harry Watson (now with second wife Alice Hutchings) show the continued popularity of immigrant humor; initially a great many acts imitated these successes.[21] But while teams like the Coles in "Our German Cousins" and Fielding and Walker in "Back to Erin" must have highlighted traditional differences between the new life and the old, their material was not necessarily nostalgic; some routines may have voiced disillusionment with the old country, a sentiment presumably expressed in an act by Susie and James Dillion called "Ireland Ain't What It Used to Be."[22] Indeed, by the late seventies many immigrant sketches were concerned not with nostalgia for the old country, but with life in the workaday world of America. Several male-female teams depicted domestic workers; the Hugheses played "Irish Servants" from 1877 to at least 1881, the Murphys showed "High Times in the Kitchen"; Frank Bennett had an Irish sketch called "Kitchen Domestics" which he did with three successive female partners between 1876 and 1883.[23] Harry Watson played a butler in "Dutch Deception," and probably the deception involved was Watson's attempt to masquerade as a competent, experienced—i.e., American—butler: the comedy derived from his awkward attempts to carve a turkey and pour water into inverted goblets.[24]

But though the stage domestics may have mirrored the real-life status of many an immigrant in the audience, they did not reflect peculiarly immigrant concerns; there were native Americans with status as low. A number of teams who cannot be identified as immigrant acts also portrayed the comic side of servant life.[25] Such routines became rarer as the eighties wore on. Greenhorn comedy, the domestic servant sketch, and the homeland-nostalgia sketch had practically ceased to be performed by male-female teams by the mid-eighties.

Besides, there was a new theatre hit which male-female teams could not fail to notice, or afford to ignore. Whereas the models of the early seventies had been such acts as Delehanty and Hengler with their rambunctious "Fun in a Kitchen," or J. K. Emmett's blatantly Dutch "Fritz," beginning in 1878 Harrigan launched his phenomenally successful Mulligan series at the Theatre Comique, in which immigrants escaped both the scullery and the

Old World; Harrigan treated the adventures and cares of true-to-life characters in their own homes right in downtown New York with humor, sympathy, and loving detail.[26] Most Irish and German mixed teams who continued to be popular updated their repertoires accordingly.

Andy and Annie Hughes, who became even better known in the second half of the eighties, used what sounds like old-fashioned Irish material on at least one occasion, in "The Emigrant's Arrival." But their other sketches from the mid- and late eighties are "Norah's Birthday," "Katie's Surprise," "The Masquerade Party," and "Teddy's Misfortunes," titles which suggest a different appeal from the unsubtle nationalistic boasting of their earlier "The Limerick Pair"—and though they were renowned in the seventies as "Irish Servants," now the Hugheses went as "Ireland's Great Sketch Team."[27] Likewise, John and Lea Peasley—billed as "The Galway Pair" for the 1877-78 season—were performing "Mollie's Victory," "Sparking in the Park," "Jerry's Fortune," and "The Fifth Corporal" in the eighties, sketch titles recognizable as Irish only because of the characters' names.[28] The older teams' former focus on a mythical life in the mother country and Irish servant life in this land was exchanged for a new emphasis on Irish characters as individuals; now the sketch titles sound softer, more universal. As for the Irish and German teams who were new in the late seventies, none did nostalgic or greenhorn comedy.[29] The emphasis in the new sketches was on personalities, on everyday life in America—picnics, families, target companies.

Rogers and Vickers performed in variety for only a few years, but they were the most sought-after German team during that time and apparently played their immigrants with the lighter touch. Mattie Vickers, daughter of comedian R. P. Vickers, joined the stock company of Wood's Museum in 1876, playing Nan in *Good for Nothing,* and remained there until the spring of 1877, when she began performing in variety with her husband Charles Rogers. They worked as a sketch team through the 1882-83 season, when Mattie, managed and supported by her husband, began starring in plays, and earned praise for her "well known ability as a German dialect comedienne." During their variety tenure, Rogers and Vickers had a repertoire of three sketches, "Stagestruck," "The Attic Thespians," and "the Debutante."[30] The routines probably poked fun at "Deitchers" whose droll attempts to go either on the stage or into society made the upstarts look even more foolish. If the comedy showed immigrants still occupying a lowly place in society, it nevertheless suggested that some immigrants were more attuned to American values than in previous times.

By the eighties the Germans and the Irish had been an established part of the American scene for decades: historians use the date 1880 to demarcate the end of the "Old Immigration." This wave had begun sixty years earlier in 1820 and peaked in the 1850s; by the eighties some Irish- and German-Americans were well into their third generation.[31] Thus, while new arrivals were dwindling, the number of American-born Irish and Germans was constantly increasing, and the foreign accents, dress, and social customs of their ancestors were naturally becoming more muted. To themselves and to others, people of Irish and German background must have seemed less foreign all the time.

Moreover, although in the seventies German and Irish immigrants may have still looked outlandish, recent arrivals to Ellis Island made them look downright familiar. By 1880 the second wave of American immigration was beginning; Eastern European Jews were the first to come, with the Italians close on their heels. Eastern Jews, with their poverty and uncouth appearance, their Yiddish tongue and the traditional folkways they clung to, were a race apart; as for the swarthy Italians, they were equated with Negroes, and the two groups made Irish and Germans seem more like ordinary Americans by comparison.[32]

American prosperity and respectability was what these last two groups aspired to, and in the eighties, large numbers of Irish and Germans were at least in sight of the goal. It had been a natural process for the Germans. After 1870, there were increasingly fewer peasants and more industrial workers and artisans among German immigrants; many brought substantial savings. Apprenticeship training in the crafts was rigorous in Germany, and German carpenters, masons, printers, cabinet makers, painters, and shoemakers quickly established a reputation for quality work in the United States. In fact, the large number of post–Civil War resolutions of some German groups, which make reference—with alarm—to the Americanization of Germans, is evidence of their rapid assimilation.[33]

It had been harder for the Irish, the great mass of whom lacked money, education, or craft. But because they spoke a language that could be understood by English-speaking Americans and were long accustomed to political involvement in Ireland, their talent and huge numbers gradually effected their political ascent. Irish political power made jobs increasingly available to them; in the eighties the Irish "cop" and the Irish fireman were familiar stereotypes. By 1893 the Irish had completely surrendered their pick-and-shovel monopoly to the unfortunate Italians.[34]

As the Germans and Irish rose in life, they literally rose geographically in New York. Below 14th Street on the East Side, nearly everyone was of foreign birth; but as the inhabitants became more prosperous, noted a contemporary guidebook, they pushed farther uptown. Whereas the Jewish population was clustered at the east end of Canal Street, near Ludlow and East Broadway, and the Italians in the notorious Five Points neighborhood, for the most part the Germans and Irish had left these squalid tenements behind. From Houston to 14th Street was mostly German, flanked by the Irish closer to the East River. Irish and Irish-Americans could also be found between First and Second Avenues, from about 20th to 30th Street.[35]

While they could not be called middle class, they made a decent living superior to the masses in the far downtown. The Irish and Germans frequented the upper Bowery, whose dime-museums, pawn-shops, and retail shops, although "of the shoddy sort," had become the thoroughfare of "the respectable lower classes"; on Saturday night these wage earners were abroad with their earnings. On Broadway near Union Square could also be found "sons of toil and work-girls," some of whom were well-dressed although not fashionable.[36]

Neither above nor below, but precisely in this area could be found the variety houses. There were none below Grand Street and none either above 30th or in Madison Square, the center of fashionable life. But between these geographical boundaries were the London Theatre, at 235-237 Bowery near Rivington Street; Harry Miner's on the Bowery, near Broome Street; Aberle's, on 8th Street near Broadway; the Novelty Theatre, at 113 Bowery; Harry Miner's Eighth Avenue House, between 26th and 27th Street; Koster and Bial's, on 23rd Street; and Pastor's on East 14th Street, between Irving Place and Third Avenue.[37] It is an attractive assumption that the "ladies and gentlemen" so avidly sought by these shrewd managers were the nearby Irish and German wage earners and their families—in other words, the types actually described by Harrigan in his plays: barbers, cops, firemen, grocers, butchers, boarding-house and saloon owners, pawnbrokers, laborers, hack-drivers, and the like.[38]

Of course, the native Americans in this area must also have constituted a part of the audience. There were decent-looking tenements on either side of the prosperous brownstones in mid-Manhattan north of Union Square; and there was a neighborhood of third-class boarding houses, mostly inhabited by poor clerks, below 4th Street between Second and Ninth Avenues, concentrated on Bleecker and MacDougal.[39] But if sizable numbers of second-generation Irish and Germans were in the audience, that provides a convenient explanation for the kinds of routines being performed. They had not yet forgotten their ethnicity, and they still enjoyed seeing it portrayed in the variety theatres. Irish military organizations even reserved entire blocks of seats to see their caricatures onstage at Harrigan and Hart's.[40] But as offstage racial characteristics became blurred, the process was mirrored onstage.

The blatantly retrogressive routines were understandably the first to disappear. The upwardly mobile Irish- or German-American was not interested in yearning for a land across the sea which he probably had never seen. On the contrary, the assimilated immigrant often took fanatical pride in his Americanism, and scorned recent immigrants. Such a one was the Irish girl in Harrigan's *Squatter Sovereignty,* who rejects a wooer because after four months he was not acclimatized; "He doesn't even know what ice cream is yet. I'd sooner marry a Turk," she exclaims passionately.[41] Similarly, the more prosperous second generation did not care to see the scullery side of metropolitan life portrayed; they did not want to be reminded of their parents' early poverty and social ostracism. Immigrants who espoused middle-class values were tiring of harsh satirical pictures of themselves in putty noses and outlandish clothes; they preferred softer portrayals. Acts like the "Four Shamrocks"—famous for knock-down, drag-out comedy staged by brawling Irish laborers—were being superseded by the defter comedy of stars like Pat Rooney, clad in a cutaway coat and fancy waistcoat, with his jaunty Irish songs and graceful dancing.

In such routines it was often not the nationality depicted but the skills displayed that was the attraction, as this advertisement for Gallagher and DeVere's Irish act suggests:

> Billy GALLAGHER & DEVERE Ada
> IN THEIR ECCENTRIC IRISH SPECIALTY, ENTITLED
> "ALWAYS FOOLING,"
> Introducing Songs-and-Dances, Flashes of Wit,
> Quick Changes; also their artistic Statue-clog
> and Waltz-clog.[42]

The main appeal of this act was obviously the skillful "fooling." Appeals other than nationality were particularly important for immigrant acts that featured flirtation between a "Fritz and Lena"; flirtation scenes now tended to make points with the romantic interaction, with less focus on German or Irish character comedy.

Immigrant lovemaking continued to be a popular theme in the late seventies,[43] but around 1880, the number of immigrant teams personating lovers on the stage increased significantly. There were Frank and Fannie Davis in "Mahoney the Masher," Ellis and Moore in "Love's Labors" and "Swiss Courtship," the Ringlers in "Heinrich's Courtship," Boshell and Mack in "Irish and German Lovers," and numerous others.[44] What these couples offered as entertainment is suggested by a song called "Flirding in der Dark mid Lena," which appeared in an 1879 *Clipper,* dedicated to Wills and Adams. Between 1879 and 1882, German team John Wills and May Adams were popular with a routine called "Larks."[45] The lyrics below match the title:

> Id's nice to have some breddy girl
> Vhen you go on a "lark"

> Dot don'd make some obshecdions
> To Flirding in der dark;
> I tell you, you have lots of fun,
> Und lots of kisses, too,
> Und odder dings too numerous
> To mendion now to you.
>
> Mosd efery night 'boud den o'clock
> Vill find me in der park,
> Mid Lena sidding by my side—
> Flirding in der dark.
> Ve look us ob some liddle pench,
> Mid room for only two,
> Und dher we sid, und sid,
> Und sid, und—wouldn't you?[46]

More verses follow, whose appeal has little to do with the couple's being German, aside from the still present dialect humor. Not a single joke is concerned with immigrant life or peculiarities; instead, the humor is dependent on the telling of the couple's "spooning." The Dutchman always breaks off before telling what really went on in the dark on that little bench. He explains they do things "too numerous / To mendion now to you," and excuses their intimacies by saying "Der pench ve use vos verry schmall, / So damb, und awful cold," no doubt with a gleam in his eye. If the feeling of this song, with its sexual undertone, is typical of the male-female acts of the day, routines contained a bit more emphasis on male-female involvement than previously. Now the emphasis is on "flirding," not on reaffirming nationalistic bonds.

The content of this song, along with the extant titles, suggests many immigrant boy-girl acts were fairly broad, with loud comical mashers and some elbowing hints of sex. Nonetheless, even if some comics winked an eye at the audience and smirked when referring to flirting, it can be assumed routines were less crude than in earlier variety days. If there was any correlation between the reality and the reporting of it, variety entertainment had come a considerable distance from an earlier act like "The Haymakers," in which boy after boy simperingly visited a girl behind a haystack, and returned to the stage one by one in disordered clothing, indicating with obscene gestures and expressions what had happened.[47]

And some stage couples may have conducted "prettier" flirting than in "Larks." The experience of the managers of the day told them "refinement" was the best drawing card for women, and the concurrent popularity of the courtship and marriage act suggests it fell in the category of what was considered more refined—i.e., more toned down, quieter than traditional immigrant humor. Thus, whereas in the early seventies, the Fieldings were billed as "the funny Irish couple," in 1880, Redmond and Blake were "the genteel Irish couple." By the mid-eighties, the ever-innovative Peasleys were bowing to the times with a routine called "Etiquette" and were billed as doing "refined character sketches"; Redmond and Clifton did "parlour sketches."[48]

The point was to assure families that the variety hall was as safe a place to visit as their own parlours. Harry Osborne and Fanny Wentworth cleverly advertised as the

> LAD AND LASS FROM IRELAND, the most NATURAL and TRULY refined representatives of Irish characters that ever appeared before the public. Their ready wit, sparkling merriment, lively humor, and outbursts of silvery, ringing laughter, together with the innocence and simplicity of the character of their representations, inspire the audience with the comfortable feeling of being at home.[49]

The ad concluded with a reminder that the team was coming soon to Tony Pastor's; this type of act must have been peculiarly well suited to the kind of theatre Tony Pastor was trying to develop. Families could be assured that while attending Pastor's they would have "the comfortable feeling of being at home." A comedian might roll his eyes at the men in the audience at certain points, but this was presumably no more than occurred in many working-class front rooms or at any rambunctious gathering—as at a Bavarian Fest Tag of the early eighties, where the small retail dealers and their wives and children present exhibited "considerable romping and kissing, not exactly *comme il faut,* but no conduct beyond the bounds of decency."[50]

What with the growing marketability of "parlour" entertainment, and the new emphasis on the boy-girl interaction in dialect flirtation acts, the time was ripe for routines about courtship divested of the immigrant trappings. With traditional racial stereotypes having less and less relevance for both immigrant and native patrons, it was a natural process for male-female teams to specialize in what was, for them, an obvious kind of humor.

One of the earliest teams to do a purely romantic routine without dialect humor was Jeppe and Fanny Delano. Jeppe Delano, born in Charlestown, Massachusetts on 9 August 1845, became a jeweller for his brother's firm, Guild and Delano in Boston; he had a beautiful voice and was in great demand as a singer in the sixties at temperance meetings in and around Boston. Perhaps it was at these meetings that he became friendly with Eddie Peak, for the Peaks, from Medford, Massachusetts, had always been musically inclined, and were often invited by temperance lecturer John B. Gough to perform at gatherings. The Peaks eventually became professionals, singing and playing on the organ, harp, guitar and banjo, and after a troupe of Swiss bell ringers imported by P. T. Barnum disbanded, Mr. Peak bought the bells and the family toured America as the Peak Family of Bell-Ringers. In 1869 Jeppe Delano visited his friend Eddie Peak on tour in Maryland. By the end of a week he had adopted the stage as a livelihood.[51]

In the company since childhood was Anna Sutter, a fine singer known professionally as Fanny Peak; Jeppe and Fanny were married around 1871, despite Mr. Peak's objections that they had more stage appeal as unmarried singles.[52] Sometime afterwards the Peak company's success suddenly dwindled so much that the company disbanded. Jeppe and Fanny went on the road in an act with Professor DeCastro, a magician; the Delanos sang and assisted the professor with his Indian box trick and his aerial suspension act. Three seasons later Fanny and Jeppe joined a touring variety company, "Brown & Campbell's Comedy Co." The company closed at Bloomington, Illinois, and then, according to Jeppe, "wee wifey, and I went to Chicago and played dates at the Coliseum, and St. Louis"[53]—and in fact, a 21 October 1876 notice in the *Clipper* announces that the Delanos are playing at the Coliseum in Chicago.[54]

Jeppe recalled that "we then played our way East, opened at Tony Pastor's, and made a grand impression, our sketch being different, with not a funny line in it. We prided ourselves we were the one sketch team that did not finish our act with a song and dance."[55] Presumably the Delanos' apprenticeship as temperance singers (a native-oriented, more genteel milieu than variety) and with the bell-ringing Peaks did not foster the development of comic talent, especially immigrant comedy. Their attractions were their singing ability and (as Mr. Peak hinted) their youthful good looks, and these appeals were easily utilized in a frothy flirtation act.

If not the first, the Delanos were among the forerunners of a new trend, the sentimental non-dialect sketch. Into the mid-eighties they would entertain audiences with pretty-sounding routines, "Flirting in the Street," "Pretty Little Roses," "Flirtation under Difficulties," and one of their most popular vehicles, "The Bashful Lover." Two sketches dedicated to the Delanos were published in the *Clipper,* and presumably are similar to routines actually performed by them. One was "The Elopement,"[56] and the other was "Tell Me, I Pray, Would You?" In the latter the female character enters and sings:

> I know a youth with golden hair,
> And eyes that beam so bright;
> With happy face so sweet and fair,
> And heart so fond and light.
> He's merry as the joyous birds,
> And says he loves me true;
> Yet I can scarce believe his words—
> Tell me, I pray, would you?

The boy then holds the stage alone for a similar song, and finally the two meet onstage:

> He: Come, tell me, sweetest little pet,
> You'll love no one but me.
>
> She: While life shall last, without regret,
> I give myself to thee.
>
> Both: And as we journey on through years,
> We ever shall be true;
> We'll never shed regretful tears—
> Tell me, I pray, would you?[57]

This number is identical in structure to the early flirtations between stage immigrants, in which boy and girl declared their love to the audience and then to each other in alternate verses; just so, in this routine the boy has only to say, "Tell me, sweetest little pet, / You'll love no one but me," for her to reply "While life shall last, without regret, / I give myself to thee." Likewise, in "The Elopement," there is no real male-female dynamic; parental opposition is the only complication, a flimsy obstacle overturned as soon as the two meet onstage. Jeppe claimed they made a hit because their act was not funny, but these routines seem to have an amused awareness of their own preciosity. Presumably their style became still more lighthearted, for an 1875 song dedicated to Jeppe went:

> I'm all the rage among the ton
> And flirting's my forte
> I'm a "bonanza" in my line,
> So all the ladies say.[58]

The verifiable fact is the frequency with which this couple appeared on variety bills at the end of the seventies. Perhaps the growing number of women in the audience liked the Delanos' flowery style, which, even if women did not take it seriously, must have assured them variety was wholesome. To managers and reforming journalists, the Delanos' fripperies were the essence of the style they were promoting—so-called refined entertainment—for the Delanos were one of the earliest teams to be described as refined. Perhaps their stage image was Tony Pastor's inspiration; when they came to New York City in March 1877 the Delanos first appeared with Tony Pastor, who advertised "their refined entertainment," and they were signed for Pastor's summer tour, billed as "Society Sketch Artists."[59] Their style was new to variety; whenever the Delanos performed, it was their tastefulness, perhaps more than any great skill, that was appreciated:

> Jeppe and Fannie Delano were cordially welcomed, and their performances in the musical sketch of "Strolling by the Old Mill Stream" were characterized by grace and refinement of manner, while their vocalisms were frequently redemanded.[60]

Years later vaudevillian Al Fostelle recalled, "I can see them now in their neat and classy song and dance—the quintessence of refinement and beau ideal fashion plates of the vaudeville stage."[61]

Making "their usual hit" as late as the 1885-86 season,[62] the Delanos were by then one of the many teams with sketches about courtship between stage couples who had abandoned immigrant characters.[63] The first important successors to the Delanos were Emma Rogers and Harry McAvoy, appearing that same season with their sketch called "Jealousy," which would still be on bills in the 1884-85 season. McAvoy played Charles Brown, a "young man addicted to late suppers, fast horses, etc.," Emma Rogers "a young lady of the period, who thinks two can play at that game." Subsequent Rogers and McAvoy sketches were "Caught at Last," "Dick's Sweetheart," "Love in a Letter Bag," and their best-known, "Love in a Horn," still popular in the 1885-86 season. The team was still performing in 1892.[64] Their courtship act must have been comical, for, as mentioned earlier, a herring figured in it at some point; nonetheless, the team did not hesitate to advertise as "America's Greatest and Most Refined Society Sketch Artists." One supporter claimed Emma Rogers's acting would not be out of place on the legitimate stage.[65]

Of course, titles can mistakenly imply that songs and sketches were sentimental; the broad tendencies of ironically titled marriage sketches is illustrated by a song called "Love, Oh Love" from a gagbook of the day:

> Love oh Love is a very funny thing
> It bothers the young and the old
> It is just like a plate of boarding house hash
> And many a man it has sold
> ....
> So boys keep away from the girls I say
> And give them lots of room
> For you will find when you are wed
> They will bang you till your [sic] dead
> With the bald headed end of a broom.[66]

Nonetheless, both audiences and professionals believed, or wanted to believe, that variety was on a higher plane than it had been.

The number of teams with courtship routines continued to increase in the eighties.[67] Not only were routines like "Hymenial Happiness Happily Handled," "Somebody Kissing Outside," and "Love Letters" practically fitted to a stage duo of opposite sexes, but the boy-gets-girl scenario reaffirmed traditional male-female roles, at a time when the traditional definition of woman was coming under attack. The variety house class of audience was probably not consciously bothered by the woman's rights movement; the women who came had never been on a pedestal and were probably not educated or leisured enough to spend time wondering why things were the way they were. But variety audiences undoubtedly knew about the woman's movement.

Although the first American feminist document was drafted for the Seneca Falls Convention in 1848, not until 1868 was the first known demonstration held for woman's suffrage, when several women were refused the vote in New Jersey. By the eighties such demonstrations were frequent: readers of the *New York Times* learned of women's attempts to vote in Flushing, Long Island in 1881, and in New York City in 1885 and again in 1887; of women denied admission to the bar in Kentucky in 1880, Maryland and Massachusetts in 1881, and in Philadelphia in 1883; of women denied admission to Harvard Medical School in 1882; and of the 1882 woman in New York City arrested for wearing men's clothing.[68] Throughout the decade there were yearly meetings of women's rights organizations on national, state and local levels, and as regularly as clockwork state legislatures discussed—and vetoed—the suffrage question, occasions given conspicuous coverage in the press.[69]

In fact, anyone who could read the newspaper (contemporary writers claimed everyone did) was exposed to a barrage of opposition, supposition, and emotion regarding woman's rightful place in man's world. Editorial and news reports pondered "Women's Mathematical Powers," whether women could sue husbands for assault and battery, women's right to business training, and the mystery of "Women Earning Money for Pleasure." However slow and minute were the public's changing perceptions, clearly woman's sex role was being questioned: the upshot was that any expansion of this definition was seen as a threat to men. To the reigning sex, female emancipation was tantamount to usurpation of masculine privilege: "Women's Demand for the Ballot and the Trousers" was the *New York Times'* revealing summing-up.[70]

In bars and over supper tables, working men and their women may have scoffed indignantly at the ridiculous new-fangled ideas of feminists. Most immigrants were conservative, and disliked feminist schemes. For example, Irish newspapers such as the *Irish-American* upheld traditional ideas of womanhood, marriage and family, and ridiculed such innovations as "free love" and the "unfeminine and undelicate gyrations of the Amelia Bloomer class." Both Irish and German newspapers scoffed at the "barefaced attempts of women to unsex themselves." In their history of woman's suffrage, Susan B. Anthony and Ida Husted Harper blamed their failure to win the vote in the eighties and nineties on an electorate largely "composed of foreign-born men, bringing from the Old World the most primitive ideas of the degraded position which properly belongs to women."[71] Fortunately, for both men and women troubled by the shake-up, answers to the questioning reaffirmed the status quo: articles on "Woman's Inferiority to Man," on woman's "Public Position Forfeited by Marriage," on women's unbusinesslike ways, and articles revealing that higher education was injurious to feminine health—all provided the reassuring reply desired.[72]

Certainly the female rights speaker was enough of a commonplace to be burlesqued in variety entertainments. Since the early seventies, stump speech performers like Frank Bell had delivered comical, malaprop-laden discourses on female rights. A song in variety performer Billy Wylie's extant gagbook marvels at women's absurd ways, asking in its title, "Wonder What They're Going to Do Next?" and in a short male-female sketch in the gagbook called "Matrimony," Duvall and his discontented wife Clara have a physical tussle in which Clara bests Duvall, then "gets on top of him and crows": "Womans rights for ever."[73] Similarly, the extant, somewhat more genteel gagbook of Jerry Cohan—compiled some time in the early eighties—contains a poem called "Woman's Rights Man Must Respect," a title which the conclusion of the poem revealed to be an unconsciously ironical pun:

> The Male sex is brave and strong and can fight for right and wrong
> While weak woman must subdue with mind and tongue
> ....
> Yet each ruffian should reflect, when the sex they disrespect
> That his mother was a maid till called a wife
> There's a true unfailing plan, how to tell an honest man.
> The true gentleman you can easily detect
> He's always eager to resent evil words at women sent
> And prove that woman's rights man must respect.[74]

Of course, the woman's rights insisted on are her "right" to occupy a pedestal and be protected—i.e., submissive. The point is that Wylie's and Cohan's audience was familiar with the issue of woman's rights, and enjoyed entertainment which supported the status quo and made fun of feminism.

For whether or not simple people consciously knew they were implicated, the already changing status of American women may have been exerting subtle new pressures on them. Female job activity among the working class had increased markedly since the Civil War. There had been a surplus of women after the war who had had to find jobs; in the 1870 census, more than 300,000 women were working in factories and other plants, especially the cigar-making, textile, and laundry industries. The depression of 1873 had drawn still more women out of their homes and into the marketplace; in the eighties restaurants began to use waitresses, stores to use female clerks, and the U.S. Post Office began to hire more women. Female breadwinners in the United States rose from two-and-one-half million in 1880, to four million in 1890. In 1882 in New York City alone, of 840,000 tenement-house dwellers, 100,000 were women who worked in textile factories, made paper boxes and bags, assisted makers of carved furniture and upholstery, worked as typesetters and press-feeders, and manufactured cigars and cigarettes.[75]

The statistics can easily be substantiated, but what they leave unrecorded is the new anxiety and tension that must have existed behind some closed doors. It is easy to look back and see the broadening scope of women's activity as a natural and necessary development, but to a single working-class family—one with old-world values, accustomed to wife and mother as kitchen fixture—when the woman had to take a job in a factory or store, the clashes that might result could cause continual headaches. To any such people, bothered by a new tension between the sexes which they were perhaps hardly aware of intellectually, a courtship sketch in which sexes fulfilled traditional expectations may have been unconsciously reassuring. No doubt more than a little wish-fulfillment went on, as married folks watched stage couples unencumbered by reality's tensions indulge in kissing and spooning.

And for spectators too hardened for the cooing of onstage "Turtle Doves" like Billy and Mamie Williams, the appearance for the first time of sketches featuring more belligerent male-female interaction may have been more satisfying. By the 1878-79 season the Burgesses were staging "Trouble in the Family," and the Brimmers showed "The Marriage Saved"; Craven and Hedges depicted "Domestic Difficulties" in the 1879-80 season, the Sheerans "Marriage, A Failure" in the 1889-80 season. In the 1884-85 season audiences could have seen Clarence and Warner in "A Matrimonial Duel," and in the 1885-86 season, Mr. and Mrs. Dan Lacy in "I Was Here First—a real 'Mr. and Mrs.' argument."[76] A perennial target must have caused comical troubles in Thorne and Willett's 1885-86 sketch, "My Mother-in-Law," likely also in Girard and Earle's sketches "Her Parent" and "His Parent."[77] Such routines may have enabled many a husband or wife in the audience to work out vicariously a few unspoken desires.

Sketches about domestic matters also reflected practical box office considerations. The gradual replacement of the enticements of female minstrels with sketches like the Sanfords' "That Wife of Mine," Hodges and Bliss's "My Young Wife," the Fields' "Who Owns the Baby?," and Delmay and Archer's "Home"[78] reveals the influence of a new family audience interested in entertainment depicting its own domestic concerns. This audience was clearly gaining ground, for the rationale of the managers who constructed the bills was not the dictates of morality or even taste, but what was most successful financially.

That "refinement" and financial success went hand in hand in the eighties is illustrated by the career of Hallen and Hart. The earliest mention of the husband-and-wife team of Fred Hallen and Enid Hart comes around 1880, when they appeared in New York City in a sketch called "Pinafore in 15 Minutes." By the 1882-83 season they were already one of the favorites of the city, with "Lolly-Pop," "The Lodger's Stratagem," and "Over the Stile" in their repertoire. In 1883-84, along with these, they performed "The Mashers" and "The Love Chase," and in the 1884-85 season they added "Leap Year," perhaps their most popular routine. These last three routines clearly used the hottest stage commodity for mixed teams, romance; by then Hallen and Hart were described as doing "refined and artistic sketches."[79]

Whatever the true degree of "artistry," their style paid off, for in the summer of 1884 the team surpassed the lot of the typical mixed act with a big business venture, the organization of their own variety company for the coming season, "Hallen and Hart's First Prize Ideals." According to a spring, 1885 newspaper, the company's first season was very successful, and Fred Hallen was off to Europe in the summer to look for new talent. The couple was back on the boards in the fall of 1885 with a reorganized company, advertised as "New, bright and clean."[80]

One on-again, off-again member of the company was Joe Hart, mentioned earlier, who was presumably related to Enid. In fact, although the male-female team of Hallen and Hart was still in existence, Joe Hart had become Fred Hallen's business partner before 1886, when the *New York Dramatic News* declared that "Messrs. Hallen and Hart have one of the best vaudeville shows ever seen in this city."[81] By this time the success of the Hallen and Hart organization was such that there were hints that Fred Hallen planned to graduate to legitimate theatre, for in the spring of 1886, *New York Dramatic News* readers were assured that Fred Hallen had decided to stay in variety after all—because variety makes more money than legit, it was claimed.[82]

At any rate, the highly successful male-female act was still on the variety circuit in the 1887-88 season, and in December 1887 husband and wife showed a new sketch, described as "a satire on the 'Highest Bidder,' called 'Under the Hammer, or, A Bid Higher.' " Fred Hallen played an auctioneer, a reviewer wrote, calling it "a very pretty sketch." This "prettiness" was seemingly Hallen and Hart's main appeal: the quality was apparently reinforced by their natty dress, for there are references to their "excellent costumes."[83]

Some insight into their sartorial image is provided by a picture of Fred Hallen, heading an 1887 variety news column. He is depicted beside a bench, in dressy suit with a boutonniere, a cane, and a straw hat; "The picture which represents him above is the way he appears on the stage," claims the caption. Here is another clue to Hallen and Hart's popularity; they were (along with the Delanos) one of the earliest teams to abandon exaggerated comic costumes for dress clothes. It must have given their act a more elegant look; presumably their songs and dialogue fit this image. The newspaper blurb goes on to describe Hallen as "manager of one of the best paying combinations on the road," and as "most gentlemanly and refined."[84] Again and again financial reward and refinement (real or assumed) had been associated with Hallen; thus the two qualities must have been related. Eventually Hallen's business acumen did convince him there was a spot in the legitimate theatre for so gentlemanly a performer. The 9 June 1888 *New York Dramatic News* announces that after that week, Mr. Hallen and Miss Hart are to retire from the variety stage, Miss Hart permanently — she had long had health problems and died soon afterwards — and Fred Hallen to star with Joe Hart in a legitimate comedy, *Later On*.[85] This is one of the last mentions of the male-female act of Fred Hallen and Enid Hart.

There was an important exception to the box-office power of "refined" variety acts. One entertainment that was anything but elegant was enjoying noticeable new favor — the male-female blackface act. Whereas before 1878 only three mixed teams appearing in New York City can be identified as working in blackface, in the subsequent ten years at least sixteen blackface mixed acts performed in the city, with one of these a "star" team, three of them "extremely popular," and four being "regulars" in the city. One blackface team, Huber and Allyne, were members of the stock company at Miner's Eighth Avenue Theatre for at least six seasons, thus had tight hold on their audience's affections.[86] Yet blackface work was the exception that proved the rule: these teams offered "grotesque" dancing and "eccentric" characterizations, skills that reflected the "natural" qualities of blacks.

Many blackface teams still personified antebellum Southern darkies in a plantation setting, especially in the late seventies, and a few even in the mid-eighties.[87] John Healey, for example, in his act with his wife Nellie, played his famous character "Old Black Joe" in New York every season from 1885 until the late nineties.[88] But a non-traditional piece of business contributed to the Ameses' success during their engagement at Tony Pastor's in 1878:

Emile and Pauline Ames scored a success in a sketch called "The Return from the War," in which Emile, of diminutive figure, gave a comical and clever impersonation of an old plantation negro, while Pauline appeared as an elderly lady with uncorked face, and after a rapid change of make-up and attire, as a youthful negro girl with great aptitude and fondness for singing and dancing.[89]

The entertaining novelty of the "quick change" was also an important attraction in Lew and Pauline Parker's 1879 blackface act, and in Tommie and Annie Dayton's 1880 routine called "Old Age vs. Youth," in which "particular attention is solicited to the rapid and distinct change by Annie Dayton from Old to Young."[90] This new specialized skill enhanced the shopworn appeal of the sentimentalized darky; it also sounds as if Pauline Ames and Annie Dayton were doing more to carry the act than earlier women in darky acts.

Carrie Swain may have been the first woman to attempt the acrobatic comedy typical of male blackface work. She was working in variety with Sam Swain in 1877 and 1878, but sometime in the eighties became involved with a man named Frank Gardiner, who eventualy amassed a huge fortune. The two moved to Paris to spend it, with Carrie living as Mrs. Frank Gardiner.[91] Their high lifestyle there was the object of much attention; it was said that Carrie's jewels were worth $80,000. The romance came to an end when Gardiner deserted her for a French shopgirl, and in 1904 Carrie Swain sued Gardiner for $5,000,000 of his $25,000,000 fortune. It was a notorious case, revolving around the nicety of whether Carrie Swain was legally Gardiner's wife. In 1906 a French court of appeals decided in Carrie's favor.[92]

The sensational suit made frequent newspaper headlines between 1904 and 1907, and naturally Carrie Swain's former career in variety was dredged up. One newspaper described Carrie Swain as among the first women to put burnt cork on her face, and as the first woman to do knockabout work.[93] Whether or not she was the first, the Swains were the earliest male-female blackface team to attract attention in news columns. Their knockabout work was advertised as their major drawing card:

> THE SWAINS, Sam and Carrie, Male and female Acrobatic Song-and-Dance Artists, MISS CARRIE TAKING THE PART OF A MALE PARTNER, and executing all the various feats of tumbling as performed by song-and-dance men generally.[94]

Carrie Swain literally "took the part" of a male partner, according to a later account:

> She was formerly the wife of a minstrel, one "Sam" Swain, and in conjunction with her husband did a "song and dance" in the variety theatres some ten years since, in which both "blacked up," and the lady, dressed as a boy, performed a somersault!...She has

a strong musical voice, and is especially happy in her dancing and imitations of negro eccentricities. She is of the order of "rough soubrettes," and, properly fitted, possesses excellent gifts of entertainment.[95]

Perhaps by the mid-eighties, "rough soubrettes" able to do those routines "performed by song-and-dance men generally"—i.e., physical business and imitations of eccentricities—were more numerous; one possible reason for the sudden gain in blackface teams may well have been that the number of women able to work in the traditional blackface style had increased. Seemingly more women were blacking up with their male partners, and as it became less uncommon, women had more license to attempt this work, thus more opportunity to develop skills in this line. Nonetheless, it is unlikely that blackface would have continued as an alternative for male-female (and other) teams, had the routines themselves not changed from what they had been. The happy slave, strumming his banjo in an idyllic Southern setting, had less relevance as the plantation lifestyle faded into the more and more distant past. Besides, just as immigrants had adapted to meet the challeges of city life, so had the Negro; the slaves who drifted to the city just after the war may have been child-like and shuffling at first, but they either changed or were unable to survive.

The minstrels and male variety performers were the first to develop more timely caricatures. Tom Heath's Hennery, for example, a big-mouth know-it-all, was what city folks knew in real life. Johnny Wild's stage character was neither slow nor slack-jawed, nor did he wear the mismatched clothes of the Southern darky; he was an urbane, cocky ne'er-do-well, whose flashy duds were patterned after the actual dress of the Negroes dwelling on South Fifth Avenue below Washington Square.[96] Of course, the coon pretensions of a Hennery or a Sim Primrose were preposterous: they were another kind of darkey fool for a white audience to laugh at and feel superior to; although the Negro might be free and even dandified, he was still firmly entrenched at the bottom of the social ladder.

Like male routines, the titles of many mixed blackface routines of the eighties suggest a sketch in which the foolish Negro's would-be competence is a source of amusement. Bryant and Richmond, for example, were best known for their routine "Opera Buffers," also called "Opera Buffoons," an act consisting "of Bryant continually interrupting Miss Richmond's singing."[97] The hilarious incongruity of a darky presuming to sing opera must have provided a variety audience with lots of gratifying laughter—ironically so, since the opera house was culturally and financially off-limits for them as well. Other routines in which the appeal may have been the outrageousness of darky-buffoons trying to perform white folks' tasks were the Nelsons' "The Jockey," from an 1884-85 bill, and "Amateur Road Agents," performed by Frank and Lillian White in the 1882-83 and

1883-84 seasons.⁹⁸ The Whites had "star" status in New York City—in the 1889-90 season they had more engagements in the city than any other male-female team—and "popular comedian" Frank White was rivalled by Fred Huber, touted by one admirer as "undoubtedly the best negro comedian that holds the boards today." Since he was said to be "the only man that reminds us of Johnny Wild in the days of the old Theatre Comique," Huber and wife Kitty Allyne must have portrayed the eccentric urban black, not the old sentimentalized Southern darky.⁹⁹ Clearly more "urbane" Negro types were being portrayed—the title of Kennedy and Allen's 1885 male-female sketch, "Nigs of the Upper Ten," speaks for itself.¹⁰⁰

In other words, the blackface male-female act was changing in ways analogous to the change in immigrant acts. Both had become less sentimental about the past. Just as the "Dutch" or Irish act was no longer concerned with immigrants' homesickness and patriotism for the old country, so the blackface act served less often to buttress white people's nostalgia for pre-war days. Now both types portrayed subjects more relevant to a citified audience living in a fast-paced metropolis.

Just how far from tradition the mixed blackface act had come was best illustrated by popular team John F. Byrne and Miss Helene, who attracted notice in New York City for the first time in the 1884-85 season. They offered a "peerless impersonation of funny darkies," but the following review of a performance they gave while touring in England reveals that the comedy was not at all racial in nature:

> Extraordinary success, we understand, has been gained at this hall by Mr. John Byrne and Miss Helene, who adopt the hue of solemn black, but whose business is entirely unconnected with the style of entertainment tendered by the old burnt-cork substitute for the peripatetic piccaninny from the Potomac. Like many of his compatriots from the other side of the herring pond, Mr. Byrne introduces himself by means of song and dance—such a dance! Acrobatic it is certainly, but with the settled melancholy of the acrobatic dancer replaced by a liveliness, quaintness and originality of step that is irresistibly amusing. At the conclusion of the dance, Miss Helene, attired in a most extraordinary flounced costume, without waist, and distended from the neck downwards by an enormous hoop, joins her partner in a burlesque sketch of melodrama of the blood and thunder school.... [I]ts very ugliness is original, and the lady who wears it exhibited conspicuous talent both as dancer and actress in a duet and American jig, which immediately preceded another variation in the business of these clever people. Mr. Byrne includes among his varied powers of entertaining a talent for drawing. He sketches rapidly in colored crayon a portion of the Oregon river, with a moose deer in the foreground; he then outlined in black the figures of gladiators wrestling, and finally limns in charcoal the well-remembered features of Lord Beaconsfield. The hackneyed phrase "a host in himself," may be most truthfully applied to Mr. John Byrne.¹⁰¹

The burnt cork merely licensed this team to utilize all sorts of out-of-the-ordinary, unrefined appeals—unusual acrobatic dance, outlandish costume, rapid crayon-drawing, and a boisterous burlesque—skills appreciated for their own sake.

Male-female teams were thus developing new ways to entertain audiences, in addition to, or in place of, the inherited traditions of blackface and immigrant stereotypes. In fact, when Byrnes and Helene included a burlesque of blood and thunder melodrama in their blackface act, they were utilizing another of the popular new alternatives to dialect comedy—the sketch about theatre.

Nineteenth-century popular entertainers had always kept their eyes on the legitimate stage, a rich storehouse of stage materials for the taking to be aped, mocked, blown up, watered down, or otherwise rearranged to suit exigency or whim. In addition to the burlesques, one ironically appropriate theme borrowed by minstrels and variety performers was that of the would-be actor; many itinerant entertainers knew all too well the comical disparity between the ambitions and actual achievements of the aspiring actor. Beginning around 1880 the bit about acting and the theatre was eagerly adopted by immigrant and non-dialect teams alike, as needed variation from stock material. Just as the German characters portrayed by Rogers and Vickers were "The Attic Thespians" and the Irish Davises had "A Quiet Rehearsal," so non-dialect-talking teams were "stagestruck" and could be found "Interviewing an Actress," "Organizing a Company," and having a "Parlour Rehearsal."[102]

The increase in sketches about acting and theatre perhaps reflects the growing importance of theatre for the audience, many of whom may never have been to a legitimate theatre, but were used to taking their entertainment in the beer gardens or in the streets. But as they improved their status, formed the habit of variety theatre-going, and learned who and what their favorites were, variety audiences became more aware of the workings of theatre, more sophisticated in their tastes. The laugh-getting antics of a sketch like "Actors in the Kitchen" depended on the audience's knowledge of the difference in talent between amateurs and professionals. Some working people took part in amateur theatricals; as early as the fifties Germans had formed theatre societies, and performed plays and variety shows before a German audience, "which if not very elegant, was yet of a perfectly respectable stamp." A contemporary observer of a Bavarian Fest Tag in 1882 noted an amateur drama was part of the festivity.[103]

No doubt a segment of the variety audience was familiar with the more popularized or most publicized offerings of the legitimate theatre, and these people were probably gratified when variety acts treated them to songs or plots lifted—or claimed to be—from more opulent attractions. The Forresters, for example, introduced "gems from the latest operas," supposedly. Hallen and Hart's repertoire included an act called "Pinafore in 15 Minutes," and a later version billed as "Pirates of Pinafore," then "Penzance Pirates in a Nutshell." It was clearly a short—i.e., some fifteen minutes'—take-off on the then-popular *H.M.S. Pinafore,* afterwards modified to poke fun at *Pirates of Penzance,* when that operetta took New York by storm in 1879.[104] Such routines had added prestige by association.

Its subjective appeal for audiences and performers aside, the story-line of routines like "A Rehearsal" or "I'm Bound to Be an Actor" provided a convenient way to introduce singing and mugging. Joe Laurie classed the "theatrical" act among the earliest type of variety sketch; according to the formula he recalled, the curtain rose on an actress opening a letter which reveals her partner cannot make the show, at which point a young man delivers her trunk, providing her with a sudden inspiration: "Say, you look like a bright young man. How would you like to be an actor?"—whereupon they begin "rehearsing" and go into their repertoire.[105] Crude as this rationale for a song and dance was, it was a welcome change from just stepping to the footlights for a number.

A team which typifies the expedient ways of the old-time school is Henshaw and Ten Broeck. Born in 1858, John Henshaw had become a minstrel at age eleven or so, and became, according to one admirer, "one of the best bones players in the business." By 1876, he was performing immigrant sketches with female partner May Ten Broeck; when next heard from in the 1880-81 season, they had apparently already dropped the dialect comedy, and by 1882 Henshaw and Ten Broeck had become one of the starring male-female teams in New York City. In addition to "Interviewing an Actress" and "Deception," their repertoire included "Yes My Dear" and "Mistakes," on extant 1885-86 bills, and "Diamond Cut Diamond," on bills between 1885 and 1887.[106]

A twentieth-century writer, looking back on early vaudeville, believed that

> John Henshaw was a sprightly chap, naturally witty, with a fine talent for flinging quips across the gaslights. His partner, May Ten Broeck, long since dead (as is now John), was a lovely lass with a pleasing voice and come-hither manner. The pair were a top team, capable of lifting ordinary stuff to something more than passable.[107]

Certainly the opening of "Deception," preserved by this same writer, is "ordinary stuff":

> They used a full set and at rise Miss Ten Broeck was discovered reading a letter.
>
> May (with wild delight): Good heavens! The Count de Suckaire is calling on me! (Runs off, and enter Henshaw: moth-eaten fur-collared coat, greasy vest, fading shiny clothing—an actor on the lam. The old mistaken identity. Reenter May and they go into a song and at finish terrific crash backstage)
>
> May (reassuring audience): Nothing but a house fell in. (Exit May, and Henshaw turns on monologue)

Henshaw (confidentially): I am an actor. (Crash) I have just concluded my engagement with the Hardly Able Dramatic Alliance—hardly able to get from town to town. Last night I appeared in Sing Sing. Not having the necessary funds to liquidate my expenses I have made my escape and wandered here. If I can stay here until the sheriff gets by I'll be all right. In the meantime I'll go in search of food. People imagine that actors never eat. Actors do eat—occasionally. I had a meal last fall.[108]

These surviving lines reveal that the sketch could be interrupted at any time for a song or some one-liners, as when a crash intervenes, explained as "Nothing but a house fell in"; this flimsy joke got May offstage so Henshaw could deliver a funny monologue. The audience was obviously not in the least disturbed by these interruptions. Why should they have been, when the interruptions—the duo's singing and Henshaw's wit—were what the audience had come to see? Although Henshaw's monologue did contribute to the plot, each line of his monologue was a joke which could stand alone (e.g., "I have just concluded my engagement with the Hardly Able Dramatic Alliance—hardly able to get from town to town"), and each joke's *raison d'être* was to elicit laughs moment to moment.

No doubt the majority of the teams of the day performed sketches with equally slight complications, concocted just for this purpose. Thus, though the sketch themes chosen are a barometer of audience taste, it is best not to make too heavy weather with them. On the one hand, the increase in non-dialect sketches about courtship and theatre, and the popularity of such subjects as the Conways' "Summer Comforts" and "Recreation," Foreman and Meredith's "Lawn Tennis," the Maxwells' "A Summer Vacation" and "Strolling by the Seaside," and Beane and Gilday's "Rural Felicity," the Whitings' "The Music Teacher," or Delmay and Archer's "The Music Lesson," suggests that audiences (both immigrants and native Americans) were less concerned with the old shocks of immigration and civil strife, and more interested in the pleasures associated with middle-class lifestyles. But on the other hand, sketch-lines could be the most trivial of excuses for performing a mélange of skills, with the number and kinds of skills displayed varying from act to act. For example, "Just Out," the Murphys' sketch, "gave them plenty of scope to show off their abilities in the song, dance and comedy flash line."[109]

One noteworthy feature in many contemporary descriptions of male-female acts is the mention of "talk." Whereas the skill of joking and punning was almost never referred to in newspaper descriptions in the early seventies—acts were invariably described as "musical sketches"[110]—by the eighties reporters were forever mentioning wit, along with song, as one of a mixed team's important skills. Burdell and Saunders, for instance, did "songs, dances, tricks and puns"; Filson and Errol offered a sketch "in which they introduce songs and funny sayings in a pleasing manner."[111]

The frequent use of the term "songs and sayings" to describe an act, rather than "sketch," suggests the extent to which plot could be subverted.[112] Teams often did a familiar sketch again and again, simply adding new songs and/or jokes to update it.[113]

In other words, the delivery of songs and jokes was now recognized as a skill important in itself, different from the attractions of sketch, i.e., plot and character impersonation. This is also borne out by descriptions of acts in which sketch, and song or wit, or both, are listed in reviews as separate skills. Harry and Gracie Emmett, for example, "introduced lots of laughable comedy, sketch, singing, and witty sayings" in their Irish act.[114] These descriptions show the inverse of the new consciousness of "songs and sayings": the "sketch" portion of an act was also becoming a distinct appeal. For just as some teams seemed to be putting more stock in one-liners, other teams may have been telling more of a story.

That this was the case is implied by no less an authority than Jerry Cohan. Cohan is remembered today because he was the father of the famous George M. Cohan; but in the late nineties the four Cohans—Jerry, his wife Helen, and their children Josephine and George—were well known on the big-time vaudeville circuit, and even before that Jerry Cohan had not done too badly for himself. He had begun his long career in 1866 at the age of eighteen as a minstrel, with an Irish comedy and clog-dancing turn. Cohan soon began taking out a handful of performers to do short versions of "Under the Gaslight," "The Octoroon," and other melodramas between minstrel engagements. By 1872 he had his own Irish comedy company, a long list of short dramatic skits all written and staged by himself, and the invaluable aid of a panorama of Ireland for a backdrop.[115]

Their best-known piece was the "Molly Maguires." In the early 1870s, a series of murders and dynamite explosions in the Pennsylvania coal fields had been blamed on the Molly Maguires, a secret Irish labor organization, and this episode had brought down a chorus of denunciation upon the Irish race in general by native Americans.[116] But in Cohan's version of the incident, the Mollies were depicted as innocent victims, as the sensational advertising for the play reveals:

> Never has a play been written with so many startling situations as presented in this drama. The Grand Conflagration Scene of the Coal Mine Breaker and the charge of the Pennsylvania regiment on that memorable night of blood and carnage, are of the most thrilling character. The play abounds in sentiment, elevating in its nature, showing how political intrigue, wire pullers and capitalists, used the secret order of the Molly Maguires to carry out their wicked and tyranical [sic] designs.[117]

Describing the success of the "Molly Maguires" in Baltimore, Jerry Cohan remembered the drawing power of the pro-Irish sentiments:

> Baltimore at that time was a great city for Irish comedy.... It was about the time of the trouble in the coal regions of Pennsylvania, and the piece took well here.[118]

Cohan played the leading role of "Mark O'Dare, the engineer of the Black Diamond Express," and in 1875 his new young wife, Helen Costigan of Providence, Rhode Island—who had never even been in a theatre before her marriage, according to Cohan—took the role of leading lady, supposedly because the company soubrette deserted.[119]

In the late seventies—during the period the Cohan children were born—Jerry often performed his Irish turn alone, but by 1881 husband and wife had begun their off-and-on career as a male-female team, which was to last until 1889, when the entire family performed as the Cohan Mirth Makers.[120] Jerry and Helen were not among the most conspicuous mixed teams; they rarely performed in New York, and there is no evidence that they were well-known outside the New England area. But their repertoire consisted of short dramatic sketches which were precursors of the playlets soon to take vaudeville by storm.

This much was claimed by Cohan himself, speaking of his and his wife's appearance as a team on the opening bill of the Keith house in Providence in 1887:

> When I came here for Keith I had two plays, "The Molly Maguires" and "The Owls of New York." They're making a good deal out of the present practice of running short plays, but I was putting on that sort of thing before some of those now in the business were born.[121]

This was an obvious choice for a team with their past experience with small stock companies; "Molly Maguires" had been done by their company in the seventies, of course; their other playlets also may have been condensed versions of short dramas done earlier with a supporting company. Other two-person sketch titles known for the Cohans are "A Noble Sacrifice," "The Tramp and His Daughter," "Retiring from the Stage," "The Old Man's Wife," and "the roaring farce, Thompson's Dead."[122] The first three sketches are contained in the extant manuscript of Cohan's gagbook. These pieces show Cohan no longer utilizing the appeal of Irish characters—presumably an acknowledgement of the changing audience profile.

"Retiring from the Stage" concerns the down-and-out actor Jonathan C. Ranting, who tries to win the heart of his landlady's daughter Nanny, along with credit for the $40.00 back rent he owes her. In the role of Ranting, Cohan entertained his audience with take-offs on well-known actors, and with monologues laden with jokes for their own sake; e.g.:

> American actors must emigrate and become foreigners to be appreciated. I assumed an English accent and appeared for a position at Wallacks. I could have told them

anything when they thought I was a Londoner. And Maynard and Drew recognized my ability. They said I was peculiar—not precisely like Irving but peculiar. One day I said Eether for Either and my nativity was betrayed and I was discharged, bounced, fired! I applied to a dime museum for the position of lecturer. They said they wanted no more freaks.[123]

"The Tramp and His Daughter," showing the rescue of a tramp who has deserted his family to devote himself to the pleasures of saloon and gutter, gave Cohan the opportunity for a comic song and two hilarious comic soliloquies, each of which like the one above, was a turn in itself.

But even these rollicking pieces gave way to sentiment in the end. "Retiring from the Stage" ends with Nanny inheriting $10,000 and a farm and casting her lot with Ranting, who retires from the stage to share his name in return for her money; "tis astonishing how my love for you grows with the size of the farm," he cracks. As for the tramp, he is persuaded to abandon the bottle by his daughter Jenny, who sings a maudlin temperance-plea to the tune and theme of "Father, Dear Father, Come Home with Me Now." "A heavenly change o'er my nature has come / And we will all be happy again," cries the tramp in an on-the-spot conversion.[124]

The growing efficacy of this sentimental element was probably what inspired the remaining sketch in Cohan's gagbook, "A Noble Sacrifice"—the most conspicuous sacrifice being Cohan's vivacious witticisms for soap-opera stuff. The sketch concerns the affairs of a domestic servant-girl, Susan Sweetapple, and Bob Ticket, heir and nephew of her now-deceased master. The playlet begins as follows:

Susan: Well that's always the way Mr. Pugwash was paying his attentions to me because he expected that my dear old master would remember me in his will and now it's turned out that [   ] has left all to his nephew Bob Ticket. Mr. Pugwash sends me a note declining the honor of escorting me to the servants calico party tomorrow night...oh well a sweet heart like that isn't worth having. I [   ] that will love me all for my self. I once thought I had a little love for young Bob Ticket...(noise without goes L looks off) The omnibus from the city its the young master at last...oh he's a nice looking young man what a pity he's so harum-scarum. [H]e'll soon spend all of master's property....

Bob: Enter Bob Ticket L.H.... Hallo! Who's at home. [H]ere is the new proprietor of the establishment coming to take possession....[125]

As might be expected, the new master tries to seduce Susan, and the virtuous miss is forced to resign. But first, she asks the presumptuous young man to examine her trunk before she leaves, to assure him that she takes nothing from the estate with her; and inside the trunk, hidden in a calico dress left to Susan by the deceased uncle, Bob discovers the true will—leaving the entire estate to Susan, and to him, one shilling. After a struggle with his conscience, Bob reveals the contents of the will. Poor Bob has nothing to his name and nowhere to go, so Susan hires him for her houseboy, and proceeds to repay him for his ill-treatment of her by making him call her missus, and giving him humiliating tasks to do. But soon disillusioned by her new moneywon popularity, Susan ends by tearing up the new will, thus reinstating Bob as master. Fortunately for her, Bob instantly proposes marriage, which Susan naturally accepts on the spot, and the curtain goes down on the happy couple looking forward to sharing life and fortune.

This sketch is different from Cohan's other two pieces. Whereas "Retiring from the Stage" and "The Tramp and His Daughter" are in the family of loosely constructed comedy sketches with "Deception," "A Noble Sacrifice" contained the germ of a new genre. Unlike Henshaw's monologue in "Deception" and Cohan's in "Retiring from the Stage"—literally stand-up comedy routines—the purpose of Susan Sweetapple's opening monologue is the giving of information, and throughout the playlet, the dialogue exists to move along the story, which is everything.

And the appeal of the situation is its sentimentality. Although the clash between the sexes depicted has serious implications—the man tries to take sexual advantage of the economically dependent woman, who promptly dominates him when the tables are turned—the situation is magically resolved by her yielding mastery of the fortune to him, and by his subsequent offer of marriage. How soothing this ending must have been to any in the audience consciously or unconsciously fearful that proper relations between the sexes were endangered! The kicker was the assurance that those who live right will get the bag of gold at the end, thus making use of the centuries-old middle-class equation of morality with love and money. This sugar-coated little homily was perfectly suited to variety audiences' growing concern with wholesomeness and sentiment, and their enjoyment of "dramatic" qualities akin to the legitimate stage.

The Cohans came up with this combination not only because of astute insight into their audience, but because their offstage characters made the elements of sentiment and romance just the thing for them. Although she had wedded a career in variety, Mrs. Cohan was from a respectable working-class family, and she was very protective of her reputation as a "lady." Jerry Cohan recalled that whenever he played the Hopkins and Morrow's Theatre Comique, "I had to play there alone, for my wife would never appear there. It was not a place for ladies." In fact, he confided that "Mrs. Cohan never wanted to play in Providence because of having come from here."[126] Sam Harris (George M. Cohan's partner) pointed out many years later that wholesomeness was always the Cohans' trademark onstage and off:

> The aristocracy of vaudeville consists of the Jerry Cohans, the Helen Cohans, and the old timers like them.... And Jerry Cohan and his wife always stood highest in that aristocracy, because, in a day when the very word "variety" usually implied dance hall improprieties, Jerry Cohan and his wife steadily held to a form of entertainment that was like their own lives—sweet and wholesome and decent.[127]

But something else was also at work. The Cohans' creation of "A Noble Sacrifice" was the result of a gradual process of specialization. The elements of sentiment and plot had been present in their routines from the beginning; it was a natural evolution for them to specialize in a sketch which emphasized qualities suited to them as a team and as personalities.

In fact, while most teams still used an aggregation of skills, by the mid-eighties there was a tendency to emphasize a single skill. With the number of male-female teams multiplying each year, doing one element expertly was a way to survive in a competitive market. In addition to "talk" and sketch "acting," teams were displaying expertise in skills rarely mentioned in the seventies, some quite exotic. Bruns and Monroe, for example, advertised their sketch "Conductor and German Sweetheart" as "Introducing their Celebrated Paper Tearing Act, Blindfolded." Throughout the eighties, Minnie Oscar Gray and W. T. Stephens did three short "thrilling" melodramas, "Roughing It," "Saved from the Storm," and "The Oaken Bucket"; the unique element was that the team was assisted in their efforts by five dogs.[128] There were also cat routines, with the difference that the cat noises were supplied by humans. The Martens' "Cat Duet" was famous, and the Tissots' "Cat Concert and Living Pictures" was highly praised in the *New York Dramatic News:*

> The biggest share of applause was awarded to The Tissots—Amanda and Jules—who introduced a specimen of amusement it is only a pity we have not something more of a similar kind by way of a change, that of their Living Pictures and their Cat Concert. They are behind a screen with their heads through holes at a convenient distance representing a pair of cats holding a levee at midnight, and "carry on" accordingly.[129]

Publicity for such novelty acts was fiercely insistent on uniqueness. Dilke and Gray proudly billed themselves as the "only Bottle and Tomato Can Duettists in the World." Edward and Carrie DeHaas, ignoring the existence of club-swingers Clarence and Warner, announced that they were "The Only Team of Novel Club-Swingers and Globe-Artists in America." The DeHaases were even praised by one reporter simply for having a one-of-a-kind stage decoration, a revolving light.[130]

But if acts were generated whose only appeal was the dubious one of novelty for its own sake, specialization had other more valuable by-products. Specialization of any sort, whether it was joking, drama, or paper-tearing, encouraged (and resulted from) the most important development in the mixed act, the increasing importance of female partners. The very fact of *both* performers in a team having exceptional talent in a skill encouraged them to concentrate on that specialty. Thus, along with the appearance of teams who specialized in instrumental work came the first mentions of female team partners with outstanding instrumental skills: a reviewer of Matthews and Harris claimed a hit was made "especially by the lady's cornet solo — her playing on the instrument shows careful practice"; advertisement for the Whitings' musical act boasted that Annie Whiting was "the only lady trombone soloist in the world."[131] It was a cause and effect development.

Granted, in many mixed two-acts, women were still the less talented team partners. In the majority of immigrant acts, it was still the man who had the dialect skills,[132] and even in non-dialect acts, it was more often the man who supplied the comical character role, while the female played the straight role and contributed a song or dance, or both.[133] Another contribution monopolized by male partners was writing and arranging acts. Frank Jones was "inventor" of the sketches done by Jones and Montague; Fred Huber (who wrote for others) presumably wrote the Huber and Allyne sketches; Jerry Cohan arranged the Cohan family acts for two decades; Jeppe Delano wrote "The Bashful Lover" and probably other Delano sketches.[134] But although women were almost never praised for their dialect, writing, or comic abilities, the mixed team's talents were surely more equally distributed than before, given the more competitive market of the eighties. In several teams, the woman's performance was a drawing card in itself. For example, one reviewer thought that John Byrne was the best male dancer alive, but that his partner Miss Helene could "give her associate 100 points and discount him dancing, and there you are!"[135]

Probably the most admired woman working in a male-female act in the eighties was Fanny Beane. Born in 1853, Fanny Beane was the daughter of George Beane, a comedian. She made her debut at the age of four, dancing a Sailor's Hornpipe at the National Theatre in New York. After a round of children's parts, in the seventies she played Columbine in *Humpty Dumpty* opposite George L. Fox for three years. Then she migrated westward, appearing on the St. Louis stage in her father's play, *Lost and Found,* and in burlesques such as *Yeast Lynne.*[136] She won some favor as an actress and as a vocalist and dancer; a January 1877 *Cincinnati Times* declared:

> This versatile little actress, who, by the way, is one of the prettiest little ladies on the stage, has attracted considerable attention. A perfect gem of a comedienne, a striking resemblance to Lotta, and as sweet and pretty a lady as ever graced the stage.[137]

That same month the *Chicago Times* contained this tribute:

> The new protean actress MISS FANNIE BEANE is exceedingly clever. She sings like a canary, dances like a sylph, and has more fun in her little finger than most comediennes have in their whole anatomy.[138]

Somewhere along the way she married Charles Gilday, a comedian and grotesque dancer; by September 1878 the two were appearing individually at the same theatres, and they were billed together at Pastor's in late November.[139] For the next ten years, Fanny Beane and Charles Gilday were one of the teams in most demand with New York City variety managers. This long streak of success did not end until 1888; Beane and Gilday departed for Europe on 16 June 1888, apparently to play the English music halls. Charles Gilday died during the return trip.[140]

The names of several sketches from Beane and Gilday's repertoire are known, but the titles provide little clue to the type of act done: "The Picnic," "Spices," "Rural Felicity," "Salvation Army," "Waffles the Waiter," "Frog Hollow," and others. The fact of an early "The Servant's Holiday" and a later "Love Letters" and "Collars and Cuffs and Chic Coterie" does suggest they were influenced by the trend towards refinement.[141] These routines were described as "exceptionally funny pieces," "in which songs, dances and funny sayings are introduced," and were said to "afford the clever little artist, Fannie Beane, and the humorous Charles Gilday plenty of opportunity to display their versatilities to the best advantage."[142]

Their best-known "versatilities" were Charles Gilday's joking, and Fanny Beane's dancing. In later years, Fanny would proudly recall, "My husband was a man of wit, and kept the audience in roars of laughter."[143] But Fanny's dancing seems to have had the greatest appeal for audiences. One bill omitted mention of Gilday and informed fans that "incidental to the act, Miss Fanny Beane will introduce her model Song-and-Dance...." On another occasion, a reviewer praised in particular "Fanny's artistic dancing, which scored for them round after round of applause."[144]

Many years later, Fanny Beane told interviewers that she was the originator of the idea of using sand for dancing, and that she hit upon the idea of wearing a red wig on stage; this innovation was so popular, said Fanny, that she became known as the "original red-headed girl."[145] Fanny Beane also claimed that she was famous for her sneezing song. But, "Oh, how I loved to dance!" she reminisced longingly in old age to one reporter. "I see dancers nowadays in elegant costumes and covered with diamonds, but I've never seen my 'stuff' used. My dancing was an innovation."

> At this point Mrs. Beane could contain herself no longer, and she rose to show just how she danced. One—two—three—she sidestepped, then struck a pose like a Spanish

dancer. There was something pathetic in the sight, but every move that she made displayed the artist even if the picture was cracked with rheumatism.[146]

"I always used a fan," she continued. "There was nothing stereotyped in me, I tell you. I had the habit of saying 'There!' the moment my dancing was finished, just before the house range with applause."[147]

But women were also beginning to develop skills other than singing and dancing. In the eighties come the first indications that some immigrant acts were joint efforts, in which each member displayed some dialect skill. Frank and Fanny Davis, for example, were billed as "dialect specialty people." Clara Moore, already known for her act as an Irish songstress, continued to do Irish roles after teaming up with her husband, Charles T. Ellis, who specialized in German characters. Theirs was one of the few male-female acts featuring partners in different immigrant roles, evidence that Clara Moore's old Irish woman characterization was too effective to be ignored when she teamed with a husband performing another dialect.[148]

By necessity, the new vogue for subjects that involved women meant that female partners would have to take more responsibility for the character comedy. The snappy give and take of a successful flirting routine, or a fast-paced marital brouhaha, required skillful performances from both male and female partners, whether straight or comic. In effect, the tastes of the women coming to variety in growing numbers were creating new opportunities for the variety soubrette.

The possibility that at least some female partners had "acting" talent, either comic or straight, is supported by the increasing number of sketch titles which feature female characters, e.g.: the Murphys' sketch, "That Woman"; "Interviewing an Actress," by Henshaw and Ten Broeck; "Lena's Birthday," by Morosco and Gardner; "Mollie's Victory," by the Peasleys; "That Girl from Vassar," from Daly and Derious's repertoire; "The Little Widow," by the Burgesses; "The Debutante," by Rogers and Vickers; "The Widow DeWitt," acted by the Whitings; "Nora's Birthday" and "Katie's Surprise," both by the Hugheses; "Linda's Wedding Day," by the Sheridans; "Dick's Sweetheart," McAvoy and Rogers' routine; "The Old Man's Wife," by the Cohans; "The Milkmaid," offered by the McCarthys; "Girls Will Be Girls," by the Conways; and so on. Even this incomplete list is impressive; at least some of these routines must have required a substantial contribution from the female member of the team.

The very fact that so many male and female members of variety teams graduated into the ranks of the legitimate stage suggests that variety was a good training ground for both male and female ability. By 1884, Mattie Vickers, of Rogers and Vickers, and Maggie Fielding, of the Fieldings, had begun legitimate stage careers. In the 1885-86 season, the roster of male-female teams was deserted by Moore and Vivian, for the *Our Jonathan* stock company; Murphy and Wells, for a play called *Rudolph's Ambition;* and McCarthy and Coleman for *True Irish Hearts.* The 1886-87 season brought vacancies left by McAvoy and Rogers, who joined the *Two Johns* company; Stanley and Conway, off to the *Peck's Bad Boy* company; Farrell and Leland, into the *Skipped by the Light of the Moon* road company; and Bryant and Richmond, who left variety for the comedy *Keep It Dark.*[149] Sometime in 1887 or so, Henshaw and Ten Broeck formed a stock company and toured the country until 1894 as stars in their own musical farce productions, *Tactics, Two Old Cronies, The Nabobs,* and *The New Nabobs.* Between 1894 and 1905 they would be involved in such musical extravaganzas as *The Passing Show, Man in the Moon,* and the Henry Savage productions of *Little Boy Blue* and *The Sho-Gun.*[150]

However, the departure of fairly large numbers of performers into more "legitimate" theatre is a telling comment on the status of the variety of the day. Despite the insistence of journalists, theatre managers, and performers that variety was "polite" entertainment by and for ladies and gentlemen, even the most successful variety teams seemed eager to leave the field for more glamorous, or more stable, ventures. The variety house was still a second-class theatre whose shabby past had not yet been forgotten, and the type of entertainment onstage still echoed more carefree, more boisterous times.

The entertainers, for all their pretensions to refinement, were funmakers unencumbered by the Victorian prudery and over-niceties of the upper classes. Henshaw and Ten-Broeck, for example, kept it clean, but an extant photograph reveals May dressed in tights that did not exactly discourage ogling.[151] Fanny Beane may have worn a fancy pink silk dress, but she had no qualms about donning a funny red wig and doing an unladylike sneezing song or "cigarette" song. Comical racial types were still peddling broad slapstick, and laughter at the bumbling stage business of a Harry Watson was a mocking reminder of unresolved ethnic anxieties. The male-female acts of the eighties were probably not ribald, but they were certainly full-blooded.

Nonetheless, the male-female teams of 1885 were more concerned with professional standards than teams fifteen years earlier, and more assured of regular engagements in decent theatres. The edges of immigrant humor had blurred; male-female teams were developing new ways to entertain that appealed to a more cosmopolitan audience and were inherently suited to performance by a man and woman. It was a slow process, but gradually the status of variety and its audience was rising. The smoky saloon air of honky-tonk was being replaced with the harmless yet fun-loving atmosphere of the working-class parlour. Both managers and performers were keeping their eyes on a new box office, and a more toned-down entertainment was being produced, calculated to attract a wide family audience of any ethnic background, and to offend none.

Indeed, by the end of the eighties, advertisements for male-female teams betray an excessive concern with propriety. Sanford and May boasted they were "a decided hit in their Parlour and Musical Sketch, introducing Banjo and Bone Solos, together with Song and Dance...a strictly First Class Act, with Elegant Wardrobe, and the reputation of being strictly refined."[152] Hughes and Farron were a western team, "somewhat unknown to Eastern managers," whom they assured that "their act is a Refined Comedy Sketch, which causes ROARS OF LAUGHTER. The SPECIALTIES...will please the most fastidious." S. F. Hodgedon, general superintendent of Keith's Gaity and Bijou Theatre, added his testimony that Hughes and Farron "ARE ARTISTS, do a good long turn, FREE FROM VULGARITY AND ROUGHNESS, create hearty laughter and will prove a VALUABLE ADDITION TO ANY VAUDEVILLE SHOW IN AMERICA."[153] By the end of the decade, then, variety was fast being tidied, redecorated, and stuffed into the package offered up in 1893 for mass consumption as "Continuous Vaudeville."

4

Male-Female Sketch Teams and Polite Vaudeville, 1893–1905

Sometime in the early 1900s, Jerry Cohan told an interviewer: "There's a good deal of difference between the present and the old days in Providence.... We had a pretty hard pull to get along at times then."[1] The difference was that by the 1900s the talented male-female team could lead the good life; variety, with its raucous company and dubious name, had been reformed as the wholesome fun, the respectable crowds, and the decent paychecks of what had come to be called "vaudeville."

The adoption by 1896 of continuous vaudeville performances by all the New York managers was concrete proof that vaudeville was a financially stable enterprise: now auditoriums could be filled, show after show, three or four times a day, and performers as well as managers were realizing new profits. The rise in salaries enabled performers to enlarge their territories, and by the late nineties most acts were crisscrossing America; the newly established booking profession made the setting and filling of distant dates operate like clockwork. Vaudeville managers were feeding their new riches back into the business: new theatres were everywhere, with large ornate auditoriums, comfortable dressing rooms, bright scenery, and adequate lighting equipment. With audiences expanding, theatres proliferating, and performers willing to travel for good pay, eventually several large vaudeville circuits were formed, controlled by 1900 by a few powerful businessmen.

The kings of the new era were B. F. Keith and his partner E. F. Albee, aptly described as robber barons who

> made of entertainment a specialized regimented industry; were products of their time—in organization and development for financial gain this pair was to vaudeville what Frick and Carnegie were to steel, the elder Rockefeller to oil, the elder Morgan to banking.[2]

Like Rockefeller and Morgan, B. F. Keith's impetus was creating a vast fortune, but for the wise businessman materialism and morality were linked. Keith's early experience had proved the value of wholesome amusement; he insisted that his entertainments meet middle-class standards. The warning signs hanging backstage in Keith theatres are now a legend:

> Don't say "slob" or "son-of-gun" or "hully gee" on this stage unless you want to be cancelled preemptorily. Do not address anyone in the audience in any manner. If you have not the ability to entertain Mr. Keith's audiences without risk of offending them, do the best you can. Lack of talent will be less open to censure than would be an insult to a patron....[3]

Keith's deference to upper-middle-class canons of taste was but one expression of a broader social phenomenon. In the second half of the nineteenth century, there was a self-conscious movement among members of the educated class to discipline and refine the growing masses below them; it was these genteel Victorian reformers who established the tone of culture in late nineteenth-century America, who founded the country's great museums, art galleries, libraries, and symphony orchestras. But, "of critical importance to their success as cultural arbiters was their ability to enlist the support of influential shapers of the nascent mass culture, who echoed their tone and carried their message to a broad audience"—i.e., the mass publishers, lecturers, and artists who commercialized and popularized genteel values, and clever entrepreneurs such as P. T. Barnum who mastered the "rhetoric of moral elevation, scientific instruction, and cultural refinement in presenting their attractions."[4] B. F. Keith must also be counted among those "popular impresarios" who carefully packaged mass entertainment with middle-class respectability, and made a fortune in the bargain.

But with Keith, more than money was at stake. Unlike Tony Pastor, Keith did not just pay lip service to the rhetoric of refinement, but was fanatically insistent that even his audiences behave strictly as ladies and gentlemen. When he opened his first Philadelphia house in the late eighties, Keith actually stood in the gallery during intermission and personally lectured the audience on its behavior. Caps and ladies' hats had to be removed, smoking was forbidden, and all stomping, whistling, spitting on the floor, and the crunching of peanuts was banned; two strategically placed bouncers lent force to Keith's sermons.[5] Certainly Keith was more than willing to do his part to make vaudeville high class; when his new Colonial Theatre opened in Boston in 1893, $670,000 was spent just on the interior decoration, with the $89 red velvet carpet in the coal bin an attraction in itself.[6]

Keith's insistence on polite behavior and the earmarks of status betrays, perhaps, his own class-sensitivity. A former circus grifter, his personal fortune had risen with the variety business; he wanted vaudeville to be not only wholesome but also high-class, presumably because its status mirrored his own. Like Keith, most of the successful vaudeville producers had begun in the humblest capacities in the entertainment business, and they were anxious, self-conscious arbiters of the vaudeville audience's taste.[7] Martin Beck, for example, stubbornly backed "class" acts such as fine concert musicians and ballet dancers. Joe Laurie, Jr. recalled:

> He didn't care if those kinds of acts went over with the audience (many of them were a way over the heads of the vaude patrons of that time). When they would flop, Beck would shake his head and say, "They got to be educated."[8]

By Victorian standards of taste, certainly many in the audience needed to be "educated." Throughout the nineties and through the turn of the century, people with "unrefined" tastes were still in the vaudeville house. Some portion of the audience still preferred the uproarious comic melees of old; male team Keno and Welch were said to "knock each other about" — "to the great delight of those who favor rough and tumble work."[9] A large number of the audience were indifferent to Keith's efforts to provide them with culture and classy acts. At one point in 1901, a boisterous "East-Side" male-female sketch called "Brockey's Temptation" was playing at Tony Pastor's simultaneously with one of Keith's cultural offerings, prompting the observation that

> although they had "The Temptation of St. Anthony" in the living art studies over at Keith's, it is a safe bet that the Pastorian element comprehend Brocky much better than they could've understood the estimable saint aforementioned.[10]

A 1903 review of a Will Cressy sketch implied that, even then, there were still those who preferred the "crude" sort of act:

> The attention with which the audience follow the unfolding of the sweet, human little plot should convince vaudeville managers that the clientele has a mind for something better than horseplay and crude parodies.[11]

There was enough horseplay in vaudeville for those who liked it; presumably this type of patron could simply endure the "class acts." But there were more and more sketches on the bills with a "sweet, human little plot," and there were also more and larger vaudeville houses; a large portion of the audience obviously acquiesced to class-conscious managers' attempts to raise the tone of vaudeville.

By the late nineties, vaudeville was attracting new patrons who shared the class-sensitivity of the vaudeville entrepreneurs, people who feared being offended by any coarse jokes and suggestive allusions. The new clientele was clearly of more consequence than the old, because performers and critics catered to their tastes. In 1895 Bonnie Thornton's songs caused a great deal of hilarity "in the regular houses" among the men "of whom the audiences are largely composed," but during her appearance at Keith's she had to sing only songs calculated to appeal to "the refined audience who are characteristic of Keith's."[12] That same year the *Mirror* printed an article headed "A Hint to Comedians," i.e., a hint to refrain from mentioning harelips, cross-eyes, hunchbacks, lame legs and red hair:

> It is time for a reform in this matter, and if the managers of the elite vaudeville theatres expect to retain the good will of good people, they must put their feet down, hard and heavy, on this kind of "fun."[13]

In the mid-nineties, vaudeville fun-making could still be less than polite, but there was a class of "good people" attending who found this low humor offensive. There was also a portion of the audience, presumably these same good people, who were said to approve the more highbrow male-female acts. The dramatic acting of Charles Dickson, an import from the legitimate stage, seemed

> peculiarly suited to the tastes of the patrons of the vaudeville houses, as they become tired of the serio-comics and knockabout teams, and the dainty sketches in which he appears come as a welcome relief from the usual monotony of the regular variety turns.

When the noted violinists Mr. and Mrs. Wilczek appeared in 1898, the "applause they received shows that even the vaudeville-loving public can appreciate good music."[14]

Who was this "vaudeville-loving public"? It was most likely the group referred to by modern historians as "the new middle class." The rapid expansion of vaudeville shows it must have drawn its support from growing segments of the population. In fact, between 1870 and 1910—the same years that vaudeville, and other expressions of popular culture such as Coney Island and Atlantic City, experienced their greatest growth—the "new middle class" grew almost eightfold: from 756,000 to 5,609,000, or from thirty-three per cent of the population in 1870, to sixty-three per cent in 1910.[15]

A still more specific hypothesis can be posited. If turn-of-the-century society were to be divided into four categories—"upper-class," those in the *Social Register* and the wealthiest nouveaux-riches; "upper-middle-class," doctors, lawyers, editors, substantial businessmen, and high-ranking administrators; "lower-middle-class," white-collar workers, tradesmen, and prosperous skilled workers; and "lower-class," factory workers, laborers, and domestics—probably the ambience of the turn-of-the-century vaudeville house was lower-middle-class, with a smattering of the classes above and below it, varying with the bill, the theatre, and its location.

The continued popularity of knockabout suggests the presence of people with uncultured taste, a taste that probably cut across the lower-middle-class and lower-class patrons, although this group was now largely relegated to the gallery. Thus, when old-timer Paddy Murphy—an Irish comic who had flourished in the seventies and eighties—appeared with his female partner in 1896, he "made several successful bids for the applause of the gallery."[16] The rather tawdry cast of the vaudeville milieu is revealed by the location of the vaudeville theatres at Atlantic City. They were at the lower end of the Boardwalk, an area famous for its beer gardens, shooting galleries, carousels, weight-guessers, rental-bathing-suit hawkers, and its scores of stalls selling cheap souvenirs.[17]

Of course, it took money to indulge in recreational buying and also to enjoy vaudeville, and neither the money, leisure, nor frame of mind for such pleasures was available to the very poor, especially the non-English-speaking recent immigrant. A 1907 study of the wages and costs of living of Greenwich Village wage earners—all those making below $1200 a year, whether blue-collar or white-collar—showed that from a sample of two hundred families, none of the 13.5 per cent making below $500 a year (e.g., laborers, kitchen helpers, cigar-makers, pressers, street cleaners) spent anything on entertainment. On the other hand, the group of families averaging $1050.70 a year (policemen, longshoremen, masons, grocers, etc.) spent $17.72 a year on recreation on the average. At the turn-of-the-century prices of 15¢-25¢-50¢, vaudeville was accessible recreation.[18]

The recreation expenses of those spending $10 a year for it consisted of a couple of trips to Coney Island and Fort George, with only a few visits to the theatre in the winter. But trips to the theatre were made more frequently by those spending more. The surveyor noted that

> the amount which some of the more prosperous families spend on the theatre is surprising. Some of the women go regularly every week all winter to Proctor's, Weber and Fields, or the Fourteenth Street Theatre, but they rarely go to an uptown theatre. They buy fifty-cent seats.[19]

Other factors besides income could also affect a family's fondness for theatre; native-born families (of immigrant or non-immigrant background) frequented the theatre more than first-generation immigrant families, and class aspirations could be a spur. For example, a native-born draftsman in an architect's office who made $850 a year (the median income for all wage earners) and lived in a comfortable middle-class home, went regularly once a week with his wife to the theatre all winter, spending about $16. Several summer trips with the two children to Coney Island brought the total spent yearly on recreation to $50. In contrast, an Irish fire-stoker who made $895 a year and an Irish harness-cleaner making $870 a year spent none on recreation; for some families, visiting and church-going were the only recreation.[20]

If Greenwich Village's theatregoers rarely went uptown, the uptown theatres must have contained fewer lower-class patrons and a larger portion of upper-middle-class patrons than downtown vaudeville houses. The prosperous middle-class residential districts stretched northward from 23rd Street on the east and the west, and by degrees, "as you move up Sixth Avenue the shoppers begin to look more prosperous, more alert, and more sure of what they want." The crowd on 23rd Street, where Proctor's Theatre was located, was "orderly" and wore "good clothes."[21]

But the class-consciousness of vaudeville journalism betrays its lower-middle-class soul. The turn-of-the-century reader of the *New York Dramatic Mirror* was bombarded with vaudeville's boasts: that Bennett and Kent "drew large and fashionable audiences," that the Garrisons please "discriminating" theatregoers, that vaudeville audiences are "usually harder to please than those who see nothing but plays." The continual insistence that the vaudeville audience had high-brow tastes was too shrill, too self-conscious; performers were still over-eager to bill themselves as "refined," "high-class," "artistic," or as a "Society Duo."[22]

One factor that tended to fill a vaudeville orchestra with decorous patrons was that women and children—no longer fearing any honky-tonk goings-on—could now attend vaudeville matinees unescorted. It was a valuable audience to tap, and the wholesome variety show must have been an equally welcome discovery to the middle-class woman, with her increase in leisure and freedom at the turn of the century.

New labor-saving devices were making housework less grueling, but at the end of the century the typical woman still devoted more than forty hours a week to housework; her burden was most dramatically lightened simply because she bore fewer children. Thanks to obstetrical and pediatric advances and spreading knowledge about birth control, women were bearing the same number of surviving children yet undergoing fewer pregnancies, so that by 1900 the annual birth rate had dropped forty per cent from what it had been at the beginning of the nineteenth century. Fewer pregnancies meant that the last child was born earlier and gone from home sooner; in addition, female life expectancy increased four years between 1850 and 1900.[23] Even younger women with children were stepping out more; now that pregnancy and infant care were less traumatic, many mothers were spending some of their twenty-odd child-caring hours per week in the vaudeville house. As early as 1893, manager F. F. Proctor claimed to be "astonished at the large number of women and children that seek admittance the moment the performance begins."[24]

In the late nineties there were increasing references in theatre newspapers to the female vaudeville audience, notices that a certain sketch "pleased the women especially," or that an actress "pleased the women and children with her 'cute' specialty."[25] When the happy ending of one play seemed unrealistic to a certain reviewer, he reasoned that "the ending must have been arranged to suit the ladies and children who attend vaudeville houses in the afternoons." George Wilson, who did a minstrel turn, was thought wise to cater to the female audience:

> He has the secret of knowing how to make the female portion of an audience laugh heartily, and any man who can do that is sure of success on the stage. Women, as a rule, do not understand poker, jokes, and lots of other things, and Mr. Wilson wisely avoided the methods of many well-known entertainers who do not pay enough attention to the very important point of pleasing the ladies.[26]

An amusing example of a child's response to any too-boisterous stage behavior occurred in 1896. At one point in the Nawns' Irish turn, Tom Nawn picked up a sugar bowl to throw at his female partner. Just as he was taking aim, a child's shrill voice cried, "Oh, Mama! dat man is goin' to frow somefin at de lady!" No doubt a sudden increase in the number of middle-class women and children coming to vaudeville accounts in part for vaudeville's tendency, beginning in the mid-nineties, to become still quieter, even less rollicking. Act after act was described as "dainty," "charming," "pretty," and "cute"—qualities which would certainly not have pleased the all-male audience of the early variety shows.[27]

An important innovation that increased the number of "dainty" acts was the successful introduction of the dramatic playlet by legitimate performers, the majority of them male-female teams. Hugh Stanton and his leading lady Francesca Redding are traditionally credited with being, in 1893 or 1894, the first performers to do a playlet. Of the several accounts, the most likely explanation is simply that Keith saw an opportunity to improve his box-office:

> Mr. Stanton had for several seasons been leading man of the famous old Forepaugh Stock compnay, and had become an immense favorite with Philadelphians when the discerning Keith bethought himself of the probable tremendous drawing card Mr. Stanton would be in vaudeville, which was just then budding into popularity. A tempting offer to Mr. Stanton was the means of putting the idea to a test, which proved the wisdom of the Keith judgement, overwhelmingly.[28]

The result was "A Happy Pair"—a "thirty-minute act which told a clean domestic story in which no singing, dancing, gagging, or topical allusions occurred." There had been forerunners, but "A Happy Pair" seemed unique because performed by legitimate performers and pretentiously billed as a "society comedietta."[29]

About this time, J. Austin Fynes, manager of Keith's Union Square house, began actively pursuing legitimate stars in order to attract some of the legitimate theatre audience to his theatre. The "legits" still looked down on vaudeville in the mid-nineties, but a few were unable to resist the money dangled by Fynes; his first recruits were Maurice Barrymore, Robert Hilliard, and three mixed teams, Charles Dickson and wife Lillian Burkhardt, John Mason and wife Marion Manola, and Mr. and Mrs. Sidney Drew.[30]

Each of these three mixed teams appeared in vaudeville for the first time in the 1895-96 season, with playlets described as "dainty." The Masons performed a sketch called "Criss-Cross," which concerned a quarrel between a leading actor and an actress who lived in the same boarding house. The Dicksons had a sketch called "The Salt-Cellar," and were "stars of the bill" in a "comedietta" called "Two Can Play at that Game"; the Drews' "dainty and effective little play, In Clover," involved a young married couple who have a quarrel and make up in the end.[31] Two-acts featuring husband-wife spats had been seen before, but these legitimate players were viewed as more artistic, and their "acting" skill was praised; for example, Mrs. Drew was said to have "made a great hit by her quick changes from one mood to another. She played in an earnest, convincing way, and her performance could scarcely be improved upon." The three teams were in a class by themselves and were deliberately compared: the Drews' sketch was rated as "a great deal better than either The Salt-Cellar or Criss-Cross, which have been presented here by the Dicksons and the Masons."[32]

An illustrious "pioneer" convert to the vaudevilles the following season was matinee favorite Johnstone Bennett, who made her vaudeville debut at Proctor's Pleasure Palace in New York, teamed with S. Miller Kent in "A Quiet Evening at Home." Miss Bennett had been one of Richard Mansfield's entourage, performing eccentric character roles in his productions of *Prince Karl, Monsieur, A Parisian Romance,* and *Beau Brummel;* in the early nineties, she had starred in Charles Frohman's hit *Jane.* Kent's credentials were also impressive; he was a graduate of Purdue University who had turned to theatre, and had supported such stars as Dion Boucicault and James O'Neill. Their vaudeville debut was presumably inspired by the monetary reward, for it was reported that

> the big vaudeville managers are vying with one another to secure Miss Bennett at figures which would astound some of her confreres who affect to turn up their noses at what they call "the variety business."[33]

In reality, it is likely that most legits turned to vaudeville because of flagging careers.[34] At any rate, the three hundred to five hundred dollars offered the dramatic acts—a substantial increase from the seventy to two hundred fifty dollars usually paid two-acts[35]—sufficed to attract a sudden influx of legitimate performers. "The vaudeville ranks are constantly being increased by new recruits," claimed the *Mirror* in 1896; among the debuts that season were the Grandins, William Blaisdell and Clara Levine, Bert Coote and Julia Kingsley, and Eben Plymton and Agnes Proctor. Lizzie Evans and Harry Mills joined them after "seeing the demand for good performers in the high class vaudeville theatres."[36] Male-female acts were by far the most conspicuous recruits from the legitimate stage; a man and a woman provided the bare essentials for a playlet—a kind of act which utilized their dramatic training, was convenient, and perfectly suited to vaudeville's developing tastes.

The light comedy sketches by legitimate performers must have attracted new patrons as well as old; certainly managers would not have continued paying out money to legits unless they brought substantial box-office returns. In 1898, when Milton and Dolly Nobles joined the vaudeville ranks, the *Mirror* happily noted that

> the genuine success achieved by these sterling legitimate comedians indicates the improved conditions in vaudeville. They are drawing to the vaudeville houses a large percentage of their old clientele, the majority of whom never before attended these theatres. This gives a commercial value to their names, which shrewd managers have recognized promptly and liberally.[37]

Such an act probably did attract some fashionable "slummers," even if not a "large percentage."

Thus, by the turn of the century vaudeville's audience had become quite diverse, with several tastes represented. The businessmen who controlled vaudeville were catering to the lower-middle and upper-middle class, especially women; but their audience still contained enough of the old variety crowd for the gallery to exercise a potent influence, During these years, then, the most important quality a vaudeville act could have was the ability to appeal to a wide spectrum of people.

It was not always easy. In 1904 Milton Nobles recalled a time six or seven years before, when a dramatic sketch with legitimate actors or a straight singing turn would be "guyed."[38] It is not unlikely that the response of the gallery to "class acts" was deliberately unmentioned in some reviews. An 1898 review of the singing turn of Attalie Claire, former prima donna of the Castle Square Opera Company, claimed she was appreciated as thoroughly by the regular habitués of Proctor's as by those who came specifically to hear her—but then the reviewer added ambiguously that both classes would have been better pleased if she had chosen her songs with more discretion; Maggie Cline, who followed Miss Claire on the bill, "understood the work in hand better," and had every person in the house "with her."[39] The implication is not only that Miss Claire did not have every person "with her," but that to appeal to the different classes present was "work." Male-female routines were often said to be "constructed with a view of entertaining any and all kinds of audiences," and the act that "appeals directly to people in all parts of the house" was probably the big hit of the bill.[40]

This important trend, the shifting status of the vaudeville audience, provides the most important rationale for the kinds of male-female routines seen in vaudeville at the turn of the century. A particularly useful touchstone for the transformation of audience and entertainment is the immigrant act. There were new kinds of humor that evolved specifically to satisfy middle-class taste, but the ways in which racial comics again modified their acts to survive onstage before a new audience reflects vaudeville's changing visage.

There were mixed teams flourishing throughout the nineties and into the next century, with acts full of old-fashioned clamor. Irish teams Daly and Devere, the Dolans, the Donovans, and Sinclair and Favor had all started in the late eighties and were still doing what sound like boisterous routines. Daly and Devere, for example, had a routine variously called "The Janitress" or "Bridget's Word Goes." The latter version was done as late as 1907, and involved some female impersonation of an outrageous nature:

> Daly is a pretty sizeable fellow and he plays an Irish janitress, a most capacious female, pugnacious to a degree and anxious to air her opinions on any and all subjects. He sings several of the old-time Irish songs and dances a sure-enough Irish jig. His gyrations with a step ladder as he tries to hang a picture are one of the funniest features of the bill.[41]

But although there was enough demand for Irish "lower ten" sketches to keep such teams working into the 1900s,[42] after the middle of the first decade they were only "small-time," almost never appearing in a big-time New York or Chicago house. Daly and Devere's peak, for example, had been the years between 1888 and 1894, when they often played as many as eight weeks of the season in New York City,[43] but afterwards their popularity gradually declined, and the 1907 review above (of an act which is clearly old-time) is one of the last mentions of them. Although in 1903 Favor and Sinclair's "The Maguires"—featuring an Irish plumber and his daughter—was kindly billed as a "vaudeville classic," their sketch "Hogan's

Flat" was considered old in 1908. *Variety* condemned their musical numbers as from "yesteryear," and condescendingly suggested that "possibly elsewhere Favor, Sinclair, and Company in 'Hogan's Flat' have been appreciated."[44]

Some of the earliest hints of a change in taste are found in reviews of the Nawns. Tom and Hattie Nawn had appeared in New York City for the first time in the 1892-93 season, and were still being headlined in the 1909-10 season. From about 1895 to 1899, the Nawns did a sketch called "A Touch of Nature."[45] Thomas Nawn played a hod-carrier, and although the act was somewhat rowdy,[46] Nawn's Irishman was hailed as "life-like"; one reviewer claimed that "Mr. Nawn's Irishman was simply perfect; he had evidently studied from nature."[47] The implication is that his character was somehow different from other Irish stage characters that were not life-like—or perhaps not like the Irish audience's view of themselves. Nawn's Irishman was somehow more gratifying to a new generation.

By the twentieth century, the way the Irish looked at themselves, and the way other Americans looked at them, had changed. The majority were still working men, but the middle-class Irish-Americans were a sizable group, and the growing number of Irish merchants, police and fire officers, and civil administrators could not be patronized, however affectionately; they were clearly respectable. They were still not on a social par with the native Protestant middle class, but the Irish were viewed as, and felt, far superior to the new immigrants—they were the group "closest to being 'in' while still being 'out'."[48]

As a result, the second- and third-generation Irish-Americans were perhaps the most "class-sensitive" group in America. By the 1890s the term "lace-curtain" was already in use to describe the more well-to-do Irish families. The term not only denoted a certain level of financial achievement, but it connoted a self-conscious, anxious attempt to create and maintain a certain level of gentility. This first group of lace-curtain Irish had "a mania for the respectable and pious, the sober and genteel"; they were trying desperately to live down the "shanty Irish" image of earlier generations."[49] The transition was first conspicuously dramatized on the stage by Edward Harrigan, whose 1890 play *Reilly and the Four Hundred* depicted the misadventures of an Irish pawnbroker who makes it into high society. Unlike earlier Harrigan songs such as "Why Paddy's Always Poor" and "The Pitcher of Beer," the hit song of this play was about the social-climbing Irish middle class:

> There's an organ in the parlor, to give
> the house a tone,
> And you're welcome every evening at
> Maggie Murphy's home![50]

Vaudeville, with its pretensions of class and respectability, must have appealed to lace-curtain Irish families. (Indeed, the rising social status of thousands of Irish-Americans contributed to the phenomenal increase in the middle class during this era, the increase that explains vaudeville's expansion.) Certainly the presence of ambitious, class-conscious Irish in large numbers would explain why vaudeville audiences were responding so favorably to kinder, less grotesque Irish humor in the early twentieth century—whereas acts which portrayed the Irish as crude roughnecks, particularly the Russell Brothers' famed "Irish Servant Girls" act, were meeting with dramatic protests. On some occasions offending Irish acts were drowned out by catcalls, songs, hisses, and boos; eggs, vegetables, stones, and even theatre seats were thrown at the guilty vaudevillians. When the Russell Brothers performed in the New York area in 1907, they went onstage every night fearing for their lives, some nights not even managing to begin their act. That engagement was essentially the end of their career in big-time vaudeville.[51]

In contrast, mixed Irish teams singled out with praise for their quiet humor—Mark Murphy and wife, LeRoy and Clayton, Girard and Gardner, and the Kelceys—were among the most successful Irish acts. With a repertoire of four sketches ("The Seventh Son," "Why Doogan Swore Off," "The Coal Strike," and "Clancy's Ghost") the Murphys could be seen in vaudeville from 1900 until Murphy's death in 1917.[52] The *Mirror* applauded Murphy in 1903 for having discarded the traditional stage whiskers; *Variety* maintained that

> the two principals have within themselves the essence of real Irish humor which is a thing apart from the spurious imitations of the ordinary witticisms of knockabouts wearing green whiskers and talking with an insistently rolling "R."[53]

Similarly, Walter LeRoy, who with partner Florence Clayton first appeared around 1895, and remained popular throughout the first decade of the 1900s in "Hogan of the Hansom," "A Horse on Hogan," and "Hogan's Millions," was said to be "a good Irishman without making a whole lot of noise about it."[54]

The extent to which Irish sketches could forsake the traditional rollicking subject matter can be seen in a description of the act done by the Kelceys, who between 1900 and 1905 were seen in "In Trust"—a "simple little affair, with a touch of heart interest that is bound to appeal to any one with a dash of sentiment in his make-up."[55] Alfred Kelcey played a middle-aged Irish major in London with £25,000 entrusted to him by a dying comrade during military service in India, to be delivered to the widow. The major cannot locate her, but even though he is starving, he nobly refrains from using the money held in trust. A sympathetic widow sees his distress and invites him to share her Christmas dinner; naturally she turns out to be the very widow he seeks, there is "a brief courtship, and the curtain falls on the usual scene."[56]

The only ethnic feature in such sketches was the Irishman himself, and with the traditional exaggerated make-up disappearing, the only noticeably Irish characteristic was the brogue. But by the late nineties, convincing stage brogues were rare in vaudeville. Fewer people talked with a pure brogue in real life, and the old Irish lilt was a less easily acquired stage skill—not always well done, so more appreciated when it was competent.[57] The *Mirror* could be found complaining in 1898 of an Irish character in a farce that "his Irish brogue...had several large holes in it," and in 1901 exclaiming that "in these days of 'sponge-in-the-mouth' Irish dialects," it was a relief to hear Alfred Kelcey's "real" Irish brogue, which was "unexaggerated" and "reproduced charmingly."[58]

Had the muted ethnicity of the Irish stage character been the only development, Irish humor would probably have died a natural death long before the end of the decade. But the Irish sketches done by Thomas Ryan and Mary Richfield after 1900 gave the tradition new life in vaudeville. Ryan and Richfield had teamed up in private and public life in 1886, touring the variety house circuit with a sketch called "Dr. O. B. Careful," followed by "The Lunatic Asylum" in the nineties and later "A Headless Man," titles suggesting horseplay in the old-time way.[59]

The first decade of the 1900s set Ryan and Richfield on a new course, thanks to a series of sketches they acquired written by Will M. Cressy and in the tradition of Harrigan's *Reilly and the Four Hundred*. "Mag Haggerty's Father," probably first seen in the 1901–02 season, was the story of an Irish bricklayer who suddenly acquires wealth when his daughter marries a millionaire; the daughter sets forth to make a gentleman of her father, and starts by taking him to Atlantic City. But since "the days of the alley and the evening can of beer are uppermost in his mind," Mike finds it difficult to accustom himself to society life, and his misadventures in their pretentious resort hotel furnished the "wholesome" fun. This sketch was followed with a sequel, "Mike Haggerty's Daughter," by the fall of 1904, and with "Mag Haggerty's Reception,"[60] by the spring of 1906. In the latter the daughter is still attempting to cultivate a taste for society in Mike, and invites him to a reception at her Central Park West home. Among other failures, Mrs. Ma-Shay-On is unable to cajole her father into accepting her adaptation of the good old Irish name of McShane.[61] "Mag Haggerty, M.D.," new in the fall of 1909, showed more of the same fun on the shaky social ladder.[62]

Ryan and Richfield's comic skills won raves from reviewers,[63] but it was their timely characterizations that boosted the team to stardom.

Cressy's sketch-writing was directed by Ryan himself, who reputedly determined to portray "a type of Celtic character that would in no wise offend the members of the race. He eschewed the green whiskers, the slapstick and the bladder so often associated with Irish 'comedians' and studied out a make-up that would be typical in every way."[64] Whereas Ryan's brogue was Irish through and through—and "unsurpassed on the American stage"— he played "quietly and without the boisterousness that usually pervades such an offering." The *New York Mirror* maintained that Ryan "illuminates his portrayal by innumerable touches that could have come to him by close observances of occurences in real life." In fact, Ryan claimed his character was "studied from life at close range," based on one "old Tim Haggarty," an Irishman he had known for many years.[65] Mary Richfield was also admired for her "affable, easy, natural manner of delivering her lines that always carries conviction."[66]

Apparently what audiences liked to think was so "life-like" about Mike Haggarty was his ability to survive unscathed the social ordeals of moving up in the world. The vaudeville audience would probably have agreed with this contemporary interpretation of Ryan's Haggerty as

> that amusing, human, true-to-life type of the little Irishman, who begins by carrying the hod and ends by having money, with all his old directness, his honest conviction and his amusing peccadilloes remaining intact. Mr. Ryan is a good little mick...showing what the men of the old sod can do when they come over here, take off their coats, go to work, retain their sense of humor, loyalty and bigheartedness and end by going away up to the top of the heap.... His humor, his hardheadedness, his prejudices, many of which do him credit, and his remembrance always that once he was one of the boys in the street and shouldn't become supercilious just because he has a little money—all these things serve to make Tom Ryan's Haggerty a role which is as true to every-day life as it is an entertaining on [sic] the stage.[67]

Ryan's characterization must have been attractive to the Irish wage earner in the audience who, thanks to new prosperity and a social-climbing wife, found himself in new social situations which could leave him feeling awkward and out of place. The sympathetic, endearing portrait of Haggerty assured the anxious audience member that his old background and habits were admirable, not something to be ashamed of. The same reasoning explains why one of the popular comic strips in the Hearst papers, which had a large Irish readership, was "Bringing Up Father," a two-dimensional picture of a lace-curtain Irish matron and her recalcitrant husband. Maggie's heart is set on making her way to the opera with the Van Snoots, but Jiggs, like Mike, just wants to take off his shoes and enjoy corned beef and cabbage with the boys at Dinty's.[68]

Just so, Mary Richfield's Mag showed "some of the sentiment which of necessity must actuate the newer generation of her good and fine kind."[69] Her characterization of a graceful colleen who moved effortlessly into higher social circles had "a remarkable following among the women who are fond of vaudeville in its best form," reported the *New York Mirror*; "Another characteristic of Mrs. Ryan is her excellent taste in...costumes, which reflect her knowledge of what is of the greatest interest to women who patronize the theatre."[70] Mary Richfield's stage persona possessed the charming appearance and social finesse lace-curtain Irish women craved for themselves; they probably clucked understandingly as in sketch after sketch she made another tireless attempt to cultivate the hopeless Mike.

Irish working people practically worshipped Ryan and Richfield. The St. Louis Hod Carriers' Union visited the theatre just to see the team do "Mike Haggerty's Daughter," and after the show compliments were showered on the team in every brogue known to the Emerald Isle. On another occasion over one hundred members of the Brooklyn Gaelic Society attended the Greenpoint Theatre to watch the team perform. Earlier, the club had passed a resolution condemning the "stage Irishman" of a certain class, but commending Ryan's portrayal of "the real, lovable type of Celt," and the club made Ryan and Richfield honorary members of the Brooklyn Gaelic Society, with their dues paid forever.[71]

But the team's ability to play in major cities across the country, year after year, often for several weeks in a season, demonstrates their success with vaudeville audiences from many ethnic and social backgrounds. They were one of the most popular vaudeville acts of any kind or sex. Their depiction was not one of immigrants new to this country, but of typical Americans new to an exclusive class of society that was also above those in the vaudeville audience. The situation was one with which a middle-class audience of any ethnic background could sympathize.

Naturally Ryan and Richfield had their imitators, but *Variety* panned lookalikes.[72] In fact, by the end of the decade, few Irish teams besides Ryan and Richfield were popular. Of over four-hundred-fifty known male-female teams appearing in New York City between the 1894-95 and 1903-04 seasons, only twenty can definitely be identified as Irish teams—a significant decrease from the mid-eighties, when at least nineteen of one-hundred-ninety male-female teams were known to be Irish. Between 1904 and 1913, the number of Irish teams remained about the same, but the number of all male-female teams appearing in New York jumped to over six hundred fifty. Dutch teams suffered a comparable decline.[73]

Of course, even as the old ethnic types were on the decline, some new immigrant types were being done by male-female teams, with the Jew the most rewarding new stage type. From five thousand in 1880, the number of Jewish immigrants a year was up to eighty-one thousand by 1892; by 1897 there were almost a million Jews in America.[74] The first generation of

Eastern European Jews initially made little attempt to integrate themselves into the American social structure; the Orthodox Jews, in particular, with their unkempt beards and long black coats, were easily exaggerated into the stage "Hebes," who were "close copies of the types seen everyday on the East Side."[75]

As with earlier dialect characters, the stage Hebrew was first depicted by male performers;[76] the first Hebrew male-female act was almost surely William Hines and Earle Remington. Beginning in 1882, Hines and Remington had performed about two weeks each year in New York City variety houses with their act, "Our Railroad Boarders," and at the turn of the century, while other immigrant comedians fell from favor, Hines and Remington were at the peak of their popularity.[77] Their success was undoubtedly due to Earle Remington, who was the star of the act and wrote their material. In the nineties she had been one of the first women to sing parodies, and incurred a lot of jealousy from the male parodists of the day, until they learned Earle Remington "wrote her own stuff." She was acknowledged by her contemporaries to have introduced the first female Hebrew character in vaudeville, in the Hines and Remington sketch "Our Pawnshop," first seen on bills around 1893, and described as "an East-Side vaudeville sketch."[78] A creative woman like Earle Remington, already impersonating East Side eccentrics, must have been quick to note the presence of a type with the comic possibilities of the Jewish immigrant.

Harry Harrigan and Annie Giles were doing a joint Hebrew turn in the 1906–07 season; *Variety* considered it a missed opportunity that Annie Giles did now impersonate a Jewess throughout, since "it is a character seldom attempted and she seems competent to handle it."[79] There were never many male-female Hebrew acts because, as early as 1907, Jewish organizations were protesting the stage depictions of Jews as offensive.[80] Whereas it took the Irish over four decades to develop the lace-curtain stereotype, Jews covered the same distance in half that time. Russian Jews brought urban skills—e.g., peddling and tailoring—which were highly marketable in New York City. The traditional Jewish respect for education was invaluable in an era of big business and bureaucracy. Unlike the Irish, Jews did not romanticize the past, but seemed driven to achieve the security which had eluded them in Europe. In 1901 the United States Industrial Commission would report that "from Hester Street to Lexington Avenue is a journey of about ten years." By 1905, close to forty-five per cent of the Jews in New York claimed white-collar positions.[81]

By the early 1900s, in many sections of the city there must have been a large middle-class Jewish vaudeville audience. A late but concrete piece of evidence is a 1911 review which notes the big "Yom Kippur crowd" at the National Theatre, a family audience composed of "Mama and Papa and six or seven offspring to each team."[82] Groups like the Associated Rabbis of America, and the Chicago Anti-Stage Jew Ridicule Committee encouraged audiences to boycott any theatres where objectionable acts appeared; in areas like the Williamsburg section of Brooklyn, a Jewish boycott could ruin a theatre manager.[83]

For similar reasons, other new racial types were also not widely performed by male-female teams. Vaudeville audiences were familiar with Idalene Cotton and Nick Long's Italian characters, with the Allisons' Swedish sketch, "Minnie from Minnesota," and with "The Swede and the Happy Girl," performed by Billy "Swede" Hall and partner Jennie Coburn.[84] But in all these sketches the characters were simply eccentrics with a curious dialect, and any other type of eccentric would have served as well. In short, the new immigrant types simply did not have the social significance of the old types. By the turn of the century, second- and third-generation immigrants and native stock were being melded into a new group, the mass middle class, with more qualities in common than not. The needs and problems of urban living and industrialization, and their shared middle-class values — aspiring materialism, gentility, and morality — were concerns which bound them into a new society, and vaudeville mirrored these shared beliefs.

The new immigrant types were merely another kind of novelty for a mass audience that consumed novelties by the season; the treatment accorded these comic characters could never be other than superficial for so broad an audience. The necessary trait of a successful vaudeville act was its appeal for the nationwide mass audience; it had to work in any house between San Francisco and Baltimore. The new racial acts could rarely do this, for the new immigrants were concentrated in particular regions. In Minneapolis they might laugh at Swedes, but were little familiar with Italians; the stage Hebe was funny in New York, but had little relevance in Omaha. Such acts had less money-making potential, thus were not what bookers sought.

One other type of dialect humor offered by male-female teams, the blackface act, was declining to even smaller proportions than the immigrant-based acts. Negro life had less interest for vaudeville audiences than for variety audiences; the time when the black man's fate had been the most searing issue of the day was now long past. Certainly the thirteen and one-half million immigrants who came to America between 1865 and 1900[85] could never fully appreciate the plantation mythology underlying nineteenth-century blackface work. Thus, from hundreds of minstrel troupes at mid-century, by 1880 there were only thirty; by 1896 the number was down to ten and still falling. When minstrelsy faltered, a major training ground for blackface work was lost. Between 1895 and the teens, sometimes only one male-female blackface act per year appeared in New York City, none with outstanding success.[86]

Perhaps another important reason for the decline of male-female blackface work was the rise of competition unsurpassable in its lifelikeness: Negro male-female teams. Minstrelsy by Negroes had followed on the heels of its white inventors, and given the impetus of emancipation, by the mid-seventies there were many highly popular black minstrel troupes acting out the stereotyped minstrel images of Negroes on the plantation for white audiences.[87] But whereas white performers could turn to new material when interest in minstrel themes declined, black performers could not escape their stereotypes, and in the nineties, black talents began testing white audiences' reaction to Negro performers in vaudeville and on Broadway.

The first successful departure by Negroes from strict minstrelsy was *The Creole Show,* produced in Chicago in 1891 by Sam T. Jack, a prominent white burlesque producer, who conceived the notion of a chorus line of beautiful Negro women. The show was a sensation and repeated its success when it moved to New York in 1893. The star was former Negro minstrel Sam Lucas, who had already played a few vaudeville dates teamed with his wife. One of the highlights of the show was a "cakewalk" done by two Negroes in formal dress, Charlie Johnson and Dora Dean. Johnson and Dean were so fashionable that the *Mirror* featured a picture of "colored artists" for the first time, and Miss Dean's beauty inspired the then-unknown team of Williams and Walker to write "Dora Dean," the song with which they would later debut. Other Negro shows followed: *The Octoroons* in 1895, *Oriental America* in 1896, *A Trip to Coontime* and *Clorindy* in 1898, the last one of the biggest hits of the year.[88]

The fact that for a brief period, Negro shows featuring men and women flourished on Broadway, explains why numerous Negro male-female teams suddenly appeared on vaudeville bills. One of the first was Johnson and Dean, whose already established success made them in demand for vaudeville dates; beginning in 1898 they toured the circuits for about four seasons. Ernest Hogan, star of the Broadway success *Clorindy,* played vaudeville dates with female partner Mattie Wilkes. Others were Billy and Madrid Jackson, Al and Mamie Anderson, Fagan and Byron, Murphy and Francis, Raustus and Banks, the Woodwards, Johnson and Wells, the McCarvers, and Maceo and Fox. The number of Negro teams was always small, but it was several times larger than the number of blacked-up mixed teams. Almost until the teens there were four or five mixed Negro teams appearing in New York City each season.[89]

If they were willing to play to white audiences' expectations, Negro teams could achieve financial success, but their stage roles were narrowly defined. Negro teams continued the minstrel custom of presenting themselves as "natural" rather than as trained entertainers, thus courting white condescension and tolerance. The Two Jacksons, for example, billed themselves as "Real Coon Comedians," Al and Mamie Anderson as "Real Coon Funsters." Almost all mixed Negro teams did a song and dance, with a "break-neck" dancing finale considered "the usual." Since lifelike male-female interaction by Negroes performing for white audiences was strictly taboo, sketches were almost never done; Joe Laurie recalled that he had never seen a Negro team do a sketch. Only the most farcical male-female interaction was attempted; Brown and Nevarro, for example, played a sketch called "The Wedding of the Chinee and the Coon"—two races who no doubt deserved each other in most whites' estimation.[90]

Like Negroes in Broadway musicals, the vaudeville teams abandoned plantation themes. The darky stereotype had been an affectionate portrait, because of the slave's supposed subservience and devotion to his white *massa;* but as free Negroes migrated into Northern urban areas and competed with newly arrived immigrants for jobs in labor and domestic service, the romantic plantation image was replaced with one better suited to white antagonism. The Negro was lampooned simply as the "coon"—those "no-account niggers, those unreliable, crazy, lazy, subhuman creatures good for nothing more than eating watermelons, stealing chickens, shooting crap, or butchering the English language."[91] Negro male-female teams who desired a living on the white stage had no choice but to act out these self-debasing caricatures, applying burnt cork to create a grotesque pop-eyed, big-lipped mask.

The musical vehicle for black performers was the "coon song," with lyrics lambasting the hapless Negro, sung to the new ragtime rhythms pioneered by blacks themselves. Ernest Hogan's "All Coons Look Alike to Me," which he debuted on the Casino Roof in 1897, was one of the first coon song hits. The coon song was so much the rage that many white male-female teams (and other white acts) began doing—often in whiteface—coon numbers, such as Cawthorne and Forrester with "Dat Coon's Got a Soft Spot for Me," or Irwin and Hawley with "Dat Nigger Treated Me all Right." Eventually white performers such as Sophie Tucker and Bessie Taylor would monopolize the coon song specialty, just as white male-female team Genaro and Bailey would usurp the cakewalk and Howard and Bland the ragtime piano number.[92]

But while white teams were flourishing with Negro material, as the effects of their freed abilities were felt, Negro male-female teams received subtle but discriminating criticism in *Variety* reviews. On one occasion, for instance, Mrs. Sam King was chided for her costume with the warning that "no colored woman should wear a low-necked dress on the stage"; the woman of Murphy and Francis was admonished because "she impresses her presence upon her audiences too forcibly."[93] "Is the Coon Craze Dying Out?" went the wishful tag line of an 1898 *Mirror* article:

> For several years past the vaudeville stage has been covered with a sort of black cloud.... So much "coon stuff" has been handed out to the patrons of vaudeville that they are beginning to show symptoms of weariness and the indications are that the great army of cake-walkers, sand shufflers, vocalists, and "pickaninnies" will soon have to go back to the less pleasing employments from which they emerged when there began to be a demand for their services on the stage. It will be a case of survival of the fittest...the sooner the others are relegated to the obscurity they deserve, the better it will be for vaudeville. The really clever negro performers now before the public can be counted on the fingers of two hands.[94]

As part of the same white backlash, Negro jockeys and prizefighters began to fall from favor; in 1900 the first of a series of riots broke out in which Negroes were beaten and arrested; gradually the Reconstruction amendments passed in Negroes' behalf were nullified or evaded by "Jim Crow" legislation.[95] With racial prejudice on the rise, by the teens Negro male-female teams were no longer in vogue.

The need for new acts to fill the gap left by the declining immigrant comedy may have been one reason that Negro performers were temporarily allowed to flourish. But like the immigrant comedian, the Negro vaudevillian did not have the universality of appeal for the diverse, nationwide vaudeville audience sought by box-office-minded managers. It was the humor embraced by male-female teams in the mid-nineties that more accurately expressed the new spirit of vaudeville, for the new character types were deliberately calculated to please an audience with middle-class values and sensibilities.

One of the first new comic characters to appear in male-female acts was the juvenile, or "kid," as the type was called. Perhaps the adults impersonating juveniles were inspired by the success of child performers, a commonplace in variety until the advent of child-labor laws at the turn of the century; Pat and Mattie Rooney, Bessie and Nellie McCoy, and Johnny and Bertha Gleeson were conspicuous favorites. The Evanses and the Midgleys, both new to variety in the late eighties, were the first known adult teams to impersonate children, however. Eddie and Josie Evans were popular throughout the nineties with "Little Sweethearts" and "Little Playmates." By 1896 their act was "quite familiar," but "about the best thing in this line now on the boards," and as late as 1903 they were still making a "hit."[96]

By the turn of the century the Evanses had been surpassed in popularity by Sager Midgley. Between 1889 and 1899, Midgley had performed with his wife Fanny Midgley, but after the two broke up, he was even more popular with his new partner, Gertie Carlisle. For the next ten years Midgley and Carlisle entertained audiences with a repertoire of three sketches, "Two Cute Kids," "After School," and "Taking a Tonic," all of which featured the characters of Sammy and Sarah.[97]

Midgley played a "half stupid, but, nevertheless, witty and inventive country kid"; he had "a queer, wrinkly, crinkly sort of a face, over which now and then a thought seems to dawn abstractly, and finally a song emerges." As a "kid" Midgley was said to be unsurpassed and "simply irresistible when he allows that fearful and wonderful smile to spread over his face."[98] Gertie Carlisle was one of the most beautiful women on the vaudeville stage, yet in her make-up as Sarah, with her "black curls and diminutive physique," did not appear to be more than ten or twelve years of age. Whereas Midgley played "a very sleepy schoolboy," Gertie's Sarah was "very wide awake," and her "youthful exuberance and charm of manner" had an "irresistible fascination." As late as the 1909-10 season the duo spent four weeks in major New York City vaudeville houses, two of them as headliners.[99]

The virtue of the juvenile act was that it offended no one; such sketches made "an irresistible appeal to every lover of children"[100]—i.e., every decent person. The juvenile act had obvious appeal for the mothers and children who patronized matinees. Children enjoyed watching what seemed to be a kiddie show, probably oblivious to the precociously witty utterances which amused the adults. Perhaps the juvenile act also offered adults a temporary escape from a world that was more complicated than the nineteenth-century world they had known as children themselves.

There were numerous others,[101] but the only team to surpass the Midgley's juvenile work was Williams and Tucker. At about the same time that the Midgleys had begun impersonating rural children, a few teams had begun specializing in city children—"Bowery Kids." Adult East Side life had been the dominant image in the variety house mirror, but for former downtowners in the vaudeville audience the hard knocks of those days were now a distant memory. They had moved farther uptown, found better jobs, gained new status, and now looked nostalgically on the old East Side life. Life had been simpler then, it now seemed; life in the middle-class world could be exacting, with its competition, its materialism, its demands for proper behavior.

To others, the new middle-class patrons now coming to vaudeville, life in downtown New York was as unfamiliar as a foreign country. Middle-class consciousness of the misery and depravity in their cities was being raised in the nineties. Journalists like Lincoln Steffens and reformers like Jane Addams were telling people about the needs and hopelessness of the poor. One of the most moving accounts was investigative reporter Jacob Riis's 1890 book, *How the Other Half Lives,* which captured public attention with its reports of living quarters in damp tenement basements, of stale-beer dives and stewing sweatshops, of the rampant crime and pauperism of New York's Lower East Side.[102] But it was easier to be titillated than motivated to do something about these conditions. Public imagination was captured by the color and variety of the downtown scene, which, squalor and all, offered an exotic change of scene from the ordinary Anglo-Saxon world. Readers enjoyed the tales of Hester Street by Abraham Cahan and the Chimmie Fadden stories with their Bowery lingo, and the cartoon creation of "the Yellow Kid" took the country by storm.[103]

The first famous "tough kid" on the stage was probably Ada Lewis. In real life a seventeen-year-old fish-cannery worker with a hard-boiled accent, she was seen in San Francisco by Edward Harrigan, on tour with *Reilly and the Four Hundred;* he was so charmed by her that he promptly created the role of the "tough girl" for her, and wrote it into his play—"a saucy, self-assured, hard-shelled, worldly girl who affected a mannish walk, talked in low-class slang, and wore a seedy get-up consisting of a brown jersey that was too short at the wrists, a ragged brown dress, a shabby straw hat, and ill-fitting gaiters."[104]

It was shortly after the success of *Reilly and the Four Hundred* in New York City—and Ada Lewis's conquest of the town—that Lawrence and Harrington appeared on the vaudeville stage as Bowery kids. By 1896 their "life-like picture of Bowery existence" was "familiar." By 1901 competition was such that they boasted of being the "Original Bowery Boy and Tough Girl."[105] One competitor was popular team Dick and Alice McAvoy, the "Hogan Alley Kids," who depicted the "eccentricities of the children of the East-Side."[106]

But Eva Williams and Jac Tucker's Bowery characters (first seen in 1898) were considered novel and superior to these toughs. Their sketch was called "Skinny's Finish." Eva Williams played a little Bowery girl named Mary Ellen Poet. The character appears onstage making her toilet, and reveals that her beau, "Skinny Dooley," is to take her to the gallery of a Bowery theatre. When the "ungrammatical yet ardent" fellow arrives, played by Tucker, he brings her a bunch of flowers. She is touched, although he confesses he swiped "'em from a posy joint w'en de blokey wasn't lookin'." Their delight is ended when a policeman grabs the culprit and lugs him away. Mary Ellen stands at a window watching them, and reports what she sees to the audience. Skinny trips his captor and runs off, and she shouts "Bully!" But then her glee fades and fright appears:

> The cop is up and after the fugitive. He'll pinch 'im—no—yes—ah-h! Hully gee! What a soak? That's "Skinny's" finish![107]

The effect was described enthusiastically by the *New York Sun:*

> You see the blow of the club and the drop of the boy as vividly in Miss Williams' eloquent visage as though the knockabout itself were in sight. The girl falls to the floor in a faint and the curtain falls on the work of an Ibsen and a Duse in vaudeville.[108]

The sketch spawned a host of imitators; in 1901, for example, the McAvoys debuted "A Waif's Chirstmas Eve," which "smacks of having been inspired by 'Skinny's Finish'," and the Ushers concocted an imitation called "Tough Love" in the 1903-04 season.[109] Williams and Tucker added "Driftwood" to their repertoire around 1902, featuring the same Mary Ellen Poet. In this sketch the East Side orphan is on her way to the poor farm; after a humorous and touching talk with the railroad agent — the only person who has ever been kind to her — she departs, determined to face her fate bravely.[110]

Vaudeville reviewers, and presumably audiences, were captivated by Eva Williams's ability and stage presence. She was lauded as

> an actress whose smile is as electric as the tears in her voice are real. She possesses some of the appealing quality that makes Maude Adams beloved of all American theatregoers. She turns from the blithest, pertest mood to the realm of truest sentiment in the flash of an eye.[111]

Said another, "Miss Williams might be called the Minnie Maddern Fiske of vaudeville."[112] The frequent reference to Fiske and Ibsen testifies to new biases. Eva Williams was admired because she did the Bowery girl "correctly" — i.e., realistically, or so it was claimed:

> Nothing more realistic than this characterization has ever been done on the New York stage, and Miss Williams cannot be too highly praised for her really remarkable study of this type of New York girl. There are dozens of "tough girl" impersonations on the stage, but not one of them has succeeded in giving that slight touch of pathos which makes the creation of Miss Williams so true to life.[113]

Williams and Tucker may have tailored their offering with a conscious eye to new trends on the legitimate stage. Already William Gillette and Minnie Maddern Fiske were impressing audiences with a quieter style of acting that seemed more natural and spontaneous; Eva Williams's stage character appealed to critics who had been exposed to the new kind of acting. Mary Ellen Poet was no Salvation Nell, but the character was an innovation for vaudeville; compared to other tough girls, a portrayal which included both comedy and pathos seemed more like life offstage. The finesse of Williams and Tucker could not but show to advantage when compared with the knockabout and exaggerated make-up still seen in dialect comedy:

> The horse-play and coarse humor of the old-time variety "team" still entertain, by a way of contrast, and will probably always be an element of more or less importance in the continuous performance; but more and more the character of the modern vaudeville as maintained by Mr. Keith is approaching the art level of actresses like Eva Williams.[114]

To the new middle class, both newspapermen and audience, the old knockabout seemed gross, and coarseness was just what they wanted to avoid. They judged their vaudeville by the qualities of the legitimate stage of the day—detailed picturesque realism and sentimentality—which Williams and Tucker emulated. As if attending a serious legitimate play, a viewer of a Williams and Tucker sketch felt moved to tears:

> Though the audience may laugh at her slang expressions there is a touch of genuine pathos running through it all that even while the muscles of one's face are relaxed in a smile, causes a mist to rise before the eyes, for it deals with human nature.[115]

To a middle-class audience, who delighted in ersatz culture, such seriousness seemed more artistic, more worthwhile. Indeed, Eva Williams was believed to be "the sort of actress that lifts the modern vaudeville stage at times to the best level of the drama," with an act than which "nothing finer in its way...has ever been done on the stage. It is art in its best and truest form."[116]

Had it just been "good for you," of course, watching Eva Williams would not have been as much fun. But there was enough comedy and street patois in the act to enable one to have a good time, even while being improved by a little culture. And the pathos made it all the more satisfying; despite her unfortunate situation as a street urchin, plucky Mary Ellen was always cute, cheerful, and able to handle her lot. Eva Williams's portrayal was proclaimed "flawless," because it was thought to match real-life Bowery children whom no one could help loving—"those poor 'kids' into whose lives so little sunshine comes, but who are generally cheerful, even under the most adverse circumstances."[117]

Such a view was certainly not realistic: if Eva Williams's portrayal was a departure from earlier tough girls, her conception was equally distanced from the creatures described by Jacob Riis. Williams's acknowledged source was the quaint pictures of well-known illustrator Mike Wolff. A surviving example of his work, *Sketches of Lowly Life in a Great City,* reveals that Wolff did not depict the hopelessness and ugliness actually uncovered by Riis, but served up street urchins in a sentimental fashion designed to appeal to genteel middle-class sensibilities.[118]

The middle class enjoyed indulging themselves with the myth of the Pollyanna of the slums. One of the most popular novels of the day was Alice Rice's 1901 *Mrs. Wiggs of the Cabbage Patch,* about the adversities of a family in the slums of Louisville's factory district. The opening words of the novel—"My but it's nice and cold this morning! The thermometer's done fell up to zero"—summed up Mrs. Wiggs's philosophy. It was easier to believe in such a reassuring myth as Mrs. Wiggs than it was to turn pity into action.[119]

The companion piece to the Bowery picture was the rural act, escapism from another angle. The Midgleys' popular juvenile act had depicted country kids, but adult rural characters were an even more popular alternative for turn-of-the-century male-female teams. In the wake of the sensational success of Denman Thompson's *The Old Homestead* (early variety material dramatized as a full-length play in 1876), sketch titles began to reveal interest in rural themes; by the late nineties several rural sketches by male-female teams were seen each season in New York City.[120]

Rural humor was made important vaudeville fare by the Sidmans between 1895 and 1901. Their first act was called "A Bit of Real Life." Sidman played a country squire who visits the city and meets a city girl, played by Mrs. Sidman. Arthur Sidman was almost immediately considered "by far the cleverest 'jay' impersonator" by critics,[121] and the Sidmans wisely followed their first success with more of the same. The new sketch was "Back Home"; in this one the "old lovable character" was visited back home by the young girl he had met in the city. By 1901 the Sidmans were among the highest paid vaudevillians; however, at the height of his fame, on 12 August 1901, Sidman died suddenly of typhoid pneumonia.[122] By then, inspired by the success of the Sidmans, there were many male-female rural acts touring in vaudeville.[123]

By the end of the century, as the consequences of urbanization became more and more glaring, rural characters and settings had a new attractiveness for urban audiences. Cities like New York were visibly blemished by slums festering with crime, poverty, and disease. Municipal governments had not yet evolved sufficiently to regulate the effects of progress, and city dwellers were perplexed and disheartened by such basic problems as managing water, sewage and garbage disposal, and fire-fighting. The woes of the modern metropolis profoundly altered the way Americans perceived the world outside the city. In retrospect, the rural lifestyle of the past became an ever more romantic myth; a broad "back to nature" movement, part therapy and part nostalgia, captured popular fancy.

Between 1880 and 1920, city planners established city parks (Central Part was the first triumph) and model suburbs; socialites and middle-class families flocked to newly established seaside resorts, national parks, dude ranches, and country clubs; bird-watchers, boy-scouts, sociologists, and landscape architects embraced the Arcadian religion with the zeal of converts.[124] Of course, these urban nature lovers eulogized the great outdoors as only city people could: they valued nature's spiritual impact above its economic importance; many praised their rural childhood, but few returned to farming. Their rural retreats ideally lay somewhere on the urban fringe, "easily accessible and mildly wild," fit for polite recreation, not raising chickens.[125]

Belief in the myth was widespread; an observer noted in 1903 that the demand for nature essays came from every class in the community, and that the supply was equally catholic.[126] Virtually every popular family magazine—*Good Housekeeping, Saturday Evening Post, The Woman's Home Companion, Ladies' Home Journal*—had regular columns or feature articles on the nature movement, and the mass audience was devouring novels about simple, decent country folks. In 1898, in *David Harum,* Edward Westcott popularized the best-selling formula for later rural novelists like Irving Bachellor and Joseph Lincoln:

> The generally romantic atmosphere was tempered by a realism of the b'gosh sort, the leading character was a quaint eccentric possessed of a simple ingenuity expressed in homely philosophy, and the kindly though shrewd country folk, unlearned and commonsensical, were capable of solving problems that beset the more sophisticated city people.[127]

Joseph Lincoln's credo was that "there's enough sorrow in this world without finding it in books." Clearly this philosophy appealed to the mass market; muckraking books like Lincoln Steffens's *The Shame of the Cities,* out in 1904, could not compete with books like *Rebecca of Sunnybrook Farm,* one of 1904's best sellers. A book like the latter enabled the city dweller to forget the anonymity of his life while he read about the wholesome friendliness of small-town life and the survival of pioneer values in backwater America.[128]

The rural vaudeville sketch offered its audiences the same kind of escape. To city dwellers confronted daily with the vision of a myriad tangle of electric wires above them and assaulted by the noise of the monstrous "el," stage pictures of the countryside were romantic and consoling. Indeed, special scenery was a stock feature of the rural sketch. Views of country cottages and haystacks and foliage were picturesque, almost exotic, to a city audience. The Midgleys' act, for example, was done against a backdrop representing "with realistic beauty and effectiveness...an old country home with a wealth of rustic detail that give it picturesque appeal."[129]

Realistic rural scenery, of course, also reflected the vaudeville audience's liking for the realism and more elaborate stage effects characteristic of the legitimate stage. Presumably one of the ways the Sidmans had "raised the standard of this class of entertainment" was with settings such as the one for "Back Home," which was "simply perfect. Every detail had been looked after, even to the old rag carpet and all the little 'props' that help make a stage scene look like the real thing."[130] The realism of rural characters was also praised. Sidman's portrait of a farmer was proclaimed "wonderfully accurate," and his joking was said to be so natural that it had no hint of the gag, but seemed to be part of his everyday life as a hayseed.[131]

Like Eva Williams, Arthur Sidman's more restrained humor was contrasted favorably with the loud, old-style comedians:

> His success proves that quiet methods are often more effective than the slam-bang, knockabout, pistol shooting practices indulged in by so many variety comedians.[132]

The Sidmans offered "the sort of merriment that does one a world of good and that one does not have to apologize for indulging in."[133] Subsequent rural acts, like the Manns with their "most kindly satire," sought the same effect.[134] Its kindly satire was an important attraction of the rural act. Whereas the old-time racial act singled out some object of mockery (possibly represented in the audience), the rural act was calculated not to offend. The patrons of vaudeville were primarily from cities or town, where the vaudeville houses were located; there were few real "hayseeds" in a vaudeville house, thus the character was someone all parts of a house could laugh at together. The effect of rural humor was to unite the diverse urban audience.

Even if any country-come-to-town folks had been in the audience, they were probably not offended, since the fun-poking was so gentle. An extant joke from Sidman's play *New York State Folks* reveals something of the friendly nature of rural humor. "Was you ever in New York?" the hayseed Ezra asks Uncle Myron, who answers:

> Yes, once. But I stayed three days. Simon Peter went with me. There's more people on that street they call Broadway any day in the week than there is here on the Fourth of July. We had an awful time gettin' along, and finally Simon Peter got tuckered out. He stopped stock still, and sez he: "I ain't goin' to stir another step till this crowd gits by!" He thought it was a procession.

"Gee, but he was green!" says Ezra, adding after a moment's thought: "Say, Myron, what was it? A parade?"[135] Just as Fourth of July orators and Frederick Turner's scholarly disciples expounded the conceit of the inherently noble American yeoman, so the rural sketch showed man at his most innocent. An older character like Uncle Myron was decent, kind, and in an unaffected way, a sort of unschooled philosopher; the silly hayseed was harmlessly amusing and touched a soft spot in audiences dealing daily with other hardened urbanites.

This beneficent view of the world was the trademark of Cressy and Dayne, a talented team which, soon after the turn of the century, was to eclipse all other rural acts, male-female or otherwise. Will Cressy's background certainly qualified him for his calling. He grew up in Bradford, New Hampshire, and was a travelling salesman for a wholesale grain and flour company. In 1889 he joined a small repertoire company in a Connecticut town, getting $24.00 for thirty-two weeks' work, and married the female lead, Blanche Dayne. In the nineties the couple played with an *Uncle Hiram* show and a *Si Plunkard* company, then Denman Thompson signed them for his *Old Homestead* company. Cressy had played the character of "Cy Prime" for six years when he attracted the attention of B. F. Keith who hired the team and told Cressy to "play a character sketch of the 'Old Homestead' variety."[136]

The sketch they opened with at Keith's Union Square on 19 December 1898 was "Grasping an Opportunity." The sketch featured a guileless old farmer who is visited by a female book salesman. She manages to work herself into an affectionate position with him and (somehow) takes a snapshot of them together. Finding himself trapped, the farmer pays her price for the plate, and drops it into the well. The *Mirror* announced at once that it was "the best thing in the rural line seen in vaudeville since the Sidmans produced A Bit of Real Life."[137]

The sketch contained components of the mature Cressy formula: the rural man who takes a loss because he helps a woman, an outsider passing through the village. This first sketch was harsher than Cressy's mature sketches; in the sketches after "Grasping an Opportunity," the woman is never designing, but is helpless and in trouble; the man is not tricked, but willingly sacrifices his own desires to benefit the woman, all because of his manly decency. Cressy recreated this formula in sketch after sketch, until by the 1906-07 season the team had a repertoire of seven sketches: "Grasping an Opportunity," "The Key of C," "A Village Lawyer," "Bill Biffins's Baby," "The Wyoming Whoop," "The New Depot," and "Town-Hall To-Night."[138]

"A Village Lawyer" was typical. Cressy played Squire Tappen, an old New Hampshire lawyer whose sole ambition is to possess a clarinet that costs eighty dollars; every time he gets the money saved, someone will drop in and borrow it. But now Squire Tappen has sixty dollars, and he vows that as soon as he gets that twenty dollars it is going right into an envelope and off to the store in Boston. He gets a twenty-dollar check in the mail as a retaining fee for a female client, prepares his order, and is off to mail it, when the woman arrives. She is seeking a divorce, but as her story unfolds, it is clear to the old lawyer that she really loves her husband. Squire Tappen counsels her until she cries and changes her mind, then he returns her money and sends her back to the husband—absent-mindedly tearing the order for the clarinet into pieces as he watches her leave:

> The moonlight shines upon his face.... He throws the fragments of the order out into the road. "Mebbe I couldn't have played the blamed thing anyhow," he says, and the curtain falls.[139]

According to the *Mirror,* the audience was delighted:

> The whole sketch is as dainty and pretty as could be imagined, and it is full of delicious comedy lines that sparkle with the quaintest of rustic humor. The long speech that makes the young wife cry is a gem of sincere dramatic writing, and the play, beautifully mounted, was splendidly acted throughout by both Mr. Cressy and Miss Dayne.[140]

Unfortunately, reviews of the sketches reveal only their plots, and not a line of the "dry Yankee wit" Cressy was famous for. But at one point Cressy had a syndicated newspaper column called "Continuous Vaudeville." It often contained the gentle cynicisms of his vaudeville persona, Squire Tappen:

> Funny how a little feller will marry a fat woman, an' then kick all the rest of his life 'cause his side of the bed is the highest.
> How is it that a Prohibitionist allers knows where to git it when he has a stomache ache?
> I don't see as that Mormon business is so bad. I know a lot of wives that would be better off if they had two or three other wives to help 'em support him.
> Why do some fellers risk their lives dodgin' across the street in front of a automobile, an' then stand five minutes lookin' in the door of a movin' picter show?
> I don't see what the advantage of these proposed trial marriages would be; strikes me that's the kind we're usin' nowadays anyway.[141]

That Will Cressy's humor was published as well as heard onstage is another indication of how popular it was. Cressy and Dayne's appeal went beyond the rural acts' reactionary nostalgia for the simpler life of the past. The team was not only the most popular of all rural acts, but one of the best-loved teams in vaudeville.

One reason was that Will Cressy was an exceptionally capable writer of vaudeville sketches. By 1914, Cressy had written 136 one-act vaudeville sketches; at one point in 1901, thirty-three of his sketches were being done simultaneously in vaudeville.[142] Almost all were for male-female teams, including such well-known teams as Matthews and Harris, Ryan and Richfield, Gardner and Maddern, and Davis and MacCauley. In the known Cressy plots, the theatrical roles of male and female always mirrored the status quo; the men were either nobler, more sensible, or less materialistic than the women, who were either sillier, more helpless, or somehow had less "character." In particular, each of Cressy's two famous male roles, Ryan's Haggerty and Cressy's Squire Tappen, was in his own way a character able to maintain his dignity and integrity despite immediate temptations. Each embodied Victorian values more and more at odds with those of the urban twentieth century. If Ryan's Haggerty presented the comic lesson that man must resist woman's urging to embrace materialism, certainly Squire Tappen provided a Sunday School lesson on the necessity for male sacrifice to save the more helpless sex from herself. Like Haggerty, Squire Tappen was the soul of the sketch; the female character provided him with the opportunity to exhibit his virtues, and also served as a less glistening foil.

The Cressy-Dayne sketches were unabashedly sentimental: not only does the Cressy hero always sacrifice the very thing he wants most, but he is so virtuous that he is even happy about it. Members of the upper classes intent on refining those below them viewed Cressy and Dayne with special approval. "Mr. and Mrs. Cressy are public benefactors," said one editor; "they preach better sermons than all the ministers in Chicago put together."[143] An Ohio minister announced that "No thanksgiving sermon preached in this or any other city carried a weightier lesson or struck home to a greater number of hearts."[144] Thus, the "lovable" Cressy character had guaranteed box-office appeal; whereas racial humor had been at the expense of a certain group, Squire Tappen's optimism could—and should—appeal to anyone. Who could publicly resist a "kindly whitehaired, simple, benevolent old fellow, with an upending sense of humor and a rosy viewpoint of the world?"[145]

There were other new comedy types popular with male-female teams in the late nineties, all based on these same appeals.[146] Like rural and juvenile characters, the stage burglars, tramps, Westerners, and hotel servants provided comic butts that a middle-class urban vaudeville audience of almost any racial or occupational background could laugh at, with no one offended.[147] But it is indicative of the huge number of male-female teams now playing in vaudeville that although there were dozens of male-female teams creatively involved with such characters, the mainstream of male-female humor was represented by still another kind of act: the confrontation of the two sexes in courtship and marriage.

The sexual interaction offered the male-female team a unique way to compete; so long as the appeal of their act was a non-sexual type—a tramp, a drunk, a Jew, etc.—the male-female team was pitted against male singles and two-acts. In addition, doing these types hampered true male-female teamwork; tramps, Negroes, and immigrants were played as grotesques, and grotesquerie was an unwomanly quality by middle-class Victorian standards. If a male-female team decided to do one of these types, it was invariably because the male partner already had experience at it, with the result that the man carried the act. Besides, a grotesque needed a foil to work best theatrically, and since a pretty woman was a natural straight, women often were just appendages to such acts.

Theatrically, then, playing a comic wife or girlfriend offered a comic actress the widest range for her abilities. Professional sexism might have been at work here; perhaps some male partners could more easily share the comedy limelight with an actress when it necessitated her becoming a caricature of her sex. Still, a male-female theatrical confrontation (such as a domestic quarrel or a flirtation) involved both partners to some extent, thus exploiting possibilities for male-female teamwork. Since this was the one appeal no other type of two-act could offer, it was the most rewarding and obvious one for male-female teams; more and more mixed acts turned to entertainment relying on sex-role interaction. Between the 1882-83 and 1887-88 seasons sixteen of 190 male-female teams who appeared in New York did routines featuring a male-female confrontation (romance or quarreling). In the ten seasons between 1895-96 and 1904-05 at least 110 of the approximately 550 teams appearing in New York City performed such comedy.[148]

But whereas flirtation sketches depicting the prettier aspects of male-female relations had been popular in the eighties, spontaneous "cooing" between stage couples had practically disappeared by the late nineties. Couples still ended up in each other's arms by the time the curtain fell, but their stage relations were rarely problem-free. Even courtship sketches were concerned not so much with wooing as with obstacles to the pairing — the difficulty of meeting in the modern world, or else social or parental disapproval.

Introductions and courtships were problematical in an urban society in which family and religious structures had weakened, but new mores had not yet clarified. Sketches like Stanton and Willard's "A Wife by Advertisement," Burkhardt and Flood's "Dropping a Hint," the Bartons' "Twentieth Century Flirtation," and others, mirrored modern answers to a new dilemma. Hallen and Fuller's "A Morning Plunge" showed how the problem of propriety could be circumvented: a young girl who needs a chaperon to go bathing utilizes a rubber dummy as a father figure; she confides her love for a certain young man to the dummy, only to learn the young man has secretly switched places with the dummy, and the curtain falls with the couple entwined.[149] Social etiquette also figured in "A Proper Impropriety," Frederick Bryton and Grace Filkins' 1897 act. Bryton played a Californian on a visit to New York City who sees a widow on the street and falls in love with her. He calls ostensibly to return eye-glasses she had dropped, then reveals the real reason of the visit. The body of the sketch was a discussion of proper and improper etiquette, ending with the couple's decision that they should go to California, where they can be properly introduced by mutual friends. He is leaving, when suddenly she boldly invites him to dinner; "he stays, and the curtain falls with the couple standing very close together, and apparently about to embrace."[150] Traditional courtship and marriage customs were avoided altogether in Linton and Lawrence's "An Auto Elopement" and in Forbes and Bowman's "A Gasoline Honeymoon"—a very modern solution.[151]

The sudden flouting of social rules always turned out for the best in vaudeville. In a number of sketches a young couple have been betrothed sight unseen by their parents, and the boy or girl is resentful and refuses to comply; one girl runs off with a dramatic company. Invariably the betrothed couple meet accidentally and, unaware of each other's identity, fall in love—against parental wishes, they believe—only to learn that they are in love with the very person intended for them.[152] The best-known sketch of this type was "All the World Loves a Lover," performed by popular team Rice and Cohen throughout the first decade of the 1900s. The scene is Archie Forrester's bachelor apartment, where a luncheon is spread for Dorothy Stevens, his wife-to-be whom he has never met, because their fathers arranged the match. She calls to say that she is delayed and cannot join him; he calls a close girlfriend, who also cannot come, but says she will send over her friend, a chorus girl Archie has never met. In blows Dorothy after all, and she is naturally mistaken for the chorus girl. She grasps the situation and plays along, even pretending to get drunk, all the while sizing him up. He likes her and vows he wishes she were Dorothy. A timely telephone call reveals she is not the chorus girl, Dorothy gives her real identity, and "all ends joyously."[153]

Such routines probably reflected the real-life anxieties of both parents and youths about modern courtship. Although nineteenth-century mate-selection had not been rigidly "parent-run," parents exerted significant influence on mate-selection and parents' approval was considered necessary. But urbanization meant that parents had less supervision over their children than in rural society, where youths worked alongside their parents. Also, the prolongation of education and the creation of child-labor laws contributed to a consciousness of a new stage in life, adolescence, and to the growth of a new autonomy for young people.[154] Although modern sociologists are not sure when "dating" first emerged, it had certainly appeared by the 1920s, and was developing in previous decades. Whereas in the nineteenth century "keeping company" had been done by couples acknowledged to be destined for marriage, sometime in the early 1900s dating came to assume the function not only of mate-selection, but of pure recreation, not necessarily leading to marriage. The new trend was a threatening one; as early as 1904, popular speakers and publications were bemoaning the inability of parents to influence their children in the delicate areas of propriety and morals.[155]

With the force of parental guidance declining, with the implications of keeping company less well-defined, and given in addition the new ethnic and religious diversity of America, many a young person or parent must have wondered how he or his child would ever find the mate Heaven had made for him. For these confused people, the courtship sketches of the day must have had a wish-fulfilling appeal; in all the sketches, despite society, parents, or even lovers themselves having made it the more difficult, the boy gets the girl, and invariably "in the midst of a fast descending curtain the couple are seen entwined after a thirty minutes acquaintance"—a soothing picture given the unsettling new trends.[156] Sketches depicting novel courtship patterns—flirting, courtship over the tennis net, automobile eloping, defiance of betrothal—also had the effect of teaching audiences about the new facts of life.

But after a stage couple were paired, true love hardly ever ran smooth. Married quarrels were already on the increase in the eighties, and between the mid-nineties and the teens, sketch after sketch featured squabbling mates. Among others there were Dean and Jose in "a sketch showing the infelicities of married life"; "Taming a Husband," in which Kent and Proctor were judged "excellent" as a quarreling husband and wife; Gardner and Gilmore, in "A Lover's Quarrel"; Mr. and Mrs. John T. Chick in "Matrimonial Mishaps"; Wordette and Kussell in "A Honeymoon in the Catskills," reviewed as one of those honeymoon quarrels sure to please the average audience; Johnson and Darling in "A Matrimonial Warfare"; and Dupree and Sherry in a married argument, one which "ends happily as they always do."[157]

But not always. In "Who's Safe," done by a team and an assistant in 1898, a lawyer with a jealous wife and a pretty typist has a red light which glows when the wife enters his office—whereupon the typist hides in his safe. But the clever wife enters disguised as an Irish washerwoman, observes her husband's philandering, and in the final scene the "triumphant wife confronts the guilty husband with a gleam in her eye which means an immediate divorce and large alimony." Such sketches were becoming more common.[158]

The marked increase in vaudeville routines about not-so-blissful marital affairs came at a time of growing middle-class concern about evolution in the family structure, or "the breakdown of the family," as it was put in the early twentieth century. The rate of divorce *was* rising. From seven thousand divorces in 1860, the number of divorces had risen to almost ninety thousand in 1910. The rate of increasing divorce was greater than the rate of increase in population. The United States had the second highest divorce rate in the world. The need for alarm was made official in 1905 when President Roosevelt gave special attention to divorce in his annual message to Congress, claiming it was "one of the greatest sociological phenomena of our time, it is a social question of the first importance, of far greater importance than any merely political or economic question can be."[159]

The reasons were as complex as modern society, with urbanization the most obvious way to explain it. With urbanization, the conservative influence of the rural community's tight-knit circle of friends and kin was replaced by the fast pace, anonymity, distractions and temptations of the city. Urbanization took men away from jobs that, in the rural nineteenth century, had been in the home or close by; the continual expansion of the city gave rise to streetcar suburbs, making the distance and commuting time between men and their families still greater; the increase in jobs for women made wives less dependent on their husbands than ever before.[160]

These disruptive trends were occurring simultaneously with the development of a new view of the family. As the urban home served less and less as the site of economic, educational, and religious activity, marital and parental love became its important surviving function; the harshness and competition of the industrial world also buttressed the need to view marriage and family as a source of emotional support and pleasurable companionship, and "home" was idealized as a retreat from the urban wilderness. In addition, at the turn of the century, the Victorian ideal of prudery was tarnishing; there was a growing acknowledgement of female sexuality and of nonprocreative marital sex. Paradoxically, the new importance of love, affection and compatibility in marriage was accompanied by a rising divorce rate. The new middle-class ideal created marital expectations which some couples found difficult to fulfill; and "the divorce rate was probably only the tip of the iceberg of discontent."[161] Likewise, the increasing number of vaudeville sketches about marital quarrels, infidelity, and divorce were probably indicative of submerged concerns—although audiences almost surely saw no relation between their laughter and anxiety about the crisis of the family.

Whereas the "crisis" is easier to analyze in retrospect, the observations of the day were far from objective, ranging from petty to apocalyptic. On the one hand, educated opinion gave men their share of the blame. Turn-of-the-century journalists, ministers, and female reformers censured men for living for business and money-making, and having no time or emotion left for their families. The loudest accusation was that all too often husband and father was coming home drunk, penniless, and sometimes even diseased. In reality, the actual culprits were a minority, but the anger and zeal of reformers was aroused against universal masculine vice. There was a "purity movement" afoot, seeking such diversified reforms as the eradication of liquor, pornography, prostitution, venereal disease, and Mormon polygamy. The temperance crusade was the most consolidated, with the Women's Christian Temperance Union its most militant champion, with "their object of attack...always a man."[162]

Certainly beleaguered stage wives were equally untiring in their efforts to cure their intemperate spouses. A favorite ploy was for a woman to pretend to be inebriated herself, thus shocking the man into reforming, as is successfully accomplished in the Royles' "The Highball Family" and Filson and Errol's "A Daughter of Bacchus." In Ross and Fenton's "Just Like a Woman," the woman's tears and reproaches over her husband's intemperance end with her deciding to go home to mother, whereupon the husband sees his mistake and asks her forgiveness.[163]

Another reason for female consternation onstage was hubby home late and with no excuse, or even more blatant evidence of masculine philandering. In a popular sketch called "Even Stephen," performed by Isabelle Urquhart and John Burke, the husband wants to attend a French ball without his wife, and disguises himself in a fake beard and wig. The wife sees through his disguise, and pretends he is her lover, kissing him and roasting her husband. The jealous husband grows so agitated that she gives him some medicine, and then pretends she gave him cyanide of mercury by mistake. He is terrified, wants a doctor, and frantically tears off his wig, until finally the gloating wife explains.[164]

But would-be male infidelities were treated lightly by vaudevillians, and though in some sketches the husband gets his just desserts, more often than not the jealous wife is mistaken in her suspicions, and turns out to be the silly one.[165] Even when the issue was the undeniable one of intemperance, the stage husband was most often the triumphant one. In Sibyl Johnstone and Edward Eagleston's "A Woman's Way," for instance, the husband arrives from the club "under the weather" and the wife tells him what she thinks of him. He says nothing while her diatribe goes on and on; in the end, however, he simply produces jewelry, and "the sketch ends in the usual kiss-and-make-up fashion." The wife in Gardner and Maddern's sketch, "Jimmy's Marie," has a husband who has developed the club habit, and she decides to teach him a lesson. She pours two whiskeys, and proceeds to become drunk, talking glibly of pugilism and other male sports; her glass held only tea, of course, and it is all a sham. While she is out of the room the husband finds a letter explaining the trick and he decides to turn the tables. When she returns, dressed in a suit as a young man, he pretends to go on a wild jag, then frightens her still more by producing a rat in a trap and threatening to release it. He makes her cry for mercy—

"The fact that she still has the trousers on does not lessen her fear in the least," gloated one reviewer—and forces her to put her dress back on.[166]

In the hands of the male-female team, the age-old comedy of the drunk was another occasion for a contest of wits, with the reformer always the wife, the intemperate one always the husband. The numerousness of such sketches suggests the topicality of the issue had not gone unnoticed, but in vaudeville it was amusing when the women's efforts floundered. Whereas the "blue-blooded middle-class" reformers and W.C.T.U. members would have choked on the sexist symbolism in the Gardner and Maddern sketch, "the piece made a big hit with the Pastor patrons."[167] The temperance movement did have class connotations, for it was directed primarily against the urban immigrant, who brought a fondness for beer and liquor to America. Whereas a lower-middle-class Irish matron might vent her lungs on her drunken spouse, it is likely she did not feel that he was morally impure and contributing to the downfall of the social order. Indeed, during Milton Noble's "realistic and amusing" jag in "Why Walker Reformed," the "husbands and wives in the audience nudge each other frequently during its presentation and then laugh till the tears come."[168]

On the other hand, the vaudeville sketches and educated opinion were in perfect agreement where aberrant female behavior was concerned. Offstage, the "New Woman" was a universal scapegoat. Massive dosages of alarmist newspaper and magazine articles told the common man that if the New Woman's goals were achieved—the vote, higher education, careers—the family would crumble. If wives entered the job market, naturally the home would suffer from the neglect of the sex entrusted with homemaking; the employed woman was told she "commits a biologic crime against herself and against the community." The desire of some women for a higher education also meant the end of the family, as the low rates of marriage and fertility among college alumnae clearly proved to anyone. "The first danger to woman is over brainwork," explained renowned psychologist G. Stanley Hall; "It affects that part of her organism which is sacred to heredity." As for "those damned suffragists," at the turn of the century they were beyond the understanding of normal people; they were rumored to favor replacing the American family with "free love," state phalansteries for children, and even polyandry.[169]

Whether or not vaudeville audiences thought seriously on the New Woman's destructive effect on society, they certainly enjoyed laughter at her expense. In the fall of 1895, for example, monologuist John Byrne talked humorously to the audience on the New Woman; that same season male team LeClaire and Leslie had a new sketch burlesquing the New Woman's mania for bloomers and bikes. But the subject was especially well-suited to male-female teams. In the fall of 1895 Ryman and Berger debuted a new sketch, "The New Woman and the Old Man," which "showed in an amusing way the two sides of the new woman question." Apparently neither sex sided with the minx; according to the *Mirror* reviewer, "Of course the man came out victorious in the end, and the men and women in the audience joined in the applause with equal heartiness."[170] Likewise, Filson and Errol, in their well-known comedy sketch "Women vs. Men," "brought many laughs with their references to the New Woman"; on one occasion their sketch was said to have brought a good many laughs from the married people in the audience in particular. And by the turn of the century, Earle Remington had created her new role of a New Woman tramp, probably a profession thought to be well-deserved by the New Woman.[171]

Of course, such routines did not actually explore the two sides of the New Woman question. The interpretation of the New Woman question offered by Irish bartender "Dooley," spokesman for the middle class created by newspaper humorist F. P. Dunne, is probably similar to the vaudeville treatment of the New Woman, and demonstrates the comic potential of simplified, distorted versions of the issue.[172] Vaudevillians were interested in the New Woman because she provided good safe comic material — disproportionately conspicuous, but represented by a minority of women: the genuine New Woman was found in the colleges and in the professions rather than the vaudeville house. Feminists themselves acknowledged that the ordinary woman was either hostile or indifferent to the New Woman's credo; Susan B. Anthony admitted in 1902 that women did not want the vote and complained that "they are more conservative even than men."[173]

None of the male-female routines in the nineties and early 1900s lampoon the suffragist; the suffrage movement was still not taken seriously.[174] But although there were few legal gains for women, the era was a time of large personal gains for women. The nineties saw an impressive growth in the number of women's organizations.[175] There were thousands of clubs devoted to such genteel pursuits as the reading of Shakespeare and Browning, and by the early 1900s a majority of women's clubs had turned from reading and chatting to implementing needed reforms in the community: cleaner, better ventilated schoolhouses; sanitary drinking fountains; free public libraries; parks, playgrounds, vacation schools, and so on.[176] Also, although it may not have seemed a personal gain to most, during these two decades more and more women found themselves in the job market. Another nationwide depression in 1893 meant that many wives had to work, while the cost of living continued to rise. From one-seventh in 1880, by 1900 one-fifth of the labor force were women.[177]

The "Woman Question" was beginning to have relevance for almost everyone; the reforming woman and the working woman had become familiar butts in male-female vaudeville acts. The woman who tried to cure her souse husband was only one type of the reforming woman; there was a whole gallery of these new types onstage who presumed to think they could run the world more effectively than their betters. One of the more ambitious female reformers, in a sketch called "Dr. Deborah's Elixir" by Minnie Dupree and Theodore Brown, is working on an elixir to change bad men into good ones. She has a boyfriend, whom she is too busy to encourage, but he persuades her to agree that if she gets a chance to try her elixir on a subject and it fails, she will marry him. He re-enters, disguised as a tramp, and pretends to let her test it on him. Suddenly the remaining elixir explodes; she is terrified, fearing the effects of the potion consumed, and he "piles on the agony until she is on the verge of collapse." But finally, he explains all; "she embraces him and promises to give up meddling in chemistry and devote herself to the study of cook books, and while the piano plays the wedding march the curtain falls." Apparently the reviewer thought "Dr. Deborah" was an accurate picture of her offstage sisters, for he believed that no one could excel Miss Dupree in portraying "the genuine American girl."[178]

Likewise, the *Mirror* concluded that Stanton and Modena's sketch, "For Reform," "teaches a good lesson to women who neglect their homes and devote their time to 'reforming' the rest of the world." The sketch depicted the domestic difficulties caused by a wife's attendance at the "Women's Reform League"; "by adopting rigorous methods the husband convinces his better half of the error of her ways, and she promises to give up her reform ideas and attend to her duties at home." The audience expressed its approval by loud laughter, claimed the *Mirror*;[179] Stanton and Modena were still doing the sketch as late as 1906. "For a long time Mr. Stanton has had a new sketch ready to produce," noted the *Toledo Blade*, "having tired somewhat of For Reform, but managers absolutely refuse to book him in anything else, asserting that its popularity and drawing powers with the vaudeville public are still increasing rather than diminishing—the highest sort of compliment indeed."[180] Audiences loved seeing a meddlesome woman thwarted.[181]

Working women were also fit subjects for farce, especially professional women. The kind of treatment accorded a professional woman at the hands of a vaudeville team is well illustrated by Mansfield and Wilbur's sketch, "A Bird and a Bottle," extremely popular in the early 1900s. Mr. Wilbur played a young lawyer whose cousin, a football player, is ill (as a result of an alcoholic celebration of a football victory); the lawyer sends for the nearest doctor, and is horrified when a woman doctor arrives. To keep this creature from attending his cousin, he pretends to be the patient himself, and is compelled to swallow noxious medicine. To get rid of her, he pretends the medicine has had a violent effect on him, and acts so crazed that the "fair medico" beats a hasty exit. The *Mirror* thought Miss Mansfield was admirable in this "new character to the vaudeville stage, that of a woman doctor."[182] But the humor underlined the idea that a woman was not fit for doctoring, and could not withstand violent reactions from a patient.

The upshot was that women in the real world, by working and reforming and thinking, were acting in ways inappropriate for their sex; this very incongruity was now the source of the comedy in most male-female vaudeville routines. However consciously, middle-class people were aware of—if not disturbed by—the fair sex's new ways. The courtship and marriage act addressing the question of sex role was not only a more popular choice for male-female teams than the old dialect humor, it also outnumbered the newer kinds of male-female acts. Comedy based on their sexes enabled male-female teams to objectify and explain a new social phenomenon in American life, one as important as immigration or urbanization: the changing role of woman, and by implication, man.

Thus, like other new kinds of humor performed by male-female teams at the turn of the century, the "drama of the sexes" betrayed audience anxiety about a world that was rapidly transforming in response to the pervasive forces of industrialization and urbanization, a world that seemed indeed to have changed overnight. And like the rural act or the juvenile act, the domestic sketch offered assurance that the values of the past still reigned, and with its forced happy ending offered escape from acknowledgement of changing mores. The domestic sketch celebrated the values of the rural past and dramatized the widespread apprehension that these values were now in flux, yet at the same time also taught ordinary people about new phenomena such as the New Woman.

The male-female domestic sketch also had the universality required for what was becoming a national entertainment. The sketch about male-female relations—like other new themes—was a way to appeal safely to everyone; everyone in the audience except the children had had experiences that enabled them to appreciate the drama of the war between the sexes. But the domestic sketch particularly reflected the influence of the most important new audience in vaudeville, middle-class women, whose lives were male- and home-centered. Indeed, no act was a better indicator of the new nature of variety: its thoroughgoing "domestication" as "vaudeville" by the turn of the century.

The courtship and marriage act was an important antidote to the bawdiness, the masculinity, and the rambunctious racial comedy of the variety house. The romantic theme had been growing in importance since variety days, but its features were crystallized by the influx of legitimate performers around 1896 and the years following. The large majority of the legits were men and women teamed for the occasion, and vaudeville male-female teams emulated them. The result was that the playlet form was most often performed by male-female teams, who were thus largely responsible for injecting the values of the legitimate stage and its middle-class audience into vaudeville.

Now, teams were praised for acting "in a quiet, effective way that is very refreshing," for their "delightful skill, refinement, and intelligence." Humor was not so often rowdy now, but was ideally a blend of comedy and sentiment; one male-female sketch was "full of pathetic and humorous touches so well blended that one does not know whether to laugh or cry."[183] It was these values—sentimentality, plot, quiet acting, and what purported to be imitating of life (as it should be)—that widened the gulf between vaudeville and the variety theatres with their emphasis on vocalists, slapstick, and blackface burlesque.

Thus, the male-female team was an important instrument in the transformation of variety into a "polite" entertainment in accordance with the doctrines and values of the Protestant upper-middle class. The humor in the new male-female acts—with their kindly fun-poking and their reassuring endings—was the kind best tolerated by the upper-middle-class establishment. It was only with the triumph of the genteel sort of playlet that the dramatic press and the spokesmen for the upper-middle class, such as educators, ministers, and magazine editors, began to extend formal recognition to vaudeville.

The embracing of these values by vaudeville also testifies to the upwardly-mobile nature of its audience. Still not secure enough in their new status to formulate their own values, the newest members of the middle class emulated the values of those above them to prove their worth to themselves and others. The new kind of vaudeville humor thus enabled its lower-middle-class audience to make a snobbish identification with their "betters." Of course, in the sketches it was always the woman who aped the upper classes and who was sensitive to matters of status. It was the Mag Haggertys who were the would-be snobs, and the Mikes who had their feet on the ground. Whether or not this reflected a truth in real life (it seems more likely men were letting women express their own secret wishes) the class-consciousness of the humor apparently appealed to women, who were now so influential in shaping vaudeville's offerings.

The women coming to vaudeville seem to have been particularly fond of the male-female playlet. The husband-wife complications in one sketch kept the audience laughing, "especially the feminine portion"; it was probably because of its subject matter that "Our Honeymoon" was considered "the right sort of material for vaudeville."[184] An important appeal in these sketches were apparently the actresses, for new attention was paid them in reviews, presumably for the benefit of a new kind of admirer. Inez MacCauley, for example, was said to be a "very charming actress. She is pretty, refined, has good taste in dress, and plays with a subdued breeziness that is delightful." Miss McIntyre was "perhaps, the prettiest girl in vaudeville, a dainty, winsome actress."[185]

In effect, the presence of the female audience was creating new stars, stage women who provided models of glamour and refinement for the women in the audience. When Mrs. Blondell wore her hair in a new way, the reviewer noted that it would probably become a fad with the women. Even male performers were being judged by traditionally "female" criteria; one male partner was praised for having "an engaging presence"—a standard which would never have been applied to an early variety actor.[186]

In more ways than one, American society had fallen under a new influence. Family life had acquired the associations of a romantic refuge; religious leaders had adopted a new, more intuitive, "heartfelt" approach; education, nursing, and librarianship had become altruistic, almost maternal professions.[187] Likewise, vaudeville was embracing qualities that had traditionally been defined as feminine: quietness, sentiment, morality, prettiness, kindness, and gentility. Just as other aspects of the life of the day were being influenced by female values, so the variety house might be said to have been "feminized." Male-female teams, with their domestic comedies, their charming heroines, their sentimental and genteel humor were therefore an important ingredient in the new flavor of the typical vaudeville bill.

5
Male-Female Teams on the Big Time, 1905–1912

It is unlikely its spokesmen would have ever admitted that vaudeville had been "feminized," but shortly after the turn of the century, they were indeed claiming that vaudeville had changed, had "progressed," as it were. For example, an act called the Military Octette, which appeared at Hammerstein's Victoria in 1905, was said to set a new precedent. It featured eight women and eight men, and several scene and costume changes; the *New York Dramatic Mirror* predicted the act would establish new criteria for success in vaudeville:

> If any proof were needed that vaudeville has progressed, it was given here last week, when the Military Octette and the Girl with the Baton, one of the most elaborate acts so far shown in vaudeville, was given here for the first time in this city. A few years ago managers would have laughed at the idea of putting on so large a turn, but times have changed, and henceforth the honors and the money will go to the men who can arrange and produce acts of this kind.[1]

Three years later the *New York Star* would proudly announce a new column, one devoted only to "really artistic vaudeville acts—those acts that have something out of the ordinary to recommend them in the matter of artistry. This difference from other acts may be in superb lighting effects, in beautiful scenery, in handsome costumes, in dramatic depth or high comedy methods."[2] The men who were doing the producing and the money-making took great pleasure in pointing out their successes to the vaudeville public. In 1908 Jesse Lasky professed to be "amazed" at the progress made by the "Big" act and explained that a few years before, an act with six people had been big, but now acts with twenty-five people, a business manager, musical director, wardrobe mistress, stage manager, carpenter, etc. were the norm. "I think in the vaudeville of the future that the productions will play a most important part," predicted Lasky with obvious satisfaction. Martin Beck happily declared that vaudeville was just beginning to realize its "richest, most ambitious, and most artistic possibilities."[3]

The vaudeville business could congratulate itself without risk of offending its constituency, for the new century's vaudeville audience was just as pleased with itself. The middle class was no longer the insecure group of the nineties; it too had "progressed." The upwardly-mobile wage earners of the nineties, although without a well-defined identity and status of their own, had known they did not fit in with either the lowly laborers, recent immigrants, unemployed, and other ne'er-do-wells crowded into the Lower East Side tenements, or with the educated, well-to-do people who constituted Victorian society. Anxious to establish their respectability, the emerging middle class had embraced the genteel values of their "betters"; they were pathetically eager to look and act successful, to be known as upright citizens.

But by the twentieth century, the rampant urbanization and industrialization that was changing the face of America, a combustion fed by thousands upon thousands of rural migrants and European immigrants, had sparked a population explosion in the urban middle class; now their massive numbers made them the most visible force in society, and gave an undeniable weight to their own impulses and beliefs. Magazines like *Ladies' Home Journal* and *Saturday Evening Post* were learning the rewards of mass advertising, and these organs of urbanism and democracy were introducing millions of Americans coast-to-coast to middle-class ways of living, thinking, and consuming.[4] Before the first decade of the twentieth century had ended, the masses had a new awareness of their likeness, and seemingly a new feeling of confidence. It had become clear that it was "respectable" to be one of the middling folks, for almost everyone else was, and the position was well-established as "solid."

As a result, ordinary people no longer had to ape the values of a higher class to attain a sense of worth in their own eyes. It was no longer a necessity to affect Victorian propriety and morality for fear of seeming undesirable. From sheer force of numbers the middle class now represented a mass market of increasing importance, and its buying power meant its inherent desires would be catered to. Thus, there was a steady democratization—or vulgarization—of culture. Now manufacturers, retailers, entertainers, and journalists, themselves middle class, were by a gradual process articulating the true values—not the assumed ones—of the mass audience.

Even before the teens, it was becoming apparent that the true middle-class values were not the thrift, soberness, and gentlemanliness of the old Protestant agrarian class, but were instead the very urbanism and industrialism that produced the new group: the speed, utilitarianism, sensationalism, and materialism of city and machine. The urban masses were those people and their children who came from the American farm or European village; they survived and remained in the city not because of the simple goodness of the yeoman, but because of their ability to adapt to new conditions, to cast off any dress or language, any beliefs or even people who impeded their success. Those with the instinct for survival in the city had the ability to talk fast and think fast, to get there first, to look after themselves often to the detriment of someone else. Twentieth-century urbanites were "street-wise," or "smart." In the city, money and smartness were the badge of status, not birth, and this awareness heightened the incentive to make money and spend money—rather than cultivating the nineteenth-century virtues of thrift and prudence.[5]

As the metropolis grew and attracted tens of thousands more, it bred, by its very nature, a new kind of national character. After decades of exposure to the complexities of the city, urbanites forgot old loyalties in the process of experiencing the problems and demands of urban life shared by all. The need to conserve energy and privacy when jostling daily with crowds of strangers develops habits of indifference, reserve, even hostility. The competitiveness inherent in city living—at work, on streetcars, in ticket lines—encourages aggressiveness and tenseness. Since one is unknown to others and judged by first impressions, fashion and other forms of conspicuous consumption, along with knowledge of slang and fads, are what establish identity. The plethora of goods on view also accentuates the value of materialism; the urban person is a sophisticated consumer, who knows what and how to consume. And life alongside the machine and skyscraper, divorced from nature, enforces a view of the world as a product of man, not God, further creating a pragmatic, coldly objective, despiritualized view of life.[6] It was a mass urban audience of just this temperament that patronized early twentieth-century movies, sporting events, amusement parks, and of course, vaudeville.

After 1905, newspaper descriptions evoke a picture of a more demanding, more sophisticated vaudeville audience. Whereas vaudeville houses in small towns and certain areas of cities still had simple family audiences, less knowledgable of fads and slang, the audiences in major big-city houses were getting "smarter." The Forty-second Street and Broadway audiences were described as "sophisticated and wise to a degree," and they liked "spice" and "well-seasoned" fare. Big-city audiences were well-educated in vaudeville conventions. It was suggested that only Lambs Club members were wiser to "refinements of stage slang" than Hammerstein's audience.[7]

As the entire middle class expanded, its upper portion also increased, and the upper-middle-class segment of the vaudeville audience appears to have grown. There were more acts depicting upper-middle-class characters—stockbrokers, college students, lawyers, and doctors[8]—and there were newspaper references to a classier segment in the audience. A 1912 Riverside Theatre audience was thought to look "like class"; the Colonial Theatre audience was the "come-in-automobile" kind; a "smart" audience often arrived in time to see a particular favorite, then left immediately after the act.[9]

As the urban middle class established its own identity and values, vaudeville and the male-female act changed accordingly. Vaudeville was both teacher and quick pupil of the mass audience, and a whole new set of criteria for judging acts was evolving. Perhaps an audience in a small town with only one vaudeville theatre appreciated whatever entertainment came their way, but urban audiences could respond to a comedy routine as fast as a performer could put it over. The vocabulary of reviews of male-female acts had become saturated with adjectives like "droll," "bright," "lively," "slick," and "snappy."[10] The successful male-female teams had "all sorts of 'go' and ginger."[11]

This new emphasis on energy was inherent in a metropolis where life had become dominated by the clock. In contrast to the country, whose slower tempo made precision unimportant, all organized actions in the city were geared to time: the five-day week, the eight-hour day, the 4:00 train, "rush hour." With its ever-agitated crowds and the constant whir of carriages and streetcars, the city was a place of perpetual movement, and its momentum demanded youthful energy and drive. The entertainment world kept up with the city's new pace. The manager of one mass amusement, Luna Park, concluded that

> speed is almost as important a factor in amusing the millions as is the carnival spirit, decency, or a correct recollection of school days. Speed has become an inborn American trait. We as a nation are always moving, we are always in a hurry, we are never without momentum....the thousand and one varieties of roller-coasters are popular for the same reason that we like the fastest trains, the speediest horses, the highest powered motor-cars, and the swiftest sprinters.... To keep up the carnival spirit everybody and everything must be on the "go."[12]

Indeed, male-female teams were criticized for not working fast enough, or else for letting the strain of the speed show;[13] Ollie Young and April, a juggling act, were told by a reviewer that their act should be "quickened up," with precious seconds between tricks eliminated.[14] Players were almost scorned if not familiar enough with each other to ad-lib.[15] Speed was considered an essential virtue for the entire bill, in fact: a Colonial Theatre bill was praised by critics as the classiest seen there in some time, because it started with "the lever in the high speed notch" and "remains there until the very end." Audiences could be restless if the pace of the show stalled; a certain bill at the Orpheum didn't go over, because "there were moments of delay between the acts, attracting to the attention of the audience a bit too much of the mechanics of conducting a vaudeville entertainment." The reviewers for *Variety* were admiring when a house offered "good clean fast vaudeville" or when a bill maintained an "astonishing pace."[16]

The trade paper *Variety* was an important influence on developing the new century's vaudeville standards. Founder Sime Silverman and associate Epes W. Sargent were critics whose honest and caustic reviewing styles had hitherto kept both out of work, and from the first edition of 16 December 1905, *Variety* was uncompromising in its objective assessments of acts—unlike other theatrical newspapers, which awarded effusive praise to any that advertised with them. Under the epithets of "Sime" and "Chicot," Silverman and Sargent and their colleagues were dangerous foes for the lazy standards and bathos which had often characterized turn-of-the-century vaudeville.[17] They told it as they saw it, and of course male-female teams got their share of advice. The woman in Barry and Halvers was told her dress needed to be cleaned, another female partner that she should examine her stockings before going onstage. Will you please cut out that cheap and silly street car encore? a certain team was asked, and the Barringtons were bluntly told that their dialogue was "excruciating."[18]

Variety was an important arbiter of vaudeville taste, but it was also a weathervane of forces already at work in vaudeville. Although *Variety* did help create a new vaudeville jargon, its reviewers echoed the new, more "hip" argot already being spoken in Broadway lobbies and night clubs, on Tin Pan Alley and Forty-second Street. With its pithy, racy, idiomatic style, *Variety* embodied the atmosphere and standards evolving in vaudeville itself, and the very fact of a newspaper named *Variety* reflected the new importance and growing professionalism of the business.

One standard emphatically demanded by *Variety* reviewers, and presumably by the hip audience they spoke for, was novelty. With each passing year, it seemed, jokes were used up faster; improved transportation and communication made it possible for a West Coast audience to hear a New York comic's joke before he appeared there himself. Situation after situation in male-female acts was damned as old by *Variety*—dropping over chairs, the woman who's never seen a man, the device of putting a stove under a comedian's chair while he plays cards, the "tough dance", and the use of the same old restaurant opening for a juggling act.[19] Male-female team Walsh and Eddy were vilified for their opener:

> man: If you went in to buy your dog a muzzle and the man wouldn't put it on for you, what would you do?
> woman: I'd put it on myself.

"By the time this man and woman were forgiven for this one," sneered the *Variety* reviewer, "they pulled the one about the drunken king beating his three wives because a king full beats three queens anytime."[20]

The success of the bill at the Columbia Theatre on one evening in 1911 was simply the newness of the acts—any newness is an attraction, it's so novel, groused *Variety*. A sketch done by one male-female team was praised as different from the norm, and "for this reason alone will make good." Rock and Fulton's act was "delightful" because "every exit and every step in the act is different from the usual order of things, and its result was a hit of the largest possible proportions."[21]

Not surprisingly, the popular character types of turn-of-century male-female acts were now outmoded, because they were no longer novel, but also because their sentimentality was unsuited to an assured middle class audience in the process of rejecting the pseudo-morality and propriety it had previously affected. Thus, after 1905, lachrymose depictions of Bowery waifs declined in popularity. In 1906 *Variety* thought the McAvoys' "A Waif's Christmas Eve" "at times...approaches dangerously bathos"; that same year Williams and Tucker debuted a new sketch, "Skinny's Return," but the dialogue was now "mostly for laughs." In 1909, when Williams and Tucker did "Driftwood" in New York City for the umpteenth time, they appeared "to diminished advantage." They worked up to a capital bit of pathos at the end, it was admitted, but the preceding parts were "a bit tiresome."[22]

Similarly, by mid-decade most rural acts appearing in New York City were resorting to new appeals to put their acts over. In Mr. and Mrs. Jack McGreevy's act, for example, he played rube, and she was in short dress "a la 'Sis Hopkins.'" They did an eccentric dance, then did talk, with "some rather 'blue'"; next he fiddled country-style while she "vamps" on the "tube." A blue-talking rube and a vamping Sis Hopkins were a far cry from Cressy's rural "sermon." Tyson and Brown decorated their rural act with "very pretentious" scenery and novel special effects—four live pigs, two chickens, a simulated rainstorm, and an assistant who played a Dutch farmhand.[23]

But few rural acts were successful. "The sketch may find room on certain circuits," *Variety* said of Jones and Walton's act; Mr. and Mrs. Dick Tracey's "Courtship at Cowslip Farm" was described as "nothing exciting." The occasional exception proved the rule: Sam Kelley was a "mighty good" rube and "does not depend upon weekly funny papers for material," *Variety* noted approvingly, implying that there was a fund of material which was all too familar.[24] Just how familiar is revealed by a review of a rural sketch in Cressy style by Hennings and Middleton in 1911. Describing it as a "rehash of all the Cressy mush bucolic pieces," *Variety's* reviewer complained that "these rube sketches with a pathetic plaster are about due to run in new grooves now, for Mr. Cressy has succeeded in killing the old style on both sides of the ocean."²⁵

In fact, though Cressy and Dayne's big name kept them booked solid throughout the decade, and though they generally won kudos while on tour, in New York City they were reviewed dubiously. In 1907 the former hit "The Village Lawyer" was called "shop-worn," and the finale to a new sketch called "Wyoming Whoop" was thought absurdly pathetic." In 1910, when Davis and MacCauley debuted an act written for them by Cressy, it was called "not much of a sketch"; Cressy hasn't had a new idea since variety began, sniffed *Variety*, adding that vaudeville in the East had changed while Cressy had been in the West.²⁶

One popular answer from male-female teams to the demand for fresh material was the act that contained a combination of several of the old stock characters plus a new one or two. Leavitt and Dunsmore's act provided the audience with the comedy of an Italian, a policeman, a ranchman, and a veterinarian; Gardiner and Vincent's act featured a tramp, a moon queen, drunk business, romance, and the use of motion pictures. Keno and Morris seemed determined to entertain the audience in any way possible:

> They start with a "kid" song ending with a dance, which went well. Miss Morris' pleasing voice was then heard in a "coon" number of pretty melody called "You'll Come Back." Keno's individual work consisted of an acrobatic dance that was a revelation. He has a funny makeup and is a good comedian. The little talk was good. It is mostly "gags" concerning hotel life. The act closed with the two dancing together, giving snatches of the "Apache" and "Hypnotic" dances.²⁷

The hard-to-please urban audience seemed less interested in sitting through an entire sketch with plot and detailed character-drawing; the regular vaudeville patrons were so familiar with the conventions that they could assimilate a rapid-fire succession of five or six types in a single act.

But the slower pace of the old plot-oriented sketch was not its only problem; although the sentimental realism of the Bowery kid and hayseed had once been successful because it was modelled after the legitimate stage, now vaudeville audiences were less impressed with legitimate stage standards and material. Vaudeville bills still featured acts indebted to legitimate stage fare, and many new male-female sketches had more than just a touch of the serious, making them seem close in tone to a legitimate play.²⁸ The degree of the "dramatic" seen before was thought to be surpassed by the Nobles in spring, 1908, in a sketch called "The Thief in the Night," in which

> the intense grip that this little play takes upon an audience has rarely, if ever, been equalled in a vaudeville production...it held a packed theatre in breathless intensity for eighteen minutes, and at its finish the audience fairly rose at it.[29]

But then, eighteen minutes is not a long time by true legitimate theatre standards, and the Nobles' sketch received curtain call after curtain call because it ended happily despite its seriousness: "The silent, quick and unexpected 'happy ending' after the suspense comes as a complete surprise, and leaves the audience in the best of humor."[30]

For the most part the reaction of vaudeville audiences and reviewers to dramatic sketches was unenthusiastic or critical. A vaudeville version of "The Bells" done in 1908 was said to be anything but satisfactory; "It is not difficult to imagine what the effect of the gruesome death scene would be upon a matinee audience composed mostly of children," complained *Variety*. Lionel Barrymore and McKee and Doris Rankin did a dramatic sketch called "The White Slaver," in which an Italian discovers that a young girl forced into prostitution is actually his niece, and in retaliation stabs the slaver repeatedly to death. *Variety* acknowledged that the prostitution traffic was a necessary subject for muckraking magazines, but criticized it as out of place in vaudeville. As for a one-act version of *Candida* by Arnold Daly and company, it was deemed a complete failure because the audience was uninterested in—or ignorant of—*Candida,* Shaw, and also Mr. Daly.[31] Whereas audiences were praised for enduring "class" acts ten years earlier, now neither audience nor critics were willing to suffer being bored, depressed, or seriously engaged for the sake of culture. Vaudeville audiences no longer needed the pseudostatus previously thought to be conferred by legitimate-influenced stage fare.

The change in the relationship between the legitimate stage and the vaudeville theatre is well-illustrated by the changing fortunes of the male-female travesty team. Numerous male-female teams had made their living in the late nineties doing travesties of legitimate drama;[32] the biggest stars in this line were Charles Ross and Mabel Fenton. Favorites throughout the nineties with their travesties of *Fedora, Virginius,* and *The Heart of Maryland,* and members of the famed Weber and Fields company between 1897 and 1903, they continued to be seen in vaudeville with their *Cleopatra* travesty into the teens.[33] Also popular with the Roman theme were Jules and Ella Garrison, who between 1895 and 1905 had a sketch which included a travesty of Spartacus' speech to the gladiators as done by John McCullough.[34]

But as the demise of the famous Weber and Fields company demonstrated, travesties of legitimate plays were not popular in the twentieth-century. With the rise of popular amusements calculated to appeal specifically to the mass audience, the legitimate stage had become a highbrow affair; the popular nineteenth-century repertoire, which had been all things to all people, was dying, and with it the travesty art. Charles Ross complained that the travesty art was difficult in 1911, because "we have no players today sufficiently great with marked mannerisms to make them recognizable to the audience, and no great plays.... We have no more Fedoras, no more Virginius [sic], Cleopatras or Camilles."[35] Thus, Ross and Fenton supplemented their travesty work with a domestic sketch and musical comedy appearances.

The exception that proved the rule was Murphy and Nichols, the only popular travesty team after Ross and Fenton. Will Murphy and Blanche Nichols debuted in the 1901-02 season and by the 1905 season were described as "headliners"; throughout the decade, they played at least four weeks a year in Manhattan, and kept busy all over the country for the remainder of the season.[36] Their famous vehicle was a "screamingly funny" sketch called "From Zaza to Uncle Tom." They usually employed one unbilled female assistant, but also did the act alone.[37]

The act depicted a stranded *Zaza* company; once a stock company of sixteen performers, now hard times have reduced them to three. They decide to do a production of *Uncle Tom's Cabin,* to get some food and passage back to New York. The leading man and manager Howland Rant (Murphy) undertakes Uncle Tom and Marks and others, the leading lady (Miss Nichols) performs Simon Legree and Little Eva, and the soubrette plays Eliza and all other female characters—but the manager reassures them he can kill off most of the characters in the first act to make it easier for them. Naturally all sorts of catastrophes break up the play, such as Little Eva's miscue on ascending to heaven; the "ice" consists of rocking blocks of wood, and Eliza's perilous journey is interrupted by ridiculous flounderings. "No one can realize how funny a good old melodrama like 'Uncle Tom's Cabin' can be until it is cleverly burlesqued," wrote one reviewer.[38]

Uncle Tom's Cabin was perhaps the one play a mass audience could be counted on to know. However, the butt of the "funny things that happen" was more the impecunious stock company than the play itself; anyone who had ever seen a group of amateurs botch up a play could enjoy the sketch, even if he were not familiar with *Uncle Tom's Cabin.* In fact, in Murphy and Nichols's addition to their repertoire after 1909, "A School for Acting," no particular play was travestied, but simply the half-baked efforts of an amateur company.[39] Such a sketch was closer in spirit to the comedy sketches about rehearsals and theatre life than it was like the true travesties.

But the two-act sketch about "life in the theatre" had also changed.

Popular since variety days, it reached the height of success at the turn of the century, when vaudeville's preoccupation with "real" theatre was at its peak.[40] Unlike the travesty team, this type of male-female act remained popular throughout the decade, but there was a significant change in emphasis: from 1904 on, at least half of these sketches were specifically about vaudeville.[41] The implication is that vaudeville was less concerned now about its relation to the legitimate stage, more secure in its own status. The former preoccupation with legitimate standards lost its immediacy, now that vaudeville could successfully compete for its share of the respectable audience. The sketches also showed that audiences were knowledgeable about the vaudeville profession; they knew about such things as auditions, broken contracts, and the difficulties of making long jumps on the circuits. In the twentieth century, vaudeville was a socially acceptable, financially rewarding profession, with an awareness of its own importance shared by performers and audiences.

Besides, it was needless for vaudeville to envy the legitimate stage, when vaudeville's own "legitimacy" had been so dramatically demonstrated by its new appeal for some of the legitimate stage's biggest stars. Vaudeville captured Henry Miller and Lillian Russell in 1905, Arnold Daly in 1906, Lily Langtry and John Barrymore in 1907, Mrs. Patrick Campbell in 1910, Lionel Barrymore and Walter Hampden in 1911, and Beerbohm Tree in 1912.[42] It had become more than just a question of money; a vaudeville tour guaranteed such performers exposure to millions of new fans and enlarged their followings in a way that the legitimate theatre could now never do; the performer who caught the mass audience's fancy became a household word across America. Vaudeville no longer depended on the dictates of the monied, educated class to provide its heroes; performers like Eva Tanguay had huge followings that performers who catered to a more exclusive set could not match. Male-female teams could make a living just by imitating or impersonating vaudeville stars like Fred Stone, Bessie McCoy, Eva Tanguay, James Thornton, Eddie Foy, Johnny Ray, McIntyre and Heath, Victor Moore, and of course George M. Cohan.[43]

Greedy businessmen and willing performers gradually whetted the average vaudeville patron's taste for personalities, a taste catered to by the rise of the press-agent and his responsive tool, mass-circulation journalism. Mass-publication accounts of tidbits about stars—such as Lillian Russell's insistence on a red-velvet carpet from her dressing room to the stage—created interest in performers as personalities. By the end of the decade, performers were regularly featured in vaudeville who were not entertainers, but simply names precious to the mass audience; baseball personalities Rube Marquard and Mike Donlin, for example, appeared in sketches with female partners and made joking references to their baseball careers, yet displayed no real stage talent.[44]

Audiences' appetites for stars increased as, in response to soaring salaries, vaudeville prices rose. Audiences wanted to get their money's worth, and demanded the satisfaction of seeing a star on the stage for a good part of the bill. For instance, when Albert Chevalier appeared in New York in the 1904-05 season, he was forced to stay onstage for forty minutes each performance. It was becoming common for a house to fill up right before the headliner's act, then for almost the entire audience to leave en masse after the star's act—as it did when Harry Lauder appeared in New York City in 1908.[45]

The influx of legitimate performers, the impressive sums of money now lavished on acts, the emphasis on stars and the constant ballyhoo about their personal lives and the paraphernalia of stardom—all these signalled the increasing significance of glamour in vaudeville, a taste which, along with novelty and fast pacing, was becoming an important consideration in the creation and marketing of vaudeville entertainment as the new century approached the teens. If the characteristic of glamour has feminine connotations, then certainly vaudeville had been "feminized."

One noticeable influence of the new standard on male-female teams was the tendency to "go big." McMahon and Chapelle, who had successfully appeared in vaudeville since at least 1904 with a male-female blackface sketch, had added a chorus line of nine "Pullman Maids" to their act by 1907; they performed their old male-female routine between revue numbers by their extras.[46] In November 1911 Rock and Fulton announced they would be accompanied on their upcoming tour by "Their Own Hungarian Orchestra with Twenty People." Popular male-female act Clark and Bergman were backed up by fifteen chorus girls when they debuted their new act, "The Trained Nurses," in the 1912-13 season.[47]

But the most important ingredient of the new glamour was elaborate costume. The very first mentions in reviews of costume as a vaudeville attraction came in the mid-nineties, referring to female singles or team partners;[48] such references increased toward the end of the century.[49] Some male-female teams began wearing evening dress,[50] and by the next decade there were regular—almost mandatory—references in reviews and bills to the appeal of fancy costumes in male-female acts.[51] "You really ought to see the dress she wears in the French song," or, "girls, catch that gown," *Variety* would advise.[52] Enjoying the picture of the woman partner's glamorous costume was one of the reasons audiences enjoyed male-female teams.

That the growing emphasis on dress was not accidental, but was a calculated response to the taste of the female audience, was articulated by Sophie Tucker. In fall, 1906, eager to go into vaudeville, she went to Hammerstein's to learn about show business, to a matinee which was composed mostly of women, "all so smart looking." The women were little interested in an acrobatic troupe on the bill, but when a sketch featured a smartly dressed woman, "the women fell hard to her; they were all talking about her figure and her gown." Sophie decided then that "there's no two ways about it, you've got to dress smart. Then the women in the audience rave about you. If you ever get on the stage, think of your clothes, look smart. It helps put you over."[53]

Reporters confirmed what Sophie Tucker noticed. Miss Violette of Kelly and Violette wore three handsome dresses, noted *Variety*, "simply for variety and to draw the attention of the women present, which is undoubtedly done"; a Miss Walters' gown reportedly caused the women to buzz for several minutes. The middle-class woman who attended vaudeville obviously loved fancy clothes, especially now that modern technology had put fashion within the grasp of the ordinary person; Jane Addams reported that many working women spent most of their income on clothes.[54] For the urban white-collar population, not property, birth, or craft determined prestige, but minute gradations of consumption, especially dress. Both men and women sought the smartness of appearance that separated the cosmopolitan from the provincial or the immigrant. Vaudeville performers taught their fans the right look.

Once the precedent of an "appearance" had been set and audiences had responded enthusiastically, it was a necessary ingredient of a vaudeville act, and standards were continuously upped. Weekly *Variety* columnist Anna Marble observed in 1906 that costume in vaudeville had been revolutionized in the past year, with Valeska Suratt the smartest-gowned woman onstage.[55] Suratt, member of the male-female act Gould and Suratt, unabashedly took the credit for the new emphasis on high-quality, glamorous costuming. A former milliner's assistant, she claimed she was the first woman in vaudeville to use real velvets and silks on the stage, having reasoned that "the ladies present always had their eyes open for detail in dressing."[56] The *San Francisco Chronicle* called her stunning gowns "no small part of the act," and *Variety* ruminated on one occasion that "the building of those gowns is a constant mystery." In 1911 her wardrobe boasted an evening coat said to be worth $20,000.[57]

An act was severely criticized in reveiws if its costumes were not well-kept enough, or if it did not have enough costume changes. Conversely, correct costuming could go a long way toward assuring an act's success. Marion and Deane's act was much improved, noted a reporter in 1907, who thought this was attributable to the confidence their new costumes gave them.[58] When Mabel Hite made her much-publicized return to vaudeville in 1911, it was "heralded" by the large investment made in her wardrobe; one green beaded gown she wore was "a scorcher," and a "long pink affair draped in black" was worn winding around her body, looking as if she "needed a key to unlock it." One act on the "small time" in 1912 had ten costume changes in fifteen minutes; in the Dehavens' 1913 act, Mrs. Dehaven's costume changes got individual applause. Rock and Fulton even advertised their 1911 act as a "Sartorial" Revue.[59]

Like costuming, staging became an increasingly important appeal in male-female acts early in the 1900s. Scenery had been crude in the old-time variety houses,[60] but the value of elaborate scene effects was learned from the legitimate stage in the late nineties. When legitimate performers Bennett and Kent made their vaudeville debut in 1896, their act featured a special interior setting designed by Voeghtlin—"equal to those seen in the best legitimate houses." The short vaudeville versions of legitimate plays often used the original scenery; for example, when Melburn MacDowell and Pauline Willard did their condensed version of Sardou's *La Tosca* in 1904, they used the "rich stage settings and appointments" of the original Davenport production.[61]

Such productions provided a stimulus for growing emphasis on scenery; male-female teams competed with their visual impact. The Garrisons' act, billed as having "Special Scenery, Electrical Effects and Auxilary Corps," opened in the interior of a pyramid, then came a special drop showing fierce lions, and the third scene was the gardens of Cleopatra on the Nile. The *New York Dramatic Mirror* thought "the properties, accessories, and effects made the production one of the most complete and satisfying ever seen in vaudeville."[62] William Robyns's "Shore Folks," seen in New York City the next week after the Garrisons, had special scenery designed by Joseph Physioc, elaborate light effects, and accessories "worthy of highest praise"; "Mr. Robyns has spared no expense," the *Mirror* maintained, "and he deserves to be awarded with a full book of dates."[63]

By the end of the decade, with full scenery the norm, lavish outlays of money or unique mechanical effects were necessary to attract attention. Even teams with well-established reputations for their stage skills seemed to believe scenic display would enhance their acts. In the 1911–12 season, singing and dancing stars Rock and Fulton introduced their new routine in a French cabaret set with chandeliers and small tables, a small balcony with one table, and opposite it a large balcony containing a five-piece orchestra, plus a large staircase in the rear from which all entrances were made. The act employed altogether fifteen people, and cost $8000 to produce. The first view of the set alone won the audience, claimed *Variety*; it went beyond anything seen in vaudeville, and one thought came to mind first: "That will be the expense incurred."[64] For middle-class audiences, viewing these sumptuous scenes was a way to experience vicariously the splendor of upper-class life.

Motion picture techniques were especially popular with vaudeville audiences. Forbes and Bowman's act featured a song and a conversation between a couple in auto attire; at the end, the "stage is darkened, and the curtain rises over a special drop, the couple being seen in a lighted limousine car going at top speed in front of picture panoramic effect."[65] A team supposedly from Holland billed as "Klaus and Trina" opened their act with a film showing them in Holland in peasant attire, giving a street entertainment. At the end of the reel the pair rushed down the aisle in person and onto the stage and began their two-act. Mabel Hite's 1911 act—billed as the "classiest" ever seen at the Majestic Theatre in Chicago—featured, in addition to the elaborate costumes already mentioned, a slideshow showing her in different characters she had made famous and also shots of her husband-partner, baseball player Mike Donlin.[66] Donlin was still on the diamond when the 1911 vaudeville season opened, so for the time being he was replaced onstage by his film image.

The new popularity of mechanical stage effects, especially various kinds of "moving pictures," probably reflected vaudeville's attempt, however conscious, to compete with the relatively new but already popular motion picture business. Originally a lower-class amusement found in immigrant neighborhoods, movie theatres proliferated in more affluent areas after 1906. By 1907 there were between four and five thousand nickelodeons in America, attracting over two million viewers a day; by 1913 there were thirty thousand movie houses. The number of daily moviegoers in New York City in 1908 was estimated at two hundred thousand—three-fourths of whom were women and children.[67] By the end of the decade, then, there was already a generation familiar with and appreciative of the conventions of the cinema. The availability of this exciting new medium, with its emphasis on verisimilitude and rapid movement of image, made it all the more attractive for vaudeville to incorporate these qualities into its own magic-making. Cinema intensified the preoccupation with speed and spectacle already present in vaudeville.

Vaudeville also felt the influence of another development in entertainment—the popularity of two evolving forms, the musical comedy and the revue. On the rise throughout the century's first decade was a new sort of musical show; hits such as *The Wizard of Oz, The Merry Widow,* and *The Chocolate Soldier* were spreading the taste for fast-paced collages of captivating lyrics and tunes and eye-filling spectacle, in place of the old farce comedy. Also, after a modest start in 1907, by 1913 Ziegfeld was creating a sensation with his revues of lavish costumes and sets and beautiful chorus girls.[68] As early as spring 1904, Dutch comic Sam Bernard, a graduate of vaudeville himself, would note the influence of the new kind of show on vaudeville: "The death of the gag and the passing of the slapstick as a source of fun has been brought about by the present style of musical comedy."[69] The success of the musical shows encouraged vaudeville's tendency to incorporate the elements of glamour on every bill.

But although revue, musical comedy and film contributed to the vaudeville patron's greater sophistication, these new forms were a response to factors already reshaping vaudeville. The rise of the mass audience created an enormous demand for popular entertainment which no one form could satisfy; vaudeville, revue, circus, musical comedy, the amusement park and the movies were all multiplying haphazardly to provide amusement for the millions. The gradual reduction of the work week, the rising standard of living and per capita income, and the pressure of a more routinized labor day in office or factory made the search for pleasure all the more intense. The preferences of this mass of pleasure-seekers were what determined the shape of musical comedy, revue, and vaudeville.[70]

For the stage manager and performer of the day, strict definition of form was not a consideration; they created shows deliberately calculated to appeal to their paying customers, and whatever pleased was kept in the act, or show. In other words, musical comedy, vaudeville and revue were developing by parallel accretion, with subtle differences in audience composition, not artistic rules, determining their evolution. Just as vaudeville kept its ear tuned to musical comedy's newfangled production numbers, so musical comedy and revue borrowed the brittle give-and-take patter being perfected on the vaudeville stage. In 1909 vaudeville comic John Lorenz was the hit of a musical comedy called *The Motor Girl,* and *Variety's* Sime observed that "there are many burlesque comedians who could walk away with a '$2 production' if given the opportunity."[71] It was the more cosmopolitan ways of the urban middle class that determined the kind of musical number and humor seen in both vaudeville and musical comedy.

As a result of these new tastes, after 1905 the song and dance act once again became the fashion on the vaudeville stage. Along with other vaudevillians, male-female teams offered a rapid succession of song and dance numbers interspersed with snappy jokes, a formula perfectly suited to urban audiences' demand for fast-paced entertainment. It went without saying that skillful singing and dancing or both was a necessary ingredient of these acts, but the star teams had additional qualities: their echoes of the latest musical comedy hits, their glamorous costumes, their striking good looks and charisma made them the darlings of the crowd. And a male-female team whose offstage love affair was blazoned in sensational publicity had an additional element of sexual electricity that male duos or female teams lacked.

One of the first of the new song and dance teams to win a large following in vaudeville was Gould and Suratt. Vaudeville performer Billy

Gould was appearing in London in 1904 when he met and married Valeska Suratt and incorporated her into his act. South Africa was the testing ground. Valeska was noticeably nervous the night of her debut, but reviewers thought "Miss Suratt looked charming enough to captivate the audience had she never spoken a word."[72] When the team made its American debut at New York's Colonial Theatre in March 1905, the act was an overnight success, said the *New York Morning Telegraph*, because of its "real elegance in dressing and the ease and grace with which it was carried through." Gould was virtually ignored by reviewers, who couldn't say too much about his partner—"a woman of such commanding beauty, and so clever and finished in her work, that it is impossible not to like and applaud her...."[73]

Gould and Suratt's singing and dancing and joking was thought more novel than other acts, an impression partly created by their fast yet easy, somewhat bold stage delivery: "Their songs are new, their wit is new and the way they do things makes them go with a snap," claimed one reviewer; "Gould does not try to do anything, but makes good on his nerve," noted another.[74] One Indianapolis critic maintained the act attracted so much attention simply for its impertinence:

> There was a certain freshness—very fresh sometimes—about the act that was enjoyed, although upon analysis, the act did not show a great deal that was worthwhile....The sketch is very risque—which may account for its success.[75]

Another critic called it close to ribald.[76] Shocking as it was to some small-towners, the act got a warm reception in the cities, where mores had changed. For example, whereas before 1900 "double-meaning" songs were rigidly excluded from mixed-audience theatres, even before the teens songs like "If You Talk in Your Sleep, Don't Mention My Name," were sung freely at mixed parties, and as one lyric admonished, "Be good, very, very good...If you can't be good, be careful."[77] To blasé urbanites, the Gould and Suratt act gained in sophistication for being a "little risque":

> It is a witty trifle that one would find in London music halls, in Paris cafés chantant, or even in the more refined atmosphere of Vienna, where novelties please and where a sprinkle of pepper is not blinding to the eye.[78]

Part of the act's daring and novelty was simply the way Suratt dressed: "rather unconventionally." She wore a sheath gown, tighter than any dress seen before on the San Francisco stage (a Cleveland reviewer thought the most remarkable thing on the bill was how Suratt got into her gowns and could still breathe), with an immodest décolleté in front and back, and transparent stockings. In Detroit, her gowns made the women gasp and the men utter a chorus of expressive "whews!" Her shocking effect is better understood when it is known that the first time a woman was seen in the new Parisian style of sheath in the Chicago shopping area, she had to be rescued by the police from the jeering crowd.[79] Indeed, Suratt's perfect Gibson Girl looks and dress were probably the most important appeal of the act; her glamour appealed to women, and even newspapermen waxed eloquent, claiming she wore gowns better than ninety-nine per cent of actresses, that she was "The Most Stunning Looking Woman in Vaudeville," with the "Most Perfect Form on Stage."[80]

Suratt carefully publicized her sartorial brazenness. When a reporter asked how she made her gown fit so perfectly, Suratt ingenuously answered "I don't wear petticoats," causing the reporter to sit up straight and echo her with disbelief.[81] Indeed, publicity was an important tool in creating the Gould and Suratt image. After much attention in the press for her $1500 cloth-of-gold dress—which "wins a round of applause for itself alone"—Suratt got still more mileage when she found the dress in a heap on the floor of her dressing room, slashed in six or eight pieces in the front by a knife.[82] On another occasion Suratt ruined a dress that was supposedly from Paris and worth 1000 francs by overturning ink on it—although other women on the same bill claimed to have seen cheaper dresses just like it in New York and Detroit.[83]

By 1909 the act had separated, and whereas Gould was little heard of afterwards, Valeska Suratt went into musical comedy and later film, where she was considered a close second to Theda Bara in the "vamp class."[84] But while teamed in vaudeville, Gould and Suratt, with Valeska's conspicuous consumption and blatant sexuality, and with Gould's risqué, devil-may-care patter, were tailor-made idols for a middle-class audience eager to cast off nineteenth-century morals and embrace the urban values of materialism and social freedom. They were an act which appealed to "the more blasé theatre-goers."[85]

Bayes and Norworth, who followed on the heels of Gould and Suratt, had similar qualities: the ability to project themselves boldly in the mass media and on the stage, glamorous looks, daring clothes and stage manners. Like Suratt, Nora Bayes achieved success just after returning from Europe—she studied in Paris and appeared with Guilbert on one occasion—and both performers probably picked up new styles in Europe that aided their American successes.[86] Bayes's first vaudeville appearance was in 1908 with her new husband, Jack Norworth, and their work as a team until their divorce in 1913 was influential in spreading the standards of glamour and sophistication in vaudeville.[87]

Like Suratt's, Bayes's dresses set a precedent for costliness and glamour for vaudeville, and were considered "daring." When the team appeared before the Fifth Avenue Theatre audience in 1910, considered one of the smartest vaudeville audiences, Bayes's first frock was thought to be utterly startling. It was a straight white silk dress which conformed "to the wearer's curves like wet paper" since she wore no "underdressing." It got a gasp from the sophisticated Fifth Avenue audience.[88] Bayes's sexuality was the perfect tonic for the audience of the day; she was

> Nora, the belligerent, mollifying, deliciously rakish Nora Bayes! There is nobody quite like her and she is fascinatingly lean and sinuous, is feline and bewitching all the time, being in fine fettle, a little thin and ethereal, but handsome as a picture of rajah's daughter and sumptuously attired in oriental mischiefs....[89]

For white collar workers with rising incomes, Bayes and Norworth provided a national lesson in the joys of reckless consumer spending. Newspapermen were duly informed and passed on to avid fans that Bayes and Norworth's vaudeville salary was $3000 a week, and that they received an additional $100,000 a year from royalties on their songs. The team always caused a stir when they arrived in a city, for they travelled in a specially constructed private Pullman car, dubbed "Iolanthe," which cost $75,000, with a dining room which accommodated six couples and a grand piano, quarters for her in rose and gold and in mahogany for him, separate quarters for servants and also a manager's office. Still another car brought her favorite automobile.[90] The prodigal lifestyle of such stars, most of whom had risen from lowly origins, was a gratifying spectacle for a mass audience who believed in the opportunities and class mobility of America.

The Bayes and Norworth combination—billed onstage as "Nora Bayes, Assisted and Admired by Jack Norworth"—was equally well-known for their offstage relationship. Theirs was publicized as a storybook marriage: they boasted they had not been separated for more than six hours in two years, and their published books on "How to be Happy Even Though Married" shared with fans their "Ten Commandments of Domestic Happiness."[91]

Sharing secrets of marital happiness fit the Bayes and Norworth style; they carefully fostered their image as entertainers of unparalleled generosity to their beloved fans. "I work on the theory," Bayes told a reporter,

> that your audience likes you ten times better if you are generous and seem to enjoy giving, than if you are stingy and only do what the program calls for and refuse encores. And I carry out the same theory in regard to my clothes. I have six elaborate gowns with wraps and hats to match, although there are only two acts and three dresses would be ample.[92]

The team even installed a ballot box in the lobby of vaudeville theatres where they appeared, so audiences could vote for what songs they wanted to hear. In fact, their act usually included only two songs by Bayes, and one by Norworth, and closed with a duet. This merely whetted the audience's appetite, and the real act was the protracted encores of famous Bayes-Norworth melodies, one after another, with the audience shouting themselves hoarse demanding their favorites, "and after that speeches. Speeches by one and then the other, and mixed, broken, convulsing speeches...."[93]

Bayes and Norworth's attraction for vaudeville audiences was largely a result of their successful musical comedy and revue careers. They were prominent figures in the *Follies* of 1907 and 1908; and when they broke their contract and left the *Follies of 1909*, a long legal suit followed in which Ziegfeld's maneuvers and Bayes and Norworth's counter-strategems furnished a protracted public entertainment in the dailies for over a year.[94] Their *Follies* career was followed by roles in *The Jolly Bachelors, Little Miss Fix-It,* and Weber and Field's *Roly Poly.* It was in the 1908 *Follies* that Bayes and Norworth sang "Shine On Harvest Moon," "You Will Have to Sing an Irish Song," and "Since Mother Was a Girl," all by Norworth, songs which were to remain their trademarks. In 1912, when Bayes and Norworth sang in vaudeville the songs they had sung in the comedy *Little Miss Fix-It,* managers Louis Werba and Mark Luescher sought (unsuccessfully) an injunction from the courts, causing a vast stir in the press.[95]

It was with the songs and polish of the big-time revue and musical comedy stage that Bayes and Norworth bowled over their vaudeville audiences. When they appeared at Atlantic City in the summer of 1909, their songs were old to the *Variety* reviewer, but new to vaudeville audiences, to whom Bayes and Norworth were "unusual people."[96] But Bayes and Norworth were more than mere personalities who sold themselves on the basis of musical comedy associations and sophisticated marketing techniques. Norworth was undeniably talented as a songwriter, and Bayes's voice was acclaimed as marvellous. With his "quiet and undemonstrative" style, Norworth was an excellent foil for his partner's dynamic, hoydenish stage persona. Bayes had that difficult-to-define something called "magnetism" that made audiences thrill to her singing. "A personality to be reckoned with," Nora Bayes delivered a number "as only she can sing it," and to at least one critic the Bayes-Norworth team gave "one of the greatest entertainments ever given in vaudeville."[97]

So successful was the type that henceforth vaudeville would never be without the male-female song and dance team specializing in "musical comedy in a vaudeville way" and "metropolitan smartness and finish" — performers possessing "more clothes than a Hippodrome ballet" and the ability to establish "just the right flirtatious relationship with the audience."[98]

This new vogue for singing and dancing acts was a boon to teams left over from earlier days. New as it seemed, the team who came on and did a specialty in "one," with no pretense to plot or realism, had dominated variety bills, but these acts had fallen from favor at the turn of the century when the sketch became prominent. Now several old-time variety teams still in existence suddenly found themselves more popular than before. Sam and Kitty Morton, for example, had done a popular Irish song and dance act in the variety halls in the eighties and nineties, when they were a couple in their twenties. In the early twentieth century, when skits were the rage, they devised a full-length farce called *Breaking into Society*, with their children Paul and Clara also in the cast, and performed in minor, out-of-the-way theatres.[99] Now Sam and Kitty began to perform once again as a two-act, capitalizing on the new popularity of song, dance and comedy teams.

By the spring of 1912 they had debuted an act called "Back to Where They Started," a nostalgic recreation of the act they had done in the variety halls. They appeared in unfashionable working clothes and filled ten minutes with song and dance and patter, demonstrating that "1880 jokes are as serviceable as those of 1916." Then, while Kitty changed offstage, Sam entertained the audience, peeling off his working clothes to reveal a fancy costume beneath just as Kitty breezed back in for a song and dance number.[100] Their green and white costumes were just like the costumes they used in "those days": Sam wore knee breeches of white and a coat of emerald satin; Kitty wore a short skirt of accordion-pleated chiffon and a coat to match her husband's. They sang "Sweet Kate O'Neill," the Irish tune that they supposedly used for their first stage appearance in 1881, and their dance steps were "of vintage of the early varieties."[101]

Now vaudeville was so securely established that it could indulge in nostalgia for its own past, for the very traditions which it had denied in the nineties. In 1911, Percy Williams even arranged an "Old Timers' Bill," which contained among others, James and Bonnie Thornton, singles in variety days, now teamed for the occasion in an old-fashioned song and patter act. James and Bonnie found themselves so popular they continued to tour as a team until 1920, the year of Bonnie's death.[102]

Perhaps inspired by the success of the Mortons and the Thorntons, in 1915 Hallen and Fuller created a new act which blatantly exploited the wave of nostalgia for variety days. Following his career as a variety star with wife Enid Hart, Fred Hallen and second wife Mollie Fuller had enjoyed over ten years of success in vaudeville playlets featuring the comic dilemmas of courting and married couples, from 1898 until around 1909, when their sketches began to seem outdated. Hallen and Fuller made a successful come-back in "The Corridor of Time," which *Variety* pointed out was altogether different from their previous style, since they now "eschewed all 'story plays' for an out and out vaudeville number."[103]

The act was done in "one" before a drop depicting a collage of old-time bills of Tony Pastor's, Niblo Gardens, Hyde and Behman's, and the Howard Athenaeum; in the center was a three-sheet poster of Molly Fuller in her famous 1880s role as "principal boy" Gabrielle in E. E. Rice's *Evangeline*. Hallen and Fuller completed the picture when they appeared, Hallen dressed in old-time suit and boutonniere—as worn in the Hallen and Hart act—and Molly dressed in a period afternoon frock.[104] They began by talking about the old days. Hallen boasts he can dance as well now as then, and Molly invites him to try; he offers to dance any old-style dance the audience demands, and does. Following a song by Molly, Hallen teases her about the days when she dressed as in the poster, which shows her in snug-fitting tights, revealing a shapely young figure. "Ah, Mollie, you were the toast of the town then. If you only looked like that now!" sighs her husband. "Don't I though," replies Molly, and after a lightning change to white tights, "she stands on the stage disclosing to another generation a form divine," proving that "time has robbed her legs of none of their pristine beauty." "Molly, I'll take my hat off to you," exclaims Hallen, and they go into their finale, an impersonation of variety team Lester and Allen in "The Two New Sports in Town," showing some impressive jig and clog dancing.[105]

This new interest in pure variety skills also spurred an increase in teams who did stand-up comedy talk. Male-female conversation acts had been long in developing, since the comic talk in the earliest male-female acts was usually dominated by the man. In the eighties snappy dialogue was finally becoming one of the appeals of the male-female team, but the progress of the mixed talking act was interrupted by the rise of the sketch as the dominant form of male-female act at the turn of the century.

As the teens approached, however, and audiences became more educated in the vaudeville conventions, thus more demanding, they were little interested in entertainment concerned with drawing characters and tracing plot-lines. Nineteenth-century humor had been expansive and anecdotal; twentieth-century humor was epigrammatic, clever, satirical. Telegraphic manners were necessary to smooth over the impersonality and potential aggressiveness of city life, and frenetic city people appreciated economy. In the early 1900s, already newspaper headlines, political slogans, advertisements and cartoons typified the urban trend of reducing communication to its essence.[106] Audiences' new delight in the facile phrase and in racy slang made patter for its own sake an important entertainment appeal once again, thus encouraging the rise of pure talking acts.

Beginning around 1908, there was an increasing number of male-female routines described as talking and singing acts, with the talk obviously an important part of the act; Barry and Wolford, for example, sang and "cross-fired talk at each other."[107] An occasional team was described as a "conversation act" or "talking act."[108] Reviewers began treating the joking more seriously and evaluating stage conversation as an important appeal in itself: Regal and Winsch were told they needed brighter talk, instead of mere plays on words; the delivery of Caine and Odum's talk was criticized as too quiet, and they were advised to emphasize the "snapper" of their conversation.[109]

By 1912 Jim Diamond of Diamond and Brennan was doing "kidding," and Clifford and Taylor, "Sidewalk Conversationalists," were described as a "conventional man and woman talking act." In this "conventional" act, she provided the feeding and he handled all the comedy, and the material was flirtation.[110] In fact, flirtation was overwhelmingly popular material for stage conversation between a man and woman. At the turn of the century courtship-and-marriage was already the predominant subject of the mixed act, and when mixed teams began distilling sketches into stand-up conversation, the established comedy situations naturally furnished the matter of their talk.

Wilbur Mack and Nella Walker were certainly one of the earliest teams to do the courtship sketch as a more streamlined act in "one." Their first routine was "The Girl and the Pearl," in which a fellow strikes up a flirtation with a young girl sitting on her trunk before a drop of a train station, and the flirting provided "an excellent line of conversational give-and-take." "The Dollar Bill," debuted in September 1911, was also concerned with flirtation, and was said to be on the same "idea" as their first act, different only in the material. A third Mack and Walker act, "A Pair of Tickets," featured a young man, described as nervy and persistent, who approaches a young woman, bent on flirtation; a slight plot told how, after striking up her acquaintance, he obtained some tickets by a ruse to entertain her.[111]

The "idea" of their routines was clearly indebted to the courtship sketch. But their plot line was said to be thin, and was interrupted by a few songs, too; their act could perhaps be described as the substance of flirtation without the intricacies of plot, i.e., just the banter. Their routine was described not as a sketch, but as a cross-fire act or simply as a "flirtation."[112] According to Joe Laurie, Jr., they started a new craze, the "bench act"—they sat on the bench onstage and did flirtation stuff, wrote Laurie. As Laurie had in retrospect, so Mack and Walker were thought in their day to be "originators of this style of entertainment"; "Wilber Mack and Nella Walker are peculiar unto themselves," claimed *Variety*, pointing out that it really did not matter how similar their new act was to their previous one, since it was not so much their material as their own individual, clean-cut "manner" that put them across.[113]

This manner was fast, witty bantering. One reviewer claimed their fine-strung witticisms came "at a rate of ten a minute." In an extant bit, "It's pleasant here," says Mack; "It was," she shoots back. By 1920, the duo had split, and Mack was performing an act with some assistants said to contain "flip" dialogue of the sort he handled so well.[114] Mack might be viewed as the successor to a type first done at least thirty years earlier: the masher. In early variety days male comics in mixed acts had often depicted immigrant mashers, whose thick-tongued lovemaking was conducted with broad comic strokes. Then, as more polite comedy made headway in the mid-eighties, Fred Hallen had created the dapper, flirtatious gent captured in the 1887 *New York Dramatic News* drawing of him as he looked onstage, in suit and boutonniere standing by a bench. This picture of an apparent "bench act" would seem to belie Laurie's assertion that Mack and Walker were the first such act; but in later years the sketch with its elaborate scenery and plot had so monopolized bills that now Mack and Walker's talking act in "one" seemed a total innovation. Mack's suave, well-dressed masher was the final refinement of the type. Mack and Walker dressed in smart street clothes, pretty Nella Walker in an eye-catching white suit and panama hat, in keeping with the flip sophistication of their act. "It was Mack and Walker who brought the 'class,' natural talk, and street make-up to vaude," claimed Laurie.[115]

By the teens, the "flirtation" in Mack and Walker manner was stock male-female stage fare.[116] In 1916, when Brett Page published *Writing for Vaudeville*, a manual explaining the various kinds of vaudeville acts, and the requirements for creating them, he listed six types of comedy two-acts: the sidewalk conversation, the singing two-act, the double female act, the parody-singers, the two-act using a plot interest, and the flirtation two-act.[117] The flirtation was clearly a well-defined type more specialized than "sidewalk conversation," and it was the only type necessarily done by male-female teams. Page defined its appeal as threefold. Romance is the chief appeal: "Moonlight, a girl and a man—this is the recipe," writes Page. Then, witty dialogue is what makes the flirtation "get over"; characters make the sort of speeches which we in real life think of afterward and wish we made. Third, the desired effect is "daintiness," with the dialogue, business, scenery, lights and music all directed to this purpose. Page adds that the flirtation was usually presented with sentimental songs, at least one change of costume by the woman, sometimes with a special drop, and often given the semblance of a plot.[118]

Merrill and Otto's "After the Shower," an act which debuted in Atlantic City in September 1909 and which was still around New York four seasons later,[119] was included in Page's handbook as an illustration of the type. A drop in "one" showed a pretty resort area, and a bench was placed on right. The girl enters, dressed in a fashionable gown and carrying a parasol; laughing, she glances over her shoulder at the boy, who follows a few paces behind her. He's dressed in a natty light summer suit. "I don't see why on earth you insist on following me," exclaims the girl. "I never knew why I was *on earth* until I met you," replies the boy, lifting his hat. Snappy dialogue followed:

> The Fellow: Say—you haven't told me your name yet.
> The Girl: I don't intend to. I think you are very forward.
> The Fellow: Shall I tell you *my* name?
> The Girl: By no means.
> The Fellow: You're not interested?
> The Girl: Not a bit.

After a string of wisecracks earns the boy one brush-off after another, finally he says:

> ah—ah—fraulein—mam'selle—you know, I don't know your name—besides I—I—I like you. I—I think you're the sweetest girl I've ever seen.

"Oh, pshaw!" she answers, "You've said that to a hundred girls," and so it goes unto the end, by which time the boy has earned the right to hold her parasol before them for a kiss hidden from the audience.[120]

As hopelessly dated as it sounds to modern ears, to *Variety* "After the Shower" offered excellent rapid-fire talk, and was "the neatest act seen here in many moons."[121] So popular was the flirtation act that by the end of the teens most mixed teams on the small time—the retrospective mirror of big-time trends—were doing flirtation acts too, and conventional language could be used to describe them. Winchell and Green did a "bench turn" containing "spooney talk"; Montgomery and Morton did "another variation of the old bench act," the "usual flirtation bit"; and Duffy and Mann did "one of the 57 varieties of familiar flirtation style of turn," with get-backs, flip conversation, and a double song finale.[122]

Not every male-female conversation team did a "flirtation," of course. At about the same time that Wilbur Mack appeared with his nervy, flirtatious character, another wise male stereotype was becoming popular, the salesman, with T. Roy Barnes vaudeville's favorite stage salesman. Barnes and Crawford, a classic combination of male comic and female feeder, had first appeared on vaudeville bills around 1909. Their vaudeville career was interrupted by frequent appearances in legitimate comedies, but throughout the teens and into the twenties they were a popular vaudeville team playing big-time theatres.[123] Their best-known act was "The Magazine Man and the Lady," in which Barnes played a salesman who would not take no for an answer. "My grandmother is very sick—she is dying in the next room," his partner pleaded, trying to get rid of him. Barnes looked nonplussed for a moment, then his face brightened: "I'll wait," he said gently.[124]

A version of the act has survived, and it reveals the routine was pure talk:

Bessie: If you're a salesman you'd better sail away, because I'm not buying anything today.
Roy: Madam, I'm neither a salesman nor a sailor. I've just quit my job as canvasman with the circus, and now—
Bessie: This is no place for a circus. Watch your step going out, please.
Roy: And now I'm a canvasser.
Bessie: I see. You're taking orders. Mine are "beat it."
Roy: I have here some wonderful new inventions. Here's Burbank's boneless banana—
Bessie: I never eat bananas.
Roy: Here's the latest skin food—
Bessie: Oh, what is it?
Roy: Five frankforters. Just add hot mustard and serve—
Bessie: I keep my own dogs.

The act ran along like this for many minutes, then ended thus:

Bessie: You must excuse me now. I hope you sell something.
Roy: I expect to get the order for celling the new jail this afternoon. Now I want you to take a year's subscription to our magazine. Look, my list of subscribers includes all the prominent ladies in this apartment. Here's Mrs. Brown, Mrs. Jones, Mrs. Smyth, Mrs. Casey—
Bessie: Why, Mrs. Casey moved away from here two weeks ago.
Roy: Did she? All right, we'll take her name off the list.
Bessie: I don't see any inducement to take your magazine. Do you give any premium?
Roy: Premium? Well, I should whimper. Why, you take this magazine for twenty years, and at the end of that time we give an accident policy which will protect every bone in your body.
Bessie: I don't quite see that.
Roy: Wait till I show you. If you have a leg cut off, you get a dollar. And we ask no questions.
Bessie: Oh, and I suppose if I have both legs cut off I get two dollars?
Roy: Certainly. What do we care for legs?
Bessie: Two dollars isn't much satisfaction for the loss of two of your members.
Roy: It isn't? Why, if some political parties could lose a couple of their members they'd give two thousand dollars. And then some.
Bessie: Wouldn't you do anything else to help a subscriber who had lost both legs?
Roy: Sure, we'd guarantee to teach you the turkey trot free of charge.[125]

The jokes bring a few groans but some are still funny, and Roy Barnes obviously had the ability and personality to make them work. A lot of his talk was thought to be impromptu; it was said the act was never played the same way twice.[126] In fact, there is an alternative ending to the above dialogue.

> Roy: After you have taken the magazine for ten years we give you an accident policy providing you pay the regular premium as it comes due. If you lose one leg we pay you $1. If you should lose both legs we teach you a stump speech.[127]

Perhaps *Variety* was more accurate in describing him as "an adept exponent of the *apparent* [my italics] ad lib style." But whether or not his act was really impromptu, Barnes' talk was impressively rapid-fire: he reputedly gabbed fifty-seven minutes worth of talk in less than twenty-nine minutes. He was "as fleet as he is casual, as now-you-see-it-now-you-don't as he is cocksure. He doesn't know what 'preparation' is, he throws—to baseball it—with a golden arm, and frequently the play is double."[128] Such studied casualness enabled spectators to share the accomplishment vicariously; Barnes (like baseball heroes) made it look like anyone could do what he did.

The appeal was not just the jokes, but the characterization, too. Like Mack's character, Barnes's salesman is cocky and persistent. The laughs are not only at his wisecracks, but at his zany resourcefulness, his insouciance, his unabashed obnoxiousness. He disregards his partner's "buts" and her orders to "beat it," and turns her remonstrances into reasons to buy that are clever puns and at the same time hilariously absurd. Ridiculous as he is, his ability to deliver such outrageous flimflam with totally imperturbable conviction is downright admirable. Barnes was well-suited for his role as an unctuous salesman. A real-life salesman in 1904, Barnes was considered so funny that he decided to try the stage, and he began in vaudeville as a small-time comedy prestidigitator. His stage manner was said to be extremely personal, but so good-humored that none took offense, a style aided by his astounding good looks and his utter unconsciousness of them.[129]

The character was an apt one for the era. Glibness and smartness were the popular virtues with the middle class, and no one personified these traits better than the up-and-coming salesman. From the nation of small capitalists it had been in the nineteenth century, America had become a nation of hired employees, and with the emphasis now on distribution of goods rather than production, salesmen were an expanding segment of the job force. Now the once intimate traits of courtesy and helpfulness had become a means of livelihood; the department store clerk sold not only his time and labor, but his personality. True sincerity was of course detrimental to the salesman; to deal with hundreds of strangers a day, impersonalized ceremonies evolved, with general methods of handling various types.

"Salesmanship" was a science in which any clever man could achieve status. Charm schools, personnel managers, and best-selling literature evolved to teach social skills. In place of the nineteenth-century belief in honesty, self-discipline, and serving the will of God, now success tracts preached belief in will power: "Think Success"; "Never Admit Defeat"; and "Every Man a King" were the new mottos.[130]

The vaudeville interest in the salesman character testified to a fundamental change in American society and also, on some level, to a middle-class awareness of a certain irony underlying the new values. Since the housewife, for whom recreational spending was an important outlet, was the salesman's traditional victim, it was a natural choice for a male-female team. It also served the need for new material other than the flirtation.

Davis and Darnell were another team, well-known on the big-time circuit, who used the salesman motif, and who were a male comic-female feeder combination. Their first act was "Birdseed," later described as "unforgettable," and as "for several years one of the brightest of fixtures on the two-a-day." Frank Davis played a glib-tongued travelling salesman whose *raison d'être* was birdseed. He must have shared Roy Barne's gift for gab, for when a small-time team did "Birdseed" in 1923, after Davis and Darnell had dropped it, the male imitator was said to lack "Frank Davis's glib and facile method of 'throwing the bull.'"[131] Once started, it was said, Frank Davis never permitted the audience to recover from his onslaught of snappy gags, and even other vaudevillians fell under his spell: George Burns once confessed, "My favorite act in the world was a man-and-woman act called 'Davis & Darnell in Birdseeds!'...."[132] Other popular male-female salesman acts were Keno and Green, Devine and Williams, and Rives and Arnold—with this last an act in which the woman played a female drummer and got the laughs at the man's expense.[133]

This reversal of traditional roles, the woman playing the wiser character, was indebted to the increasing importance of the female comic—one of the most important trends in twentieth-century vaudeville. At the same time that Wilbur Mack and Roy Barnes were popularizing the wise guy, a few female performers were establishing themselves as comic talkers. They were few at first because the male-dominated nature of the early variety had created a bias that inhibited the development of female comic ability for two decades to come.

Even in the era of mature vaudeville, many a male-female act was primarily carried by the entertainment skills of the male partner, with the female merely assisting and looking pretty.[134] The unequal distribution of talent in Ross and Stewart's act apparently worked well enough: "The man offers an acceptable line of comedy, song and talk. The girl dresses neatly and looks well, thus holding up her share."[135] But in the late nineties—

partly because of the infusion of female talent from the legitimate stage—female partners had begun to win more praise than ever before. Legitimate actresses usually appeared in sketches tailored to their advantage, as in "A Wife's Stratagem," in which Georgia Gardner had "all the fat."[136] Almost for the first time, many team efforts were noticed by reviewers to be the result of not one but two talented people.[137]

In particular, the popularity of domestic sketches like "A Wife's Stratagem" highlighted the importance of the comic actress's contribution, for their plots often demanded that the woman play a comic virago who insulted, nagged, and generally tortured her partner. Thus, when talking acts in "one" began to replace the sketch in popularity, the time was ripe for stand-up acts in which the woman was the comic. In fact, just as the flirtation in "one" was a distilled version of the courtship sketch, the early talking acts with female comics were virtually stand-up versions of the comedy sketch about marital woes.

The same shrewishness of the comic wife in the sketches was the specialty of the woman of Melville and Higgins, a husband and wife singing and talking comedy act touring in vaudeville by the end of the 1906-07 season. At the time, a team with the female partner handling the comic talk was considered an unusual arrangement: Mae Melville was said to be "one of those rare creatures, a really funny woman."[138] Her costume and make-up clearly distinguished her from the traditionally pretty female straight:

> As an example of grotesqueness, Mae Melville takes the cake with plenty of frosting. Her get-up from her toes to that funny little headgear makes the paint crackle on the walls of the boxes.[139]

The accompanying picture shows a chubby woman in a little hat with two large plumes, a ridiculously large bow at her neck, and a comically misshapen peplum over a billowy skirt.

Mae had a contagious laugh and a steady fire of comical lines, for the most part consisting of her jeers and shrieks at her male partner. A well-known bit was his stooping over throughout the act to pick up his hat, and her shrilly demanding "let it lay," which he meekly obeyed. Higgins took her attack with a deadpan demeanor, occasionally butting in for a remark; his line "All the time she's picking on me" was said in such a way that it was a sure laugh-producer. His appearance was a comical foil to hers; whereas Melville emphasized her fatness with busy, bulky clothes, partner Robert Higgins was extremely slender, and appeared clad in "a skin-tight suit that makes one wonder how he could ever get into it and still more how he could ever get out of it." Mae teased him unmercifully about "his ability to disappear through a crack in the stage floor."[140]

The repartee was punctuated by mugging, singing, dancing, and general horseplay. "What does Mae do over at Keith's?" asked one reporter;

> Why, she sings a little bit, walks around a little bit, makes faces, whistles — don't forget the whistle — shrieks at Robert, dances a little just to show she knows how, whistles again — and — that's about it.[141]

One newspaper suggested their antics were a travesty on an old-time song and dance team, or "take-offs on the follies of fad-afflicted mortals"; a patron of the Colonial Theatre summed it up better, perhaps: "They are crazy — just plain crazy."[142]

Reviewers invariably explained that Robert Higgins was "an admirable foil" displaying cleverness on his own account. *Variety* declared his silent comedy was an art in itself, and complained that "the general idea seems to be to overlook Robert Higgins... but to those who go a bit under the surface, Higgins is not the smallest part of the specialty." In contrast, Mae Melville's comic artistry was explained to be just natural. She is funny, said *Variety*, "just naturally so." "Mae can look as funny and wriggle herself about the stage in as funny a style as ever did any comedian or comedienne," maintained another reviewer; "She doesn't have to try to be funny." One prejudiced observer explained mysteriously that Mae was really funny, whereas an average comedienne would be only unpleasant.[143]

At any rate, the act clearly contained what had been the very gist of the old sketch depicting comical marital battles — the loud, obnoxious, unattractive hag of a wife who continually pesters her henpecked husband, giving him a perpetual pain-in-the-side. In fact, an early act by the team was called "Just Married," and Melville's tirade against the defenseless Higgins was delivered before a church drop, adding considerably to the comedy, no doubt. Their next act was "Putting on Airs," and likely featured Mae's criticism of her husband's behavior in some social situation: the act contained some remarks about watermelon wetting the ears, and about peas on a knife.[144] Perhaps Melville and Higgins's stage roles took a toll on their offstage relationship. Although still getting rave reviews in 1914, the team was separated by divorce before the 1915–16 season.[145]

In 1915 divorce had also ended the approximately seven-year career of the male-female team of Montgomery and Moore, featuring a comedienne who had become even more famous than Mae Melville. Like Melville and Higgins, William Montgomery and wife Florence Moore sang and joked, with Montgomery feeding and serving as the butt of Florence's insults. The two burst upon the stage in automobile coats, and exchanged rapid-fire patter about William's auto. "The machine kicked me in the nose," complained Montgomery; "Good!" screams Florence, "it saved me the trouble," and then, "I wish I had a moth to throw at his coat," she would say aside.[146] Florence proceeds to scold William about the car:

> Florence: You don't know how to run a car. Keeping me sitting there two hours. If only you had told me I could have brought my knitting along. Why, I could have stayed home tonight and read the telephone book. I told you if you were going to run into anything to run into something cheap, and then you run into a window of cut glass with a 5 and 10 cent store next door.
> William: Why, my machine is a forty horsepower.
> Florence: Well, thirty-nine lay down and died.
> William: I put three speeds on my car.
> Florence: I know — slow, slower, and stop.
> William: And I put a one man top on it.
> Florence: So that when it rains you are the only one who gets wet.[147]

It was Florence who got the laughs, with her "nasty banter," and in tune with the times, her delivery was fast. Whereas Montgomery's style was "quiet drollery," her stage delivery was "racy," "perky," "careless." The act seemed improvised, one reviewer thought. "Twelve-cylinder, 60 horsepower, self-starting, fully equipped, f.o.b. fun is their specialty," it was said; "They come on the stage like a whirlwind, and never for a minute does the speed slacken."[148]

Unlike Robert Higgins, however, Montgomery got in a decisive parry of his own before the routine was over; the above dialogue ended thus:

> William: Well, I put something on your car, too. Guess what it was?
> Florence: What? Headlights?
> William: No; my curse.[149]

Montgomery's crack is a key to a significant difference between Montgomery and Moore and their predecessors. Although the substance of their act recalled Melville and Higgins, unlike them, Montgomery and Moore were not grotesque cartoon figures, and Florence Moore was said to be attractive. This may have made her "nasty banter" difficult for an audience to enjoy, had it not been somewhat ameliorated. It was no doubt to soften Florence's jabs at her mate that she punctuated her invective with kisses, "as a reward," pointed out one reviewer; "that ought to console most anyone."[150] It would not be so funny for an attractive woman — one like those in the audience, perhaps — to rail non-stop onstage. Just so, unless he is clearly only a stick figure, for a male character to submit meekly to abuse would be patently unmanly; thus, although he played straight, Montgomery established his male prerogative by getting the last rejoinder — probably to the audience's satisfaction.

A number of distancing devices were also used in the routine. Although the team did not adopt outlandish costume, their heavy automobile coats set them apart from the audience. Florence Moore also disguised her womanliness in another fashion. She told that she spent a year on the stage trying to be funny, and was unsuccessful, because "I maintained a certain standard of decent looks." It was at a matinee where she was not going over that in a spirit of disgust Florence "made faces as they have seldom been made from any stage." Laughter began coming over the footlights, and when she made more faces, the laughter exploded. "After that the managers refused me work unless I obliterated every possible claim to looks while on stage," said Florence.[151]

Not only did Florence Moore contort her face grotesquely, but apparently she utilized her body as a comic prop. A newspaper silhouette shows her with an extremely angular body, with abnormally large hands, and with her hands and feet thrown out in an ungainly, stilted fashion. This caricature suggests she used her feet and hands in a stylized way which called attention to them, creating a clown-like impression. Similarly her jokes were delivered in exaggeratedly shrill tones; "Miss Moore's methods are not subtle; she does not aim at super-refinement; her voice has no pellucid notes," remarked one reviewer.[152]

Thus, Florence Moore was that rare bird, a truly funny woman—although she sacrificed most of her feminine qualities to be one. True to form, reviewers were quick to point out that Montgomery was good-natured enough to give her full sway:

> Montgomery is a meek and capable feeder, who might be a star by himself, if he did not indulge Miss Moore in having her exuberant way and capturing the laughs hands down.[153]

Florence Moore's stage work was backhandedly praised as "boyish romp," and just as with Mae Melville, reviewers excused her femaleness by distinguishing her from the rest of her sex in the business:

> Unlike so many eccentric comediennes, for whom eccentricity is a last resort and a charitable cloak, Florence Moore is real in her talent, her charming personality, her satire, her wit and her "faces."[154]

But by the end of the decade, many female partners were providing the comedy end of the act, with their mates playing straight. Mabel Hite— "funny all the way"—was famous for her eccentric clowning skill, and her baseball-player husband Mike Donlin, having no acting experience, naturally played straight.[155] One of the "snappiest" new acts in vaudeville was male-female team Innes and Ryan. Comedienne Maud Ryan's fast talk was a sensation: "Too fast for anyone from Chicago, and as fast as the speediest from Gotham." Her winning quality was that, fast as she could work,

Maud Ryan's talk was never labored; she spouted her lines so effortlessly they seemed to fall spontaneously from her lips.[156]

Even though Maud Ryan's talent for ad-lib gagging was extraordinary, *Variety* emphasized that it should not go unnoticed how hard her male partner worked to put her over: "Innes just naturally opens up all the little opportunities for Miss Ryan, knowing full well she can handle them right." Likewise, *Variety* thought comediennes Miss Douglas and Miss Dunlop needed their talented straight men to bring out their comedy ability.[157] Such observations were undoubtedly true; cross-fire talk and ad-libbing demanded skill from both comic and feeder. But whereas the efforts of female feeders had gone virtually unpraised for decades, when men had upgraded the role its importance was truly realized.

On the other hand, when a female partner's clowning became too funny, praise was grudging. The woman of Deane and Sibley was acknowledged to be a good comedienne—"she slangs him this way and she slangs him that"—but she was criticized because her "talk is much too rough for any girl to use." Although Miss Douglas handled the comedy work "exceedingly well," her praise was qualified: "She gets every word and bit of facial expression over, and that's saying a lot for a vaudeville woman nowadays."[158]

A female partner apparently had to work harder to win notice. Isabelle D'Armand certainly did her part to entertain in her act with Frank Carter: "Miss D'Armand is a gingery mite of femininity, skipping about the stage one minute, singing the next, dancing about the graceful Carter, exchanging repartee with him, playing the piano, and flitting off for another change." Even so, partner Frank Carter got more praise than the typical female dancer-assistant—he could hold up any partner with his dancing, exclaimed *Variety*. As for Miss D'Armand, after all her exertions, she was told that "it doesn't matter so much what the little lady does on the stage but she is good to look upon in her becoming costume...."[159] Most discussion of female talent was blatantly sexist, but the important development to note is that such talent was now found in increasing abundance.

In addition to being challenging models for the women in the audience, wisecracking comediennes like Florence Moore and sexual, glamorous women like Valeska Suratt, with their talent and self-possession, mirrored the emergence of a new generation of women. Mabel Hite's humor was said to be "that of the New York woman, keen, alert, and ready."[160] By expanding their roles onstage, vaudeville actresses were doing what tens of thousands of women were also doing offstage; in the real world, women were achieving significant legal and social gains.

One measure of the amount of change in the air was the sudden surge of activity in the suffrage movement. The first signs of new energy in the suffrage movement came in New York City. In January 1907 a group of

New York women, despairing of the personal friction and inactivity of the National American Woman Suffrage Association, formed a new organization designed for dramatic campaigning, The Equality League of Self-Supporting Women. One month later they were lobbying in Albany at the annual legislative hearing for a bill on woman's suffrage and presenting working-class women as witnesses, whose poignant testimony gave jaded legislators a jolt. Within months the League's increasing membership was holding open-air meetings (the first on behalf of suffrage in thirty years) and campaigning actively against political officials opposed to suffrage; in 1910 they initiated the first of many suffrage parades down Fifth Avenue.[161]

By 1910 the N.A.W.S.A. had followed suit and had functioning headquarters in New York City, and their membership was also growing. Informed estimates of the day had put N.A.W.S.A. membership at about 13,150 members in 1893, with an increase up to only 17,000 in 1905; the enrollment suddenly jumped to 45,500 in 1907 and to over 75,000 in 1910.[162] On 9 November 1910, suffrage workers across the nation were galvanized by the news that Washington State had broken a fourteen-year deadlock by granting women the vote by a majority of two-to-one. The next year the biggest suffrage campaign ever waged swung into gear in California, with the result that the woman suffrage referendum in yet another state was won. These conspicuous successes inspired a frenzied revival of campaign activity.[163]

Quick to make use of well-publicized but less than popular political matters, vaudeville comedians were having a field day with suffrage material. John and Mae Burke's act took place in front of an armory, headquarters of a suffragette army; the act was smart cross-fire between his messenger-boy role and her heroic suffragette soldier in tights, doublet and feathered hat. The Nobles followed "Why Walker Reformed" with a sequel called "Why Walker Rebelled": Walker's cause for rebellion is his new topsy-turvy household arrangements; he is forced to do the woman's work, because his wife has become addicted to her suffragette club. In a reversal of the old intemperance theme, Walker gets his wife soused and ends by convincing *her* to "reform."[164]

But although the "suffragette" provided lots of laughs, a segment of the population was getting more accustomed to her. The growing support of women of all classes was visible in the suffrage parades that became a regular sight in New York. From an attitude of hostility or ridicule, onlookers were coming to show friendly interest, even respect, as this out-of-town newspaperman noted:

> Women who usually see Fifth Avenue through the polished windows of their limousines and touring cars strode steadily side by side with pale-faced thin-bodied girls from the sweltering sweat shops of the East Side....All along Fifth Avenue from Washington

Square, where the parade formed, to 57th Street, where it disbanded, were gathered thousands of men and women of New York. They blocked every cross street on the line of march. Many were inclined to laugh and jeer, but none did. The sight of the impressive column of women striding five abreast up the middle of the street stifled all thought of ridicule. They were typical, womanly American women...women doctors, women lawyers, splendid in their array of academic robes; women architects, women artists, actresses and sculptors; women waitresses, domestics; a huge division of industrial workers...all marched with an intensity and purpose that astonished the crowds that lined the streets.[165]

One explanation of the growing support for woman's suffrage was that suffragists had changed their tone; they were starting to argue "woman's duty" instead of "woman's rights." Suffragists were now politically agreeing that woman's place was in the home and it was her duty to preserve it—by voting. With the vote she could perform needed domestic duties in the community—the care and protection of children, the regulation of health and morals—that were best done by women.[166] Already introduced to social activity in the club, the upper-middle-class woman fell right into the suffragists' hands.

At the same time, suffragists were beginning to identify themselves and their cause with working women. The dramatic 1909 Strike of the New York Shirtwaist Makers attracted new sympathy for working women, and suffragists rallied to the workers' cause. The growing understanding between comfortable women and working women reached a high point on the occasion of the notorious Triangle Fire, on 25 March 1911, which took the lives of one hundred forty-six women. Now the suffragists were embracing a wider goal, the full development of women's potential and the creation of a more just social order. Suffragists began speaking on street corners in working-class neighborhoods and distributing leaflets in foreign languages; by the teens ethnic and working women were joining suffrage organizations in great numbers.[167] With support for the movement growing from above and below, those women in between could not help having their consciousness raised on the issue of woman's rights.

But the upshot was that middle-class women were simply changing in spite of themselves. Even if a shop girl wanted only a husband, a home, and freedom from work, she made the nineteenth-century definition of womanly nature obsolete just by working. The job in office or department store took the woman out of the home, made her less dependent on a man, made her an important contributor to the family income. Under such circumstances it was patently senseless for a man to be defined as her protector and provider. The comical hit song which went

> Mother takes in washing, so does Sister Ann,
> Everybody works at our house but my old man[168]

had economic and social pointedness; wives' and daughters' paychecks changed their relation to bread-winning fathers.

Similarly, even though the proper middle-class reformer might desire only to improve the lives of children, to preserve the home, and to protect women, in effect she was enlarging her traditional role. Besides, she was reforming a man-made society, and the implication was that the stronger sex was not doing a very good job. Even those genteel diehards most dedicated to nineteenth-century expectations were often finding it difficult to be "feminine." The rising cost of living and the decline in cheap immigrant labor was making the servant girl increasingly unavailable to all but the upper-class rich, and the middle-class woman's forty hours of housework made it impossible for her to maintain the life of the lady the etiquette books described to her.[169]

By the teens the Victorian lady was a dying breed, and even the masses must have sensed her demise. At any rate, in vaudeville, the old comic situations involving a man and a woman were becoming outdated. "Three months married and hubby home late" furnished the comedy in a 1910 sketch by Lauder and Mortland, and *Variety* complained because "the several ingredients of jealousy, suspicion, misunderstanding, and threatened separation...are approached from no particularly new angle." A few weeks later Miller and Atwood played out "the familiar wrangle between husband and wife," with the comedy furnished by "the hackneyed device of a drunk husband who returns home," and the resulting "commonplace puns." Likewise, Gordon and Warren's domestic quarrel was panned as "small-time," and Walters and Franks' row was "along the lines as old as variety itself."[170]

Part of the disenchantment was the urban audience's growing demand for novelty. But clearly the old depictions were obsolete now, and by the end of the first decade of the 1900s, most new big-time sketches featuring male-female relations had lost the farcical tone. Lockney and Fletcher's "lady burglar" sketch is typical of the new mood. The sketch opened with the woman discovered burglarizing a man's apartment; a luncheon is spread to which she helps herself, and when she is discovered by the man, she talks to him brazenly and picks his pocket. He calls the janitor, and instructs him to summon the police, but she points out that with his wife away in the country, it will be a compromising situation for a woman to be arrested in his apartment at night. She tells the janitor to call her a taxi,

> and so saying, with the satchel full of plunder, the man's watch and a big roll of bills which she has extracted from his clothes, she goes out with the janitor. The man flops into a chair to say the tag: "Don't that beat hell?"[171]

Perhaps the tag-line summed up more than one spectator's feelings about the way some women were acting.

The old stereotypes were still seen, of course; in November 1908 Winona Winters entertained audiences as "The Little 'Cheer Up Girl'," making a delightful picture in pink, with youthful looks and a girlish manner. But a few weeks later New York City vaudeville audiences watched the actress Patrice portray a female lobbyist, who, intent on securing the passage of a railroad bill through Congress, manipulates a young Congressman. When he denounces her she faints in his arms, a picture is snapped of them, and she threatens him with blackmail to obtain her ends. *Variety* thought that "the character of the woman, and the methods employed by her to secure her ends are not at all pretty and are not just what we like to connect women with."[172]

By 1910, the woman with professional aspirations, a jesting matter in earlier years, was treated with deadly seriousness in an act called "Sincerity." The well-known S. Miller Kent played Hal Thomas, a Wall Street stock broker, with Miss Ray Beveridge appearing as his wife, Sincerity, with a female assistant in a maid role. The time is three in the morning, and the couple have just returned from the premiere of a play written by the wife. Although her play is bad, the wife is blinded by thoughts of success, and forces her tired and unwilling husband to rehearse her in a newspaper interview. Finally the papers arrive; they are uniformly damning:

> Then the husband tells her that he knew she was self centered and artificial and that he had payed [sic] the expenses of the show to teach her a lesson, knowing well that it could never make good. A phone call from the manager tells her that the show is closed. She sees the truth.[173]

According to *Variety* the act was "well liked," a hint that at least a portion of the audience was resentful of these women trying on new roles.

But not everyone. In September 1912 some real suffragists were tolerably received at Hammerstein's Victoria. Willie Hammerstein, always eager to capitalize on the sensation of the day, allowed the women to appear at each performance for a week and tell about their cause and troubles. They may not have had many active followers, but they apparently did not arouse any hostility. The *New York Dramatic Mirror* thought "they came out a lot better than had been expected," and

> Inez Miholland made such an unqualified hit by her beauty alone that no man in the house would have dared vote otherwise than as she wished.[174]

A feminist may have considered this kind of support of dubious worth; nonetheless, one senses a new note.

In fact, by 1912, suffragette sketches with more ambiguous rhetoric were occasionally seen in vaudeville. Vedder and Morgan, for example, in a straight dramatic sketch, portrayed a young millionaire mill-owner and a suffragette; by making him believe that he ran over a pedestrian and she witnessed it, she tricks him into calling off an impending strike.[175] The team's intentions are ambiguous; neither character is wholly sympathetic. There is a hint they were playing to both sides of the question. That such an approach might be rewarding is indicated in a *Variety* review of an act by Carter and Waters in the spring of 1912. The woman entered in a travestied suffragette costume—"gaining laughs by itself"—and delivered a suffragism monologue, lambasting men to a frazzle. The man walks across the stage behind her with a baby carriage, and stops to give some suffrage talk of his own. The finale was a duet "vaudeville song." The reviewer thought the non-suffragette finish weakened the act and should be dropped; his advice was:

> The couple after doing their singles could join for a hot "suffragette" debate between them, trying to work the house through the sexes in front. To hear a woman pan men as this one does is really funny, and it catches the sympathy of the women auditors while it amuses the other gender.[176]

By 1912, some of the women in a typical vaudeville audience could be sympathetic, at least to a degree, with the notion of suffrage. In fact, films, which drew upon the same audience, were also beginning to ridicule Victorian views of women. In *Down With Women* in 1907, for example, a well-dressed man condemns woman's suffrage because the weaker sex is incompetent. He leaves the meeting, and meets a woman selling bread, a woman sweeping the road, a female musician playing for children, others driving cabs and trucks. A woman saves his life, and when he is arrested a female lawyer defends him in court. Beginning in 1912, popular serials such as *The Perils of Pauline*, *The Hazards of Helen*, and *Dolly of the Dailies* featured working girls as heroines who were robust, adventuresome, and self-reliant.[177]

Indeed, it was the growing sympathy of women—and men—for the suffrage movement and for a more free female behavior that made the more conservative segments of the population, especially men, so outraged. The above *Variety* reviewer hints of a schism in sympathy between men and women; this difference could explode into violence on occasion. In Washington, D.C. in 1913, for example, a group of suffragists led by militant Alice Paul were insulted and physically threatened by angry men. As one male observer had warned a few years earlier, if women insisted on usurping male rights, "sex antagonism would be substituted for gallantry," and men would put down women's opposition with brute force.[178]

Whether or not the middle-class man or woman consciously acknowledged that the male-female relation was showing new signs of strain, by the end of the decade physical antagonism between the sexes certainly had box-office potential. The sensation of several seasons was a violent male-female stage clash, the "Apache" dance. The dance had begun in Paris; it was introduced to New York audiences by Gould and Suratt upon their return from a European tour in 1908. After five other song and dance numbers, they unveiled the Apache for the finale. The dance described in "forceful pantomime" the jealous fury of a thug as he dances with his paramour, whom he suspects of faithlessness: "The two dance a slow waltz step with faces close together, and from time to time the man strikes the terrified woman or strangles her without interrupting the dance."[179]

Within days of the Gould and Suratt performance, William Rock and Maude Fulton unveiled their more elaborate version of the Apache. The set was an elaborate cabaret-celler scene, filled with extras as Parisian desperadoes and their female companions. Rock entered in the role of a pimp in search of his woman; Miss Fulton played the prostitute, who goes immediately to her master and gives him money. He orders drinks, and though she does not want to drink, he forces her. They quarrel, and then the dance begins, "a particularly brutal performance in its thinly veiled significance"; at its end, he throws her aside and approaches another woman. The rejected woman creeps up behind him, plunges a knife in his shoulders, and staggers out.[180]

Some reviewers insisted audiences were opposed to the new dance; according to *Variety*, "American vaudeville audiences, to their credit, do not care to see a woman ill-treated, even though it be for 'art's sake.'"[181] But unpleasant as it was claimed to be, it could not be denied that the Gould and Suratt act "scored tremendously," and that "the audience was impressed" with the Rock and Fulton exhibition.[182]

By the spring of 1909, a male-female dance team straight from the Paris cabarets arrived in New York, Molasso and Corio, with "L'Amour de l'Apache." Their act had an imposing realistic set, "only exceeded in realism by the first act of 'Salvation Nell,' the most licentious dramatization ever flaunted before a civilized community." *Variety*'s reviewer claimed that

> vaudeville doesn't care for this phase of lower life. Although some of us know that some things are, we don't care to have illustrated before us a woman who removes money from her stocking upon demand, passing it over to her financial director, and though we may know of this, there are others who do not and need not be educated.[183]

Ironically, the reviewer himself revealed that audiences were able to assimilate such shocks; this Apache dance isn't going to set New York afire, he sneered, for its only interest is its elaborate set, since New Yorkers are already used to the tough aspect. And, in fact, in July, French and Eis's

"Vampire Dance" would make the Apache look "lamblike."[184] Audiences could plainly become inured to violence.

Done by big-name personalities in exotic costumes against an elaborate set, the male-female Apache number, with its risqué dance movements and its sophisticated, cynical treatment of relations between the sexes, was representative of the new atmosphere which had evolved in vaudeville—and in society—by the teens. New York's elite were beginning to flaunt their wealth and their disregard for an older generation's values. In lavishly furnished cabarets and nightclubs like Jesse Lasky's Folies Bergère, the "Best People" were dancing uninhibited new dances with primitive names like the "Turkey Trot" to "hot" new music played by black musicians. Mingling with the men, who had always had a sporting life, were unchaperoned women of respectable backgrounds, now seen smoking and drinking, and showing their ankles and curves in dresses like those formerly worn only by loose women.[185]

Some of these same people were slumming and taking in vaudeville shows, and vaudevillians were attracting a cult following among the rich, who "took them up" as the darlings of the moment.[186] Indeed, the elite were embracing some of the same values the immigrants had brought from Europe—their love of festival, of drink and dance, their acknowledgment of sexual pleasures.[187] Whoever was aping whom, people in the middle class, either because they were licensed by society leaders, or because they now felt secure enough in their identity to pursue true values merely obscured by genteel affectation before, were also shedding the Victorian norms of turn-of-the-century cultual leaders.

By 1910 the respectable middle class seemed caught up in a whirl of pleasure-seeking. Not prudence and self-restraint, but getting and spending, success and pleasure, seemed to preoccupy the masses. Consumer spending had created new mass industries: the advertising of goods was a million-dollar industry; huge department stores were warehouses of luxuries; and a man named Henry Ford had discovered the notion of mass-producing goods. Even recreations such as baseball and vaudeville had become big business.

Just as baseball officials had devised new rules to speed up the moments of spectacular action in the game, and had introduced protective equipment so players could safely make the rough and exciting plays audiences demanded,[188] so vaudeville's aim was to be action-packed and novel. The polite turn-of-the-century acts with their pathos and prettiness had been outdated by the glitter, the costliness, the fast pace and cleverness of "big-time vaudeville." The expectations of critics and audiences were high: a classy appearance and lavish accoutrements, a fresh, dynamic routine with a flippant delivery, and an irresistible personality marked the headliner. The most successful act had to be "live wire" material, with "every line hitting the high water mark," an act that "even the most blasé of vaudeville goers will laugh at...." Even a good vaudeville bill would be criticized if it didn't have enough of the "ringing lively stuff"; a bill was praised when "thrills, novelty and class were evident at all times."[189] Vaudeville audiences seemingly sought a new sort of jolt than before.

The desire to be jolted explains the sudden popularity of shocking routines such as the Apache dance, with its decadent blend of glamour and violence. Soon even its novelty would fade. Eventually the desire for ever greater "thrills," ever more spectacular shows, was to take its toll on vaudeville. But in the early 1910s there was no sign of this as yet. There were more talented and experienced male-female teams on the boards than ever before in vaudeville; there was an ample supply of both male and female comics, and utilizing their special brand of humor, they had evolved fast, funny routines which required a new sort of teamwork. There was a new breed of team, who were true partners, thus twice as talented as their predecessors. These teams could be seen at the fabulous Palace.

6
The Standard Male-Female Teams, 1912–1925

By the teens there were more than one thousand theatres playing standard vaudeville acts and four thousand small-time theatres, and the circuits were still growing. George Burns marvelled that a vaudevillian could spend two or three years on the road before playing again at the same theatre.[1] Of these theatres, about eighty were large, prestigious houses playing star attractions to an urbane audience; this was the "big time." Each big city had one or more big-time houses known for luxuriousness and high-priced attractions: there were the Prospect and the Orpheum in Brooklyn, the Majestic and the Palace in Chicago, and the Keith houses in Philadelphia, Boston, Washington, Detroit, and other big cities. The opening of the Riverside Theatre in 1916 brought the number of big-time houses in Manhattan alone up to five.[2] Making the big time was what every vaudevillian lived for: "a full route sheet, play-or-pay contracts, good orchestras, able stagehands, good hotels, decent food, comfortable rooms, and playing the Big Time to reserved seats and maybe ending up at the Palace...."[3]

"Maybe ending up at the Palace"—the New York Palace at Broadway and 47th was the "Mecca," the "Taj Mahal of vaudeville," "the seventh Heaven of the vaudevillian's dream." To the American vaudevillian, playing the Palace was what a command performance was to the British actor, explained Sophie Tucker; it was "something to live for. Something to boast about all the rest of your days."[4] Perhaps Jack Haley best described the thrill of playing the Palace:

> Only a vaudevillian who has trodden its stage can really tell you about it. Audiences can tell you who they saw there and how they enjoyed them, but only a performer can describe the anxieties, the joys, the anticipation, and the exultation of a week's engagement at the Palace. The walk through the iron gate on 47th Street, through the courtyard to the stage door was the cum laude walk to a show-business diploma. A feeling of ecstasy came with the knowledge that *this is the Palace,* the epitome of the more than

15,000 vaudeville theatres in America, and the realization that you have been selected to play it. Of all the thousands upon thousands of vaudeville performers in the business, you are there. This was a dream fulfilled; this was the pinnacle of variety success.[5]

Ironically, the Palace's first bill on 24 March 1913 was a flop. *Variety*'s notice was "a delighted funeral oration," attacking everything and everybody involved under the headline, "PALACE $2 VAUDEVILLE A JOKE." The bill cost about $7000 to assemble, and the week's gross box office receipts came to only $4000.[6] But on 5 May 1913 history was made when for the unheard-of sum of $1000 a day, Sarah Bernhardt made her first appearance in New York City vaudeville, at the Palace. Prices were raised for her engagement, but people gladly paid to see the First Lady of the Theatre. She remained for four weeks; the third week the theatre grossed $27,000.[7] The magic name of Bernhardt gave the Palace an edge over its competitors that it never lost. The Bernhardt engagement showed the management that paying exorbitant salaries to secure stars was the solution; the roster for the second season at the Palace contained names like Fritzi Scheff, Joe Jackson, Nora Bayes, Nance O'Neill, Marie Lloyd, Ethel Levey, Bert Williams, Cissie Loftus, Vernon and Irene Castle, Maggie Cline, Sam Bernard, Trixie Firganza, Fanny Brice, Eddie Foy, the Avon Comedy Four, and Anna Held.[8] Thanks to bills top-heavy with talent, the Palace opened its third season playing to "turnaway business." By 1916, there were so many starry-eyed actors hanging around the Palace marquee that the police had to hand out summonses for obstructing the traffic.[9]

The Palace set a precedent for class that was emulated by the other major houses. In the teens and early twenties the "big time" was synonymous with glamorous, star-studded, sure-fire entertainment. Prices rose and larger theatres were built, but big-time vaudeville houses were usually filled, standing space as well as seats.[10] On a typical evening in 1917 at the Royal Theatre, patrons had to fight to get to the door; to observers it looked as if everyone in the Bronx was trying to get in. Scalpers did a profitable business out on the sidewalk before the best houses, and could always be found down the block from the Palace, selling the $2.50 tickets for at least $3.85, sometimes for as much as $10.[11]

The most sophisticated vaudeville audience was the audience at the Palace; the Palace had what Jack Haley labelled a "hip" audience, full of gamblers, professional theatre people, and of course Manhattan's tourists. Audiences at all the big-time houses were "smart"—people who because of money or lifestyle had "know-how" about the ways of the city and about vaudeville. Performer Will Ahern described Boston, New York and Chicago audiences as "show-wise," and whether or not they were well-off they looked it; the audience at the Riverside suggested a grand opera affair. Bigtime vaudeville was an "event," reminisced George Burns, to which dinner dress was worn. A big-time audience was a bustling, demanding, diverse urban crowd, like the one at the Hippodrome, when it opened as a vaudeville theatre in 1923, and "stars of the social world rubbed elbows with stars of the stage, the underworld and the overworld and all the rest of one of New York City's great cosmopolitan gatherings...."[12]

In the teens almost everyone went to a vaudeville house at one time or another. Even "society," although they did not consistently patronize vaudeville, sometimes came for special performers. When Ruth St. Denis appeared at the Palace in 1916, more than one-half of the audience were people who seldom attended vaudeville, and the street beside the Palace was jammed with Rolls Royces when Lady Duff Gordon did her fashion show act to aid war-destroyed villages in France. Woodrow Wilson had a box reserved for him every Thursday night at the Keith's in Washington, D.C.[13] Lower-class people saw small-time vaudeville in the neighborhood houses—often a certain ethnic group predominated at a "pop" house—and sometimes on the big time. One-time *Variety* reporter Bill Smith recalled being very poor when growing up in the teens, yet attending the local small-time house regularly, occasionally saving 25¢ to attend a big-time house.[14]

It took in both ends of the social ladder, but the majority of vaudeville's audience was the huge middle class, uncultured but quick-witted, prosperous and self-confident—just plain folks. Mae West described a week's audience out on the road in a typical American town as including everyone from the top society crowd to family groups and fraternal organizations, to working-class people and of course children, especially on Friday nights. A typical audience at the Riverside Theatre, observed a *Variety* reporter, was the " 'better class' of prosperous 'family audience' "—most of whom have their own autos and are fancily dressed. But they were only good to look at until they talked, he complained:

> Monday evening one, accompanied by her husband and her mother, wearing a fur coat that represents an ordinary working man's salary for two years, remarked to mamma: "Ain't it nice to come to a crowded house and meet everybody!"

But refined or not, admitted the reporter, they are appreciative, know their favorite artists, and are not hesitant to express approval.[15]

These audiences had ample opportunity to learn the potential of the vaudeville art. There were probably over twenty thousand vaudeville acts, and given the array of talent to choose from, the big-time bookers could with little effort assemble impressive, talent-laden bills. Jack Haley pointed out that with eight acts usually on the Palace bill a week, fifty-two weeks a year, only about 416 of the thousands of acts available could play there, even fewer in reality, since most stars returned within the year.[16] The Palace was not being terribly presumptuous when it added the following warning to its program in 1914:

> Note: — The position which an act is alloted [sic] on the program does not in the least affect its merit. When a bill is made up almost of headliners — a state of affairs not unusual at the Palace — every number is frequently worthy of the "star spot" on ordinary vaudeville bills....[17]

During the teens, with vaudeville at its zenith, at any big-time house audiences could see half-a-dozen famous performers in a single evening. It was routine for reviews to dub a big-time bill a hit from start to finish, especially Palace bills: "One of the greatest vaudeville shows that has ever been assembled on any stage"; "Hits followed each other like beads on a string...": this was typical praise.[18]

The talent of the performer who finally reached the big time was no accident. His polish was the result of years of practice, experimentation, and seeking the perfect act. Jack Haley tells that every performer began with the small-time:

> That's where you learned your craft, and then you were selected to play the big time. What made vaudeville so wonderful was the freedom, the tremendous freedom. You could do whatever you wanted onstage, as long as it was in good taste. Managers would never bother you. They weren't creators, they were producers. You received immediate appraisal of any new creation you might think of. You'd get a funny idea and you tried it out. If it was any good, got audience approval, you kept it in. If not, you threw it out. Consequently, a perfection was attained because you could polish a bit, keep it smooth and make it part of your act. The field of artistic development was in vaudeville. It was probably the most ideal life for an entertainer.[19]

As critic Gilbert Seldes observed, the materials may have been trivial, but the treatment was accurate to a hair's breadth.[20]

When all went as intended, the pace of the entire bill was a masterpiece of timing. The ideal vaudeville show was intended not only to give an audience a taste of every variety of entertainment, but a sense of building excitement which culminated with the appearance of the headlined act — ideally a wallop of talent that sent the audience home with a feeling of complete satisfaction, content that its money and time had been well spent. Absolute precision in creating mounting expectation and climax underlay the successful working of the vaudeville format, with the two essential elements speed and comedy. The first was necessary to generate the accelerating tension, and the unrestrained hilarity created by the comedian was the punch that left the audience properly spent at the show's end. The successful vaudeville show was not a mere aggregation of entertainments, but a perfectly-timed, unified whole; a 1916 Colonial bill reviewed as "a well diversified program, running along like an oiled machine," was considered an excellent show.[21]

Between 1914 and 1925, a time when excellent shows were commonplace, there were around two hundred "standard" male-female teams—teams who got regular bookings in big-time theatres and big welcomes from fans—and over six hundred different male-female teams appeared at the top five or six New York City vaudeville houses. Since this number represents only a sample, the total number of male-female teams may have represented from one-tenth to one-twentieth of the total number of acts. This much is certain: the typical vaudeville bill, indeed, most vaudeville bills, featured at least one male-female team.[22]

Ultimately, the special appeal of the male-female act was the sexual interaction. There was a certain dynamic present when a sentimental hit tune, a comical quarrel, or a sensual modern dance number was performed by a man and a woman, which was lacking when it was presented by either a single or a team of two men or two women. But it is a testimony to the versatility and talent of male-female teams that all the components of a typical bill *could* have been supplied by male-female teams—though of course there would never have been an entire bill of mixed acts. Only a handful of male-female teams show up on the "ideal" bills often made up by vaudeville-lovers, and compiled as they are from so vast a pool of talent, perhaps it is not surprising. But surely a star bill of male-female teams would not leave its audiences wanting, and the surviving bills provide proof that male-female teams routinely and ably filled every spot in vaudeville, from the innocuous opening position to the comedy-punch of the next-to-last position.

Many mixed teams performed the obligatory "dumb" acts necessary to open and close a show. As Palace booker George Gottlieb explained, the opening and closing acts had to be silent numbers such as animal or dance acts, whose good impression would not be ruined by late arrivals seeking seats or patrons hurrying off at the evening's end. Ideally the closing act was also a big "flash": "Whatever the act is, it must be a showy act," said Gottlieb, "for it closes the performance and sends the audience home pleased with the program to the very last minute."[23] During the teens and early twenties, big-time audiences were accustomed to seeing bills opened and closed by such novelty two-acts as the Brightons, "artistic rag pickers," who "built" attractive landscape views, profiles, and animal pictures from a collection of innocent-looking rags; Gordon and Rica, Rose and Dell, and Mortimer and Clegg, with their trick bike riding; Mr. and Mrs. Loyal's Canine Novelty; Will and Gladys Ahern's lasso tricks and dancing;

LaHoen and Dupree's sharpshooting act; Arnold and Miss Florence, who balanced on bottles; aerialists Lohse and Sterling (Joe Laurie thought they were great) and Togan and Geneva on the tightwire; and the many male-female juggling and acrobatic acts.[24]

One of the most glamorous dumb acts was the roller skating team of Reynolds and Donegan. Both were proven champions offstage: Earl Reynolds had won the 1895, 1896, and 1897 National Speed Ice Skating Championships; Nellie Donegan boasted of being the Ice and Roller Skating Champion of England and Australia in 1904. Reynolds won public attention in 1906 when he was featured in a roller skating scene with Anna Held in *The Parisian Model,* so when Reynolds appeared in vaudeville teamed with his wife in 1908, they were a success from the beginning.[25]

The two were not mere roller skaters, but did dances on their skates. In their first act, Nellie Donegan did a buck and wing dance to the tune of "Happy Days," and played "The Merry Widow" waltz on the banjo while swiftly spinning on her toes; in a later act they did the twists and glides of the popular Apache dance. The *Mirror* claimed they did every dance step possible and impossible on their roller skates, that they were equally "skaters who dance, or dancers who skate."[26] It was said that the most famous dancers might well envy their skill and grace, and acrobats had cause for envy too. Singly and in tandem they performed tricks on wheels, which according to "Sime," one would never dream could be accomplished.[27]

Their fame certainly eclipsed that of the average "dumb" act. In 1909 Reynolds and Donegan were credited with responsibility for a roller skating craze which had swept the United States and Europe. Then, when indoor ice-skating became the rage, they gave lessons to New York's "400," including Mrs. Clarence McKay, Miss Helen Gould, the Vanderbilts, Astors, and Ogden-Millses. Not every vaudeville team achieved their international success; "E. Reynolds and His Wife Rouse Berlin," proclaimed one headline, and in 1916 they gave a command exhibition before the King and Queen of England.[28]

Reynolds and Donegan were an ideal act for closing a vaudeville show as well as opening it, for their dazzling maneuvers and fancy costumes provided the kind of "flash" booker George Gottlieb described for the closing act. Extant pictures show Nellie Donegan in showy costumes trimmed with beads, ribbons, jewels and fur. She wore $10,000 worth of costumes in their 1916 act, with each gown designed by her husband to maintain her reputation as one of the most gorgeous dressers on the stage.[29]

If a bill were opened by a flashy full-stage act like Reynolds and Donegan, an act in "one" was convenient for the number two position on the bill. Now an act was needed to settle the audience and prepare it for the show, and a man-woman song and dance act was a frequent choice for this spot.[30] After witnessing a display of some skill such as skating or wirewalking, it was time for an introduction to the pleasures of song and dance, two of the most important components of a vaudeville bill.[31] There were dozens of mixed song and dance teams in mature vaudeville; Joe Laurie, Jr. believed it "represented real vaude more than any other kind of an act."[32] Kalmar and Brown, Millership and Gerard, Sully and Houghton, Morton and Glass, McKay and Ardine, Cross and Josephine, Nesbit and Clifford, Gould and Ashlyn, Clark and Bergman, Norton and Lee, Donahue and Stewart, John and Winnie Hennings, Stone and Kalisz, Miller and Bradford, Tracey and McBride, Mason and Cole, Cantwell and Walker, Dooley and Rugel, Bronson and Baldwin, and Cartmel and Harris were all standard song and dance teams on the big-time circuit.

It was probably the most popular choice of act for a team, because it was a versatile form offering two performers a wide scope for displaying their abilities. Each big-time song and dance team somehow differed from every other song and dance team. Some did a pure song and dance routine, while others did an almost equal share of talking, and some acts were virtually miniature musical comedies. Many teams performed their skills straight, and others did comic singing and dancing; in some acts each partner was an outstanding singer and dancer, while in others, one partner handled the bulk of the dancing, the other the singing. The point was to have a fast-moving, varied act which could be done in "one" in ten to fifteen minutes.[33]

A classic song and dance team was Rooney and Bent, one of the best-loved teams in vaudeville. Son of the famed variety hall comic Pat Rooney I, Pat II had gone on the stage as a young child after the death of his father, in a song and dance act with his sister Mattie. Their debut was sometime around June 1889, at Tony Pastor's, and their act was appropriately called "Two Chips Off the Old Block."[34] Beginning around 1898, Pat appeared in vaudeville (uneventfully) with Emma Francis, his dance partner in several musical shows at the time.[35] Soon after marrying Marion Bent in the summer of 1904, Rooney learned Emma Francis was leaving the act, which was booked on the Orpheum circuit that fall. Rooney sheepishly went to Martin Beck to explain, who shrugged unconcernedly: "Vell, you've got a vife, ain't it? Vy you don't put her in your act?" "My wife isn't a dancer, Mr. Beck," objected Rooney; "Dots all right, take her and put a little talk in the act," said Beck, disarming Rooney's buts with the rejoinder, "I don't book for da talk, I book you for da feet, und dey are always da same!"[36]

Many teams were overnight successes, but Rooney and Bent's career is a reminder that most stars were the product of years of hard work. Their first act was called "The Busy Bellboy"; Marion contributed a song or two, "without being a singer of note," and although Pat attempted some jokes, it was noted that "Rooney is a dancer, not a comedian."[37] In 1909 they had a new act called "At the Stand," done in "two" before a newsstand set; Rooney was a news dealer, Marion Bent an actress. The entire front page of the *New York Times* was pasted upon the stage, and when Marion made her entrance shouting "Where is the boy who runs this stand?", Pat would break through the newspaper and say, "Pardon me, for being a little ahead of the 'times'." "Oh, papers from all cities. Have you the Squeedunk Star?" asked Marion; "Whay [sic] do you want with a Star, when you're a star yourself," replied Rooney. "I've seen you on the stage many times. I love the stage. I love the ballet girls and the way they dance." Pat would illustrate by doing a couple of ballet steps, and would fall on his face.[38] Marion next picked up a song book, a cue for a song by her, which developed into a duet with Pat and Marion taking alternate lines:

> You be my Ootsie,
> And I'll be your Tootsie,
> Your loving hugging boy;
> You be my Piggie,
> I'll be your Wiggie;
> Your Angel cake and joy.[39]

More dancing followed, with Marion thought to do better work in this sketch than before, and Rooney's "Yiddish hornpipe" was a hit. It ended with a sand dance by Rooney, who had the clever idea of doing it with a broom, with which he swept the stage during the encore.[40]

However old-fashioned it sounds to modern ears, the act was becoming more and more popular with vaudeville audiences; in 1912 Rooney and Bent moved from the three-a-day into the two-a-day.[41] By the teens Pat Rooney and Marion Bent were an established star turn with "Twenty Minutes with Pat and Marion." They performed before a drop of the exterior of a five-and-ten-cent store; Marion emerged from the store, dropped a bundle, and Pat appeared and picked it up; singing and dancing and snappy patter followed:

Marion: What are you doing?
Pat: Skating.
Marion: Well, what are you doing with three skates, when you only have two feet?
Pat: I'm not going to be on my feet all the time![42]

A second drop fell showing a ballroom interior, and they reappeared in evening clothes to do a succession of new-fangled ballroom dances.[43]

Rooney's inimitable dancing was still the featured attraction. He was "almost a synonymous term for dancing"—"a dapper little bundle of steel springs, constantly in motion, constantly graceful, constantly startling through the agile manner of his dancing." A Milwaukee newspaper declared that many of his steps were new to that city and thought "it is doubtful any other dancer could do them." Critics rarely tried to analyze his powers; "What's the use of talking about his dancing?" exclaimed *Variety;* "He's Pat Rooney; that's enough."[44] Though not Rooney's equal in talent, Marion Bent was an expert (thanks to years of experience) at accompanying her husband; it was claimed that "there were never two who more thoroughly understood each other or worked together more effectively." She was complimented for her comeliness, her beautiful coifs and dresses, and her magnetism, and was so popular that a hearty hand of applause always accompanied her stage-entrance.[45]

For in addition to Pat Rooney's amazing dancing ability, the couple had another quality that accounted for their stage following—an image of overwhelming likableness:

> They had the common touch. They were the family next door. You would no more miss the Rooneys than you would miss the St. Patrick's Day Parade. They had become part of the American tradition.[46]

The jokes were pure hokum, but they were wholesome; "The jokes my first wife, Marion Bent, and I used to tell were so clean a Congressman commented on it in the Congressional Record," boasted Rooney many years later. The team inspired unusual devotion in fans; when they appeared at the Alhambra after an absence of several years, they were greeted with "Welcome Home" signs and were presented with a loving cup. In 1925 Rooney and Bent were still one of the five top acts in vaudeville.[47]

In reality, Rooney and Bent, or any really popular song and dance two-act, usually escaped the number two position. It was still early in the evening then, and the audience was not totally settled yet; Fred Astaire called it "the lousy number-two spot on the bill."[48] A big draw like the Rooneys worked well for closing the first half of the show, in the number seven position on a nine act bill, even in the next-to-last spot. The beauty of the song and dance in "one" was that it was completely flexible, and could be juggled around according to the backstage requirements of the other acts.[49]

The number three position on the bill was one of the least flexible and invariably reserved for the sketch of the bill; it was even referred to as the "sketch position."[50] "With 'number three' position we count on waking up the audience," explained George Gottlieb, and ideally the number three sketch was "a playlet that wakens the interest and holds the audience every minute with a cumulative effect that comes to its laughter-climax at the 'curtain'...."[51] If a song and dance act were the second number, clearly an act emphasizing comedy situation and character-drawing was also a good variation to follow it. Some bills even had two sketches, and if that were the case, the second sketch was usually in the number seven position, thus creating a well-balanced bill.[52] It was increasingly rare for a bill to have two sketches, however.

The popularity of the sketch had declined since the turn of the century, when vaudeville audiences preferred entertainments modelled along legitimate theatre lines, and there had often been as many as three male-female sketches on a single bill. By the teens, with the mass audience's love of variety skills re-established, the sketch had become merely another kind of specialty. With only one spot on the bill regularly going to the sketch team, their numbers declined, and few new teams did sketches. In fact, a list of the most popular sketch teams in the teens is largely made up of already long-established teams: there were Mason and Keeler, McConnell and Simpson, Grapewin and Chance, the Barrys, the Ushers, the Connellys, Nicholson and Norton, Hyams and McIntyre, and Dolan and Lenhaar. With the exception of McConnell and Simpson and the Connellys, all these teams had begun their careers around the turn of the century; as a result most sketch teams continued in traditions established over ten years earlier.

For example, Dolan and Lenhaar had devised a "burglar" sketch in 1898 when the theme first became popular, and they continued to tour the circuits with a very similar sketch at least into the 1915-16 season. Likewise, Victor Moore and Emma Littlefield never replaced "Change Your Act, or Back to the Woods," a theatrical sketch using the time-worn device of "rehearsing" to exhibit song and dance, first offered by them in 1903. In 1911 *Variety* marvelled that the old sketch still "wears like steel" and 1924 found them performing the same sketch for the ten thousandth time.[53] Even teams who were blatantly outdated were still granted "routes" each season, apparently because there was so little competition for the sketch position. Hyams and McIntyre, teamed up since 1905, were still staging "The Quakeress" in 1914, a theatrical sketch they had debuted in 1908, even though it was criticized as old. At some point they acquired a sketch called "Maybloom," still on the boards in 1920, although described as one of those pleasant turns that one likes but never raves about.[54] After seventeen years as a sketch team, by 1916 the Barrys were deemed old, but showmanlike, and a 1920 reviewer noted that everyone knew by heart the lines in "The Rube,"; nonetheless, the Barrys could still be seen at the Palace in the 1925-26 season.[55]

The most successful teams tried to give old topics something of a new twist. Mason and Keeler's well-liked sketch, "Married," was one of the more successful redoings of tired commonplaces. The plot concerned a female amnesia patient who regains consciousness in the room of a hotel—thanks to a blow on the head by a burglar (played by an unbilled assistant), still hidden in the hotel room. She immediately calls her doctor, who tells her to rest in bed until he comes. Naturally the man staying in the room returns—extremely drunk, of course—finds the girl's clothes and throws them out the window, and then sees the girl in his bed. She awakens and screams, and the man, sobered by his predicament, concludes that they must be married. They try to determine how and when they got married, but neither can remember the past few days. At this point, the burglar comes out of hiding and tries to escape, and the young man catches him; simultaneously, a call from the doctor reveals the pair are not married, since both just disappeared from the same sanitorium. But the young couple are thoroughly in love by now, and when the burglar reveals he is really a kleptomaniac minister, they get married on the spot.[56] It was a clever combination of several of the old themes—burglars, romance, mistaken identity, and drunkenness, along with a variation on the old escaped lunatic theme.

After a full-stage sketch, the fourth position on the bill was ideal for more singing and dancing in "one." The number four spot was frequently filled by a mixed song and dance act considered too strong for the number two position.[57] It was a good position for any kind of musical turn, in fact, and a song and piano act fit well here. "Song and piano" teams were often composed of singing wives and piano-playing, song-writing husbands, with Connolly and Weinrich, and Mayhew and Taylor among the best-known. Dolly Connolly's voice was described as a "ragtime voice"; if she sang "Holy City" it would have come out a swing. She sang about five numbers in the act, with a change for each; while she changed, husband Percy Weinrich played a medley of the choruses of some of his famous songs, whose published versions had sold into the hundred thousands—"Moonlight Bay," "Silver Bells," and "Put on Your Old Grey Bonnet," among others.[58] Fat, jolly Stella Mayhew was best-known for her coon songs, with "Under the Chicken Tree" and "Way Down in Alabam'" two favorites in her repertoire. Her songs were "not the riotous, brazen coon-singing that addles and beats your brain into numbness—but soft, drum-like negro singing that carries a little note of melancholy in the lilt of its notes no matter how happy-hearted it is"; her songs were the type "that get right into your blood and sing there." But she was equally at home in any funny number, and the act also included funny chatter between songs. Husband Billy Taylor presided over the piano, served as straight in the talk, sang a number or two himself, and wrote all their songs.[59]

Then, in the number five position on a nine act bill, the first part of the bill most often ended with a good comedy act. By this point the audience was alert and ready to appreciate some rapid-fire wit, and the hilarity of good comedy would—it was hoped—leave the audience at just the right pitch, still buzzing about the jokes during intermission, excitedly anticipating the second part of the bill. Clearly the fifth act had to be a big name, a headliner, for it was the culmination of the first part of the show.

This spot was often filled with male-female teams, for by the teens there were many highly successful man and woman comedy-talking acts capable of providing a high moment of the bill, either here or in the next-to-last position. In this "ideal" bill, the talking acts will come on next-to-last, but representative of the kind of infectious humor that served well here or in the later spot were Brendel and Burt, and Williams and Wolfus—two man-woman teams distinctly different from their fellows: the appeal in these two acts was not funny dialogue so much as it was comic business; and both teams were throwbacks of a sort, for each was almot totally monopolized by the man.

El Brendel and Flo Burt's Swede act was the only important male-female dialect routine during the teens. Contrary to the common belief that El Brendel was a Swede, he was the Philadelphia-born son of a Bavarian and an Irish colleen; "I realized when I decided to go on the stage I must have a trademark," explained Brendel; "There were hundreds of Jewish comedians but few Swedish comics, so my wife and I did a specialty in which I played a Swede." Their debut was in 1913; before that, Brendel was a "shill" for Indian Jack, a purveyor of "snake oil" at tent shows, then a regular in Gus Edwards's playground sketches.[60]

In vaudeville Brendel played a "boob," fed in cross-fire by his wife Flo, who sang and cracked "nifties" herself, and they also did comedy dancing with difficult ankle work.[61] But the appeal of the act was Brendel's incomparable clowning. One well-known laugh-getter was their "kissing bit"—he hit his hat from the back as he was facing Flo, causing him to kiss her, whereupon he innocently looked back to see who had pushed him. Another gag featured Brendel's antics with one end of a string tied to his aching tooth and the other to a brick.[62] The funniest bit in the show, however, was when the Swede tried to save his vanishing wardrobe. Brendel performed the finale in a special evening suit, which fell apart before he could leave the stage. Brendel returned to take his bow holding a little screen before him, which fell apart. For the second bow, he came on in a bathrobe, which disintegrated; then he came on in a barrel, which collapsed. Finally Brendel came back onstage in the dark, with a lighted match to show his way to his quest, a small bottle of booze. In 1925, this famous finale was still furnishing the "howl" of the show at the Palace.[63]

The appeal of Williams and Wolfus's act was also sheer craziness. Born Herbert Schussler Billerbech, Herbert Williams wanted to be a concert pianist and was classically trained at the Philadelphia Conservatory of Music. He and his songstress wife started in vaudeville sometime around 1910 with a straight act, but soon became a comedy team. Legend has it that they were both gripped by stage fright at their debut, stumbled all over each other and the piano stool, and Herbert kept knocking his music off the piano. Their terror kept the audience in stitches, and as a result they got three months of bookings, for all the wrong reasons.[64]

They were a sight gag in themselves: near-sighted, bald and clumsy, wearing pince-nez spectacles, a wrinkled, ill-fitted evening suit, and huge yellow shoes on the wrong feet, Herb looked "like a country store keeper who has drifted into the theatre by mistake...." Skinny and flat-chested, Hilda hid her good looks with "the weirdest costume any human bean-pole ever brought onto the...stage."[65]

Herb comes out first. "Spot l-l-light," he shouts imperiously, and immediately the stage is plunged into darkness. A moment later Williams reappears onstage with a lighted candlestick, yelling in agonized tones, "Spot l-l-l-i-i-i-ght!" Eventually the footlights come on and he bows ceremoniously and adusts the piano stool, which is too low. When he climbs up on it, suddenly it whirls so high he cannot reach the keyboard; he climbs off and lowers it, but the minute he sits down it falls so low he still cannot reach the keys.[66]

In this manner, from foolishness to more foolishness, the act progressed. Piano keys stick, and a cat in the piano is the problem. Herbert gets thirsty, pulls a beer spigot out of the piano, and nonchalantly draws a stein of beer. Hilda sings and tries to do a recitation to the piano lamp, but is pulled offstage; Herbert plays the piano while standing on his head; in one version of the act, he fell on his knees, raptly listening to "those bells"—which always remained inaudible to anyone else.[67] An act of such unrestrained zaniness would not likely be forgotten during intermission, and would keep the audience charged with excitement, expectant and ready for more entertainment when the show resumed.

Nonetheless, opening the second half, spot number six on the nine act bill, was a difficult position, observed George Gottlieb: the first act after intermission "must not let down the carefully built-up tension of interest and yet it must not be stronger than the acts that are to follow." "Any sort of an act that makes a spendid start-off is chosen," explained Gottlieb, "for there has been a fine first half and the second half must be built up again—of course the process is infinitely swifter in the second half of the show—and the audience brought once more into a delighted expectant attitude."[68] A singing duo was one good choice for this position;[69] with some people still seating themselves, certainly it was not a good position for an act with rapid-fire talking. But a really snappy singing act quickly recaptured the high spirits, which may have slightly dissipated during intermission, and stirred up even livelier emotions, preparing the audience for the headlined stars to follow, the final peak of the bill.

George Whiting and Sadie Burt were probably the most famous mixed singing act. George Whiting had come up the hard way. In the nineties, at age twelve, he had begun singing in saloons Irish songs his mother had taught him; in the following years he worked on show-boats, in medicine shows, circuses, honky-tonks, and museums. In the early 1900s he began singing at cafés, became well-known, and earned about $100 a week (in later years he was acknowledged as the first paid singing waiter). About this time he collaborated with Irving Berlin on "My Wife's Gone to the Country," a song which caused a sensation, and Whiting suddenly became quite famous; he soon received as much as $1000 a week singing in cafés.[70] Sadie Burt became his partner around 1911—their on-the-road romance broke up his first marriage—and by 1914 they were making a hit on the big time. They were such stars that they sometimes earned the next-to-last position on a bill, unusual for a singing team; at the Palace in 1917 they reportedly stopped the show, and a 1920 Palace appearance gathered twelve bows.[71]

Why were they so popular? Whiting's ability to write their songs probably gave them an important edge on many competitors, who shared popular material with the thousands of other performers whose acts included songs. The Whiting and Burt repertoire was second to none. They sang some comical character songs, but for the most part they did romantic numbers. A 1919 appearance featured "I'll Buy a Ring and Change Your Name to Mine," "Chip, Chip, Chippewa, Won't You Be My Little Squaw," "The Love Strike," "Wait Till You See," "Please Tell Me Why," and "I'm Sorry I Made You Cry." Among Whiting's compositions were such well-known favorites as "I'll Be Blue Just Thinking of You," "Don't Let Your Love Go Wrong," "Strolling Through the Park One Day," and, with collaborator Walter Donaldson, "My Blue Heaven."[72]

The team also projected personality. Sadie Burt was "in there in every way on the cute thing," and *Variety* maintained that "anybody who could resist li'l Sadie Burt when she sings 'I'm Afraid of the Wide, Wide World' needs an operation." As for Whiting, although his wife maintained he did not have a very good voice, he was universally considered a great artist: "The Master of Song; A Genius," said Damon Runyon; "The Barrymore of Song," said Lou Holtz; "The Greatest Entertainer that Ever Lived," effused Will Rogers.[73] Asked to explain his success in an interview, Whiting replied:

> I strive to please; I begin by regarding everybody within earshot as my friend; it works out that way.... I try to understand my songs and let my understanding be known to

audiences. I study every song I sing, I do not mean that I merely study the words, but I endeavor to discover the various shades of meaning in the "ditty" giving my idea of the words in the manner that I sing. It is a real benefit to me to do this and I think the public in turn is delighted.[74]

It sounds simple, but in the twenties the team was earning $3000 a week, much more than the average vaudeville team.[75]

Either in this spot, or in the seventh spot on a nine act bill, could often be found a sophisticated pair of "modern" dancers.[76] Although minor dance teams might appear in the number two position, it was considered too early on the bill for an "artistic" act like ballroom dance.[77] In the teens people were going dance-crazy, and dance acts were usually star turns, thus well-suited to this late spot on the bill. Position seven had to be held by an act stronger than the sixth, preferably a full-stage act, and a big name.[78]

The great popularity of theatrical dance teams in the teens followed from the popularity of social dancing, which by 1910 was taking the nation and Europe by storm. It was one more example of expanding leisure activity for the continually enlarging middle class, like baseball, vaudeville, and biking. Traditionally dance had been an activity for the upper classes at posh private affairs, or for the lower classes at disreputable dance halls; now respectable dance halls were springing up, and hotels were adding ballrooms. Whereas before 1910 dance bands were created for an occasion, and were not full-time professional groups, after 1910 "dance bands" were an institution.[79] The new interest in dance followed and was inspired by the innovative popular music that had been flourishing since the turn of the century, ragtime. Now there was a music that belonged to the people, and the novel syncopated rhythms created an urge for new, livelier, less formal kinds of dances. The appearance of simpler versions of ragtime—like Irving Berlin's hit, "Alexander's Ragtime Band"—was both a stimulus and a symptom of the widespread interest in dancing as was the growing popular sheet music business (previously published specifically for professional pianists and singers).[80]

New social dances like the Bunny Hug, Turkey Trot, and Grizzly Bear were frenzied, crude, and simple; in fact, the steps were of little importance, and could be learned by anyone able to walk in time with the music. It was the new rhythm that was the attraction. It was freer and less formal than the old waltzes done by the upper class, more individualistic and expressive than folk dancing; in a sense, dancing had been democratized.[81] The Castles, and others like them, raised the popular diversion to the level of art; as done onstage, the modern dancing was elevated above its rather vulgar social counterpart into something graceful, refined, and skillful. With their classy good looks, their elegant costumes, and their association with "society," the new dancers—often called "society dancers"—were folk heroes and heroines whom audiences could worship, but also identify with and imitate. Women copied Irene Castle's haircut (the first bob) and her clothes, and tried to dance like her. In 1914 the Castles published a book telling fans how to dance, what to wear, and how to give a *thé dansant*.[82]

In the mid-teens, the one-step, waltz, tango, fox trot, and the like were exhibited onstage by such popular male-female teams as Bankhoff and Girlie, Jennie Dolly and her husband Harry Fox, Riggs and Witchie, John Jarrot and Joan Sawyer. Maurice and Florence Walton rivalled the Castles, and popular child stars Fred and Adele Astaire became still more famous during their adulthood in the twenties. Both dances and dancers, of course, varied periodically in popularity, with new fads always appearing to replace old ones. Popular vaudeville dancers in the twenties were Roye and Maye, Rolls and Royce, the DeMarcos, and Berk and Saun, with the shimmy and the Charleston the most long-lived of the later dance crazes.[83]

One team who successfully outlived fad after fad was Adelaide and Hughes. Adelaide Dickey, as "La Petite Adelaide," had been in vaudeville as a perpetual child performer—until her marriage in 1900 revealed she was an adult, not about fourteen as implied. She never made the transition to adult success, however, until she teamed up in 1910 with J. J. Hughes, who became her second husband in 1913.[84] The team was regularly given headliner status at the Palace; they sometimes stayed there for several consecutive weeks, once for ten weeks and another time for twelve weeks, the all-time record for any vaudeville act during the two-a-day era. Adelaide and Hughes often spent as many as six consecutive months in New York City theatres, and like the Castles, were socially in demand.[85]

Adelaide and Hughes's secret, in addition to their elaborate costumes and elegant image (prerequisites for dance acts) was their diverse and theatrical repertoire. Not only were they among the best ballroom dancers, but their acts usually contained a variety of dances from the minuet to modern, with Adelaide's "toe dancing" the featured turn. One routine showed the most spectacular dancing feats of the current musical comedies. Most of their acts also contained a descriptive "story" dance, such as their Pierrot and Pierrette dance, their dance about an Egyptian girl who falls under the magic spell of a Hindu sorcerer, and during the war years, an allegorical treatment of the European situation.[86] In their 1920 act, they opened with an exhibition of popular modern dances, including an intricate jazz fox trot and a waltz, then illustrated "Dancers of the Past"—an exhibition of clog dancing and the like as done by George Primrose and other old favorites. Then Hughes demonstrated various soft-shoe dances from jazz eccentric to buck, while Adelaide changed into a black ostrich feather ballet dress for her toe speciality. The finale was a descriptive pantomime of a toy soldier and mechanical doll flirtation.[87]

After a visual, extravagant act such as this, the audience was primed for the high point of the show. Indeed, after two hours of entertainment featuring ever bigger stars, ever more exciting numbers, the audience *needed* the climax of the star turn. The next-to-last act of the bill was the *scène obligatoire* of the show, the act the audience had been waiting for. It was the most desirable position on the bill, the position reserved for the top headliner, and was most often a comedy turn in "one." After a flashy full-stage dance number, a comedy act in "one" worked perfectly, in terms of stage mechanics, pacing, and variety. Now it was time for the comedy knock-out of the evening, an act that would have the audience roaring until the tears came, and leave them exhausted, exhilarated, and well-satisfied with the evening's entertainment. A famous team like the Avon Comedy Four would be good here, or a single comedy star like Walter Kelly. But many male-female comedy teams were accustomed to the next-to-last honor—Ryan and Lee, Dooley and Sales, Broderick and Crawford, and in later years, Burns and Allen. In all these teams, the comic was the woman.

Times had changed from the days before 1910, when Florence Moore and Mae Melville had been the only well-known comediennes. As Joe Laurie, Jr. tells it, " 'Funny women' were at a premium;" thus the male comics tried to develop their female partners into comediennes: "At first they would let the partner get a few laughs in the act, then maybe next season the lady got 50 per cent of the laughs (alternating funny answers)."[88] Laurie's implication is that men—the ones who understood comedy and trends in the entertainment business—tutored their female partners in comedy; i.e., ultimately men were responsible for creating the comedienne in the male-female act. But it seems equally likely that the profusion of comediennes in male-female acts was at least partly related to a growing pool of female talent needing an outlet, a possibility Laurie neglects to mention.

One development that may support Laurie's interpretation was that the majority of comediennes were very different from their predecessors, and the new type may well have been more appealing to male partners than a Florence Moore or a Mae Melville. The new character was developed, or first brought to attention, by the now-forgotten team of Ryan and Lee, one of the most influential male-female talking acts in mature vaudeville.[89]

Comedian Ben Ryan and partner Harriette Lee had formed a vaudeville team sometime by the 1911-12 season, and had done only moderately well; but when they returned to New York City in early 1914 in "You've Spoiled It," to their utter surprise, they were hailed like long-lost children; they were an instant sensation. That same season, both Melville and Higgins, and Montgomery and Moore, would disband, leaving a noticeable vacancy in the ranks of comic women. Coincidentally, critics had noticed the need for something new in the way of male-female acts. But no doubt their turnabout success was largely because, in the interval on the road, Harriette Lee had developed into the comedienne.[90] *Variety* announced immediately that Harriette Lee was one of the best comediennes on the vaudeville stage, and applauded Ryan and Lee's "brilliant" teamwork: Ryan was deemed a perfect feeder, leading cleverly up to each joke, with Harriette never failing to make the desired point.[91]

Comediennes were no longer novel by the mid-teens, but in 1916 Harriette Lee did "an unusual act for a girl."[92] Ryan and Lee played tough Bowery kids, and although like Mae Melville and Florence Moore, Harriette Lee did get the laughs, she was different from them. She did not make "nasty banter," did not win laughs by getting the best of her partner: she was not "wise" — she was "dumb."

What is known of the famous Ryan and Lee turn called "One and Won is To" [*sic*] shows them at work. The act opened with a comic wrestling match; Ryan has a book in his hand and Harriette Lee is trying to take it away from him. She tosses him around for a minute or two of physical comedy. But the substance of the act was their talk about the book, which is a dictionary. He tries to explain the mysteries of the book to her. She tries without success to look up an animal she has been called; she then remembers it is eaten for breakfast, and turns to "cantaloupe." Finally Ryan deduces she is thinking of "antelope." Another dumb *mot* was her story about a man who stole "$10,000 and two bugs." After much cross-examination Ryan realizes that the poor girl read a headline about a bank cashier who "stole $10,000 and flees!" The same joke is found in a surviving script in which the girl says that whenever she has a cold, she follows the directions on the medicine bottle and "steals silverware." "The directions on the bottle say 'steal silverware,' " exclaims her partner; "Well, it says take two teaspoons after every meal," she replies.[93] It was the kind of joke described by reviewers as Harriette Lee's "inimitable dumb talk." Her mind was as unfathomable as Gracie Allen's would later seem: "There's no telling what makes Harriette do what she does...."[94]

Reviewers fretted in print that the new act was difficult to describe. Ryan and Lee's style of teamwork was "not listed in the category of conventional vaudeville acts and they have few equals as laugh producers," said one; another agreed that "it's a little away from the conventional idea of what is termed in vaudeville classes 'team artists.' "[95] The novel feature was that both partners handled comedy; Ryan was not a mere straight-man, but was allowed to indulge in a little kidding himself. An extant piece of dialogue has Ryan making a crack or two:

> Ryan: This tiny package can't be yours.
> Lee: Certainly; it's my grip.
> Ryan: You don't mean to say you keep your clothes in that?

Lee: Certainly.
Ryan: What do you do, anyway?
Lee: I'm a chorus girl.
Ryan: Oh, I must see this show! Where do you live anyway?
Lee: At the hotel just around the corner. I pay $6 a day for my room.
Ryan: Six dollars a day! Say you ought to be able to get a pretty good cup of coffee for $2.25, oughtn't you? Say, you're a freak. You ought to be with Barnum.
Lee: Barnum? Why, he's dead!
Ryan: I know it.[96]

Another bit ended just as callously:

Ryan: Say, you are a pretty girl.
Lee: Do you think so?
Ryan: You have lovely teeth.
Lee: O, now—
Ryan: Both of them.[97]

The two exchanges resemble the flirtation formula—what do you do, where do you live—with the significant difference that the flattery and growing familiarity set up an insult, and the conversation indicated that the laughs were at Harriette Lee's expense, whether she or Ryan did the feeding.

A female boob, or "dumbbell," was a new type to the audiences of the day, who clearly found her funny; the team was capable of holding the next-to-last spot on the Palace bill, and on one occasion won thirty-nine laughs in twenty-four minutes.[98] Perhaps it was easier for audiences to respond to Harriette Lee as a butt, because she was just a "kid," and a Bowery kid at that. Presumably both Ryan and Lee used Lower East Side accents, and Harriette Lee did "baby talk"; one reviewer found it jarring after a while and wished she would talk more naturally.[99]

But aside from her exaggerated talk, there were apparently no other stylized features to the act. Harriette Lee did not have to resort to Florence Moore and Mae Melville's grotesque mugging or comic costumes. Although Ryan and Lee played Bowery characters, pictures of the team in character show them in the ordinary street clothes of downtown New York. Also, Harriette was a former chorus girl and was considered downright pretty, and there is no evidence she tried to hide it.[100] Although audiences had been made uneasy when an attractive woman handled comedy and abused her male partner, it was obviously less discomfiting if a pretty girl played dumb and was used as a butt.

The team soon had many look-alikes onstage, with Ben Ryan providing the scripts for some of them. Henry and Adelaide did a cross-fire sketch by Ryan called "One Hundred Per Cent Dumb," which was said to resemble still another from Ryan's pen. Henry and Adelaide's East Side kids were both a little dumb; the boy illustrated what a hard head he had by cracking a soda cracker on it.[101] Ben Ryan was also said to have authored the first sketch done by a new team who appeared about the same time as Henry and Adelaide—Burns and Allen.[102]

These were small-time teams, but big-time team Blanche McLaughlin and Jim Evans were also revealed to "work somewhat like Ryan and Lee." An early Ryan and Lee routine was "Hats and Shoes," and it was said of McLaughlin and Evans that "in place of hats and shoes they use baker's rolls." The act was called "A Bowery Courtship" and the team worked in front of a tenement house drop, with Blanche McLaughlin's accent a burlesque of New York's "Four Million"; "Some of the wit is deep and all of it is broad," said *Variety.*[103] Andy and Louise Barlow's small-time act was said to be similar, as was Millard and Marlin's "Honeymooning," described as the Ben Ryan type of neighborhood sketch, in which tenement inhabitants do their usual line of gags.[104]

Aside from Ryan and Lee, and McLaughlin and Evans, no other standard big-time act used the East Side part of the characterization. With two successful big-time teams doing "tough" roles, there was little room for competitors; moreover, the Bowery act had limited value on national circuits where universal themes were the most profitable. However, comediennes playing "kids," divested of the Bowery trappings, became more popular than ever. The kid had universal application, and it permitted a woman—especially if pretty—to be a comedienne in a role which did not threaten the vanity of male partners and the men in the audience. It also allowed female patrons to laugh at a woman with no danger of identifying with her. Although most stage "kids" were old enough to "flirt" (singer Sadie Burt played a "baby vamp" in one number), comedienne Gracie Deagon's kid was a child. Her child impersonation was "cuteness personified," and was free from the studied mannerisms of most kid work, said *Variety;* both she and straight-man Homer Dickinson worked in an easy manner, without resorting to the low comedy usually used by kid acts. During a week at the big-time Riverside Theatre in 1919, Dickinson and Deagon closed the show, and earned four bows at 11 p.m., an achievement any talking act should be proud of, noted *Variety.* By 1923 Gracie Deagon had a new partner, Jack Mack, and Deagon and Mack were still performing in the 1925–26 season.[105]

After Harriette Lee, however, the most admired kid work was probably done by Aileen Bronson. When she and her new husband, Joe Laurie, Jr., first appeared at small-time theatres around New York in the 1915–16 season in talk and songs, the opening talk was flirtation stuff, until she protests she is married. He says he'll give her all he has, and strips down to trousers and undershirt to prove it. *Variety* observed that the team needed more refined material. But by the fall of their second season together, they were working at big-time houses, and *Variety* now thought they had an abundance of endearing personality and a repertoire of original comedy; by the following September they had clicked at the Palace.[106]

Laurie was originally the comedian, but at some point Aileen Bronson took over the comedy honors — probably by the time of the Palace appearance, since she got the credit for their success. The act was largely put across by the unusual personality and impeccable showmanship of the girl, said *Billboard,* and one false move on her part could ruin the turn, but it was a scream if it went right. An "unvarnished nut act in one,"[107] the routine was a sidewalk conversation called "Lost and Found," and the following bits of dialogue survive:

> Joe Laurie: What about it if you have an ocean? Are you going to buy a boat or something?
> Aileen Bronson: Not an ocean, a notion.
>
> Joe Laurie: Your head's as good as new. You have never used it.[108]

Part of each joke is clearly missing, and these lines certainly do not reveal anything about Aileen Bronson's comic ability. But Laurie's last crack shows that, like Harriette Lee, Aileen Bronson served as "dumb girl" butt at least some of the time for her semi-straight man. By January 1919 they were doing a routine called "Let 'Er Go," in which Aileen Bronson played a naughty, child-like kid; unfortunately, like many a male-female act, the team was dissolved by divorce sometime between July 1920 and January 1921.[109]

Whether simultaneously or not, the Laurie and Bronson repertoire had contained flirtation, dumb girl, and kid work. *Variety* maintained Ryan and Lee were "the pioneers of a school of vaudeville talking acts which afterward developed Laurie and Bronson and others."[110] Joe Laurie himself described his mixed act as in the Ryan and Lee tradition, although he did not mention that the Ryan and Lee team came first:

> Later Ryan & Lee and Laurie & Bronson brought a new type of mixed act to vaude — the "dumb girl" type comedienne and the smart-cracking straight man, depending on cross-fire "semi-nut" comedy, using a song-and-dance finish.[111]

Later, Burns and Allen would be placed in the same tradition: in 1937, when the disbanded Ryan and Lee team came together for a radio appearance, they were introduced as the team "who helped set the comic pattern that is now used by Burns and Allen."[112]

It seems more than coincidental that in all three acts the man was originally the comic, but turned the laughs over to the woman, because she was funnier. "It hurt his pride plenty," said Laurie, speaking generally, "but it was good business."[113] Having begun as comics, however, neither Ryan, Laurie, nor Burns became complete straight-men, but what Laurie calls light comedian straights. They kept some laughs for themselves. And since each was foil to a comedienne getting laughs for her dumb cracks, their counter-laughs were naturally for their wisecracks.

The result was a combination apparently more to the liking of the middle-class audiences of the day than the earlier comedienne and straight-man butt, and perhaps more palatable to the men whose comic roles had been usurped by female partners more talented at winning laughs. Although Mae Melville and Florence Moore were both admired, their stage characters, strident women who verbally pulverized their male foils, were less widely imitated. One proof of how audiences liked their stage women was offered in a 1915 performance by song and dance team McKay and Ardine. Their act received its biggest applause when at one point the wife sat down crying and said, "What a silly fool I've been," and her partner replied, "Don't cry, you're only a woman," whereupon "the house rocked with the hand-clapping," reported *Variety*.[114] Thus, the sexism of the dumbbell material aside, it was obviously a wise choice for male-female teams, because it worked. Paradoxically, it was also a "liberated" arrangement, for it freed both partners for comedy.

By the twenties the comically dumb woman—usually a "flapper" now—had become a tradition offstage as well as on. In 1921 the "Tillie the Toiler" comic strip was born, about a dark-haired, wide-eyed beauty whose brains were not on a par with her looks, and in 1927 Marion Davies played Tillie on the screen. So successful was their Tillie strip that King Features assigned Chic Young to create another cute but mixed-up brunette, Dora Bell, whose misadventures earned her the epithet "Dumb Dora." A few years later Young came up with "Blondie," initially a bird-brained flapper.[115] In one early strip, Dagwood's father asks Blondie to remember the college she went to, for the newspaper notice of her engagement to Dagwood:

> Blondie: Oh dear, what was it? Name some colleges—is there a Yale?—Yes, I do believe it was Yale.
> Dagwood: Yale is a men's college, dear.
> Blondie: Then it wasn't Yale—no, I remember—it was near Yale—we used to go over there to the dances and things.[116]

Whether or not the newspaper Dumb Dora was indebted to Ryan and Lee, the epithet certainly defined the kind of figure they had originated. Their 1924 act, described as their "typical," featured "Harriette Lee as

Dumb Dora." Although the nickname could refer to something distinct from a kid impersonation, a comedienne suited to one was probably able to do the other; in one of her routines, Gracie Deagon did a "flip kid" impersonation, then went into a "Dumb Dora."[117] The significance of the latter-day nickname was that it identified the essence of the type; although there were kiddish, East Side Dumb Doras, a female boob no longer had to be distanced from the audience; now dumbness was unabashedly the most important appeal of such acts.

The dumb comedienne remained a popular type in big-time vaudeville's last decade. In 1925, along with Ryan and Lee, Dorothy Murray and Earl Lavere featured the girl in "dumbbell" talk; the woman of Walton and Brant played a Dumb Dora; and Aileen Bronson was doing the old Laurie and Bronson act with Johnny Dale. In 1927 Jack Benny was appearing with an unbilled Dumb Dora, as was Bob Hope in 1929. In the act by well-known team Broderick and Crawford—later said to be in the same classification with Burns and Allen—comedienne Helen Broderick got most of the points in the cross-fire with her "wise-cracking dumbbell," which was "a comedy panic."[118]

Another dumbbell woman at the end of vaudeville's successful era was Eve Sully, teamed with Jesse Block. In 1923 Jesse Block was doing a flirtation bench act as a member of a team called Block and Dunlop, considered a nice number two on the big time. After Block's partner retired to get married, he formed an act with Eve Sully, and three years later they were married. When the team appeared in New York for the first time in the summer of 1927, *Variety's* "Abel" [Abel Green] wrote that their act was a line of talk with a laugh in nearly every sentence, and noted that "these babies have been around before and know what it's all about."[119]

Eve Sully played "her inimitable Dumb Dora," and like Ryan and others, Block was the "mugging straight." Block said that one of their best gags went thus:

> Jesse: I never met anyone as dumb as you.
> Eve: Aw, gwan, my sister is dumber than me.
> Jesse: You mean dumber than I.
> Eve: Oh, she's even dumber than both of us.[120]

Interestingly, like Ryan and Lee's "One and Won is To" act, the Block and Sully turn opened with a physical tussle. They passed onstage, with Eve suddenly turning around and starting a scrap, and ending by ruining Jesse's straw hat. She explained afterwards that she was practicing a defense against mashers.[121] Perhaps a male could more freely insult his female partner after she had physically attacked him; perhaps it established a little sympathy for the male, thus made the audience able to laugh more freely at the female.

In fact, even female straights were occasionally being insulted by their comedian partners. In the Barnes and Crawford act performed in the mid-teens, comedian Roy Barnes got some of his laughs with his jabs at Bessie Crawford. When the salesman explained that his accident policy would cover her legs, Bessie objected with "My face is my fortune"; "You're starving to death," Roy shot back.[122] The joke is similar to the one about Harriette Lee's teeth. Barnes's winsomeness may have made his insults go down more easily; besides, the profession of salesman virtually licensed obnoxiousness. It was the perfect role for some banter in which the female straight took the worst of it. Of course, it was one thing when it was salesman and housewife exchanging insults, or even husband and wife, both traditional foes. But when a male insulted his straight female partner in the context of flirtation, the implications were more ambivalent.

One early team whose routines had this equivocal quality was Diamond and Brennan. Jim Diamond had been a principal comedian in burlesque between 1906 and 1909, and had soon after entered vaudeville with a former burlesque prima donna. The 1912-13 season found him teamed with pretty Sybil Brennan, his straight woman into the mid-twenties, in an act called "Nifty Nonsense."[123] Their talk was flirtation, but Diamond's raves were almost offensive, and his last crack was a blatant insult.

James: I hate you. I hate you like Rockefeller hates oil.
Sybil: My name is Rose, sir.
James: It was sure some gardener that raised you.
Sybil: And I have a sister named Violet.
James: I'd like to go home with you and meet the whole bouquet.
Sybil: My father was a teacher and I got educated for nothing.
James: My father was a minister and I got educated to be good for nothing. Oh, she's gone to change her dress! That reminds me.... Ah, here she is. Say, you look O.K.
Sybil: What does O.K. mean?
James: One kiss. I'll have it C.O.D.
Sybil: All right. I.O.U. one.
James: All right. I'll take that kiss P.D.Q. But say, honey, keep your mouth closed so that I can find your face![124]

Jim Diamond's tone was insultingly over-familiar; Sybil sounds too ingratiating, a little dumb. At one point in a routine Jim exclaimed, "I'm going to get you yet, you pug-nosed chicken"—certainly a bold mode of flirting. One reporter thought the act bordered on the indelicate now and then; the *Mirror* thought it was too inane and broad.[125]

Perhaps Diamond's disrespectful attitude toward his female partner was an inheritance from his days as a burlesque comedian. In one bit from those days, after a girl undressed very decorously, Diamond than did a burlesque of it, using a corset with comic effect.[126] There is an almost similar touch of mocking, although lighter, in his attitude toward his vaudeville partner's femininity. By early 1922 Diamond and Brennan were using a salesman and female drummer flirtation, with "flip" cross-fire; each told what he had sold, with a "dollar-a-kiss" bit of business used. In one piece, Diamond directed his female partner's talk like a traffic cop, whistling for her to go and stop, and at the end handing her the whistle.[127] It sounds patronizing.

Diamond's careless attitude toward his partner is typical of a certain flippancy or detachment increasingly found in flirtation acts in the late vaudeville period. Whether male or female played straight or comic, their romancing was edged with an almost disdainful casualness. A flirtation done by James Doyle and Laura Hamilton in 1921, for example, was "performed unassumingly, airily with an almost supercilious daintiness"; it was "devoid of the serious 'will you be mine' slush, but more on the superficial, airy persiflage order denoting each takes the other none too seriously as yet, and thus more approaching realism." The man of Fox and Allen depicted a very cocky flirtatious chap—he outlines his success with the girls, explaining he "finds 'em, feeds 'em, fools 'em, and forgets 'em"—and a girl smart enough to take care of herself. Keane and Whitney did flirtation and proposal talk—which was undermined when each remembered being already married.[128]

In latter-day stage flirting, the emphasis was on wit, not romance. Frawley and Louise's flirtation act, for example, was "as full of nifties, wisecracks, and double meanings as a watermelon is full of seeds." In this new game the object was one-upmanship, not love. In Rolland and Ray's standard act, the joke of the opening episode was the guy-kept-waiting gimmick; again and again he says he will wait just one more minute. But when his date finally arrives, he gets his revenge by revealing that their sumptuous New Year's Eve feast will be purchased for nickels in an automat. At the end he promises her that if she is a good sport they will work up to Child's; he does not believe in "spoiling 'em," he confides.[129] Matthews and Ayers's comedy chatter also turned on the man's refusal to whet his date's appetite. When Burns and Allen debuted "Lamb Chops," it was described as being in a Matthews and Ayers vein; Burns later recalled that "the basic jokes for all girls were 'eating' jokes. You always took a girl out to dinner and if she ordered lamb chops, that meant she was a gold digger."[130]

The eating joke and other "airy persiflage" of the typical flirtation in the late teens and early twenties is found in a 1922 routine called "The Nifty Age," by James Madison. The early part of the routine gives the man opportunity to make some cracks at the female's expense. He pretends to be a palm reader, and upon taking her palm, acts very agitated;

She: (somewhat alarmed): Anything the matter?
He: Your hand is sick. It needs a cure.
She: What sort of cure?
He: A mani-cure.
She: (hunching her shoulder several times disdainfully): Sir!
He: (further examining palm): Your palm indicates that you are much in need of something.
She: (aside, exultantly): The fur garment I saw in the show window.
He: (examining further): Something, I might say, you want very badly, indeed.
She: A sealskin coat.
He: No; a cake of soap.

Finally, they get around to flirtation, but each is more interested in getting a free meal, and in making wise come-backs:

She: Well, I must be going.
He: Lady, don't go.
She: Why not?
He: I like you awful well.
She: But you know nothing about me.
He: Maybe that's the reason.
She: What made you think I would even talk to you?
He: I was taken with a hunch.
She: (with sudden enthusiasm): Oh, that's different.
He: What's different?
She: Why didn't you say before that you would take me to lunch?
He: (after letting audience see aside that his trouser pockets are bare of coin): Oh, very well, but on the way to lunch, I'd like to stop a moment at my uncle's....
She: On the way to the restaurant I want to drop in at my home for a moment.
He: Can't we go there for lunch?
She: You certainly have nerve.
He: No, merely appetite.
She: You may not believe it, but I'm a very good housekeeper. In fact, every Saturday I wash the floor, but it's bad for my knee.
He: Next Saturday I'll wash it for you.
She: What, my knee?
He: No; the floor.
She: It's solid concrete.
He: What, the floor?
She: No; your head.
He: How would you like to be my wife?
She: Since this country went dry, I don't care what becomes of me.... If I agree to marry you, promise me you will never tell a lie.
He: I promise.
She: (sighing): And now that we're engaged, say that I am young and beautiful.
He: I can't.

She: Why not?
He: Because I just promised you I would never tell a lie.
She: If I marry you what will we live on?
He: I make my living by my brains.
She: Tell the orchestra to play a funeral march.
He: What for?
She: You've been dead for years. (She leads him off to "Funeral March" air.)[131]

The man and woman act offered as typical by Joe Laurie, Jr., in *Vaudeville*—a composite of actual vaudeville bits—is similar in tone, and is probably from the same era; Laurie was in vaudeville after 1915; what he knew as "typical" vaudeville was actually its late period.[132] In such routines, women wisecracked as cynically, were as hard-boiled as men, just as offstage, the flapper adopted mannish haircuts, angular silhouettes, and aggressive sexual manners and slang. Their themes were still flirtation, proposal and marriage, but usually romance merely provided an arena for the battle of the sexes. Routines still ended with boy-gets-girl, but often winning the woman was less a matter of possessing the girl of one's dreams than it was asserting male superiority. Walsh and Ellis flirted, the man proposed, and the woman equivocated—at which point the man read her a lecture on the modern flapper: "so true that it hurts, so satirical that it gets laughter and applause," and this "leads to her capitulation."[133] In a Sully and Houghton bench flirtation called "Calf Love," the man is rather sarcastic: he says he cannot eat or sleep, and wants to get married so he can get her off his mind; he warns that he won't submit to her sway, but plans to drink, smoke, and stay out late because he's a man.[134]

Routines which celebrated being "a man" at feminine expense seemed more in vogue than ever, and the mannish woman who tried to domineer her husband was a popular butt—especially to men with "the worried look," it was said. In Gibson and Connelli's "The Honeymoon," for example, the team plays newlyweds at Niagara Falls, where the bride has taken her uncurbed temper, and her dog to cuddle instead of her groom. At the end, he turns on his wife and informs her he means to dominate. Terrified, she gives in; when she tearfully asks who told him to act that way, he says, "Your father." It was *The Taming of the Shrew* modernized, said *Variety*, and, "it simply can't fail with married men in the audience."[135] When the curtain came down, William Gibson reappeared and expressed his hope that "every married man will profit by his illustration of masculine dominance," and cheered his audience with the vow, that though "man may be down, he's never out"; he ended with this advice: "Marry 'em, treat 'em rough and tell 'em nothing." One reviewer thought the enjoyment of the audience "proves the aptitude of the old saying that a woman does not love a man unless she fears him."[136] A 1922 film starring Constance Talmadge,

The Primitive Lover, echoed the theme: only after the man treats her like a squaw, and even gives her a good spanking, does he win her respect.[137] Robert Higgins may have taken it whiningly from Mae Melville in 1910, but in an act by Ray and Emma Dean in 1922, in which the woman baited and mistreated a sissy male, the man finally clenched his fist and gave his oppressor a threatening dirty look.[138]

All these comedy routines in which the men protested so much revealed the audience's real concern: there is no topic so popular as "the modern girl," proclaimed *Variety* in 1925.[139] Newspaper comic strips like "Fritzi Ritz," "Boots and Her Buddies," and "Connie" satisfied the mass audience's curiosity about the life of the liberated, contemporary woman; beginning in 1918, Cecil B. DeMille made a cycle of saucy high-spirited pictures about brassy, adulterous women; film after film in the twenties showed the public's preoccupation: *The Flappers, In Search of Sinners, Dancing Mothers, Flaming Youth,* and of course, *It.*[140] The "chickens" in the cartoons and novels, and on the stage and screen, were distorted caricatures of the traits of the woman of the day: the routines, stories, and films satirized her mannish carryings-on and wiseness, delighted in her female frivolousness and silliness.

Why were women suddenly so bothersome? An annoying new female freedom had been noticed back in the early teens, but twenties opinion leaders thanked the war for exploding any remaining nineteenth-century convictions about "ladies." Americans had had to become accustomed to women collecting streetcar fares, driving taxis and operating elevators, even making grenades, and it was in wartime that nice girls had first begun "losing their heads"; even middle-class girls were "picking up soldiers on the street, going to shows and ice cream parlors with them, and gradually becoming demoralized."[141] It was largely as a result of the change in climate caused by the war—Americans' forced acceptance of female participation in public life, their generous feelings toward patriotic suffragists, and the postwar fervor to make the world not only safe but humanitarian—that the Nineteenth Amendment had finally been ratified in 1919, giving the vote to women at last. The masses and their spokesmen believed that with votes for women true equality had come at last; an element of anxiety was part of that knowledge. One editor summed up the public viewpoint with the observation that although men had always tried to keep women on the so-called feminine side of the fence, that fence had a large hole in it, and "only Heaven can help the men now."[142]

There was some truth behind the alarmist claims. A whole generation of young women (and men) were questioning traditional sexual politics and experimenting with new social mores. Women were adopting coarser manners, more liberated fashions, and more forthright attitudes about their sexual satisfaction—freedoms which were masculine by definition. It had all been done before, but now the new morality had infected middle-class youth; a newspaperman who toured the country in 1925 was convinced that "between the magazines and the movies a lot of these little towns seem literally saturated with sex."[143]

In retrospect, the excessive concern with dress, slang, and symbols of liberation does not appear so surprising. However awkwardly and self-consciously, a new generation was actually devising the new sexual manners demanded by the world created by their parents. Automobiles, speakeasies, office situations, and college campuses had resulted in a new physical and social mobility; urbanization, the decline in birthrate, new methods of contraception—all this and more had changed the definition of marriage and the family. Dating and petting were ways to achieve the ideal of "companionate marriage" established by the previous generation. The new behavior was the necessary result of decades of social change, but to traditionalists "Flaming Youth" was merely immoral, self-indulgent, and irresponsible.[144]

The fact that the new era was personified by the flapper betrays the mass conviction that women were at the bottom of it all. Just as the war was a convenient starting place, woman was a comforting scapegoat, a way for confused people to explain the social rebellion roaring around them. Women were permitting "liberties," and this was peculiar cause for alarm: since women were the special guardians of genteel nineteenth-century mores, the flapper rebellion seemed to portend the end of all order and sexual control. What was not said was that the flapper's denial of the paternal double standard dared women to shape their own sexual morality, and challenged men to achieve manliness on their own rather than as head of a household. Few observers were objective enough to notice that most young women still sought the traditional end—to win a husband. Besides, the offensive new feminine freedoms would be quickly curtailed in the depression since few women actually acquired economic independence.[145]

But in the twenties, the conventional majority could hardly know this, and audiences loved seeing the flapper caricatured on the stage and screen. The women in male-female routines were not real flappers,[146] but were all that flappers were to the mass audience: on the one hand, smart-alecky and mannish, on the other—the necessary reverse of the coin—as downright dumb as many people had always believed women were. The vaudeville routines did not explore the complex challenge the new woman offered; it was easier to laugh than to think.

Nonetheless, the routines revealed the public's preoccupation with the fact that modern woman was different from what she should be, and hinted at their consternation. Indeed, mixed comedy acts comparing the woman of the past and the present, or the present and the future, were extremely popular. Kolb and Harlan, for example, did an act called "Evolution." They appeared first as a courting couple in the 1860s, then, saying they will let their imaginations wander to 1920, they reappeared as a henpecked husband and militant suffragette. Bronson and Baldwin were doing an act in 1920 called "Visions of 1969." He played a maidish man, who looked after the house while his suffragette wife supported the family. Looking through an old chest he finds a bottle of something called "Scotch" and gets drunk and sings "Poor Downtrodden Man." In "It's Every Husband's Duty," Gibson and Connelli also showed a couple in the future, with the husband a homemaker, and the wife a lawyer. Women were becoming masculine and men effeminate, warned Will Durant, and on some level of consciousness the populace believed him.[147]

The preoccupation with sex roles was better than the best publicity stunt any male-female team could have possibly arranged. Male-female talking teams had at last settled almost exclusively on the stage material most rewarding for them theatrically, and one which was indigenous to the sexual make-up of the team: courtship and marriage, which invariably meant the battle of the sexes. By the late teens, this subject matter was being given every possible variation. Professionally, the male-female routine had developed to its most mature stage. After decades of specialization, there were dozens of teams who offered acts in which the appeal was pure talk, with song and dance just a convenient finale. Female talent and true teamwork were finally commonplace: with little professional sexism, many teams shared equally in the talk, with the role of comic and straight allocated according to talent, not sex. There was team after team in which the male played comic and yet the female straight was an integral part of the act, a competent feeder contributing just as the male feeder did in a male two-act. Likewise, there were many talented comediennes who were the appeal of the act, with male straights who fed their talk.

In one sense, the new comediennes ended what could be described as Victorian stage relationships. In male two-acts, the actor who played the boob emerged according to what worked best theatrically, not in deference to any sexual constraints; now male-female teams could delegate their stage chores with less concern about offstage propriety. But whereas sex was not a fetter in terms of a partner's opportunities to joke and crack and be a laughingstock, in terms of material, male-female routines clearly reflected modern biases. Now women were free to play a much wider variety of types—but they had come down from the pedestal to serve as comic butts. There were forward women and henpecked men, tightwad guys and flappers, but in the teens and twenties, the dumb woman and the wise man was the most popular combination. And whether the stage female played wise or dumb, audiences enjoyed laughs at woman's expense: the dumbbell was an obvious figure of fun, but even smart women—vixenish wives, brazen flirts, suffragettes and flappers—were satirical butts. But it was not for male-female teams to ponder the sexism or onesidedness of their characters; what they knew was that the new humor worked, that audiences were laughing harder than ever before at comediennes' self-caricatures. By exploiting the era's obsessive concern with sexual politics, male-female teams were in more demand on vaudeville bills than ever before.

The best of these comedy teams were popular enough to hold the next-to-last position on any big-time vaudeville bill. When Ryan and Lee appeared at the Palace in 1924, they brought with them over a decade of experience. Such an act had been perfected by testing every single moment before live audiences night after night, week after week, by continual pruning, shaping, and timing. In this piecemeal fashion, a team like Ryan and Lee evolved male and female stage characters and interactions which appealed to something men and women believed, or feared, about their own sexuality.

With humor meticulously constructed in response to the mass audience's tastes, these acts were direct reflections of middle-class values, but they were also more. Great teams like Ryan and Lee provided exciting entertainment; they were professionals, experts who could be counted on to send the audience home satisfied. With their timely material and their time-honed talents, they put the male-female routine in high profile in vaudeville. Like the classic male conversation acts, male-female teams had become important contenders in the ranks of great comedians, and the male-female comedy-talking act had become a valuable ingredient in the vaudeville show. The very best teams had achieved for themselves the goal of every vaudevillian, the hard-won possession of what George Burns called "17 good minutes," an act which could not be improved on—the essence of the vaudeville art.

7

Male-Female Teams and the Decline of Vaudeville, 1925–1932

Herbert Williams and Hilda Wolfus felt compelled to improve upon their seventeen minutes of comedy, even though it was already an acknowledged masterpiece. Their 1921 act boasted several new bits in addition to the proven favorites: an imitation by Williams of Raymond Hitchcock, a joke using two dogs, a Bolshevik pianist take-off, and at the end not only did the stool come apart but the entire piano, thus a baby grand was needed for the legitimate piano work finale. The *New York Clipper* observed that "the act loses out at the finish, for the simple reason that Williams gives them entirely too much. He should cut part of the act, and leave them wanting."[1]

Unfortunately, the trend in the late teens was for performers not to "leave them wanting." Vaudeville acts of all kinds, male-female teams included, were always seeking ways to make an even bigger hit; the easiest way to accomplish this seemed to be by embellishing an act with more performers, more numbers, more elaborate costumes and sets. In 1921 Brendel and Burt modernized their act into a revue production with eleven extras. They kept their old stuff, but their famous routines were now interrupted by revue numbers. By the twenties, Wilbur Mack was supported by a company of three, Armand Kalisz by a company of fourteen; male-female comedy team Elinore and Williams had added three assistants; Diamond and Brennan had added a sister dancing team and a male pianist.[2]

Almost all teams were adding the appeals of song and dance because of the tremendous popularity of big musical productions. After the war the demand for big song and dance numbers climbed to bigger proportions every year. During the month of October 1923, in New York City vaudeville houses alone, a patron could have treated himself to the following: Dave Meyerhoff and Orchestra; Oumansky's Dancers; Andre Sherr's Revue; Bobby Folsom and Jack Denny's Metropolitan Orchestra; "Yerkes' Jazzarimba," a jazz band of eleven, and another called "Jack Allyn's Aces and Alice Tyrell"; "Shake Your Feet," a colored revue with eleven performers; "Fred Jennings' Daffy-Dils," a revue act; Eddie Leonard and company of twenty; Hanlon and Xamboni and their Argentine Orchestra; Vadie and Norton and company of nine, dancers; Ted Claire and company of eleven, a band and song and dance act; Inez Courtney and company with a production skit; the Vincent Lopez Band; Paul Specht and his Alamac Hotel Orchestra; Harry Carroll and Company, a revue of nine; Hughie Clark and Band; "Dance Frivolities," a revue number; "Dancing Devils," colored song and dance production; B. C. Hilliam and Company, revue number; Imperial Russian Entertainers; the Opera Comique Russe; Moro Castle Orchestra; and Webb's Novelty Orchestra.[3]

Such acts clearly showed the triumph of musical comedy and revue. Musical comedy in America had come of age in the years surrounding World War I; in 1919, there were more musical comedy shows on Broadway than ever before—eighteen, an impressive forty per cent of all productions.[4] The operetta, an imitation of European forms, was at its height; Friml and Romberg were turning out lilting works with sentimental waltzes, charming melodies, and picturesque characters and settings. The home-grown musical was also on the ascent. Composers Cole Porter, Irving Berlin, George Gershwin, and Jerome Kern all matured in the twenties, and lyricists of the DeSylva, Brown and Henderson ilk had risen to the challenge. In hits such as *Irene* (1919), *Sally* (1920), *Lady Be Good* (1924), and dozens more, a host of native geniuses dazzled Broadway audiences with the energy, cleverness, and optimistic glow of their productions. For a relatively small admission price, Broadway offered fairyland-like shows with stars and a host of extras, special scenery, and large orchestras. In the 1925-26 season audiences could choose from *No No Nanette, The Girl Friend, The Cocoanuts, Sunny,* or *The Vagabond King,* all playing on a single evening within six blocks of one another, and none charging over $4.40.[5]

By the late teens, Ziegfeld had his formula down to perfection; he combined the scale, the melodies, and the glamour of the musical comedy production with the variety and pace of vaudeville. He packed more riches into each show than audiences could possibly absorb. He unveiled a resplendent tableau decorated with luscious beauties, which would disappear before the spectators' eyes before they could take it all in, to be replaced by one heavenly vision after another, in an unending parade of prodigality.[6] Ziegfeld insisted his shows use only the best materials, the best designs, and the finest performers. His opulent production numbers were interspersed with lightning fast comic numbers by the biggest comedy stars of the day: the 1917 *Follies* had Fanny Brice, Bert Williams, W. C. Fields, Eddie Cantor, and Will Rogers all in one show.[7]

Vaudeville could not possibly compete with Ziegfeld's astronomical budgets. By the 1920s, Zeigfeld's production costs were over $100,000 before a show ever opened; the 1927 *Follies* cost over $289,000. And Ziegfeld had by the twenties a string of spendthrift and successful imitators: the Shuberts' *Passing Show* series, Raymond Hitchcock's *Hitchy-Koo* revues, George White's *Scandals,* Earl Carroll's *Vanities,* and numerous others. Irving Berlin's first *Music Box Revue* cost $200,000; critic Arthur Hornblow described it as "a piling of Pelion on Ossa of everything that is decorative, dazzling, harmonious, intoxicatingly beautiful in the theatre — all that and more...."[8]

Musical comedy and revue were not the only sumptuous theatricals available to the consumer. Until the mid-twenties, the Hippodrome and the Winter Garden housed extravaganzas featuring such startling spectacles as marching elephants, performing horses, Sousa's Band, and simulated fires, earthquakes, and shipwrecks.[9] At the other end of the scale, entertainment seekers could hear the strains of big band music led by Paul Whiteman, Vincent Lopez, Fred Waring, and other featured leaders and their musicians. Dance bands were no longer just for dancing; now they were full-fledged orchestras and an important part of the entertainment scene; a mass enthusiasm for orchestra styles and leader personalitites that would peak in the late thirties was already forming.[10]

On the stage, audiences craved stars and spectacle in the same way that they embraced hero-worship and indulgent living in the world outside the theatre. Between the beginning of the war and 1929, advances in technology raised industrial production sixty per cent — faster than the population increase, thus profits, dividends, salaries, and labor wages rose considerably. Prodded by the enormous extension of consumer credit and the new emphasis on advertising, the consumption level of the ordinary person soared. For the first time, thanks to the new income levels, increased leisure, and mass technology, the crowd was able to participate fully in fads, fashions, and riotous spending, formerly a preserve of the wealthy.[11]

The stock market was spiralling; Lindbergh's triumph showed Americans could do anything, and the soldier and the girl back home wanted to make up for lost time. In such a climate, sumptuous entertainments flourished, even on the popular level. The variety-hall working-class audience would surely have been struck dumb by Broadway's twenties' flamboyance, but the middle-class patrons of the twenties were not shocked; Ziegfeld's *Follies* were merely a very theatrical version of their own.

As with all vaudeville, the influence of musical comedy and revue on male-female teams was overwhelmingly obvious. The change in Rooney and Bent's repertoire is representative of the trend in vaudeville bills in general. Rooney and Bent had unsuccessfully attempted two production acts in the spring of 1909; by June they were back on the stage in their established repertoire, without making another such attempt until ten years later.[12] Then, in the fall of 1919, Rooney and Bent opened at the Palace with a brand new act called "Rings of Smoke," a pretentious revue with nine scenes—such as a Spanish bull ring, a cabaret, an Irish cottage, and a Parisian flower stand—lasting forty-six minutes and utilizing thirteen people, including Vincent Lopez and his Kings of Harmony band and fashionable ballroom dancers Mlle. Marguerite and Frank Gill.[13] Audiences loved it; during Rooney and Bent's week at the Royal Theatre, 30,000 came to see the act, breaking all attendance records for that house.[14] Reviewers were equally admiring. Variety thought "Rings of Smoke" was the best thing Pat Rooney and Marion Bent had ever done: "there is more action crammed into this one-act vaudeville turn than in the average musical comedy.... [A]ny vaudeville bill that has it for a headliner will not need much more to boost it." It was "a whole show in itself," and the *Montreal Gazette* praised it as the most pretentious vaudeville act ever seen in that city, adding, "one finds such a wealth of good things, that to particularize is a problem."[15]

After touring big-time houses all season, Rooney and Bent were brought back to the Palace in the summer for a four-week run, in the coveted next-to-closing spot. Then, after three outstanding seasons with "Rings of Smoke," Pat Rooney outdid himself with an even bigger production, "Shamrock." Recounting an Irish emigrant boy's adventures in New York in five scenes of song and dance, the act had a company of twenty—dancing beauties, supporting actors, and jazz musicians; it cost $23,000 to produce and lasted an entire hour.[16] The *New York Telegraph* thought that with a little padding and some intermissions it would be ready for a regular Broadway production. Rooney modestly admitted he was "convinced that vaudeville audiences are interested in these little musical comedies, boiled down to their essence, and presented with pep and speed."[17]

One by one, other male-female teams were emerging as big production acts. In 1917 dance team Adelaide and Hughes added fifteen assistants to back up their dancing, and Rock and White debuted a vaudeville revue act which lasted fifty-five minutes. In a subsequent Rock and White revue act with eight chorus girls, the costumes alone reportedly cost $10,000. Then, in 1920, William Rock produced his own full-fledged revue, *Silks and Satins;* "The question naturally arises, however, what will become of vaudeville if all the vaudeville stars enter the revue-producers' lists," mused the *New York Dramatic Mirror*.[18] But there were still plenty of stars exercising their revue-producing abilities on the vaudeville stage. Songsters Whiting and Burt added eight assistants in 1920 to create a new forty-five minute act; Walter Huston and Bayenne Whipple, after seven seasons as a two-act, dressed up their routine with a jazz band and described it as a "novelty revue."[19] Dance two-act Jeanette Hackett and Harry Delmar were producing their fourth revue act by 1923, a full-stage spectacle with eight chorus girls and costumes small enough to fill half a handbag. The 1925 Hackett and Delmar revue number at the Palace brought "real Parisian nudity" to vaudeville; in one number Jeanette appeared nude except for rhinestone clusters.[20] Dozens of these girl and dance "flashes" were manufactured from male-female two-acts;[21] *Variety* noted in October 1919 that most male singles, female singles, male two-acts, sister acts, and male-female acts now have "productions." Given in addition the increasing numbers of big bands, miniature operetta acts,[22] and dance troupes, gradually vaudeville was becoming a different kind of entertainment from what it had once been.

Complaints that big-time bills contained too many singing, dancing, and other musical turns were more and more common in the teens;[23] *Billboard* protested of an October 1918 Palace bill that

> while there are undoubtedly some clever people on the bill, the entertainment, as a whole, is nothing more or less than a disjointed, hodge-podge of music, song and dance, with no semblance of a novelty to act as a stabilizer or even as a digestive tonic to the Brobdingnagian helping of a one-course vaudeville meal.[24]

By the end of the teens, reviewers had noticed that vaudeville was looking less like itself and more like a musical comedy or a revue. A 1919 Riverside Theatre bill was "built along revue lines"; a November 1919 Palace show had a "musical comedy atmosphere"; "in fact, vaudeville really seems to be playing now as musical comedy," concluded another reporter.[25] *Variety*'s "Sime" turned prophet in 1919, when he bemoaned the amount of singing on a Riverside bill, and voiced some fears about where the trend would lead.

> Of course, the singing thing was ever evident. Where has vaudeville gone to? Musical comedy? Or does vaudeville go to musical comedy anytime it shows anything? This dance thing from the bunk classical to the dirty shimmey just seems to have about ruined a vaudeville show since the bookers found it an easy way to fill up their programs...still vaudeville is doing business, big business, nearly all the time. But one can never tell.[26]

The problem, of course, was that the new emphasis on song and dance meant there was a corresponding de-emphasis of comedy, and its lack was increasingly deplored in reviews.[27] *Variety* described one Palace bill as

> a place to invite the soul to the dazed contemplation of a pageantry of draperies, but you have to wait long, oh, so long! for the laughs. The stage decorations pass in bewildering array of opalescent orgies and amethystine splendors...there are wonderful

gowns done in tints and fabrics for which there probably isn't a name and the men make a procession of claw hammer coats and Beau Nash trimmings. Lord—ie! What a grand lady vaudeville has grown up to be.[28]

By the early twenties, the next-to-last spot commonly went, not to a comedy act, but to a song and dance production act; Rooney and Bent's "Rings of Smoke," for example, always played next-to-last—for where else could it be placed?[29] Usually lasting almost an hour, such acts were too long and too showy for any earlier spot.

But lavish display was not real vaudeville entertainment, and there were loud hints that many vaudeville shows were boring. One vaudeville fan, interviewed by *Billboard,* publicly declared that he and others like him are "paying weekly for variety—and are getting monotony." He had attended an average of two or three vaudeville performances a week for five years, and had seen the program develop into a dance carnival, he pointed out with disgust.[30] "They's a whole lot of show at the Palace this week but they ain't a whole lot of entertainment," mused an observer of another all-too-typical bill.[31]

There was simply too much "show" to be truly appreciated, and the succession of equally big names destroyed the pace of a bill. "Deluged with stellar talent," a bill at the Los Angeles Orpheum "just did not seem to make headway"; a 1924 Palace bill was "toned so high it almost chokes itself."[32] Vaudeville audiences were quite naturally becoming jaded. "Wanted: A few drops of condensed pep from some place in the universe to stir up the Palace audiences these days," *Billboard* announced; "One by one the weeks have been going by and a jammed house sits in calm acceptance of bills that a king's ransom could scarcely buy." Now many shows often just "never seemed able to reach the crest."[33]

Ostensibly, business was booming. Houses were full; scalpers were still doing big business down the block from the Palace marquee. But as audiences became accustomed to the diet of glamorous stars, lavish costumes, and elaborate production numbers, managers had to put together ever more impressive bills, which would themselves grow stale. As a result of its inclination toward pageantry, vaudeville's exclusiveness was vanishing, and its audience was diluted: why go to vaudeville for spectacle when you could see bigger and better for a bit higher price in musical comedy and revue?

Nonetheless, vaudeville bookers doggedly spent their meager budgets to create one or two breathtaking production numbers in the Ziegfeld style with disastrous results. Expensive acts like "Rings of Smoke" monopolized a budget and left little money for the remainder of the bill, which suffered in comparison. With vaudeville unable to afford them, big-time comedians were lured to film and the musical stage.[34] More and more often, reviewers in the twenties, announced that a show was mediocre, or simply bad.[35] A 1922 bill at the Palace earned this rating:

> Holdovers, returns, "names" with little but past performances to back them up, and one or two good and healthy old-style flops, combine to make this week's show one of the sort that makes a "regular" appreciate a rocking chair near the radiator, his own wife, and a thrilling trade paper or a snappy seed catalogue.[36]

One 1925 act was praised as a pleasurable interlude, in "the usual vaudeville morass of nothingness." And although prices were higher than ever, perceptive critics noticed that many of the same acts could be seen in big- and small-time.[37]

Variety noted rather incredulously in 1920 that three of the turns on the Colonial bill had spent considerable time in the three-a-day. A few weeks later the Palace bill was surprisingly reported to be a "curious mixture" of big-time and small-time acts. When a male-female team that had clattered around the small time was an unqualified hit at the Palace in 1924, *Variety* theorized that a good small-time turn could now make just as big a hit at the Palace as it could in "supposedly smaller company."[38] Occasionally it was noted that a vaudeville joke had actually been heard the same day in burlesque, and sometimes it had been used on the burlesque stage first;[39] indeed, circus acts and even freak acts were finding a niche on the big time.[40] Unable to afford the comics with big-time finesse, vaudeville was gradually falling back on the habits of an earlier lifetime: physical comedy, grotesque costumes and make-up, even "blue" material. By 1922, *Variety* could exclaim that "the Palace may be the classiest vaudeville audience in America, but they're assuredly strong for hoke—not the mild sort, but the pure, unadulterated burlesque brand."[41]

Of course, there were many big-time male-female teams from the years of vaudeville's greatest vitality still performing, but it was the new male-female teams who typified the new trends. For example, one of vaudeville's hottest new acts in the twenties was Bert Lahr—"the funniest man in burlesque"—and his female partner Mercedes. After several years in some lowly "school" acts, in 1917 Bert Lahr debuted on the Columbia Circuit; from 1920 to 1922 he was principal comedian with the "Roseland Girls" and "Keep Smiling" burlesque companies. He played a German cop, using an inarticulate "Dutch" dialect, exaggerated make-up, and broad facial work and gestures. One reviewer thought "his funny make-up, with his piggish eyes and tiny Germified upper-lip decoration," was hilarious, and it was said he "kept his eyebrows and forehead moving overtime." His work was also very acrobatic, featuring neckfalls and flops. Mercedes began as a chorus girl in the same burlesque company, and moved up to soubrette status in the fall of 1920.[42]

They debuted in vaudeville in 1922 at the small-time Fifth Avenue Theatre, with fifteen minutes of comedy in "one." "Looks like a mixed two act from burlesque," *Variety* sneered, calling it on only a small-time keel. Exactly one year later, back in New York in another small-time theatre, Mercedes and Lahr were encored again and again, and *Variety* conceded that the big time could use them in any spot. By the following season they were regulars on what was left of the Keith big time. Their act still smacked of burlesque, but now audiences loved it. When they appeared on a big-time bill with standard mixed comedy team Crawford and Broderick, a reviewer observed that Lahr "paints his comedy with a much broader brush" than the former, and the Riverside customers "fancy the contrast."[43]

Their act was a pick-up scene called "What's the Idea?". Lahr kept to his old "Dutch" cop character and grotesque make-up. To his own nose he added a "large false proboscis" and his suit was several sizes too large; Mercedes dressed like a burlesque soubrette, in a short skirt over tights. Lahr still did pratfalls and sang "S'Peggy O'Neil" in an awful voice, while Mercedes sang and played the sexy straight to his funny talk and did a hootchy-kootchy dance.[44] The talk was low comedy. Critic Fred Morgany's drawings of the duo show Mercedes shaking her anatomy in a scant dress, and Lahr, in cop dress, crying "Stop—it's again' the law to shimmy or vibrate any part of the human astronomy!" In another drawing, Lahr is saying, "In the name of the station house—stop shifting your gears!" Mercedes had lines full of easy innuendo: "They call me 'vaccination'—I never catch anything"; Lahr claimed he "socked" her to sleep, and quipped, "If I ain't stewed I'm out 7 bucks."[45] Bert Lahr does not hide his burlesque training, reported *Variety,* "and this low comedy to vaudeville is like feeding starving Armenians." By June 1925 they had played the Palace and were listed among the Keith-Albee "All Star Acts."[46]

Ted Healey was another graduate of the burlesque circuits. In 1917 he was a comedian with the "Cuddle Up" company, and after a brief stint as a vaudeville blackface performer, he teamed up with his new wife Betty Braun, probably in early 1923.[47] While perhaps not as broad as Lahr, Healey was described as "The Funniest Fellow of all the Fools," one who clowned every second and kept his audiences screaming. Fred Morgany caricatured him in blazer and straw panama, shouting, "I want to go to the shoe college—it's higher than Oxford!" Betty appears in Morgany's cartoon strip in a scanty chorus-girl tutu, leggy and with bobbed hair, saying "I shot at a rabbit—missed him by a 'hair.' " Whereas Ted was the "furious funster," Betty was the "dazzling blonde" who capered back and forth adding atmosphere to his antics. Ted also contributed a burlesque of an aerialist, and a rendering of "Mammy" a la Jolson.[48]

Ted was famed for his ad-libbing, and sometime in the late twenties, during a New York appearance, he asked two boyhood friends to appear onstage with him for some impromptu fun. Moe and Shemp (joined afterwards by Larry) went over so well he kept them in the act (and divorced Betty in 1932), billing them as his two, then three stooges. When the foursome went to Hollywood in 1933 (with Shemp replaced by brother Curly) to make movies, Ted and his "face-slapping, skull-cracking, eye-poking maniacs" became still more famous. Ted was credited with being the man "who made the United States stooge-conscious." After his death in 1937, his three stooges continued to perform without him.[49]

Burlesque graduates were becoming more conspicuous on the vaudeville stage,[50] but many teams not known to be from burlesque did slapsticky low comedy. Bert Wheeler had come to vaudeville from a Gus Edwards schoolboy act and married Betty while still a teenager; after a year or so as members of a rather off-color production number, "Fun on the Boulevard," they formed a two-act.[51] There are few descriptions of their routine, but Bert's comedy was called "hoke comedy," and not only did he utilize an inflated bird, but he did most of his routine lying down! Bert must have done some mugging, for it was said that his "wrinkles" amuse, and he was known for his impromptu funmaking—walking into others' acts and making wisecracks, as when he mischievously called out to the orchestra leader, "Benny, you'll die drinking that stuff."[52] Like Mercedes and Betty Healey, Betty Wheeler was a dancer and "satiates the eye satisfyingly with her good looks, breezy manner and cute appearance." The two-act was abruptly terminated, however, when Betty Wheeler ran off with another performer, sued Bert for mental cruelty, and was awarded $34,000— and obscurity, whereas Bert enjoyed several decades of fame and married three more times.[53]

They were one of many male-female teams in the twenties in which the man supplied low comedy, the woman sex appeal. Ed and Birdie Conrad's act featured Ed's "hokum," contrasted with the "sweetness" of Birdie; Al Trahan did low comedy, his partner Vesta Wallace was a "looker" who sang. Old teams broadened their humor. Hyams and McIntyre jettisoned their sentimental sketch "Maybloom" for a new act in which McIntyre impersonated a red-nosed comedian, with "hoke" the brand of humor employed. Similarly, wisecrackers Keno and Green created a new act full of stage falls and "low comedy wallops," and Conlin and Glass's act was now "hoke stuff."[54]

Almost all of the new male-female headliners did physical comedy, almost a necessity in the huge vaudeville houses being built in the twenties.

Famous mixed conversation team Dooley and Sales had a hard time when they appeared at the Hippodrome, because the huge house was "impervious to gags."[55] It was visibly funny slapstick and comedy falls that went over now, as in the act done by Toney and Norman. Jim Toney and Ann Norman, comedian and straight woman, were teamed as early as 1911, but not until 1917 did they attract any attention in New York City and establish themselves as a standard big-time act. It was a conventional flirtation and began with a sidewalk pick-up, but was constructed to show Jim's specialty, his amazing falls: he would strike a pose, hold it a few moments, then crumble to the floor in slow motion. His costume was a comic version of a sidewalk conversationalist's—a slipshod business suit and a prop derby. "It would make a monkey laugh to watch Toney in his nut stuff." raved *Billboard*.[56]

A team composed of members of two famous stage families was also doing stage falls to great applause in the twenties. Gordon Dooley was teamed with his new young wife, Martha Morton, daughter of old-timers Sam and Kitty Morton and a seasoned veteran in the rambunctious sort of comedy. While Martha tried to sing a ballad, Gordon interrupted with a dive over the footlights and right into the piano. He scrambled over to Martha and brought up the subject of their marriage; "Didn't your old man raise hell!" he crowed, slapping her roughly on the back, whereupon she punched him on the jaw, giving Gordon opportunity to go into a series of somersaults. Their finale was a double song and dance with Gordon in dame dress. This knockabout act might have been unacceptable to audiences earlier in the century, but it now "had 'em eating out of their palms" and enabled the team to "write their own ticket."[57] In a later act they did a double comedy tango in Spanish costumes, and a slow motion bit of boy meeting girl which featured knockabout; at one point, Gordon kicked Martha in the rear.[58]

Ann Codee, of Orth and Codee, was another woman whose specialty was "physical comedy of the kind that one could see over and over again." Frank Orth, in vaudeville since 1897, had been teamed successfully with several male partners in male two-acts in the teens, but he joined up with his wife in 1918, and during the mid-twenties they became big-timers in a mixture of knockabout and songs called "Franchy."[59] The act opened with Ann's song complaining about all the men who follow her, during which Orth entered in boob get-up, following her as she sang. During the talk Orth got all sorts of rough handling from his taller wife, and his comic pan added to the laughter. The high point of the act was a double song, "The Proposal," during which Orth took a "glorious shellacking," and was finally picked up bodily, spanked, and hit with a chair.[60] Just as boisterous was "The Last Car," by Wayne and Warren, whose jokes reveal the rough edge of humor in latter-day vaudeville: he makes wisecracks about the girl's father, and says that if her father had one more hair on his chest he'd have to live in a tree; she says that one more crack like that, and she will knock him so cold she will be able to walk home on the ice.[61]

In fact, the declining subtlety of vaudeville humor in the mid-twenties partly explains the continued popularity of the Dumb Dora. Although the theme had the potential for nuance, it could easily be milked for "hoke" — as in Clifford and Marion's act, in which the woman played a boob type, with "make-up suggesting nothing less than an unfortunate half-wit." *Variety* thought they carried it too far, and disliked all the talk about the woman being "as dumb as she looks."[62] Given vaudeville's reborn fondness for vulgarity, the dumbbell increasingly came across as a dumb "broad." A routine by James Madison, called "Dialogue Between Master of Ceremonies and a Dumb Dora," illustrates the indelicate possibilities of the character.

Master of Ceremony: (to one of the female performers): If you do well this week, I may hold you over.
Dumb Dora: Hold me over what?
Master of Ceremony: I mean I'll renew your engagement.
Dumb Dora: Has it been broken?
Master of Ceremony: Has what been broken?
Dumb Dora: Our engagement.
Master of Ceremony: We're not engaged. Getting married is foreign to my thoughts.
Dumb Dora: That's all right; I'm a foreigner.
Master of Ceremony: (overcome by her dumbness): You intrigue me.
Dumb Dora: What's that?
Master of Ceremony: I said, "You intrigue me."
Dumb Dora: Not while all these people are watching.
Master of Ceremony: Say, do you know what intrigue means?
Dumb Dora: I don't care. Now that I have you I needn't wear tight shoes any more.
Master of Ceremony: Why did you ever wear tight shoes?
Dumb Dora: It was my only chance of getting squeezed.
Master of Ceremony: (with some warmth): If I stay around you much longer, I'll lose my self control.
Dumb Dora: Well, I can't remain here all night.
Master of Ceremony: I can tell by looking into a girl's eyes, just what she thinks of me.
Dumb Dora: How very annoying.
Master of Ceremony: Do you object to petting?
Dumb Dora: That is something I have never done.
Master of Ceremony: Petting?
Dumb Dora: No; objecting.
Master of Ceremony: Suppose I tried to kiss you.
Dumb Dora: You'd have to use force.
Master of Ceremony: In that case I don't think I'll undertake it.
Dumb Dora: Oh, that's all right. You're stronger than I am. (She purses up her lips.)[63]

The small time had always permitted offerings with a tinge of "blue"; when a male-female duo at the small-time 58th Street Theatre resorted to "semi-suggestive material," the applause was thought to show what the average small-time audience wanted.[64] But "damns" and innuendos increasingly found their way into male-female (and other) acts at big-time theatres: Doyle and Cavanaugh's turn at the Riverside in 1922 had "some 'blue' notes"; the "blue" in Tighe and Leedom's act at the Colonial appealed to the gallery; Gilfoyle and Lange made a hit at the Riverside in November 1923 with "blue" material.[65]

Extant "blue notes" reveal the predictable. In Frey and Rogers's act, the man asked, "Are you married?" "That's my business," she snapped back; "How's business?" he cordially replied, after some broad pondering. A skit done by Wanzer and Palmer, a standard twenties team, featured conversation between a society lady and an unsavory coal wagon driver. She's a reformer, but he tries to get sociable. She asks his views on liquor, and he offers her a drink from his hip flask. But when he discovers she's married he tries to leave, saying he had trouble with a married woman seven years ago. She responds that her husband is in Baltimore; yeah, that's what the other one said, he cracks, but he came back for his rubbers or something.[66] A James Madison routine, this one from 1930, shows the trend continued.

(At rise lady enters from left and starts walking across stage.)
Man: (following her): Lady! (She pays no attention to him.)
Man: (repeating in louder voice): Oh, Lady!
She: (turning around): What is it?
He: I've been shouting at you for the last half hour.
She: I didn't know you were addressing me.
He: Maybe you're not used to being called a lady.
She: (coldly): Let us not mince words. What is your business.
He: I'm a horse doctor. Any of your folks sick?
She: If they were, they wouldn't send for a horse doctor.
He: I also treat jackasses.[67]

By 1925 the Keith office was finding it necessary to make cuts in performers' material all over the East, censoring curse words, sex business, and two-way gags, such as "Mother is home sick in bed with the doctor"; or, raising one's skirt and announcing "I'm a show girl."[68] The vulgarity made the big time's resemblance to small time still more pronounced, and made audiences less willing to pay big-time prices. Besides, the portion of the audience who delighted in horseplay and innuendo could enjoy still zestier acts on the flourishing burlesque wheels. Defeated in its attempt to rival Ziegfeld's flights of fancy, vaudeville discovered that in the meantime a full-blown version of its lower nature had emerged as a competitor.

But there were still other competitors. By the twenties vaudeville's hit singers and jazz bands could be heard in a fan's own home, on records. Record sales were soaring in the twenties, and performers like Al Jolson could earn $7000 a side recording for Columbia, more than twice the best salaries paid for a week's work—twice a day—in vaudeville.[69] Although radio was not yet attracting many big names, already comparable entertainment could be heard on the "set." Radio sales first gained momentum during the recession of 1920; a set was only $10.00, so cheap it seemed like entertainment for free. Sales increased almost sixfold between 1922 and 1924, and by then there were six hundred stations. Performers were discovering "Radio Paying More and More," and "K-A [Keith-Albee] Dead Against Radio," as *Variety* headlines announced.[70]

The middle class was saturated with demands on its leisure, for there was more to see and hear and do than ever before. Undoubtedly, however, vaudeville's most deadly competitor was film. Only a novelty at first, by the teens film offered drama, and filmmakers began competing for performers, hitherto unbilled and lowly paid by the early, technically oriented companies. The star system was established almost overnight, salaries soared, and film began bidding against legitimate theatre and vaudeville for talent. Even a valued performer like Florence Turner, the Vitagraph Girl, was paid only $5.00 a day in 1906, but by 1917, Douglas Fairbanks was commanding $15,000 a week—while the top vaudeville stars usually made only $3500 a week.[71] Vaudeville stars began experimenting with the lucrative medium, usually during the summer between seasons; Rooney and Bent, for example, made several pictures based on their famous vaudeville routines in the mid-teens. In 1915 the United Booking Office warned that vaudevillians who performed in film would have their salaries decreased, or else not be booked.[72]

Beginning in 1914, the big film houses gradually encroached on the Palace territory: the Strand, the Rialto, the Rivoli, the Capitol, the Paramount, and then, in March 1927, the Roxy. These colossal theatres had an atmosphere of "deluxe" far surpassing the vaudeville temples, and had high profits, given their low operating costs, gigantic seating capacities, and continuous shows. Besides, once produced, a film was enacted again and again at no further cost to its producers;[73] vaudeville could produce equally lavish shows, but then had it to do all over again the next week, and the next. Spectacle and stories were not film's only achievement; it was learning to surpass vaudeville at its forte, slapstick. Vaudeville comics could simulate eye-poking and endure real kicks-in-the-rear onstage, but a Keystone comic could suffer much worse than a pie in the face and emerge unscathed a moment later, ready to suffer harsher trials. Slapstick could be faster, harder, more exaggerated, thus funnier on the screen. Vaudevillians had only one resource film could not, for the time being, top: an earful of rapid-fire witticisms and raggy tunes.

Given its supreme advantage, vaudeville houses felt safe in adding more and more films to their bills as a way to compete; in the twenties, even a big-time house like the Riverside had five film reels on a bill.[74] By then, some people were going to theatres for the motion pictures and not for the vaudeville, as an overheard conversation between a couple at Loew's State revealed: "There's vaudeville here, too. I thought you said Pictures," said she. "Sure—vaudeville. But it will be over soon and then we'll get the picture," he replied.[75]

In the mid-twenties, however, the film industry dealt a series of blows that felled vaudeville. The first was the appearance of the "superspecials"—longer films produced at greater cost, which were successful at the expense of the vaudevillian: the higher cost of renting a big motion picture meant the vaudeville portion of the show had to be cheaper.[76] It was equally devastating when, profitting from vaudeville's example, the prestigious film houses did the obvious and added live, big-time vaudeville acts to their picture bill, calling them "Big-Name Presentations." As a result, while vaudeville's box office sales plummeted in the 1925-26 season, the audiences at presentation houses were usually so huge that not everyone could get in.[77]

But vaudeville managers still refused to see the truth. "Nothing Will Supplant Vaude," Proctor told reporters. Each year brought new excuses from vaudeville spokesmen for their bad business—e.g., daylight-saving time, bad weather—along with a succession of novel plans that would bring vaudeville back to health: revues with local talent; holding over big bills two weeks; longer contracts; selling tickets in drug stores; "unit shows," and so on.[78] The Keith-Albee management persisted in building still larger and more grandiose big-time theatres, although existing ones were losing money.[79]

The publicists protested, but the facts told the truth. Reviews in the twenties increasingly noted half-capacity houses at the big-time houses; in January 1925 the two-a-day was running as much as $5000 a week behind its corresponding grosses of a year earlier.[80] One by one, vaudeville theatres were forfeiting their big-time status.[81] A Keith-Albee agent made headlines early in 1926 by having a nervous breakdown.[82] Many male-female teams must have felt anxious. With less than eleven big-time weeks of work available in the East, vaudevillians had to play all sorts of theatres to make a living—the big time, presentation houses, and three- and four-a-day vaude-film houses. Some standard big-time acts were working from booking to booking, at whatever price they could get. Sam and Kitty Morton, who had played only Keith big time since the turn of the century, were forced to sign with Loew's four-a-day circuit.[83]

Then, in 1927, came what would later be interpreted as the final blow. When *The Jazz Singer* opened on 6 October 1927, it did not create a sensation and reviews were lukewarm, but customers quietly kept coming and coming. Even the major film studios did not realize the potential of sound films for almost a year, and vaudeville did not feel threatened. Nonetheless, several weeks after *The Jazz Singer* opened, the average weekly gross at the Palace—$28,000—had dropped $8,000.[84] Although the Keith-Albee office had bravely announced it was "prepared for one of the most brilliant years in its history," the 1927-28 season saw most of vaudeville fall by the wayside. The season had opened with twelve houses, but one by one they added films and extra shows.[85] In September *Billboard* suggested that "what had been known as two-a-day vaudeville is either dead or tottering on its last legs," and one month later its headlines proclaimed, "Death Knell Sounded for 'Big Time.' "[86] Any remaining big-name acts would soon leave vaudeville; bookers could arrange only about ten weeks for them, and in any case could not afford their salaries.[87] A Palace booker was horrified when an act chose to appear at the Roxy instead of the famed Palace, with the argument that "we'll be at the Roxy longer than all the time you can give us."[88]

Thus, even before the depression, what remained of big-time vaudeville was "almost comatose." For it was the talkies, not the depression, that immobilized live theatre—the legitimate as well as vaudeville. Between 1927 and 1929, before the depression, the number of admissions to film houses almost doubled; in contrast, of eighteen theatres on Broadway in 1927, by 1929, before the crash, seventeen of them were already talking pictures, with the Palace the only exception.[89] Although there were still hundreds of vaudevillians working live, performing in the colossal movie theatres as a sort of "presentation" to a big movie feature was not vaudeville. Even the Palace was not "doing business." In 1930, its new management, Radio-Keith-Orpheum, was spending tremendous sums to construct weekly live entertainment composed of big vaudeville names now making good in radio or film, who had to be lured back to "Mecca." The Palace was being artificially sustained, week by week, with costly transfusions, at a loss of $4000 a week.[90]

After several seasons of long runs, special shows, big bands, and offbeat personalities, in May 1932 the Palace added two extra daily shows, at $.50 to $1.00 prices. But even cheap vaudeville was no good, when down at the Paramount audiences could see a film and Fred Astaire in a tabloid version of his hit *The Band Wagon;* at the Capitol, in addition to the film there were Burns and Allen, Arthur Tracey, and Cab Calloway's Band; Loew's State had a film plus Smith and Dale and a shortened version of the Broadway hit *Girl Crazy*. With such competition at the lowest ebb of the depression, the Palace could not get out of the red. "SIX ACTS, FILMS IN N.Y. PALACE JULY 9," announced *Variety* in its 28 June front-page headline. After twenty years of vaudeville the famous Palace became just another grind house, and before the depression had ended, it would become a straight film house. Any living male-female teams who would henceforth play there would be names to "ring only the faintest bell...."[91]

8

George Burns and Gracie Allen

Although vaudeville as a business arrangement was virtually dead, the vaudeville art was very much alive. The thriving live entertainment circuits of decades past had fostered the development of a vast pool of performers with popular stage skills, and these entertainers did not vanish overnight, although the financial structure that supported their livelihood had crumbled. With the opportunities to do live stage work shrinking, there was a surfeit of talent finding its way into the radio, recording, and film industries. Vaudeville's finest performers now had to make a living divorced from the audiences and milieu that had created them, but they brought the rewards of a long tradition into these new venues of entertainment. The patter and crooning heard on the set, the mugging and comedy falls seen on the screen, indeed, every nuance of the uprooted vaudevillian's stage style, was limned with the hard-earned lore accumulated by generations of troupers working in tandem with their fans just across the footlights. The gifts of vaudeville lived on in the performances of Jack Benny, Eddie Cantor, George Jessel, Bert Lahr, Pat Rooney II, John Bubbles, and many others. Like all these performers, George Burns and Gracie Allen ventured into this new, still unsettled kind of show business world bringing an ability to "sell" that was anything but new. They were, as *Variety* put it in 1927, "a real vaudeville turn."[1]

Like so many others in vaudeville, George Burns—born Nathan Birnbaum on 20 January 1896—had grown up in a poor family on New York's Lower East Side. From his debut with the Pee Wee Quartet on Bowery street corners as a youngster, he was in love with the idea of being an entertainer.[2] By the time he teamed up with Gracie in 1923, George had been the "Company" of "Fry and Company," the Williams of "Brown and Williams," the Glide of "Goldie, Fields, and Glide," the Links of "Burns and Links," had performed a skating act, worked with a seal for three days, and done ballroom dancing with a sixteen-year-old female partner stage-named Hermosa Jose, whom he married, supposedly so her father would let her go on the road—in other words, "anything to stay in show business."[3]

In 1922 George was doing a song and dance act with male partner Billy Lorraine, called "Broadway Thieves" because they did imitations of Broadway stars such as Eddie Cantor, Al Jolson, and of course George M. Cohan. Since they had rarely seen these stars perform, it was a horrible act, and after years of trying, George was finally convinced he could neither sing nor dance and was looking for a female partner to do a talking act, when he was introduced to Grace Allen.[4]

Like George Burns, Grace Ethel Cecile Rosalie Allen described herself as stagestruck since childhood. Daughter of a song and dance man in San Francisco, she had sung and danced and performed since age three. During summers in between schooling at a Catholic convent, she performed some in vaudeville.[5] At about age fourteen she left school for the stage, and was soon performing in an Irish act with Larry Reilly and several other girls. Her colleening ended, apparently because of salary or billing squabbles, and her unsatisfactory tenure with an unreliable partner named Boylan Brazil was even briefer. When Gracie met George Burns she was out of work, in secretarial school and hating it, and as desperate as he was to get an act together.[6]

Gracie had a two-act written for her by a writer—her fiancé—but a three-hundred-dollar drop was required to perform it, which the new team could not afford. George had an act, too, put together from joke books and the like, so they started with that act.[7] It was a flirtation routine, and, as has often been said, George was the comedian, Gracie the straight. It was probably the smart, sarcastic kind of flirtation then in vogue in which even the female straight came across as wise, for George later said that "the act was bad for Gracie because it was out of character for her. It was wisecracks...." George was presumably the comic masher, and like Joe E. Brown, he wore wide pants, a big red bow tie, and a hat turned up in front.[8]

Although both George and Gracie later claimed George rewrote the act after its first performance,[9] they kept their original roles somewhat longer than claimed, for reviews by *Variety* in April 1923 and again in June 1923 identify George as the comic. In the April act, George was "a smooth worker of the lounge-lizard, finale-hopper type, with not much to spend, beyond conversation," and with "his efforts at lovemaking consisting of 'wisecracks.'" *Variety* did think the boy had a good delivery for this type of talk, and that the girl was an excellent foil, with both having "more than average" personalities. But several of the gags were old—the skit reminded *Variety* of the one previously done by Matthews and Ayres, a standard flirtation team—and the talk needed to be strengthened.[10]

They ended with a comedy "stop time" double dance broken up by gagging, with George getting laughs cueing the orchestra leader for "music!" George claimed later that "we were the first ones ever to do what 'Laugh-In' has been doing for years," but at the time *Variety* thought it was "more or less of a purloined idea." By June, Burns was still doing a "wisecracking hick," and Gracie was said to handle talk competently too. Already the act was "well delivered," and the team showed ability much above their material; but with their present routine they were judged only three-a-day fare.[11]

As late as November 1923 they were offering "some wise-cracking chatter that didn't take them far" — although by this point Gracie may have been doing the wisecracking. For however long it took, the team had discovered the audience was not responding as intended to their act. Gracie had an "isn't-this-silly-what-is-this-all-about" air in her straight lines right from the start. "If she asked me a question, they would laugh and I didn't expect a laugh there," said George. "While I was answering her, I talked in on her laugh so nobody heard what I had to say." But the more serious Gracie tried to act, the more laughs she got. "Finally, I saw the light," concluded George. "I started playing the serious, exasperated male, leading up to Gracie's nitwit gags."[12]

Thus, Gracie became a dumbbell. There were other comic female types to choose from, but George insisted the audience gave Gracie her stage character. After giving Gracie her first jokes, George gradually learned "that certain jokes were not good for her. The audience would tell you.... They didn't want sarcasm from Gracie." The audience "didn't want her to be smart," and George began to collect Dumb Dora jokes.[13] No doubt there was something in Gracie's personality that made the audience respond best to her as a dumbbell; in fact, the team's earliest reviewer had noticed Gracie's "lack of sophistication," a quality well-suited to the Dumb Dora stereotype.[14] Then, too, perhaps George, however consciously, felt most comfortable with Gracie as a dumb comedienne. Making Gracie comedienne was a difficult decision for George — it "broke my heart," he later confessed — and Gracie recalled that George got lots of kidding for giving her the laugh lines.[15]

But another reason they turned so quickly to the Dumb Dora character may have been that they already owned some dumb girl material: the act written for Gracie by a man both she and George described as her fiancé, a writer named Ben Ryan — the same Ben Ryan who had created the earliest known dumbbell character for his partner Harriette Lee. The act Ryan wrote for Gracie was presumably the act she performed with Boylan Brazil, an act that featured flirting (a Ryan specialty) between a jewelry salesman from the city and a country girl named Sally Simpkins. If the act by Ryan for Gracie did feature a comic dumbbell—and the name Sally Simpkins suggests as much—then Gracie's subsequent sudden emergence as "natural" comedienne is all the more understandable, since she had certainly already rehearsed the Ryan act. Gracie herself told of rehearsing it for several weeks with two different male partners; she also said she had lost the drop for the Ryan act on the way back from Canada, which is exactly what happened after she performed with Boylan Brazil in Montreal.[16]

Of course, it is not certain whether or not Burns and Allen ever used any of the Ben Ryan material. Still without a drop, they clearly would not have used the Sally Simpkins characterization, but they could have used the idea and some of the dumbbell jokes. In fact, more than one contemporary viewed Burns and Allen as a product of Ryan and Lee. Performer Benny Rubin tells that in 1923, he chummed around with three fellows, one of whom was

> Benny Ryan, who worked with his wife as Ryan and Lee. Those three guys were also song writers and even wrote a song for me, one I could sing and dance to—"When Frances Dances with Me." Ryan's wife became ill and Ryan hired a girl to replace her in the act. She was a little dancer working with an Irish jig troupe. You know her as Gracie Allen.
>
> Then Benny Ryan decided he didn't want to troupe and hired George Burns to do his act with Gracie Allen. So Burns and Allen played the circuit as a small-time act. Then Al Boasberg, a jewelry salesman who later became a full-time comedy writer, sold them a sketch, "Lamb Chops." They tried it, liked it so much they left Benny Ryan, married each other, and worked in their own act.[17]

Certainly there were also plenty of other sources for the Dumb Dora material, the newspaper comics and jokebooks like *Whizbang, College Humor,* and *Madison's Budget,* among others.

At any rate, their first act was called "Sixty-Forty,"[18] and in December 1923 Burns and Allen were doing it around New York, at the Fordham Theatre and a small-time Flatbush theatre. The act opened with Gracie coming onstage with a spotlight on her, looking for George, who walked on in the dark lighting a cigar. Then Gracie saw him and started bawling him out, saying he was no good, always late, and so on; finally she said, "Here I've talked to you for three minutes and you don't even answer me. Aren't you going to say something?" George then turned, looked at her, and said "Hello, Babe"—and went back to his cigar.[19]

"I thought if I smoked, I would look like an actor. So I started smoking cigars when I was sixteen and I have been smoking them ever since," George explains. But no doubt the business was also something which enabled him to maintain his sangfroid onstage. George Burns has often confessed how awkward he was onstage at first: "I was self-conscious on the stage. I used to stutter and stammer."[20] The "Hello, Babe" line worried George the most, for it was either a big laugh or it fell flat on its face; "I'd walk down the street saying 'Hello Babe,' in every possible way. 'Hello, Babe—no that's not right. *Hello*, Babe. Hello, Babe!' And so on." At an engagement at the Columbia Theatre, a burlesque house whose Sunday vaudeville was an important showcase for bookers, sometime in late 1923 or early 1924, George was so nervous that he could not even get out the line![21] The cigar may have allayed his anxiety; many years later George explained that what an actor should do with his hands is a real problem if no specific business is called for; "I would be lost without that cigar."[22]

Not much else is known about "Sixty-Forty," but the jokes were obviously not the greatest, for Burns and Allen remained a small-time act for over two years. They played the little theatres in New York, New Jersey, and Connecticut, and in Sunday vaudeville shows at burlesque houses, as a "disappointment act," i.e., they waited by the phone to fill vacancies caused when more successful players fell ill.[23] But beginning on New Year's Eve in 1925, Burns and Allen were booked for nineteen weeks in and around New York City on the "big" small-time Loew's circuit, and by then they were doing a version of "Dizzy."[24]

This early "Dizzy" routine opened with George onstage talking to the orchestra leader, and went something like this, recalled George:

                Me: This little book I'm carrying is a book of systems.
Orchestra leader: What kind of systems?
                Me: All kinds. How to win at horses, how to meet a girl—everything.
Orchestra leader: How would you meet a girl?
                Me: You take an impossible name like Mamie Dittenfest, then you go up to a girl and say, "Pardon me, aren't you Mamie Dittenfest?" She'll say no. You say "Well, you certainly look like her." She'll say, "I'm not, though," then the next thing you know you're buying her a cup of coffee.

At that point Gracie made her entrance, and George whispered to the orchestra leader, "Watch this," then said to Gracie, "I beg your pardon, is your name Mamie Dittenfest?" "Yes," answered Gracie—causing George to turn and walk offstage, fast.[25]

It was on the Loew's circuit that George came to truly understand Gracie's part, and they gradually worked out her character.[26] In fact, their best joke, which gave the act its name, sounds like the Gracie of a later day; it came when George said, "You're dizzy":

        Gracie: I'm glad I'm dizzy. Boys like dizzy girls and I like boys.
Me [George]: I'm glad you're glad you're dizzy.
        Gracie: I'm glad you're glad I'm glad, etc. etc.[27]

The joke remained in their repertoire.

The team must have been improving, for around September 1925, Burns and Allen were booked (for $400 a week) for eighteen weeks on the Orpheum circuit—what remained of big-time vaudeville in the Western states.[28] Ben Ryan had asked Gracie to cancel the tour and marry him, but this important venture could not be passed up. Since George had been in love with Gracie from the beginning, he was thrilled at the opportunity of eighteen weeks on the road with Gracie. The story goes that thanks to Gracie's subsequent appendicitis, Ben Ryan's failure to send flowers despite the telegram George swears he sent Ryan, and George's persistent courting, Gracie finally fell in love with George, and they were married at the end of the tour, on 7 January 1926.[29]

Coincidentally, the marriage marked the beginning of real success for Burns and Allen. At the time of the marriage they were outside Cleveland on the small-time Gus Sun circuit, breaking in a new act they had acquired called "Lamb Chops," by a then-unknown writer named Al Boasberg.[30] The team had been praised for their personality and delivery from the beginning, and now that these were combined with the top-notch material of "Lamb Chops," Burns and Allen had it made. Five weeks after their marriage, they played "Lamb Chops" in Syracuse, and were such a hit that the manager called the Keith booking office. Thus, when they opened next at the lowly Jefferson Theatre in New York, Burns and Allen were seen by a Keith talent scout, who signed them to a five-year contract for $750 a week. "We were what is termed 'hot' and from then on we got steadily hotter," claimed Gracie; "Six weeks later we played the Palace," echoed George.[31] By August of that same year, 1926, the team had indeed made it to the Palace, and *Variety* was enthusiastic: the laughs were fast and many, and it was a "tiptop comedy interlude for the best vaudeville."[32]

George later published "the act we did the very first time we played the Palace," some of which went like this:

(Play-on music:)
(George and Gracie enter holding hands. Gracie stops, turns, looks toward the wings, and waves. She lets go of George's hand and walks toward the wing, still waving. Then she stops and beckons to whomever she is waving to come out. A man comes out, puts his arms around Gracie, and kisses her, and she kisses him. They wave to each other as he backs offstage. Gracie returns to George center stage.)

Gracie: Who was that?
George: You don't know?
Gracie: No, my mother told me never to talk to strangers.
George: That makes sense.
Gracie: This always happens to me. On my way in a man stopped me at the stage door and said, "Hi ya, cutie, how about a bite tonight after the show?"

George: And you said?
Gracie: I said, "I'll be busy after the show but I'm not doing anything now," so I bit him.
George: Gracie, let me ask you something. Did the nurse ever happen to drop you on your head when you were a baby?
Gracie: Oh, no, we couldn't afford a nurse, my mother had to do it.
George: You had a smart mother.
Gracie: Smartness runs in my family. When I went to school I was so smart my teacher was in my class for five years.
George: Gracie, what school did you go to?
Gracie: I'm not allowed to tell.
George: Why not?
Gracie: The school pays me $25 a month not to tell.

....

George: Hazel must be the smartest in your family.
Gracie: Oh, no. My brother Willy was no dummy either.

....

George: What's Willy doing now?
Gracie: He just lost his job.
George: Lost his job?
Gracie: Yeah, he's a window washer.
George: And?
Gracie: And...he was outside on the twentieth story washing a window and when he got through he stepped back to admire his work.
George: And he lost his job.

....

Gracie: When Willy was a little baby my father took him riding in his carriage, and two hours later my father came back with a different baby and a different carriage.
George: Well, what did your mother say?
Gracie: My mother didn't say anything because it was a better carriage.
George: A better carriage?
Gracie: Yeah...And the little baby my father brought home was a little French baby so my mother took up French.
George: Why?
Gracie: So she would be able to understand the baby—
George: When the baby started to talk?
Gracie: Yeah.
George: Gracie, this family of yours, do you all live together?
Gracie: Oh, sure. My father, my brother, my uncle, my cousin and my nephew all sleep in one bed and--
George: In one bed? I'm surprised your grandfather doesn't sleep with them.
Gracie: Oh, he did, but he died, so they made him get up.[33]

After a song and dance by Gracie, about ten minutes more of dialogue followed, which included the famous joke that gave the routine its name.

Burns: Do you like to love?
Allen: No.

Burns: Do you like to kiss?
Allen: No.
Burns: What do you like?
Allen: Lamb chops.
Burns: A little girl like you? Could you eat two big lamb chops alone?
Allen: No. But with potatoes I could.[34]

The act ended with a typical boy-girl song, which led into a double dance interrupted by jokes: e.g.:

George: Stop! (Music stops)
Gracie: My sister Bessie had a brand new baby.
George: Boy or girl?
Gracie: I don't know, and I can't wait to get home to find out if I'm an aunt or an uncle.
George: Music! (Music starts, and dance continues).[35]

The success of the stop-music joking showed the duo had acquired new expertise during their three years of small-time trouping. It was an old bit from their first week together, which had fallen flat on its face then, but it was a smash at the Palace: "The bit was just as good then," declared George, "but *we* weren't."[36]

The team returned to the Palace later that season in the headlined position, and "had the Palace bunch eating out of their hands after the opening and never lost them." Henceforth, into the thirties, Burns and Allen performed in the best of the remaining vaudeville theatres, and had successful London engagements each year between 1927 and 1931. They were now considered one of the top vaudeville acts, comedy stars who ranked in critical estimation with the famous male two-act Smith and Dale. When Burns and Allen appeared at the Palace in March 1931, they came on fourth, an important spot; Smith and Dale were the other comedy hit of the bill and played next-to-last, the more coveted position. The reviewer was quick to note, however, that "Burns & Allen can hold down that best spot anytime."[37]

They had a "new offering" by Al Boasberg for that particular 1931 Palace booking, called "Dizzy" because the Dizzy joke was featured; people remember the big jokes, not the small ones, said George. By 1931, the team had many "big jokes" which could be combined according to mood and occasion, and with whatever new jokes George took a liking to. They did "bits and pieces of 'Dizzy,' 'Lambchops,' 'Sixty-Forty,' and anything else I thought of," recalled George.[38] In that era of vaudeville before they got their own radio program, Burns and Allen had already articulated their mature two-act formula. They had developed certain bits which would be used successfully by them again and again throughout the remainder of their long career, always surviving the test of time; indeed, the test of new material was how well it suited the established prototype.

Two excellent examples of this perfected formula survive from the early thirties. In 1930, Burns and Allen recorded the following version of "Dizzy" for Columbia records:

George: Well say hello to everybody.
Gracie: Hello everybody.
George: Now that we're started what are we going to do? Oh I know what we'll do. I'm going to ask you something, you ask me the same thing, then I'll tell the answer. If I should say to you why are apples green, you must say I don't know, why are apples green. Do you understand that?
Gracie: No.
George: No, well you wouldn't. Look, whatever I say, you say. Do you understand that?
Gracie: Not very well.
George: It's going to be hard for you.
Gracie: Yes.
George: Oh I can see that. Well anyway here we go. What fellow in the army wears the biggest hat?
Gracie: Why are apples green.
George: I expected you to say that. Look, when I say what fellow wears the biggest hat, you must say I don't know, what fellow wears the biggest hat. Whatever I say.
Gracie: Oh.
George: Do you understand that?
Gracie: Well...
George: Well here we go. What fellow in the army wears the biggest hat?
Gracie: The fellow with the biggest head.
George: Oh yes, you understand that.
Gracie: That was good.
George: That was too good. Somebody must be helping you.
Gracie: Oh no.
George: That's awfully good. Well we'll try one more. What is it that sings and has four legs?
Gracie: Two canaries.
George: I picked out a good game. I stepped right into your backyard. Well this is the last one. What gives more milk, one cow or two cows?
Gracie: Oh.
George: What's that?
Gracie: Well I guess I'll be going home now.
George: Going home? I'll take you home in my car.
Gracie: Oh no thank you. I'm too tired. I'd rather walk.
George: Yes I'll walk you home. I'll walk home with you if you give me a kiss. I'll take you home.
Gracie: Well if you take me home I'll give you a kiss.
George: But just a minute, before I take you home I would like to find out whether or not your mother is home.
Gracie: She is, but my father wouldn't let you kiss my mother.

George: Oh you're dizzy.
Gracie: Well you're silly.
George: Well I'd rather be silly than dizzy.
Gracie: I know I'm dizzy. I'm glad I'm dizzy.
George: You're the only dizzy girl that I know that's glad she's dizzy.
Gracie: I'm glad I'm a dizzy girl, because boys like dizzy girls and I like boys.
George: I'm glad it's over. I'm glad it's finished.
Gracie: And I'm glad I'm dizzy.
George: All right. This can go on for years, let's talk of something else.
Gracie: Oh all...let's do something.
George: Let's do something.
Gracie: Let's do crossword puzzles.
George: That would be fun.
Gracie: I'm very good at them now. You know, I make them up.
George: Well make one up.
Gracie: All right. What is it that starts with c and, uh, well, I don't know how many letters, what is it?
George: Hmm, that's very good. You made that up.
Gracie: That came right out of my own head.
George: I'd have it stuffed.
Gracie: My head?
George: Your head.
Gracie: Oh I have brains you know.
George: Have you?
Gracie: Oh I have brains I haven't even used yet.
George: I see. Well leave 'em alone. Don't disturb them...It starts with c and you don't know how many letters, what is it. Does it jump?
Gracie: No.
George: Does it swim?
Gracie: No.
George: That's all right. Now give me another one.
Gracie: Well, no, you didn't guess that one.
George: I give it up.
Gracie: Well, look. Men shave with it.
George: And it starts with c.
Gracie: Yes.
George: Well, the only thing that I can think of that a man shaves with is soap.
Gracie: Soap! That's it. That's very good George. Now you make one up.
George: Why don't you go to a doctor and have him examine your head, and if the doctor finds a brain, have somebody examine the doctor.

Gracie: How can we start this side?
George: We'll start with a riddle. Will that be all right?
Gracie: Yes.
George: All right, we'll start. What's the difference between kissing a girl five years ago and kissing a girl fifty years ago?
Gracie: Oh. I don't know. What's the difference?
George: Forty-five years.
Gracie: Now don't tell me, let me think of the answer. Uh...no...No. I don't know.
George: You give it up.
Gracie: Yeah.

George:	Well, the answer is...is a...is...Horsefeathers. Do you see it now?
Gracie:	Horsefeathers? Horsefeathers. Horse...Oh yes! That's very good.
George:	Well I don't know, maybe I'm wrong. You're kind of glad you're living.
Gracie:	Yes.
George:	You're good and dizzy.
Gracie:	Yeah. I know I'm dizzy. I'm glad I'm dizzy, boys like girls...
George:	Well. Just fine. We had that on the other side. I think we'd better sing. (go into double number).[39]

The cross-fire in a 1933 recording, billed simply as "Comedy Skit," was equally lunatic.

George:	Well, Gracie, say hello to everyone.
Gracie:	Hello, everybody. What do I do now?
George:	Well, just make something up, you know.
Gracie:	Oh, all right. I'll make up a riddle. I'll give you three chances, and if you can't guess it, you win.
George:	If I can't guess it I win? Well, what happens if I guess it?
Gracie:	Well, uh, then it's a tie.
George:	It's a tie?
Gracie:	Now what's the difference...
George:	Just a minute Gracie. This one is on me. A fellow was in a restaurant, he orders spinach, mashed potatoes and cheese cake. How did I know that he was a soldier?
Gracie:	Ohhh, is that the one where the fellow had on a uniform? Yeah, oh, that's very good George. Tell that one.
George:	Listen. What I'd like to know is how do I allow myself to get mixed up into these things.
Gracie:	Oh, that's very funny. Now I'll make one up. Not only can I make up riddles, George, I also can tell you what you're thinking about. I'm a mind-reader.
George:	Listen, Gracie, is there anything that fazes you?
Gracie:	I don't think so.
George:	No.
Gracie:	All right, think of something.
George:	Well, all right, I'm thinking.
Gracie:	Uh, is it green?
George:	Is what green?
Gracie:	Does it hang from the ceiling and whistle?
George:	Does what hang from the ceiling and whistle?
Gracie:	Does it run along the floor and sing?
George:	Listen, uh...
Gracie:	Does it climb up buildings and swim?
George:	Just a minute. I thought you said that you could read my mind.
Gracie:	Well, George, how can I read your mind if you keep on asking all those silly questions?
George:	I'm asking...listen, let's talk about something else. Well, Gracie, I'm sorry to hear about your missing brother.
Gracie:	Oh, that's too bad, George, because my brother's missing too.
George:	Well, the only difference between me and you is that I have the power of mind over matter and you have no mind, and it doesn't seem to matter.

Gracie: Oh, I bet you tell that to all the girls.
George: I still would like to know how is your brother?
Gracie: My brother? Well, I think they ought to open up all the prisons. It would help prosperity.
George: Wait a minute. That's the wrong answer.
Gracie: No, that's the right answer but you asked me the wrong question.
George: Uh...
Gracie: Now, look, it costs the government seventy million dollars to feed all the prisoners.
George: Yes...
Gracie: And when they're out they only steal sixty million dollars a year.
George: Well...
Gracie: Now, that gives the government a ten million dollar profit right there, don't you think so?
George: I think so. I'll see you later, Gracie.
Gracie: Now take my brother Harry.
George: You take him.
Gracie: Well, they got him.
George: They got him?
Gracie: He's ruining Sing-Sing. He eats them out of house and warden.
George: House and warden.
Gracie: Yeah. And my other brother, Willy, well there's an appetite for you. He bit Harry.
George: Without ketchup?
Gracie: No, with ketchup.
George: Yeah, it's better with ketchup.
Gracie: Yeahhh. Willy goes to San Quentin.
George: He *goes* to San Quentin. He takes his books and he *goes* to San Quentin.
Gracie: Yeah. Well, I'll never forget when my brothers got out. How proud my father was. As they left the gate, my father was standing waving from his cell.
George: Your father *waved* from his cell.
Gracie: Yeah. He said, "Good-bye kids."
George: Hmmm.
Gracie: And they hollered back, "Good-bye Pop."
George: Nice family.
Gracie: Yeah. "Tell Uncle there's some toothpaste left in cell 22."
George: In cell 22.
Gracie: Yeah. My father didn't like prison, though.
George: Bad, huh?
Gracie: Yeah. They won't let him gamble. They said it gave the place a bad name.
George: Listen, Gracie, how is it that it's so easy for you to talk and so hard for me to listen?
Gracie: There you go.
George: Oh, yes, there I go and you're going with me.
Gracie: I can't. My shoes shrunk.
George: Your shoes *shrunk*?
Gracie: Yeah. George, what do they make shoes from?
George: Hide.
Gracie: What?
George: Hide.

Gracie: Oh, I'm not in the mood to play games. You hide.
George: Hide! Hide! The alligator's out-side.
Gracie: Ohhh, well, if the alligator's outside, let's all hide!
George: Oh, quiet.
Gracie: George, I've got some wonderful news for you. My brother got married, but it's the carpenter's fault. You see, my brother was crazy about...
George: I know that, Gracie. But what do you mean it was the carpenter's fault.
Gracie: Well, you see, my brother was crazy about a girl who lived on the third floor...
George Yes...
Gracie: But the carpenter made the ladder too short, and he eloped with the girl on the second floor.
George: But what about the girl on the third floor? Bet that made her pretty mad.
Gracie: Oh, well, she didn't seem to mind it. But her husband was so disappointed he could hardly hold the ladder.
George: But how could your brother get a license to marry a girl he didn't know?
Gracie: Oh: well, he got two licenses, one marriage license and one hunting license.
George: A hunting license?
Gracie: Yeah, because as soon as he marries her, she'll have to hunt for a job.
George: But does your father approve of things like that?
Gracie: Oh, my poor father, he couldn't say anything on account of his black eye.
George: Black eye...well all he had to do was just put a piece of steak on it.
Gracie: Well, if there was a piece of steak in the house, my mother wouldn't have given him a black eye!
George: A black...Gracie, if you had a brain you'd be smart, and if you knew how to use it, you'd have a brain.
Gracie: That's very good George. But I still like that one about early to bed, early to rise, makes you healthy, wealthy, wealthy and healthy.
George: A little music please.[40]

Each routine ended with the same song ("Do you believe me"), and in each case, after the song, George began humming the chorus, then broke off to explain to the audience, "We're dancing now. Hey, you're missing this and it's very nice." Burns and Allen were live stage performers in instinct and experience; the explanatory aside enabled them to suggest the visual part of their vaudeville act for radio and record listeners. Since Gracie Allen, an accomplished Irish clog and jig dancer, was unable to display her adeptness at kicking up her heels to a record audience, she made a joke about it: "George, look, I'm kicking the back of my head." "Well, maybe that's the trouble with you," George dryly replied. George's continued humming was interrupted by more jokes, and the routines ended thus:

George: You know, you're too smart for one girl.
Gracie: I'm more than one.
George: You're more than one?
Gracie: My mother has a picture of me when I was two. (Music.)

George: This is the finish. You've missed the dance.
Gracie: Good-bye!

These routines were pure vaudeville, exemplifying a model gradually developed on the vaudeville circuit; in fact, George observed in 1933 that "we've been doing the same thing for ten years." The first routine was recorded the year of their very first radio appearance; the second was done very early in their radio career, but was clearly a vaudeville act—it was specifically "Not Licensed for Radio Broadcast."[41] Throughout the thirties, until at least 1936, Burns and Allen would continue to perform live in the vaude-film houses.[42] They were a quintessential male-female vaudeville teams. From the vaudeville reviews, the recordings and scripts of their early acts, and George and Gracie's own descriptions, an understanding emerges of the workings and appeals of Burns and Allen's vaudeville artistry.

The major appeal of the act, of course, was Gracie's "adorable 'dizzy.'" *Variety* maintained that "without that dumbish personality and style of Grace Allen's, plus the voice, they wouldn't go much farther" than other teams featuring a Dumb Dora.[43] Gracie's style was different, implies *Variety*, and Gracie Allen told how:

> Now there had been many dumb Doras on the stage but the Gracie character was different. The other dumb Doras wore funny clothes and said funny things—they were sort of Tenth Avenue, if you know what I mean. I wasn't funny, I was wide-eyed and I never fell down or went slapstick or made funny faces and I made the smartest clothes I could buy.[44]

Not only were many other Dumb Doras in Bowery dress, but by this time many were funny in an almost vulgar way, more akin to burlesque. In a decadent era, Burns and Allen offered an amazingly clean brand of humor;

> You have something a reviewer doesn't see once in fifteen years in a team act, something that will keep your act always distinct from the general run of he-and-she acts. It's devilish clever, astoundingly clean for vaudeville of the current day and Miss Allen apparently has the brains to avoid doing things other girls on the stage have done to death,

explained one critic.[45] Thus, Gracie Allen's well-dressed dumbbell, who made neither faces nor innuendoes, was much less broad than the others. Extant pictures of Gracie from the late twenties and early thirties show her strikingly cute and petite (certainly she did not have the clownish, almost masculine appearance of many famous comediennes, e.g., Lucille Ball, Carol Burnett, Joan Rivers, and Fanny Brice); a reviewer noted in 1932 that, with her curly black hair and red lips, "she could have passed for the ingenue in a sophisticated farce."[46]

But although lacking the "hoke" of the Bowery Dumb Dora, in her early career certainly Gracie kept the "kid" qualities of the dumbbell. Cuteness was the important trait of the kid impersonation, but most kid work was also very broad; Gracie Allen had the cuteness without the exaggeration. In the late forties and fifties, Gracie inclined towards a rather grandmotherly dingbattiness which could be charming but sometimes almost overbearing. However, the recordings testify that in the early thirties Gracie's voice had none of its later shrillness and brassiness, but was extremely girlish and cute, in a way the older Gracie Allen could quite naturally never have sounded. In the 1930 "Dizzy," in particular, Gracie sounds about fifteen. Her voice is not loud and high-pitched as in later radio work, but is very soft and sweet, and sometimes, like Harriette Lee, Gracie's speech almost verges into baby talk.

In addition to her childlike voice, an important element in the creation of Gracie's "adorable" stage personality was her laugh. The scripts do not indicate what the 1930 and 1933 recordings reveal, that Gracie laughed continually throughout the routines. It was a tinkling, happy giggle, and contributed to the cuteness of the character, especially when her laughs were in response to things that George did not find funny: George's exasperated "How do I allow myself to get mixed up in these things?" sent Gracie into delighted tittering; "Oh, that's very funny, George," she giggled appreciatively. The frequent, often inappropriate tittering must have helped create an impression that this character inhabited a world different from George's and the audience's, a world with its own rules of logic.

It was that different kind of logic that made the stage Gracie so fascinating. Other Dumb Doras said things that were clearly stupid—and were told frequently by their partners just how stupid they were. Usually Gracie's comments did not immediately sound stupid, however; they were straightforward explanations, uttered with total conviction; but although each separate statement made sense in itself, as "effects" of the "causes" posited by George, Gracie's observations were preposterous. "Oh, no, we couldn't afford a nurse, my mother had to do it," was a sensible answer to which one's imagination could supply a reasonable question—but it became hilariously illogical when it was an answer to the question "Did the nurse ever happen to drop you on your head when you were a baby?"

Sometimes Gracie narrated a sequence of events that, given the original premise, was quite logical: if your canary hatched an ostrich egg, it would be too big for your canary to keep warm, and sitting on it yourself might be a solution. However, the craziness of her premise always eluded Gracie. Gracie saw situations with peculiar eyesight, with blinders which hid the logical interpretation of a situation, as when she said, "When I went to school I was so smart my teacher was in my class for five years."

Her syntax is logical and she sounds quite sane; but an audience would not have on Gracie blinders, and the bit would win a big laugh. Gracie's perceptions were limited to an absurdly narrow interpretation of events, as in her description of what happened to her brother, for example. When George asks what is Willy doing now, as Gracie sees it, he just lost his job. Well, he did: but when a window washer steps back from a twentieth-story window to admire his work, that's not all he loses.

Other dumbbells did not think logically, did not know what words meant, were naive about the world. But Gracie's dumbbell was articulate, was full of ideas (such as freeing all America's prisoners),[47] could even argue according to laws (hers) of reason. *Billboard* therefore described Gracie's stage character as "the sophisticated Dumb Dora"; she came across as "the quiet girl who knows her way around."[48] She knew plenty — but the assumptions which underlay her views and arguments were downright illogical to everyone but her.

The stage Gracie didn't really know her way around, she just thought she did. And audiences believed she thought she did, because Gracie delivered her nonsensical statements with absolute sincerity.[49] Her childlike conviction that she was right and George was wrong was undeniably real. She was as blissfully oblivious to George's meaning as she was to the non-sensicality of her own thought processes. When George cried out "How do I allow myself to get mixed up in these things?" she responded with perfect seriousness — and perfect incomprehension — "Oh, that's very funny George. Now I'll make one up."

George Burns thought this was the secret of success of her humor: "Gracie could do the wildest kind of jokes and make people believe them — no matter how mad the jokes were, when Gracie told them you would believe they were true."[50] Gracie's "honesty" was indeed essential, but Gracie did not exactly make her nonsense itself seem believable and true. If audiences had now known that her perceptions were absurd, there would have been no joke. As George pointed out, the opening to "Lamb Chops" was not only a good joke, but was "terribly important, because from then on you knew she was nuts."[51] On the other hand, if Gracie herself had not believed in her "dumb" conceptions, they would not have been funny. The same lines delivered with a wink or a chuckle would be either silly, obviously ridiculous, or in some cases distasteful, as in the joke about her grandfather who died in bed. "My uncle eats concrete," she explained; "My mother asked him to stay for dinner, but he said he was going to eat up the street."[52] Told by a stand-up comedian, it is just a gag, and not a very good one. Told by Gracie with her special conviction, the humor lies not in the joke, but in the character who believes it. Gracie was not a jokester or stand-up comedienne, but a character.

The motif of Gracie's family, in use by the time of the first Palace appearance in 1926, was one important tool for creating this dramatic character. Talking about unseen offstage characters made Gracie's trust in her stories more believable. It was more convincing for Gracie to believe her offstage brother had an appendicitis scar on his neck than for an onstage performer to claim to have one herself. Her credibility as a true zany was also all the more effective, because, according to George, it was enacted with total concentration on George as a character.[53] She played directly to her partner and was completely oblivious to the audience.

> Gracie's sense of concentration was so marvellous that she didn't know there was an audience. Those were not footlights. As far as she was concerned, there was a wall and even though she looked that way she didn't look at the audience...she talked to me. If Gracie had an exit and you were supposed to stop her and say, "Wait a minute, Gracie, I want to ask you something," if you forgot your line, she would go right into the dressing room and take off her make-up. She only remembered her lines if you remembered yours.[54]

Her concentration on creating her character is apparently what George referred to when he so often insisted Gracie was not a comedienne, but a straight dramatic actress.[55] But just as often, George contradicted the notion of Gracie as a self-conscious technical actress. Instead of describing any acting techniques, George maintained that "she was just herself"; Gracie herself explained, "I don't act; I just live what we're doing. George calls this being a natural." Nothing was calculated, according to Gracie; "I never seem to say the same line the same way. I say it the way it occurs to me at the moment and it occurs to me differently every time." "There's no make-believe. It's for real," she claimed.[56]

In fact, once made self-conscious of technique, apparently Gracie was at a loss. When Jack Benny came backstage and told Gracie how much he laughed at her joke, "My mother's home, but my father won't let you kiss my mother," it made Gracie think about the line and wonder why it was funny. Henceforth she could never do the line.[57] The implication is that Gracie had little conscious working technique, but an inborn way of playing her character which happened to be funny. This, her "natural" absorption in the character, the moment, and in her partner, and the resulting obliviousness — or deliberate ignoring — of the audience[58] all contributed to the effectiveness of Gracie's stage character. As George put it, she rehearsed like nothing, but was struck by "something magic" in front of an audience.[59]

But was she really just being herself? "Gracie is Gracie," George claimed; "The character George developed for me is actually a sort of caricature of me," was Gracie's explanation.[60] When George said she played herself, presumably he was referring to a certain style, a certain innocent attitude and behavior that was only one facet of the offstage Gracie, but was the entire Gracie stage character. "Off-stage she was a very intelligent, smart lady," he also maintained; "To be able to play the character like that on stage, you had to be smart—in order to play dumb"[61]

The important fact is that Gracie's audiences were almost convinced that she was really like that; she made audiences temporarily suspend their own logic and fall under the spell of her stage character. (A few people actually did believe her offstage self and her stage persona were one and the same. For example, Gracie heard regularly from a Des Moines woman who wrote that if Mr. Burns kept mistreating her and if Gracie decided to leave her husband for good, Gracie could be assured of a comfortable home in Des Moines at any time.)[62] As a result, George learned that he couldn't blow smoke into Gracie's eyes onstage, or push her or try to punish her for things she said: "The sympathy of our audiences is all with her."[63] Even offstage, Gracie did not have to encourage the public's belief in her dumbbell character, recalled George;

> Gracie would get into an elevator and say, "Ninth floor, please," and it would get a big laugh. I don't know what people thought. Maybe they thought she was really going to go to the 12th floor and walk up three flights. They made up their own stuff.[64]

On one occasion a fan asked Gracie to sign an autograph book; when Gracie innocently inquired on what page, the girl whispered to her friend, "I imagine she is so dumb that she doesn't know what page to write on."[65]

In fact, if fans or reporters had seen into the real Gracie they might have been disappointed. George was usually the spokesman for the two, since interviews were exhausting for Gracie, because reporters expected her to give something she was not prepared to give. She was plagued for years with shattering migraine headaches, "probably brought on by the chronic strain of making like someone she isn't."[66] In retrospect, very little is known about the offstage Gracie at all. In her few public utterances, she repeated the stock anecdotes in the Burns and Allen publicity legend, the same stories George tells today.[67] Her private persona was so submerged beneath her public image that it did not shatter or influence her stage image, unlike such performers as Judy Garland, Frank Sinatra, or Vanessa Redgrave. Her secretive exterior enabled the public to respond to her as the character they wanted her to be, the character they wanted, or needed, to laugh at.[68]

No doubt Gracie's character did tap a mass belief, or need to believe, that women were the dumber, more childlike sex. The Dumb Dora stereotype was still popular in the thirties, performed not only by Gracie, but in the presentation houses by Eve Sully and a host of imitators, on radio by Jane Ace, and in the delightful series of films by the Thelma Todd/Zazu Pitts and Thelma Todd/Patsy Kelly combinations. It seems more than coincidental that a society threatened by the triumph of female suffrage and by the brazen behavior of women in the twenties so enjoyed the stage stereotype of the dumbbell. But the solace of laughter at Dumb Doras also fulfilled a need after the demise of the flapper. More crucial depression concerns pushed the sexual battle offstage; nonetheless, during the thirties the public was more determined than ever to believe that women were the weaker sex, and men the protective, breadwinning sex. In the 1937 Gallup poll, eighty-two per cent of Americans agreed that women should not be out in the business world competing for jobs with men who had families to support. Three out of four American cities excluded married women from teaching positions, and the federal government ruled that the government could not hire married persons—with four-fifths of those fired, naturally, women. The 1937 Gallup poll also revealed that two-thirds of America—and sixty per cent of the women polled—would not vote for a woman, however gifted, for president.[69]

The ruling bodies ignored the fact that many of the women denied jobs were either self-supporting or the heads of families, because the discriminating attitudes soothed the anxieties of the reigning sex, men, for whom the depression was understandably a time of great insecurity. Men laid off from work became moody, uncommunicative, and over-sensitive. Many men went insane, committed suicide, or deserted their families, with the majority just staying at home, inside their proverbial castles. But family pressures mounted with an unemployed father at home. "How can you be glad to see your wife and children... when you see debts all around you and that's almost all you can talk about. And every time you think of them you know they cry to heaven that you're a failure. The wife may not say so, but she knows it the same as you do," said one man during the thirties. Many husbands turned to shouting and bossing, demanding the respect they felt they were losing; others had extramarital affairs.[70] Perhaps laughing at dumbbell women in vaudeville houses and on screen and radio was still another way of coping for such men.

In fact, the most popular film images of women in the thirties were the society madcap and the little girl; the reigning box-office figure, male or female, between 1935 and 1938 was Shirley Temple. Although depression films did show women devoted to their struggling men, women with real strength were depicted as unscrupulous, as in a succession of Bette Davis films and in *Gone With the Wind*, or as predators who must be tamed or annihilated, as in Marlene Dietrich's films of the thirties for Josef von Sternberg.[71] All these popular-culture stereotypes reflected the desire of *both* women and men to believe in men as the strong sex, able to take care of their families during unprecedented hard times.

Women liked Gracie as well as men did, despite the way she depicted their sex. Much of her mail was from female admirers, because, Gracie suggested, they were not jealous of her: "A woman can't be jealous of me when her husband either affectionately or unflatteringly terms her just like Gracie Allen." To one female journalist, Gracie was the "beloved addlepate," "whose feminine irrelevance has offered untold comfort to members of her sex for 28 long years. How often we've viewed her dizzy schemes and boastfully remarked to our own spouses, 'Now that dumb I'm not!'"[72] Men, of course, were free to believe the stage formula reflected a certain reality. "There must be women like that," George argued;[73]

> I'm sure everyone has seen and heard couples all over America carry on conversations at least a bit in our vein. Everyone has heard wives pick out autos on account of the color of the seat covers or ask their husbands why we don't pay the neutrality bill.[74]

But Gracie's popularity also transcended any mere need of her audiences to identify a certain sex with her character. George thought Gracie's conversation illustrated the way everyone's mind worked sometimes; beneath the surface of an intelligent conversation, everyone's mind races from thought to thought, often with no logical connection. "We often *think* the way Gracie *talks*," explained George, "but we pride ourselves that *we* never talk the way Gracie thinks." A *New York Evening Post* reporter agreed that "Miss Allen represents something that has been an intimate and fundamental part of our experience since the beginning of memory." Gracie was the epitome of an illogicality that either sex could be accused of; it was an appropriate attack even during a congressional debate for one senator to say to another, "You make as much sense as Gracie Allen."[75]

And many of Gracie's cracks had a touch of satire levelled at a more general object than women. When Gracie "ran for President" in 1940, the very notion of a feminine dizzy running for President was funny, but her campaign was also a comic mirror of the actual campaigns. When reporters asked Gracie questions like "What do you think of the national debt," and she answered, "We ought to be proud of it—it's the biggest in the world," her answer implied she was not the only addlepated one; some people actually voted for Gracie on election day, thus revealing what they thought of the real politicians. Likewise, when Gracie took up surrealist painting, the real butt was modern art, which ordinary people found to be ludicrous.[76]

This way of discussing the acts puts all the weight on Gracie's role, and in fact, early critics did not always attach much worth to George's contribution. "Mr. Burns is a good feeder for Miss Allen and that's all for him," said one; "He tries at times to steal the spot but he can't do it. Miss Allen is wholly master of the situation."[77] But according to Gracie, everyone in show business knew George was the power behind the team. Even when they had five writers, it was George who assembled the routine, determining which jokes went in where and which were out. Some have dubbed him the Svengali, the Edgar Bergen of the team.[78] George's feel for comedy had been developed through years of effortless offstage joking and botched onstage attempts.

> I was able to get laughs on the street corners but not on the stage. I was self-conscious about being on the stage. If I was invited to somebody's house—to a party—I was very good. Prepared stuff was hard for me to do.[79]

But George knew show business, especially vaudeville, and all the ingredients involved in putting an act together; "I knew exits, entrances, how to construct a joke, how to switch a joke, where the laughs were going to drop, how to build an act to a strong finish. And most important, I knew the zany, off-center character Gracie Allen played onstage."[80]

And the creator of the act could not help giving himself some laughs, even if he was the straight man. Like Joe Laurie and Ben Ryan, George played a wise character, thus he made cracks in his feeder role. "I'd have it stuffed," he retorts to Gracie's insistence that her joke came right out of her own head. His tone expressed the superiority of the wise guy. "Why don't you go to a doctor and have him examine your head and if he finds a brain have someone examine the doctor," he cracked. George's wiseness was not just a matter of insults; it was an attitude. Even his flirting was patronizing; he treated Gracie like a child: "Well, Gracie, say hello to everyone," began the recorded routines; "say good-night, Gracie," went his famous tag-line.

Nonetheless, once one of Gracie's inane stories or explanations was set in motion, George was left baffled. When Gracie can't understand the "say what I say" riddle, George says sarcastically, "It's going to be hard for you," in a tone which implies how wise he is and how dumb she is. "Oh yes, you understand that," he says to her second wrong answer, still sarcastically, but finally he is forced to admit, "I picked out a good game. I stepped right into your backyard." At last, in pique, George sardonically tells Gracie that the answer to the joke is "horsefeathers"; but when Gracie ponders "Horsefeathers? Horsefeathers?" and then concludes with obvious delight, "Oh yes! Now I see it," it is George who has nothing further to argue; "Well, I don't know, maybe I'm wrong," he concludes helplessly. Wise as George is, Gracie's very dumbness defeats him.

George's contribution thus had many facets. He was the source of several good laughs in a routine himself, and his feeding, of course, gave Gracie the opportunity to display her "logic." He was also an important foil; his sanity provided a contrast which made it all the more clear how "nuts" Gracie was, making her character even funnier. And just as funny as the stage Gracie's character, was that character's effect on George. Seeing George go from convinced to befuddled to totally frustrated was hilarious. It gave the routine another dimension, making it not only a depiction of a dumbbell but of the exasperation involved in dealing with one.

George thus became interpreter and representative for the audience. His reaction told audiences how to take Gracie. His tongue-in-cheek echoes of Gracie's ideas—"He *goes* to San Quentin. He takes his books and *goes* to San Quentin," cracked George, in a voice which said "sure"—underlined the outlandishness of her notions. The repitition also had the quite practical effect of letting Gracie's lines sink in, which was necessary since the lines were almost rapid-fire and often sounded more logical than they really were. In addition, George both "taught" and reflected the audience's affection and tolerance for Gracie. He never took his sarcasm too far. However amazed and exasperated he became, George always retained his composure, was never unkind, and never resented his own inability to defeat Gracie's "logic." At times he almost became a butt, yet he never lost control. Their relationship had an underlying sympatico summed up in George's refrain in the ditty sung in the thirties' recordings: "I love you, love you, love you dear, I cross my heart, I do, do you believe me?"; "I do," sang Gracie back.

As a result, George's onstage character had an appeal for both male and female audiences. The act was perhaps the perfect antidote for audiences wearied of the sexual combativeness of the twenties. Like the proper husband, he could indulge Gracie, but men could admire the fact that George was never drawn into Gracie's zany universe. One way George achieved his image of calm was probably with a knowing, unperturbed facial expression. His vaudeville demeanor is unrecorded, but in later years he had developed a deadpan look which kept him immune to Gracie's assaults on his reason. As Carol Channing, who worked with George in a nightclub act after Gracie's death, noted:

> George never does anything with his face, it's a mask; he never changes the tone of his voice, he has no mannerisms, except his cigar, and that's his style.... He doesn't twitch, he hardly moves. He *is* the stand-up comedian.... But he leads the audience with his wry modesty, patience and tolerance.[81]

His cigar was another distancing prop. He was always puffing as he listened to Gracie; his absorption in his smoke set George apart and gave him an air of bemused superiority. But he never blew smoke in her eyes; he did not put Gracie off, or her female fans. He was assured, but polite and interested. He was the wise one, but as Carol Channing explained, he was soft and likable, not haughty or insulting.

> Comedians usually rely on the slow burn or the comedy of insult. Not George. He doesn't put down anyone. He keeps his cool head while the world crashes about him. He's Samson. Nothing bothers him.... And George understands women. They're on a pedestal but he knows how to make them funny—I mean, Gracie, her sister and mother, and me—by listening patiently to their problems. He doesn't answer back with one-liners. His softness is masculine and cuddly-funny, not bitchy.[82]

It was not only his attitude toward Gracie that appealed, but his attitude toward himself and his audience. In the early years George already had that tone in his dealings with the audience that implied he was both confident yet had a sense of humor about himself. When he says in 1933, "We're dancing now. Hey, you're missing this and it's very good," it sounds just like today's George informing the audience of his excellence as a singer. His cocky attitude clearly pokes fun at himself, yet his ability to do so reveals his confidence in himself, and his tone betrays his belief that the audience is enjoying being intimate with him. His tone of familiarity with the audience is likable, and given Gracie's obliviousness of the audience, was an important trait of his character.

Publicly, both Burns and Allen made little of their abilities. Whereas Gracie maintained she was "just herself" onstage, George claimed he merely fed his comedienne-wife; being a straight man was very easy.

> Well, anybody can be a straight man if he hears well.... A straight man just repeats the questions and the comedian gets the laughs and you just wait for them and don't let them die completely at the tail end of the laugh.[83]

But to anyone who has witnessed Burns and Allen at work at the peak of their career in the thirties—either in film (*International House*, for example), or on recordings—it is obvious that, however easy it was for them, they were immensely talented performers with an impressively artful act. Whether Gracie's peculiar brand of dizzy dame was the product of conscious technique or was instead an accident of nature, the point is that she achieved the effect of naturalness for which many performers study and practice for a lifetime without success. Calculated or spontaneous, she was always consistent; "Gracie Allen's delivery is one of the few dependable elements of this undependable show business," wrote *Variety*.[84] Her voice, her laugh, her innocent yet knowing facial expressions and attitude, along with her constant flow of unconscious inanity, was consistently a source of the most marvelous humor.

Likewise, George, with his dry comments about himself and his mate, and with his pose as the sweet wise guy who must suffer defeat again and again at the hands of a dumbbell yet maintain his sense of humor and éclat, created a character heroic in its own right. He was both wise guy and boob—the alter ego of all those who feel both superior to and frustrated by the Dumb Doras in their own lives. And the relationship he developed with audiences over the years was a masterpiece. He had a directness that brought the audience into the act, made them respond to Gracie with him, thus made them react more intensely to her. Also, his tongue-in-cheek cockiness about himself as a performer made audiences like watching and hearing him. Even today George Burns is still an entertaining performer: one is intrigued by the tension between his self-confidence and his self-deprecation; it is never quite clear if he is laughing at the dumbbell, himself, or perhaps even the audience. He is like a friend whose consistent kindness makes us like and trust him, but whose superior wit and amused gleam in his eye issues a slight challenge, thus keeping us relaxed yet never bored.

Each of the two stage characters had an appeal of its own, but their workings were tandem; the appeal was above all that of the two-act. The stage Gracie could not have been a stand-up comedienne single, because Gracie the performer depended too much on her obliviousness to a straight-thinking partner and to the audience to create her character. Had she maintained her distance from the audience without a partner to direct their reaction to her, she would have projected the image of a truly insane person; she would have been pitiful and shocking, not laughable. Conversely, Gracie's intense concentration and seeming naturalness provided a justification for George's stiffness and stage-conscious personality. These very traits had kept George from being a successful wise-guy comedian on his own, but were perfect for portraying the wise guy whose sangfroid was eternally tested by an unflappable dumbbell, who was conscious of his own inability to assert his superiority, and had an audience to account to for Gracie and himself. Thus, Burns and Allen's comical and many-faceted stage personalities made the team a joy to watch or hear; as performers they were both likable and provocative because they engaged audiences on a number of levels.

They did not get their laughs simply from character, however, letting the jokes work or not as they may; they were experts at comic delivery. The 1930 and 1933 recordings show that in their first ten years on the live entertainment circuits, Burns and Allen had already developed the skills of timing, pacing, and emphasis to a fine degree. The routines were delivered almost rapid-fire—not in a jerky and frenzied manner, but at a quick, never flagging pace, with an even rhythm continually punctuated with jokes. Take, for example, the following sequence in the recorded 1930 "Dizzy":

> Gracie: Let's do something.
> George: Let's do something.
> Gracie: Let's do crossword puzzles.
> George: That would be fun.
> Gracie: I'm very good at them now. You know, I make them up.
> George: Well, make one up.
> Gracie: All right. What is it that starts with *c*, and, uh, well, I don't know how many letters, what is it?
> George: Hmm, that's very good. You made that up.
> Gracie: That came right out of my head.
> George: I'd have it stuffed.
> Gracie: My head?
> George: Your head.

Thanks to the staccato give and take, their perfectly timed pauses (often filled with Gracie's giggle), and the repetition of key phrases, the jokes moved along with the audience always involved and expectant, able to catch everything, yet never having the chance to lose interest. The recordings also reveal the team kept up a stream of almost whispered, meaningless chatter between jokes ("Yeah?" "Yeah."), which although rarely recorded in the scripts, was important in creating pace. Not only did they frequently echo the rhythms of the other, but George often repeated Gracie's words, and his sarcastic echoes of her innocent comments served as a rhetorical foil to her meanings, and were timed to give the audience opportunity to understand and laugh. Having captured the audience with their measured pacing, it was all the more surprising and comical when George broke their rhythm with an unexpected wisecrack ("I'd have it stuffed"), or when Gracie came up with one of her superbly inane insights, as in the sequence below:

> Gracie: Well, I guess I'll be going home now.
> George: Going home? I'll take you home in my car.
> Gracie: Oh no thank you. I'm too tired. I'd rather walk.
> George: That's a very good answer.
> Gracie: But if you like, you can walk home with me.
> George: Yes, I'll walk you home. I'll walk home with you if you give me a kiss. I'll take you home.
> Gracie: Well, if you take me home I'll give you a kiss.
> George: But just a minute, before I take you home I would like to find out whether or not your mother is home.
> Gracie: She is, but my father wouldn't let you kiss my mother.

Thus, their delivery was a sequence of rhythmic beats and pauses that created a spiralling, expectant pace leading to moments of surprise. This mastery of the craft of timing—their ability to sustain interest and create tension and climax—made them able to make their material even funnier than it was. In their hands repetition could become a joke in itself, as in the "Dizzy" joke:

George: Oh, you're dizzy.
Gracie: Well, you're silly.
George: Well, I'd rather be silly than dizzy.
Gracie: I know I'm dizzy. I'm glad I'm dizzy.
George: You're the only dizzy girl that I know that's glad she's dizzy.
Gracie: I'm glad I'm a dizzy girl, because boys like dizzy girls and I like boys.
George: I'm glad it's over. I'm glad it's finished.
Gracie: And I'm glad I'm dizzy.
George: All right. This can go on for years, let's talk of something else.

As talented as Burns and Allen were, their success was of course aided by their top-notch material. From his own mind and from his many writers and other sources, aided by his unerring sense of what was funny and right for Gracie, Burns produced hilarious routines for the team, many of which have become legendary. The excellence of so much Burns and Allen material is illustrated by the untitled, undated routine below:

George: How's your brother, Gracie?
Gracie: Which brother, the one who's married or the one who sleeps on the floor?
George: You've got a brother who sleeps on the floor?
Gracie: Oh yes, the one with the appendicitis scar on his forehead.
George: Gracie, your appendix is down by your waist.
Gracie: I know, but Willy's so ticklish.
George: What's Willy doing now?
Gracie: Oh, he broke his back.
George: He broke his back...?
Gracie: On account of he's left-handed.
George: On account of he's left-handed?
Gracie: Well, you see, he had a doughnut in his right-hand pocket, and he tried to take it out with his left hand.
George: Well, the next time he has a doughnut in his pocket, tell him to take it out with his right hand.
Gracie: Well, that's hard to do when you have your pants on backwards.
George: He had his pants on backwards?
Gracie: You see, Willy had a suit with two pairs of pants, so he had to put one pair on backwards and one pair on frontwards.
George: Could he walk like that?
Gracie: Not after the truck hit him.
George: The truck? What truck?
Gracie: The one with its lights out.
George: Why didn't the man in the truck have his lights on?
Gracie: Why should he, it was daytime?
George: But didn't the man in the truck see your brother?

Gracie: He didn't know it was my brother, he just saw two pairs of pants walking towards him, so he lost control of the truck![85]

This timeless, carefully constructed dialogue is almost actor-proof, and truly demonstrates the "art" of comedy conversation. Its humor was not topical, and though its appeal is certainly enriched through being performed by opposite sexes, the comedy is not dependent on any particular beliefs about woman as the dumber sex. Its appeal is inherent in its form: the structure of the conversation is the actual embodiment of how Gracie's mind works. The disordered flow of wacky assumptions explained by nonsequiturs and insufficient facts is hilarious—and not only was it hilarious done by Gracie and George in the 1930s, but it was equally hilarious performed in 1978 by George Burns and Madeline Kahn. It is the form that is funny, not the mockery of an event or belief—thus this routine and others like it are eternally entertaining. With such material in addition to their stage personalities and performing talent, Burns and Allen's success would outlive vaudeville.

Indeed, any understanding of the live stage work of Burns and Allen is influenced by their more familiar work in radio and film, and many of the above observations are based on comments by or about Burns and Allen made many years after their career in vaudeville. But although their success in 1926 coincided with the decline of vaudeville, Burns and Allen developed as a vaudeville team, and it was vaudeville that Burns and Allen carried over into the canned media. George Burns told interviewer Kate Davy that "in radio we did little routines like vaudeville routines," that "we tried to move the routines into the atmosphere of the movies, but they were mostly vaudeville routines." Davy responded, "So you would say that all the way through your career, through television, you were influenced by—"; "Mostly, we were vaudevillians," interrupted George.[86]

The team's first appearance before a movie camera came in 1929; shortly afterwards, in 1930, they performed on radio for the first time, for the BBC during a vaudeville engagement in London.[87] When their Keith contract ended in 1931, they were signed to star in Paramount shorts, and to play in Publix movie presentation houses the rest of the time.[88] But later that same year Eddie Cantor asked Gracie to appear with him on his radio show, and the team subsequently appeared on Rudy Vallee's radio show, for thirty minutes. One success led to another; the following week brought one appearance on the Guy Lombardo show, which was extended to thirteen weeks, and in February 1932 they aired their first regularly scheduled broadcast.[89] By then, Burns and Allen had already made fourteen film shorts, and in 1932 they appeared in their first full-length film, *The Big Broadcast of 1932*. In 1934 it was estimated that with pictures and radio, the team was earning about $5000 a week; by 1939 they would be earning $13,500 per radio show.[90]

In their radio and movie work, Burns and Allen continued to work with material and techniques from vaudeville, adapted as needed to new conditions. For example, when they made their first short, the team was somewhat unnerved to learn their street corner pick-up act was to be done in a realistic living room set. But, by calling attention to the medium—the lack of an audience, the presence of cameras, and so on—they were able to create artificially the "presentational" style of live entertainment, and were able to work more comfortably.[91] Their usual pattern in full-length film was to break into the story at regular intervals and do their standard routines; Gracie's piece about her brother in *The Big Broadcast* was vaudeville material, as was the routine about her uncle who shoots his dogs, seen in *We're Not Dressing*.[92]

Of course, on a weekly radio show it was much more difficult to maintain the high standards of a vaudeville act, which could be worked up to a fine pitch during several seasons of testing and polishing before live audiences. A new routine had to be secured weekly for the radio audience, and there was no trying it out—it had to be good for the one-time slot. By 1935, Burns and Allen had five high-priced writers turning out material in the famed formula, and they had turned to the crutch of a theme or event—Burns and Allen go to Honolulu, Burns and Allen tour Europe, Burns and Allen appear at the London Palladium—as the supporting structure for typical Burns and Allen jokes.[93] Another expedient was sharing the comedy; the show had an announcer, a soloist, and a band leader, and by the end of the 1936-37 season, this supporting cast was being given more in the way of comedy assignments. At the opening of the 1938-39 season, Burns and Allen remained "one of radio's choicest pieces of entertainment property."[94]

But beginning in the late thirties a critic would occasionally complain that the ancient gag of Gracie trying to make love to the singer and male guests was becoming tiring, and there were complaints of stale jokes, that Burns and Allen were letting audiences down and not delivering the "pun." One 1939 reviewer claimed Gracie blew her lines and that her timing was off.[95] Their ratings gradually declined, and they lost their sponsor; when they were finally picked up by Swan Soap in 1942, it was for half their former salary.[96]

By then, George had determined that, with both teammates over forty, "we were too old for the he-she kind of jokes we were doing at the time," and George and his writers determined to change the Burns and Allen humor to "domestic-situation" comedy.[97] The first season with Swan Soap George paid so much for writers and for top-notch band leader Paul

Whiteman that he lost money. The team also began to bolster their appeal with outstanding guest stars like Frank Sinatra, Charles Boyer, and Bing Crosby. The result was that their ratings rose again.[98]

Not only did their humor change from flirtation to husband-wife, but their style was significantly changed too. *Variety* revealed that the team had converted from "the slam-bang type of olio cross-fire" to sketches with "plot, an ingratiating brand of whimsy, suavely diffused hokum and overall good radio sense." Gracie was as dumb as ever, but "the characterization has been augmented with some easily recognizable facets of feminine impetuosity and fantasy."[99] Gracie's zaniness had been "suavely diffused" into the quieter, situational comedy of a "recognizable" female stereotype—the one next door.

The team was doing "situash comedy," and the situation usually concerned either money or some topical event.[100] Gracie was the typical (almost) wife with a hole in her pocketbook; George was the husband who held on to his money for dear life;

George: Gracie, suppose you start explaining these Christmas bills. Who got this $25 hat?
Gracie: I gave that to Clara Bagley. I've decided to break up our friendship.
George: Then why did you give her an expensive hat?
Gracie: I have one exactly like it. When she sees me with it on, she'll stop speaking to me.
George: There must be cheaper ways to lose a friend. Here's a bill for a bushel of nuts delivered to San Francisco. Who'd you send those to?
Gracie: My mother. That was your suggestion, dear. Every time I said, "What'll we send mother?" you said, "Nuts to her."
George: I should give your mother a bushel of nuts. What'd she ever give me?
Gracie: She gave you me. I'm as good as nuts.
George: You can say that again.
Gracie: I'd rather not. I didn't like the way it sounded.
George: Who got this chromium chair with the plastic seat?
Gracie: My brother, Willy. He's building his own house with a GI loan and he's crazy about antique furniture.
George: A chromium and plastic chair isn't antique.
Gracie: It will be by the time the house is built.[101]

George maintained that once they turned to husband-wife comedy, he couldn't insult Gracie. Nonetheless, in their more realistic situation comedy, there seems to be a stronger undercurrent of the battle between the sexes than had previously been present in their work—as in Gracie's 1947 scheme to worm money for a new dress out of George.

George: Good morning, Gracie. How about some breakfast?
Gracie: All right, would you like the table by the window?
George: Yeah, it's the only one we've got.

Gracie:	Now, what would you like to eat?
George:	I'll have a glass of orange juice, a slice of toast and a cup of Maxwell House...coffee.
Gracie:	Yessir. (Calls) Squeeze two, burn one and please the sponsor.
George:	What are you doing?
Gracie:	I'm a waitress. I'm calling your order to the kitchen. You wouldn't give me $85 for a dress, so I'm running this house like a hotel to earn the money.
George:	This isn't a hotel and you're not the waitress.
Gracie:	I'll prove it. Here's a glass of water. I'll bring the food two hours later.
George:	Cut out the nonsense and bring me my breakfast.
Gracie:	You'll have to pay in advance. You haven't got any luggage.
George:	Look, Gracie, you're my wife. I would pay you only if you were employed by me. This hotel deal is too much. I won't give in. I won't agree and I won't cooperate.
Gracie:	You left out one thing.
George:	What?
Gracie:	You won't eat.[102]

The show ended with Gracie winning—as she usually did. In fact, during this era, more and more of the laughs were at George's expense. One 1940s script concerned George's attempts to convince Bing Crosby to retire, so George could have the chance for the singing career that he believed he deserved, but had been deprived of by Bing's stealing the limelight.[103]

At any rate, the new formula kept them in demand with sponsors and audiences. In 1944 they were judged "one of the more consistent chuckle providers among the spectrum" by *Variety*. When their radio career ended in 1949—General Foods did not renew their contract because the $17,500 per show they demanded was too high—the Burns and Allen show still had top ratings and they were snatched up by television's Bill Paley within two days.[104] Nonetheless, although successful and "consistent," they were no longer at their thirties peak. *Variety* implied they were popular because of their familiarity—and because of the lack of new talent to challenge them.

> There's a warm familiarity about them, they're as comfortable as an old hat or a veepee's brand new ulcer; radio just wouldn't be radio without them.

The team made no claim to side-splitting "yuks," continued *Variety*:

> They were just themselves, a pair of surefooted troupers who had control of every moment, who instilled into the listener the confident certainty that, if he won't be lifted—he is at least sure not to be let down.

They have "deftness" with "old and tired" material, added *Variety*, and noted that until new talent is born, the old ones had better be kept on.[105]

The debut of the Burns and Allen television show in 1950 removed the team still further from their original formula. In the context of a true-to-life situation, a realistic set, and other live characters, Gracie's zaniness was reined in still further. Now her ideas had concrete effects on characters seen in the flesh by viewers, and the producers were careful not to let Gracie hurt anyone or drive them crazy; the new structure left no latitude for the almost fantastical flights of verbal play from the old days. Gracie and her neighbor Blanche (Bea Benadaret) hatched schemes that could have been borrowed from Lucy and Ethel, such as Gracie and Blanche's attempts to get their husbands to take them to a posh night club, or their efforts to hide Blanche's new mink from her husband Harry.[106] Fortunately, in 1955 the team hit on the notion of doing their old stand-up talking routines at the end of the show, as a separate bit.[107]

But the television show was demanding, and Gracie was "very tired" and had already had heart problems.[108] Perhaps to compensate for Gracie's need to be less in the limelight, or to prepare for an already likely future as a single, in the television years George developed still further as a comedian in his own right. Every show was introduced by his monologue, delivered leaning against a proscenium mock-up, and throughout the show George functioned as a comic chorus, commenting on the action and the medium to the audience.[109] As it had with their films, this self-conscious raillery gave the Burns and Allen show a unique rapport with its television audience, and enabled George to exercise an attractive element of his stage personality.

But the show catered to what the team had discovered in their later radio years to be a safe formula for the mass audience: easy gags and simple comedy situations. Television was new and costly, and in retrospect, Burns seemed afraid of taking chances, aiming cautiously at pleasing the lowest common denominator. Burns himself described their jokes as "relaxing," and some reviewers were critical. The Burns and Allen jokes were "what you might call the middle level," complained John Crosby, and too many of the gags were old, "as if Mr. B. felt that old jokes are soothing to old customers, that a new joke might upset our digestions."[110] But Burns and Allen were veterans able to put over mediocre fare, and their supporting cast was also good, so ratings remained respectable.

Yet, a large part of the show's popularity was obviously audiences' long familiarity with and love for the now grandmotherly yet still charmingly dumb Gracie Allen, and when Gracie left the show in 1958, George Burns and son Ronnie were unable to fill the bill alone the following season. It would be many rocky years later—and after unworkable teamings with substitute dizzy blondes like Connie Stevens—before George Burns would establish himself comfortably as a single performer. Even then his career would be sustained by his public image as a survivor, one whose lifetime exposure to a dumbbell had made him "an innocent who has outlived all surprises."¹¹¹ And until her death on 28 August 1964, there was always the hope, as one reporter expressed it, that Gracie would change her mind and return to show business.

> The real-life Gracie thinks in much straighter lines than the show-business Gracie Allen, but she's still a woman.¹¹²

Conclusion

Just as George Burns found it easier to impersonate God than to replace Gracie, so members of other male-female teams found success elusive without their mates. Famous Fanny Beane's success dwindled after her husband's death; "she seemed to lose her ambition and good fortune." Like Fanny, Guy Linton fell from favor when he and partner Lucy Adams separated, and a year or so later he was dead of starvation. Billy Clifford persisted as Billy "Single" Clifford after his divorce, but it was thought that his wife Maud Huth had

> "fed" Clifford so adroitly that he seemed almost like a real comedian, which he has never seemed since he divorced....

One bereaved male team member, James Richmond of Richmond and Glenroy, even annexed his wife's name after her death, becoming James Richmond Glenroy.[1]

Teams obviously depended on both members to do their accustomed material, and good teams with years of experience and knowledge of each other appeared to work effortlessly together. Ted and Betty Healey, for one, were said to

> never rehearse because they understand each other so perfectly.... If Ted "pulls a new one" on Betty she never fails to "catch on" as if they had rehearsed for days.[2]

Such reviews suggested the importance of both partners' contributions to their act's success. Although Dooley and Sales had previously captured Atlanta as a team, in 1912, after Corrine Sales was seriously injured in a car accident, Jim Dooley did not fare so well alone, and only later, when he returned to Atlanta with his partner, did the *Atlanta Constitution* declare that "all's forgiven." Dooley confessed that "he never appreciated how good a foil she was until after the automobile accident...."[3]

Indeed, the history of the male-female team is a story of increasing appreciation for female talent, for such recognition had not always been given. Although audiences had enjoyed laughing at the spectacle of a man and a woman making comedy in tandem, the dynamics of a man-and-woman interaction were little created by the earliest teams. These teams worked in an entertainment designed for men, in a milieu of relaxed proprieties and male camaraderie. The men came for their own purposes, one of which was to escape Victorian domestic life; thus women's tastes did not intrude on the entertainment. It was only one aspect of man's relations with woman that held this audience; female performers, like any woman in that milieu, were there to be exploited.

Even the comediennes poked fun at their own sex; the joke was that the "blondes" and female minstrels playing male roles were not men, and the paratheatrical pleasure was ogling them. "Nice" women were certainly not very funny. Thus, the comedy in the early male-female routines was invariably furnished by the man, and given the narrow role assigned to women, there was little opportunity for female talent to be appreciated. "Actresses" were best appreciated in a dance number, and even without theatrical ability could provide a feast for the eyes of a stag audience.

It took a change in the milieu itself to alter this situation. When variety managers started catering to working people and their families—to expand their box office, and to escape municipal legislation against concert saloons—the subsequent change in patronage meant different demands on male-female teams. What made a man a family was a wife, and the presence of man's better half in the audience was dramatically responsible for destroying the barroom intimacy of the variety house. These theatregoers could obviously take little pleasure in ogling ballet dancers; it was domestic comedy, reflecting their real-life interests, that appealed to them. The result was an impressive increase in the number of male-female teams doing domestic sketches, and the very middle-class values that supported the institution of the family—sentimentality, morality, and order—gradually came to govern the male-female act.

The kind of change effected by female patrons is well-illustrated by the contrast between Sam Morton, who began his career in the early variety halls out West, and his son Paul, member of a big-time vaudeville male-female team in the teens. Sam was of the vulgar, kick-in-the-rear school,

> with every muscle ready for instant action in a dance, a fight, a noise, and a leap into rowdy favor. He has exactly the sort of broad, obstreperous low comedy which introduced Denman Thompson to stardom. It is crude, burly and most shocking...of the sort very few have virility enough to present....[4]

Paul, however, was a "beautiful dancer" and "one of the Beau Brummels of the stage," a "clean-cut young man" with "the sort of personality that helps to make musical comedy popular"; with wife Naomi Glass he played "a rather 'fresh' suitor and a superannuated dandy" in an act which "might well be termed 'The Act Dainty'."[5] Vaudeville never became a solely female entertainment (like television's afternoon soap operas), but it lost its old-style "virility"; the response of variety's stag audience to Nicholson and Norton's act in the twentieth century, in which Angie Norton impulsively hugged her partner and cried, "My God, but you are a pretty man!," can well be imagined.[6]

The increase in family patronage was not only a stimulus, but also a result of the growing number of male-female teams with domestic sketches. Acts dramatizing marriage and courtship and espousing the values of family and home were probably important drawing cards at houses trying to establish a middle-class patronage. The fancy dress and frothy flirtations offered by the Delanos, or the wholesome, sentimental dramas concocted by the Cohans, must have appealed to families; such teams deliberately marketed themselves as "refined." Fred Hallen, who with first wife Enid Hart had performed one of the most "refined" and stylishly dressed acts of the day, implied he had had a hand in creating the mixed-sex audience and polite tone of vaudeville. When Hallen took his company west in 1884,

> 90 per cent of the audiences would be men. By the end of the engagement, 75 per cent would be women. For the first time they learned that vaudeville — or variety — could be clean, and wholesome and good to look upon, and that was a good deal to accomplish in those days.[7]

The new milieu gradually attracted even more illustrious performers, and by the turn of the century teams formed by legitimate stage performers could be seen in vaudeville. The large majority of "legits" did two-person comediettas, and with their dramatic (for vaudeville) acting, their fashionable dress and elaborate stage sets, and in particular their legitimate stage reputations, these teams established the still more genteel atmosphere of early twentieth-century vaudeville. Male-female teams like Sydney Grant and his wife consciously congratulated themselves for introducing the "drawing room style of entertainment" into vaudeville, and such teams were "much admired by the ladies."[8] The "comedy sketch" quickly became the preserve of the male-female team, and actresses like Eva Williams, actors like John C. Rice, and writers like Will Cressy — all in male-female teams — were hugely successful because they offered what middle-class audiences wanted: quiet, "artistic" acting; "realistic" characters; and sentimental, inoffensive plots — often featuring a wise and decent man with a silly, shrewish wife.

Indeed, although male-female teams always essayed whatever new types were popular—tramps, Jews, rubes, hotel servants, etc.—by the twentieth century the majority of teams performed domestic comediettas, and romance and marriage would more and more become the standard material for a male-female act. These acts focused on the comical and sentimental aspects of marriage and courtship—infatuation, obstacles to mating, jealousy, and husband-wife arguments. Vaudevillians had only about fifteen minutes to capture their audience, and routines immediately conveyed the very essence of the male-female relation: "Are those the best rooms you could find?" was the waspish line that opened the Drews' honeymoon sketch, telling the audience at once that a quarrel was brewing.[9] By the teens, teams would have distilled the courtship and marriage sketch into a conversation in "one," offering rapid-fire flirtation or belligerence, divested of pretensions to plot and character-drawing.

These domestic routines not only offered male-female teams a kind of material exclusively suited to them, but also capitalized on society's intense preoccupation with the New Woman in the late nineteenth century and early twentieth century. The established rules of proper female behavior no longer explained the ways women were acting. The very facts of urbanization, working women, and divorce necessitated new courtship procedures; and wives' new predilection for trousers and suffrage clubs, reforming and the professions, meant new marital disputes and issues to be resolved. The old social scripts for man and woman were outmoded, and like their offstage counterparts, men and women in vaudeville routines were having difficulties not found in the old scripts. Whereas in early flirtations like the Delanos', love, courtship, and marriage were automatic, and stress between onstage couples nonexistent, by the turn of the century flirtation and marriage were problematical. Observers noticed that male-female vaudeville acts had real-life significance. A sketch called "The Honeymoon," in which a bossy wife was reduced to subservience, was said to have "a moral, and a serious one, too"; the female character in the sketch "is happy in finding a master," claimed one reviewer, and her husband tames her "much to the amusement of the men portion of the audience."[10]

While the routines do not explain the complexities of what audiences thought about such issues, the offstage preoccupation with women does help explain why the topic was so popular with vaudeville audiences and so often chosen by teams. For audiences bothered by the fair sex's unsettling new behavior—and the outpouring of novels, sermons, editorials, and films proves just how disturbed people could be—it must have been reassuring when recalcitrant female characters demurely agreed to love, honor and obey their spouses, or when women acting other than God intended them to were viewed as laughable. Routines in which boy and girl ended up in each other's arms at the end of a fifteen-minute courtship (despite parental disapproval or outdated etiquette), or in which wayward wives wearing pants and frequenting reform clubs were forced to put on their skirts and swallow their complaints, were easy, soothing entertainment for an audience probably dismayed about new social developments. With their happy endings, these routines reinforced sentimental beliefs that an old order still reigned—that tradition was good and the New Woman was not.

Male-female teams were peculiarly suited to portray domestic concerns, for the sexism and tensions of the real world existed between partners, who were often husband and wife and had their own offstage prejudices. Male-female teams often shared the audience's views about marriage and family, and about proper relations between the sexes. Gracie Allen, for example, "certainly had no desire to be a liberated woman," claimed her husband; "She enjoyed all the little niceties that were normally extended to women."[11] Male-female teams also brought a very realistic sexual electricity to their acts. The two-act was especially convenient for teams married or dating (so convenient, that teams who were not romantically involved often were after a season or two—Block and Sully, Burns and Allen, Adelaide and Hughes, and Johnny and Emma Ray, to name a few), and sometimes very romantic couples betrayed their smugness; lovebirds Mabel Hite and Mike Donlin, for example, could not refrain from mentioning their family affairs onstage, until one reviewer concluded "that neither of the performers dislike themselves very heartily."[12] Certainly the frequency of teams broken up by divorce suggests the more combative tensions which could enliven an act, or even mar it—in 1917 Lew and Bonita Hearn had to withdraw from Keith's because of domestic problems she could not help showing onstage.[13]

But as the twentieth century wore on, a more widespread strain between the sexes was apparent in many male-female acts. Offstage, the escalating demands of women for "rights" had given new sharpness to the age-old battle between the sexes. Suffragists and feminists were no longer a joking matter, and the more serious fears and anxieties about the New Woman were expressed in vaudeville routines. Female professionals and reformers were treated less lightheartedly, and some stage couples were having vicious confrontations that were hardly funny. Some routines were self-consciously aware of a split in their audience; male and female characters could be pitted against each other to play on the divergent sympathies of their audience. Even physical antagonism between the sexes had a certain amount of box-office appeal.

What most revealed the new strain between the sexes was that, by the mid-teens, insult humor was no longer found only in husband and wife battles, but had found its way into flirtations. In flirtations in the 1910s the women were smart enough to take care of themselves, and sparring and insults were inevitable in staged street pick-ups. Even the innocuous eating joke had social implications: men would refuse to cater to women's needs if women insisted on usurping male power; women would forfeit their position on the pedestal. Callous as they could be, the new stage relationships were a comical version of the sexes' attempts to create new dialogues in real life, and in a sense the stage routines taught people the new etiquette. Men and women of the younger generation were trying to interact as equals by the twenties, and the forced attempts to be offhand and cynical in the routines hint at an underlying uncertainty about the new rules. But the stage couples did know that the old etiquette was an inadequate guide now, and they mocked Victorian manners: "And now that we're engaged, say that I am young and beautiful," said one stage flapper, "sighing," reveals the stage direction.[14]

The new relations between vaudeville men and women were perhaps most obvious in male-female routines featuring female comics. By the twentieth century it was not as unusual for a woman to be "a gingery comedienne...not what's generally known as 'the other half of the sketch.'"[15] Women like Florence Moore and Mae Melville beshrewed their men like wives in the old marital battles, but with the difference that they were running the show, handling the wisecracks, and often getting in the last word. The most disconcerting thing about such women was that they were not acting like women; women were not supposed to be funny.

> Take women as a separate and distinct specie[s] and you do not find much in her to arouse your sense of humor—meaning no disrespect to the sex, of course. Measured by the ordinary standards of humor she is about as comical as a crutch, due, no doubt, to the excellent wisdom of the Lord in making her from a man's ribs instead of his funnybone.
> A women was made to be loved and fondled...she certainly was not made to be laughed at,

maintained one newspaperman in 1909.[16]

Dainty women were not to be laughed at, he should have said. One exception was noted by Stella Mayhew, who gave two rules for great comediennes in 1910: (1) Be fat; (2) Stay fat. Along with Mayhew herself, famous partners like Mabel Fenton, Mae Melville, Emma Ray, Ray Bailey, and Kitty Morton fit the description, as did Maud Ryan—who joked onstage that her arms were as big as her legs and that "from the waist down I'm on a diet"—and Maud Huth, who weighed two hundred pounds and, in 1899, was "one of those few and far between women who can discern a joke without an accompanying blueprint."[17] Other early comediennes like Mabel Hite and Florence Moore compensated for their slimness either with burlesque make-up or grotesque mugging.

Thus, when audiences gradually learned to laugh more freely at women in the 1910s, they were expanding their view of woman's proper role. Indeed, as Florence Moore pointed out, it could even be said that the question of woman's rights was making itself felt in vaudeville. Women should have just as much chance as men to be funny onstage, argued Florence, and if given the opportunities hitherto saved for men, there might be many more female stars in this line.[18] By redefining their stage roles, and by acquiring new responsibility as laughmakers, women in male-female teams were asserting new rights for women, just as offstage feminists were doing. In fact, there was a cause and effect relationship between women onstage and women in the audience. With their risqué new fashions, their bobbed hair, and their self-assurance, female vaudevillians were models of sophistication and glamour for the women in the audience. But the significant percentage of women in the audience added to the actress's drawing power. It was often the fashionably dressed, charismatic actresses that feminine patrons came to see; thus the new audience segment increased the importance of actresses in putting over the vaudeville acts.

In fact, it was becoming more common for women to be the stars of two-acts, and sometimes men gave up careers if their wives were more successful, as New York Giants star Mike Donlin, who teamed up with his wife because he preferred "Mabel and a home to baseball."[19] Some women even arranged their two-acts; Florence Moore organized the Montgomery and Moore combination, which may have accounted for the unusual female stridency in the act.[20] Maude Fulton was a successful writer, and it is tempting to think she concocted her imaginative contributions to the Rock and Fulton act—her Sarah Bernhardt imitation, or her imitation of different kinds of suffragettes delivering speeches. In March 1912, one reviewer noted that Maude Fulton was all her partner was and more; the following September notice was given that they would split at the end of the season, because they were "hampering" each other's advancement. In later years Maude Fulton would write and star in her own plays, work as composer, concert pianist, stage director, theatre manager, and from 1925 to 1941, as a screen writer, with *The Maltese Falcon* one of her collaborations.[21]

Such women were peculiarly threatening, because—as in society—they were poaching on men's preserve. In the course of vaudeville's history women not only won increasing praise by reviewers and showed more conspicuously their talents and involvement in male-female routines, but the skills they aquired were those previously monopolized by men: eccentric dancing, acrobatics, blackface joking, novelty skills such as skating or stage falls, and comedy. Thus, to men, female laurels and responsibility meant male loss.

244   Conclusion

Female advancement was a concrete threat to their male partners, for two-act salaries were generally assigned by amount to each partner by bookers. Sam Morton explained that however tender their family ties, teamed-up family members had a commercial relationship generally uninfluenced by affiliations of blood or affection. If a husband and wife team earned $300 a week, the wife knew what portion of the $300 she earned, explained Sam.

> She probably has worked alone and thus has had her value definitely fixed, or she has had offers at a certain salary and thus knows what her services can command, and generally she draws from the weekly salarly that amount. It is even frequently stipulated in the contracts of married couples in vaudeville that the husband shall not be permitted to draw the full sum, leaving him to settle with his wife or not as he may see fit, but that a certain percentage of the money be given to him on his order and the remainder to her on her order.

A talented female partner would obviously have a great deal of say in determining how salaries were divided. A star like Mabel Hite even signed contracts and then paid her husband herself.[22]

Given the finances and egos involved, it is unsurprising that sexism continued to be suggested where female team partners were concerned. Talented female partners were often discussed from a sexist perspective in reviews — invariably as "unusual" departures from their sex, or as "natural" (i.e., inexplicably professional) funmakers, who were given free rein and invaluable assistance by their tolerant and good-natured mates. And although women were taking greater responsibility in making acts go, in the majority of teams the man still handled the organizing of material and the business dealings, as with Burns and Allen, and Ryan and Lee. Also, men apparently expected to monopolize the comedy, and they would relinquish that right only if necessary; whereas it was not uncommon for women to assume the comic role only after men had essayed it unsuccessfully, the reverse was unknown. It is revealing that only when men took over the role of feeder was that role given the recognition it deserved — as has often happened in other professions. Indeed, for men whose partners were better at winning laughs, a new role was developed, the "light comedian straight." In this guise, men were able to be more than mere feeders, and to grab a few of the laughs for themselves.

Nowhere was the sexism more implied than in the ways in which female talent seemed most free to develop. The best-known early comediennes in two-acts played obnoxious shrews who insulted and tortured their partners. Usually women who were not particularly attractive offstage, they made their looks laughable with exaggerated, grotesque costumes or ungraceful, unfeminine gestures and faces. It later became acceptable for pretty women to assume responsibility for comedy, as either a laughably "fly" flapper, or as a dumbbell—the most popular kind of comedienne. Throughout the decades, men were funny because they impersonated an Irishman, a tramp, a Jew, a hayseed, or a darky; woman, however, was funny as a caricature of herself, as all that was funny about woman in general—the ways in which she was inferior to man, and the laughableness of her attempts to be what she was not, man's equal.

Whatever its sexist implications, however, male-female teams had developed a kind of routine in which both partners were equally important; since the comedy was invariably dependent on the sexual interaction now, both team members were equally necessary. Two performers of opposite sexes were most funny when they made comedy of their differences and the unbreachable distance those differences placed between them. When women worried and fussed and cooed, their behavior was funny simply because it was so unlike the stronger sex's ways; and when women bullied and swaggered and demanded rights that obviously did not belong to them, it was even funnier. Men were equally comical in their attempts to indulge and understand and deal with their perverse partners. The appeal of the male-female act was therefore sexual in the broadest sense; the maudlin infatuations of lovers, the fencing and flattery and fakery of the street pick-up, the exasperations and hostilities between husband and wife—all that made the relations between the sexes so dynamic and so problematical in real life was sentimentalized and revelled in, made light of and made fun of, in male-female routines on the vaudeville stage.

These comical interactions were a memorable contribution to the fund of popular humor—especially the dumbbell acts. Whereas many characters performed by male-female teams had long been part of comic tradition, the dumbbell was apparently a product of the male-female vaudeville team. In later years, dumbbells would invade comic strips and films, and even a successful Broadway play, *Dulcy*, would take up the character. The real significance of the male-female act was that it was "good theatre," that, at its best, it was hilarious.

But stage women were even funnier when foiled by their offstage counterparts, who were thought to be acting just as comically in the real world. In other words, making comedy of sexual stereotypes was a way for male-female teams to tap an important social concern, one they were eminently suited to dramatize, and which they alone could monopolize. Impersonators could act out the parts, but could not capture the sexual tensions. The male-female routine tapped a sense of dislocation in society, an unsettling tremor that lasted several decades, from the 1850s until the 1929 crash. Women were shaking up society, and the great concern with this offstage issue gave an edge to male-female routines that otherwise would have been lacking. As Henry James said, explaining why he wrote *The Bostonians* in 1886:

> I wished to write a very *American* tale, a tale very characteristic of our social conditions, and I asked myself what was the most salient and peculiar point in our social life. The answer was: the situation of women, the decline of the sentiment of sex, the agitation on their behalf.[23]

The fact of the matter is that the male-female act was more popular during the era of the woman's movement than at any other time, and the implication is that this act was peculiarly bound up with its time. The contemporaneous rise of the American city, with its break from old-world lifestyles and its high standards of living, allowed new social freedoms and experimental new social relationships; the change in relations between the sexes was one of the most dramatic creations of urbanism. Male-female routines reflected this upheaval in American society. The awareness that traditional sex roles were now passé explains the tremendous popularity after 1915 of routines contrasting old sexual behavior with new, nineteenth-century men and women and their twentieth-century counterparts.

There was even a suggestion that women were somehow responsible for all the changes in society. The world had changed from a rural country with Victorian values to an urban nation, in which the values of materialism and cosmopolitanism were now espoused by the ordinary man on the street, and nowhere was the change more obvious than in the new rights brandished by women. Women had been regarded as the guardians of all that was stable and moral in the nineteenth-century world—religion, the home, the virtuousness of man and child—and now women were embracing the modern, urban values of sexuality, materialism, sophistication, and fast living. Thus, they were inextricably linked in the public consciousness with the changes. Perhaps it was not unrelated to the public's consuming interest in the modern woman that after 1910, female performers became more dominant in vaudeville, according to one first-hand observer, and in many instances outdid the men in artistry and appeal.[24] Male-female teams, with their talented women who so often stole the spotlight from their mates, were in more ways than one a touchstone for the "feminization" of variety entertainment—and the world—in the twentieth century.

Eventually, both the real world and the theatre world would forego the frivolity of feminine freedom for a masculine tussle for survival. The depression would redraw old battle lines. As the opportunities to make a living shrank during the depression, it was women who first found themselves out of jobs; female independence was a luxury of the boom years. In the depression, women would return to playing supportive roles at home, their bobbed hair would curl femininely to their shoulders once more, and men would no longer tolerate mannish behavior by women. But these social changes were rehearsed in vaudeville. As opportunities to present live entertainment became fewer and farther between in the late twenties, male prerogative made itself felt. Teams monopolized by male comics supported by glamour-girl foils began to multiply again, and now comediennes could often be found playing somewhat unsavory "dames" and dumb "broads." "Maybe you're not used to being called a lady," gibed one male-chauvinist character to his female partner.[25]

It is perhaps not coincidental that in the thirties, with men and women resettled into traditional sex roles and feminists in low profile for the time being, few male-female teams achieved national prominence on radio, which had gradually supplanted vaudeville as the national pastime. The one team to win conspicuous success in the new medium was Burns and Allen. With her adorable, child-like "dizzy," Gracie was the epitome of what men wished all women to be. But Burns and Allen also captured all that was universal in male-female interactions; playing two characters, each convinced that he or she was right, their wacky conversations encompassed the flirtations, the insults and the arguments, the games, and the very real affection that existed between the ordinary couple. In contrast, although Block and Sully had been a successful vaudeville team, Eve Sully's Hebe dialect was perhaps too limited in appeal for radio's vast audience, which, unlike vaudeville's, was not necessarily urban.

And unlike many latter-day vaudeville teams, with their dependence on slapstick, female beauty, and eyeball-rolling innuendo, all invisible across the airwaves, Burns and Allen had depended on conversation to put their vaudeville act over. It was pure talk and just as funny on radio. It is tempting to add that Burns and Allen survived because they were the greatest male-female two-act artists produced by vaudeville. Of course, it is impossible today to know how Burns and Allen compared with such then-famous teams as Ryan and Lee, or Dooley and Sales, of whom scripts, recordings, and films have not survived to testify to their talent. The undebatable fact is that Burns and Allen were the only male-female team to achieve great popularity after the demise of vaudeville.

It is nonetheless significant, as the many histories herein show, that Burns and Allen were the product of decades of experimentation and innovation and achievement by male-female teams, and without their predecessors, Burns and Allen would never have been. "I always say that long before Block and Sully or Burns and Allen went into business, they had man-and-woman acts," summed up Jesse Block with homespun insight.[26] To the millions of Americans who laughed at male-female teams in vaudeville and to those who have loved Burns and Allen ever since, the fleeting art of the male-female vaudeville team was and is its own reason for being.

Conclusion

And to those teams who lived and worked in vaudeville, it was "a very rewarding life. Oh sure, there is television, radio, pictures—but none of this is vaudeville. Too bad that present generations had to miss it." This was Jean Carroll's assessment. Her husband and one-time partner Buddy Howe agreed: "Vaudeville gave me a wonderful life.... I was very lucky to find and meet the girl I married. It's been a love affair now for over thirty-seven years."[27] Just so, for Block and Sully, vaudeville gave them not only memories, but also each other.

Block: Anyway, that's the story. Today I'm a stockbroker. Do I miss vaudeville? Of course. It was a wonderful life.
Sully: Why don't you ask me if I miss it? Yes, I miss it. I was younger, lighter—and besides, I met Jesse. Without vaudeville—well, who knows![28]

Notes

Introduction

1. James Gleason, *The Shannons of Broadway* (N.Y.: Samuel French, 1927), p. 16.
2. "Punched Manager, Captured a Bride," *Cleveland Leader,* 18 January 1913.
3. Ibid.
4. Ibid.
5. "Ross and Fenton," *New York Dramatic Mirror,* 1898 Christmas Annual, p. 111; unidentified clipping dated 16 September 1907, Charles and Mabel Ross file, Locke Col., New York Public Library at Lincoln Center (hereafter N.Y.P.L.-L.C.).
6. *Pittsburgh Gazette,* 13 April 1913; *New York Dramatic Mirror,* 29 June 1895; unidentified clipping dated 16 September 1907, Charles and Mabel Ross file, Locke Col., N.Y.P.L.-L.C.
7. *Milwaukee News,* 21 October 1913; unidentified clipping, Charles and Mabel Ross file, Locke Col., N.Y.P.L.-L.C.; Amy Leslie, "Ross," *Some Players,* 1899, p. 589.
8. Charles J. Ross, "The Building and Repairing of Vaudeville Sketches," *New York Dramatic Mirror,* 5 July 1911.
9. *Variety,* 21 December 1907; "Charles J. Ross Dead," *New York Times,* 16 June 1918.
10. *The Stage,* September 1898.
11. *Variety,* 14 November 1913.
12. "Ross and Fenton in Clever Skit," *New York Telegraph,* 11 December 1907; unidentified clipping, Charles and Mabel Ross file, Locke col., N.Y.P.L.-L.C.; *Philadelphia Telegraph,* 22 August 1911.
13. *Radio Guide,* [1934] clipping, George Burns file, N.Y.P.L.-L.C.
14. John E. DiMeglio, *Vaudeville U.S.A.* (Bowling Green, Ky.: Bowling Green Univ. Popular Press, 1973), p. 11.

Chapter 1

1. For a study of *commedia* containing *soghetti* which show the number and role played by these male-female "couples" in early *commedia,* see K. M. Lea, *Italian Popular*

Notes for Chapter 1

Comedy: A Study in the Commedia Dell'Arte, 1560–1620; With Special Reference to the English Stage, 2 vols. (1934; repr. N.Y.: Russell and Russell, 1962); on the *Comédie-Italienne, see* Virginia Scott, "The Jeu and the Role: Analysis of the Appeals of the Italian Comedy in France in the Time of Arlequin-Dominique," in *Western Popular Theatre,* eds. David Mayer and Kenneth Richards (London: Methuen, 1977), pp. 1–27.

2. E.g., *see* Emmett L. Avery, et al., *The London Stage, 1660–1800* (Carbondale: Southern Illinois Univ. Press, 1960-1968), part 2, 527, 528–529, 587, 783; part 3, 71, 74, 226, 604, 1315; Victor Leathers, *British Entertainers in France* (Toronto: Univ. of Toronto Press, 1959), p. 20. *See also* Sybil Rosenfeld, *The Theatre of the London Fairs in the Eighteenth Century* (Cambridge: Cambridge Univ. Press, 1960), p. 46.

3. Sybil Rosenfeld, *Strolling Players and Drama in the Provinces, 1660–1765* (Cambridge Cambridge Univ. Press, 1939), pp. 14–19.

4. For a collection of contemporary writings illustrating views in Europe of desirable female attributes, sixteenth century to the nineteenth century, *see* Julia O'Faolain and Lauro Martines, eds., *Not in God's Image* (N.Y.: Harper and Row, 1973); for typical seventeenth-century English expressions of, on the one hand, distaste for the immorality of the stage and its players, and, on the other, the excitement actresses could stir in a male patron of the theatre, *see,* respectively, John Evelyn, *The Diary of John Evelyn,* ed. E. S. De Beer, 6 vols. (Oxford: Clarendon Press, 1955), III, 465–466, 510–511; IV, 422; and Helen McAfee, *Pepys on the Restoration Stage* (1916; repr. N.Y.: Blom, 1966), 237ff.

5. Harold Scott, *The Early Doors: Origins of the Music Hall* (London: Nicholson and Watson, 1946), pp. 49–50, 129, 138–141, 152–154; W. MacQueen-Pope, *The Melody Lingers On* (London: W. H. Allen, 1950), p. 114.

6. There are no references to pre-twentieth-century male-female teams in stock treatments of music hall like Scott, *The Early Doors;* M. Willson Disher, *Music Hall Parade* (London: B. T. Batsford, 1938); and Roy Busby, *British Music Hall: An Illustrated Who's Who from 1850 to the Present Day* (London: Paul Elek, 1978).

7. Bernard Hewitt, *Theatre U.S.A.: 1665–1957* (N.Y.: McGraw-Hill, 1959), p. 2; Rosenfeld, *The Theatre of the London Fairs,* pp. 19–28.

8. Laurence Senelick, "George L. Fox and Bowery Pantomime," in *American Popular Entertainment: Papers and Proceedings of the Conference on the History of American Popular Entertainment,* ed. Myron Matlaw (Westport, Conn.: Greenwood Press, 1979), p. 97.

9. Adam Hallam performed in Theophilus Cibber's Bartholomew Fair booth in 1733; in 1739 "Harlequin Turn'd Philosopher; or The Country Squire Outwitted"—which starred Harlequin and Colombine—was seen at William Hallam's fair booth (Rosenfeld, *The Theatre of the London Fairs,* pp. 39, 45).

10. E.g., *see* George C. D. Odell, *Annals of the New York Stage,* 15 vols. (N.Y.: Columbia Univ. Press, 1927-1945), I, 123, 127, 148, 168, 229, 233, 245, 258, 265, 278, 299, 300, 303, 304, 322, 323, 325. For evidence of the continued appeal of pantomime entertainment, *see also* "pantomime" in index to subsequent volumes of Odell.

11. Philip Graham, *Showboats: The History of an American Institution* (Austin: Univ. of Texas Press, 1951), pp. 40–41.

12. Graham, pp. 29–32.

13. Francis Hodge, *Yankee Theatre: The Image of America on the Stage, 1825-1850* (Austin: Univ. of Texas Press, 1964), pp. 24-29.

14. Hodge, pp. 18, 24, 38; David Grimsted, *Melodrama Unveiled: American Theatre and Culture, 1800-1850* (Chicago: Univ. of Chicago Press, 1968), p. 78; Foster Rhea Dulles, *America Learns to Play: A History of Popular Recreation, 1607-1940* (1940; repr. Gloucester, Ma.: Peter Smith, 1959), p. 111; Russell Nye, *The Unembarrassed Muse: The Popular Arts in America* (N.Y.: Dial Press, 1970), p. 147. See also Grimsted, pp. 186-201; Robert C. Toll, *Blacking Up: The Minstrel Show in Nineteenth-Century America* (N.Y.: Oxford Univ. Press, 1974), pp. 7-9, 13-17.

15. Michael Chevalier, *Society, Manners and Politics in the United States* (Boston, 1839), quoted by Dulles, p. 85.

16. Nye, p. 23; Carl Fish, *The Rise of the Common Man, 1830-1850*, A History of American Life, vol. 6 (N.Y.: Macmillan, 1950), pp. 122, 109-17. See also Arthur Charles Cole, *The Irrepressible Conflict, 1850-1865*, A History of American Life, vol. 7 (N.Y.: Macmillan, 1934), pp. 120, 123, 132, 135.

17. Dulles, p. 211; Toll, *Blacking Up*, p. 4.

18. Toll, *Blacking Up*, pp. 4-5.

19. Fish, p. 326; Arthur Meier Schlesinger, *The Rise of the City, 1878-1898*, A History of American Life, vol. 10 (N.Y.: Macmillan, 1933), p. 171.

20. Dulles, pp. 123-124.

21. Graham, pp. 9-10, 16, 21-25.

22. Dulles, p. 114; Marcello Truzzi, "Circus and Side Shows," in *American Popular Entertainment*, pp. 178-179; Gretchen Schneider, "Gabriel Ravel and the Martinetti Family: The Popularity of Pantomime in 1855," ibid., p. 242; Grimsted, p. 101.

23. Toll, *Blacking Up*, pp. 25-32.

24. Ibid., pp. 12, 34-38.

25. Ibid., pp. 136, 162, 170, 175, 176.

26. Cole, p. 163.

27. Parker R. Zellers, "The Cradle of Variety: The Concert Saloon," *Educational Theatre Journal*, 20 (December 1968), 578-579.

28. Ibid.

29. James Dabney McCabe, Jr. [Edward Winslow Martin], *The Secrets of the Great City: A Work Descriptive of the Virtues and the Vices, the Mysteries, Miseries and Crimes of New York City* (Phila.: Jones, Brothers and Co., 1868), p. 311; Junius Henri Browne, *The Great Metropolis: a Mirror of New York* (Hartford, Conn.: American Publishing Co., 1869), p. 328. See also Matthew Hale Smith, *Sunshine and Shadow in New York* (Hartford, Conn.: J. B. Burr, 1869), p. 440.

30. Browne, p. 327.

31. The New York Press, *The Night Side of New York: A Picture of the Great Metropolis After Nightfall* (N.Y.: J. C. Haney and Co., 1866), pp. 10-11.

32. Cole, pp. 155-156, 160.

33. Joe Laurie, Jr., "The Early Days of Vaudeville," *American Mercury*, 47 (February

1946), 233; Browne, p. 330; McCabe, *The Secrets of the Great City,* p. 309; The New York Press, p. 11.

34. *New York Clipper,* 15 September 1860, p. 174.
35. The New York Press, p. 10. *See also* James Dabney McCabe, Jr., *Lights and Shadows of New York Life; or, The Sights and Sensations of the Great City* (Phila.: National Publishing Co., 1872), p. 596.
36. Browne, p. 328.
37. McCabe, *The Secrets of the Great City,* p. 256; Browne, p. 332; The New York Press, p. 20.
38. *New York Evening Post,* 2 January 1862, quoted by Parker R. Zellers, "Tony Pastor: Manager and Impresario of the American Stage" (Ph.D. diss., Univ. of Iowa, 1964), p. 73. *See also The Spirit of the Times,* 12 October 1861, quoted by Zellers, "Tony Pastor," p. 73.
39. Zellers, "Tony Pastor," p. 74.
40. Ibid., pp. 75-77.
41. Ibid., p. 77.
42. For testimony that the early variety theatres were patronized exclusively by men, *see* Tony Pastor, "Vaudeville in its Infancy," *Toledo Blade,* 19 February 1898; Charles T. Harris, *Memories of Manhattan in the Sixties and Seventies* (N.Y.: Derrydale Press, 1928), p. 14; unidentified clipping, Tony Pastor file, N.Y.P.L.-L.C.; "Stage Stories by Late Tony Pastor," *Toledo News Bee,* 28 August 1908.
43. M[ichael] B. Leavitt, *Fifty Years in Theatrical Management* (N.Y.: Broadway Publishing Co., 1912), pp. 184-185.
44. The New York Press, p. 17.
45. Ibid., pp. 18-19.
46. Ibid., p. 20; *Spirit of the Times,* 16 March 1861, quoted by Zellers, "Tony Pastor," pp. 66-67; Harris, p. 14.
47. Tony Pastor, quoted by Charles Darnton, "Tony Pastor, 39 Years a Manager," *New York World,* 26 March 1904.
48. Playbill, Morris Brothers and Trowbridge's Opera House, 13 June 1866, Tony Pastor file, N.Y.P.L.-L.C. *See also* contemporary bills in Vaudeville: programmes, U.S. file, N.Y.P.L.-L.C.
49. The New York Press, p. 17.
50. Browne, p. 136; *See also* Smith, *Sunshine and Shadow in New York,* p. 215.

Chapter 2

1. Zellers, "The Cradle of Variety," p. 522.
2. Laurie, "The Early Days of Vaudeville," p. 233.
3. Whereas waiter girls received no salary, only a percentage on the drinks they sold — about four to six dollars a week — pay for ballet girls of the lowest class began at eight dollars a week, rising to four hundred dollars for premieres, such as Maria

Bonfanti (McCabe, *Lights and Shadows of New York Life,* pp. 594-95, 789; McCabe, *The Secrets of a Great City,* p. 256; "The Ballet," *Spirit of the Times,* 27 December 1873, quoted by Barbara M. Barker, "The Dancer vs. the Management in Post-Civil War America," *Dance Chronicle,* II, 3 [1978], 173).

4. Odell, VII, 433. *See also New York Clipper,* 1 January 1870, p. 311.
5. The New York Press, p. 19. *See also* W. J. P., "Tony Pastor at 444," *New York Herald,* 26 December 1921.
6. Leavitt, pp. 183-84.
7. Pastor, "Vaudeville in its Infancy."
8. *New York Clipper,* 11 March 1865, p. 882; playbill, Tony Pastor's Combination (Newark, N.J.), 25 March 1865.
9. Odell, VIII, 83.
10. Ibid., 86.
11. Ibid., 357, 360; *Sporting Times and Theatrical News,* 20 March 1869, p. 12; 24 April 1869, p. 6.
12. *See* 1860s bills in Vaudeville: programmes, U.S. file, N.Y.P.L.-L.C.; on Sheridan and Mack, and Delehenty and Hengler, *see* Odell, VIII, 85, 219, 340, 350, 504, 507, 533ff., 546, 633-635, 637, 639, 642, 654-657, 670.
13. Frederick Wadsworth Loring, "Two Song-and-Dance Men," *New York Clipper,* 22 October 1870, p. 225.
14. *New York Clipper,* 23 October 1869, p. 230.
15. "Barney Williams: Story-Teller, Vocalist, Minstrel, Comedian," *New York Clipper,* n.d., Barney Williams file, N.Y.P.L.-L.C.
16. "A Chat with Mrs. Barney Williams," *New York Dramatic Mirror,* 29 February 1896, p. 18.
17. E.g., *see New York Clipper,* 14 April 1866, p. 6; 28 April 1866, p. 23; *Sporting Times and Theatrical News,* 21 August 1869, p. 7; *The Prompter* (Phila.), January 1867, p. 6; Odell, VIII, 641.
18. "William J. Florence," *The Illustrated American,* 5 December 1891.
19. Ibid.
20. *Sporting Times and Theatrical News,* 24 April 1869, p. 7.
21. *The Prompter* (Phila.), October 1866, p. 7; *New York Clipper,* 22 February 1868, p. 367; *Sporting Times and Theatrical News,* 20 February 1869, p. 12; "The Life Story of Mr. and Mrs. W. J. Florence," unidentified clipping, W. J. Florence file, N.Y.P.L.-L.C.; *The Prompter* (Phila.), November 1866, p. 5.
22. *Sporting Times and Theatrical News,* 2 September 1871, p. 7.
23. Lauri Family file, N.Y.P.L.-L.C. *See also* Young and Daniels, *The Prompter* (Phila.), January 1867, p. 6.
24. Odell, VIII, 442-443, 507, 537; *New York Clipper,* 11 December 1869, p. 287; 1 January 1870, p. 311; 8 January 1870, p. 319; 15 January 1870, p. 327.
25. *Sporting Times and Theatrical News,* 28 August 1869, p. 7; *New York Clipper,* 22

October 1870, p. 231. *See also* Mlle. Imperiar and Mons. Victor, *Sporting Times and Theatrical News,* 24 December 1870, p. 7.

26. Grimsted, p. 105.
27. Toll, *Blacking Up,* pp. 76, 140-141.
28. Dulles, p. 116. French ballet was introduced to the New York public in 1827 (Odell, III, 264).
29. Charles B. Smythe, "The Naked Truth," *New York Herald,* 19 November 1866, quoted by Barbara M. Barker, "The Ballet Girl: Graceful, Ungraceful, or Disgraceful?," unpublished paper, p. 20.
30. Leavitt, p. 156; Nye, p. 172.
31. Mark Twain, *Mark Twain's Travels with Mr. Brown* (N.Y., 1940), quoted by Bayard Still, *Mirror for Gotham: New York as Seen by Contemporaries from Dutch Days to the Present* (N.Y.: New York Univ. Press, 1956), p. 176.
32. Leavitt, p. 308.
33. John E. Henshaw, quoted by Bernard Sobel, *A Pictorial History of Burlesque* (N.Y.: Putnam, 1956), pp. 45-46.
34. *New York Clipper,* 12 March 1870, p. 390; Odell, IX, 79; "List of Original Scripts from the Tony Pastor Opera House, Accompanying the Music, Orchestrations, and Clippings From His Music Hall," N.Y.P.L.-L.C.; Odell, VIII, 641. For bills featuring "burlesque blondes," "ballet" troupes, and female minstrels, *see New York Clipper,* 15 February 1868, p. 359; 22 February 1868, p. 367; 30 October 1869, p. 239; 27 November 1869, p. 270; 18 December 1869, p. 294; 22 January 1870, p. 334; 19 February 1870, p. 374; *Sporting Times and Theatrical News,* 16 January 1869, pp. 12-13; 27 March 1869, p. 13; 20 March 1869, p. 12; 31 December 1870, p. 6; 11 February 1871, p. 6; 25 March 1871, p. 6.
35. The New York Press, p. 19. For costume evidence, *see* the picture on the cover of the 3 April 1869 *Sporting Times and Theatrical News* of "Miss Jennie Kimball, Actress and Vocalist."
36. Odell, IX, 331, 86. On the can-can, *see New York Clipper,* 1 January 1870, p. 311; 8 January 1870, p. 319.; *New York Times,* 24 December 1874, p. 5.
37. *New York Clipper,* 7 September 1867, p. 175; *Sporting Times and Theatrical News,* 6 March 1869, p. 12; *New York Clipper,* 1 January 1870, p. 311; *Sporting Times and Theatrical News,* 31 December 1870, p. 2; 4 November 1871, p. 6; Odell, IX, 198.
38. Odell, VIII, 355; *New York Clipper,* 10 September 1870, p. 182; 22 January 1870, p. 335; 1 October 1870, p. 207; Odell, VIII, 357.
39. *Sporting Times and Theatrical News,* 31 December 1870, p. 6.
40. *Sporting Times and Theatrical News,* 27 March 1869, p. 13; *New York Clipper,* 29 January 1870, p. 343; 19 March 1870, p. 399. Still others were Sidney Frank and Emma Alford (*Sporting Times and Theatrical News,* 24 December 1870, p. 6; 8 April 1871, p. 6; 2 September 1871, p. 11); George Moore and Kitty Henderson (*New York Clipper,* 17 September 1870, p. 191; 15 October 1870, p. 223); Harry and Fanny Wood (*New York Clipper,* 1 October 1870, p. 207; *Sporting Times and Theatrical News,* 23 December 1871, p. 7; Odell, IX, 199); Charles and Carrie Austen (Odell, VIII, 86; *New York*

Clipper, 29 October 1870, p. 238; *Sporting Times and Theatrical News,* 24 December 1870, p. 6); and Fred and Emily Siegel, comic dancers (*Sporting Times and Theatrical News,* 1 May 1869, p. 7; 17 December 1870, p. 6; 2 March 1872, p. 6; *New York Clipper,* 22 February 1868, p. 367; 19 March 1870, p. 399; 12 September 1874, p. 191; Odell, IX, 199).

41. Unidentified clipping, Martha Wren file, N.Y.P.L.-L.C.
42. Ibid.
43. Odell, VII, 220; VIII, 248.
44. *New York Clipper,* 29 October 1870, p. 238; unidentified clipping, Martha Wren file, N.Y.P.L.-L.C.; *New York Clipper,* 11 December 1869, p. 286; Odell, VIII, 587, 644.
45. *New York Clipper,* 26 November 1870, p. 267; 29 October 1870, p. 238.
46. *New York Clipper,* 19 November 1870, p. 262; Odell, IX, 79, 81; *Sporting Times and Theatrical News,* 28 January 1871, p. 6; 4 February 1871, p. 6.
47. *Sporting Times and Theatrical News,* 6 May 1871, p. 6; 13 May 1871, p. 7; 8 April 1871, p. 6; 29 April 1871, p. 6; 20 May 1871, p. 6.
48. Odell, IX, 79; *Sporting Times and Theatrical News,* 4 February 1871, p. 6; 9 December 1871, p. 7; Odell, IX, 244.
49. *Crossing the Line,* done at the American Theatre in September 1833; *Delicate Ground,* first done in America at Mitchell's Olympic on 9 January 1850; and *Nan the Good for Nothing,* premiered in the U.S. in 1852, were standard British farces that also became stock pieces in the American repertoire. See Odell, III, 676; IV, 23, 162, 251, 373, 462, 598; V, 128, 457, 556, 557, 596; VI, 54, 105, 106, 110, 125, 130, 131, 153, 154, 166, 197, 205, 206, 220, 227, 236, 277, 286, 302, 341, 351, 357, 370, 383, 385, 396, 461, 475, 495, 546; VII, 67, 115, 119, 338, 393.

    "Beautiful Snow" was a popular poem in 1868, burlesqued not only in print but in an afterpiece at Tony Pastor's Opera House, and performed as a double number on at least one occasion by Adah Richmond and Pastor himself. It was a bathetic tale of a policeman saving a homeless woman (ruined and cast off by a rich brute) from a freezing death in the snow (Pastor, "Vaudeville in Its Infancy"; *New York Telegraph,* 30 October 1898; "List of Original Scripts from the Tony Pastor Opera House"; *New York Clipper,* 13 December 1873, p. 292; 10 January 1874, p. 324).
50. Harry Leslie and Minnie Grey performed together for a few weeks in Washington, D.C. before Leslie departed (*New York Clipper,* 9 April 1870, p. 7; 16 April 1870, p. 7; 30 April 1870, p. 31; 14 May 1870, p. 47.). A Joe and Iona Lang were on a bill together at an Indianapolis house; Lew and Annie Brimmer appeared at the Winter Garden in Cincinnati; on at least two occasions while in the same travelling troupe, Gus Williams and Adah Richmond—both very well-known singles—did a comic duet, "The Suspicious Wife." Others were Harry McCarthy and Lotta Estelle, and a Billy Burton and Minnie Rainforth in their "champion Zouave drill" in a St. Louis house (*New York Clipper,* 12 November 1870, p. 255; *Sporting Times and Theatrical News,* 31 December 1870, p. 6; 7 January 1871, p. 6; 11 February 1871, p. 6; *New York Clipper,* 27 October 1870, p. 231). The sporting newspapers contain other references to couples travelling together, or appearing on bills together, yet without explicit evidence of any act done together—or else refer to an act in which it is unclear whether they were supported by a company (e.g., Tom Adams and May Clifton, *New York Clipper,* 10 September 1870,

256 Notes for Chapter 2

p. 183; Fanny Florence and Johnny McVeigh, *Sporting Times and Theatrical News,* 13 January 1872, p. 7; May Fielding and George Brooks, *Sporting Times and Theatrical News,* 1 April 1871, p. 7).

51. *See* Odell, IX, 78ff., 195ff.

52. *New York Clipper,* 5 April 1873, p. 6; Odell, IX, 79.

53. *See* Dan and Josie Morris, *Sporting Times and Theatrical News,* 31 December 1870, p. 6; 28 January 1871, p. 6; Watson and Sherman, *New York Clipper,* 10 May 1873, p. 47; 13 September 1873, p. 191.

54. *New York Clipper,* 18 April 1874, p. 21; 12 September 1874, p. 191; 16 January 1875, p. 335; Odell, IX, 329.

55. *Sporting Times and Theatrical News,* 7 October 1871, p. 7; Odell, IX, 329; *New York Clipper,* 5 April 1873, p. 6; 3 May 1873, p. 38.

56. *New York Clipper,* 23 May 1874, p. 63; 12 September 1874, p. 191; 16 January 1875, p. 334; 22 January 1876, p. 342.

57. *New York Clipper,* 2 May 1874, p. 35.

58. There were the Fieldings (Odell, IX, 327), Adams and Linton (*New York Clipper,* 26 April 1873, pp. 29, 31), and James and Dollie Emmerson (*New York Clipper,* 19 April 1873, p. 22; 26 April 1873, p. 31), appearing together by the 1872–73 season; Andy and Annie Hughes (*New York Clipper,* 13 September 1873, p. 191), Ella Esmond and Archie White (*New York Clipper,* 2 May 1874, p. 35), J. H. Larkin and Carrie Armstrong (*New York Clipper,* 13 September 1873, p. 191), and William Homer and Minnie Kean (*New York Clipper,* 16 May 1874, p. 51), each performing as a team by the 1873–74 season; and Paddy and Nellie Hughes (*New York Clipper,* 9 January 1875, p. 223), Thomas and Lottie Winnett (*New York Clipper,* 19 September 1874, p. 199), May and Nic Hughes (*New York Clipper,* 12 September 1874, p. 191; 26 September 1874, p. 207), Kate O'Connor and G. B. Harcourt (Odell, IX, 599; *New York Clipper,* 9 January 1875, p. 328), Billy and Maggie Ray (*New York Clipper,* 9 January 1875, p. 323), Mr. and Mrs. George Ware (*New York Clipper,* 16 January 1875, p. 331), and James Welch and Maud LeMoine (Odell, IX, 604; *New York Clipper,* 16 January 1875, p. 335), each on the boards together by 1874–75. By the 1875–1876 season, there were Frank and Eva Bennett (*New York Clipper,* 15 January 1876, p. 335), Nat and Bernetta Blossom (*New York Clipper,* 22 January 1876, p. 343), Harry and Lizzie Braham (Odell, X, 86; *New York Clipper,* 11 March 1876), Ned and Emma Bradley (*New York Clipper,* 22 April 1876, p. 31), Lew and Lena Cole (*New York Clipper,* 8 January 1876, p. 327), Tommy and Annie (Rattelle) Dayton (*New York Clipper,* 8 January 1876, p. 327), James and Kate Edwards (Odell, X, 87), Frank and Carrie Lavarnie (*New York Clipper,* 15 January 1876, p. 335), Ed and Alice (Ross) Murray (*New York Clipper,* 5 February 1876, p. 358; Odell, X, 85), Lew and Pauline Parker (Odell, X, 84; *New York Clipper,* 22 January 1876, p. 343), John and Lea Peasley (*New York Clipper,* 15 January 1876, p. 335), and Thomas and Annie Whiting (*New York Clipper,* 8 January 1876, p. 327).

59. Unidentified clipping, Maggie Fielding file, N.Y.P.L.-L.C.; *Sporting Times and Theatrical News,* 24 April 1869, p. 6.

60. *Sporting Times and Theatrical News,* 3 April 1869, p. 6; *New York Clipper,* 6 November 1869, p. 247; 19 February 1870, p. 374; 19 March 1870, p. 399; 16 April 1870, p. 15; 15 October 1870, p. 223; 26 March 1870, p. 407; Odell, IX, 327.

61. Odell, IX, 327; *New York Clipper,* 19 April 1873, p. 19; 20 September 1873, p. 198; Odell, IX, 467, 470; *New York Clipper,* 4 October 1873, p. 214; 11 April 1874, p. 11; *New York Clipper Almanac,* 1874, p. 28; *New York Clipper,* 9 January 1875, p. 323.
62. *New York Clipper,* 25 December 1869, p. 303; 30 April 1870, p. 31; *Sporting Times and Theatrical News,* 27 January 1872, p. 11.
63. Joe Laurie, Jr., *Vaudeville: From the Honky-tonks to the Palace* (N.Y.: Henry Holt, 1953), p. 227.
64. "Thomas Winnett," obit., *New York Dramatic Mirror,* 3 July 1912, p. 19; *New York Clipper,* 4 December 1869, p. 279; 19 March 1870, p. 399; 5 April 1873, p. 7; 19 September 1874, p. 199; 22 January 1876, p. 343. *See also* Andy Hughes, *New York Clipper,* 22 January 1870, p. 335; *Sporting Times and Theatrical News,* 24 February 1872, p. 6; *New York Clipper,* 13 September 1873, p. 191; 20 September 1873, p. 199; 1 January 1876, p. 319.
65. Sam Morton, "When Women Were Prey," *Variety,* 12 December 1908, p. 41.
66. At least forty-eight double male acts played in New York City variety houses in the 1875–1876 season (Odell, X, 83ff.).
67. *Mr. and Mrs. Peter White* was first acted in the U.S. at the National Theatre in New York, on 2 February 1837, and was a standard piece in subsequent decades (Odell, IV, 144, 147, 149, 267, 430, 469, 495; V, 49, 158, 297, 431, 525; VI, 45, 71, 154, 276, 383, 389; VIII, 169, 184, 241, 383, 404, 527). "The Nerves" was perhaps based on Bayle Bernard's long-lived farce, *The Nervous Man,* first done in New York City in 1833 (Odell, VIII, 76; III, 639).
68. Teams with Irish routines were the Hugheses, the Fieldings, the McAvoys, Kate O'Connor and G. B. Harcourt, William Homer and Minnie Kean, James Welch and Maude LeMoine, Harry and Fanny Wood, James and Kate Edwards, Paddy and Nellie Hughes, Ned and Emma Bradley, and the Carletons. "Dutch" teams were Watson and Sherman, the Winnetts, Lew and Lena Cole, and Larkin and Armstrong. The Morrises and Moore and Henderson alternated their Irish routines with Dutch routines. Two exceptions were Wren and Collins, still using traditional farce material for the most part, and Adams and Linton, whose act "The Quakers" nonetheless betrayed fascination with America's ethnic and religious diversity (*New York Clipper,* 12 September 1874, p. 191; 16 January 1875, p. 334; 26 April 1873, p. 29).

    On the pervasive popularity of "racial" comedy, *see* Douglas Gilbert, *American Vaudeville* (1940; repr. N.Y.: Dover, 1963), pp. 61–85; Paul Antonie Distler, "The Rise and Fall of the Racial Comics in American Vaudeville" (Ph.d. diss., Tulane, 1963).
69. *See* picture of the Fieldings in costume (Odell, IX, opp. 316) which is much like the dress worn by male team Sheridan and Mack (Odell, IX, opp. 156).
70. *New York Clipper,* 2 January 1875, p. 316.
71. *New York Clipper,* 13 June 1874, p. 84. *See also* "Boys of the Period" (*New York Clipper,* 9 January 1875, p. 324) and "The King of Song-and-Dance" (*New York Clipper,* 8 November 1873, p. 252).
72. *New York Clipper,* 3 July 1875, p. 108. "Waiting By the River," "I am Dreaming of You Norah," "Kathleen O'Neil," "The Irish Heart," and "At the Gloaming," songs in

the *Clipper* during this period, were virtually identical (*New York Clipper,* 9 January 1875; 22 November 1873; 12 April 1873; 24 May 1873; 14 June 1873).

73. William Shannon, *The American Irish,* rev. ed. (N.Y.: Macmillan, 1966), p. 28; Cole, p. 134; Allan Nevins, *The Emergence of Modern America, 1865-1878,* A History of American Life, vol. 8 (N.Y.: Macmillan, 1927), p. 49.

74. On immigration, *see* Oscar Handlin, *The Uprooted,* 2nd enlarged ed. (N.Y.: Little, Brown, 1973); John Higham, *Strangers in the Land: Patterns of American Nativism, 1860-1920* (N.Y.: Atheneum, 1963); Marcus Lee Hansen, *The Atlantic Migration* (Cambridge: Harvard Univ. Press, 1940).

75. *New York Times,* 24 December 1874, p. 5; Browne, p. 129.

76. Richard O'Connor, *The German-Americans: An Informal History* (Boston: Little, Brown, 1968), p. 130; Smith, p. 214; McCabe, *Lights and Shadows of New York Life,* pp. 191-192.

77. McCabe, *Lights and Shadows of New York Life,* p. 550.

78. E.g., Odell recorded that the Bowery Garten and Liberty (National) Garten, in 1866 "a home of beer and gutturals, German to the last drop," would in later years become "a flourishing scene of 'variety' in English." Indeed, although in the 1875-1876 season, the new German Volksgarten had operettas in German, by February "German or not, the Volksgarten inclined, now, to 'artists' of Anglo-American names"; likewise, bills at the National Garten "were, so to speak, anglicized." By the 1879-80 season, all these houses were offering English-speaking entertainment, and were little advertised in the German newspapers (Odell, VIII, 68, 70; X, 56-57, 60, 118).

79. E.g., *New York Clipper,* 5 April 1873, p. 6; 3 May 1873, p. 38; 10 May 1873, p. 4; 17 May 1873, p. 55; 18 April 1874, p. 21.

80. *New York Clipper,* 7 September 1878, p. 188.

81. Patriotic references to the homeland were popular in the variety milieu; e.g., *see* "Dublin" (*New York Clipper,* 15 August 1874, p. 157), "The Irish Heart" (*New York Clipper,* 24 May 1873, p. 60), "Don't Go Away, Mollie Darling" (*New York Clipper,* 22 November 1873, p. 268), and "Two Flowers from Paddy's Land" (*New York Clipper,* 13 June 1874, p. 84). The Irish were romantics with a poetic love for their native land, and even Irish of third and fourth generations often expressed deep nostalgia for Ireland. See Carl Wittke, *The Irish in America* (1956; repr. N.Y.: Russell and Russell, 1970), p. 193.

82. *New York Clipper,* 26 April 1873, p. 30.

83. *New York Clipper,* 27 March 1875. See also "Dutch as Sauerkraut" (*New York Clipper,* 30 January 1875, p. 348).

84. The New York Press, p. 54.

85. German routine, "The Two Emigrants"—dedicated to a Mr. and Mrs. F. Krause, presumably a real male-female team—expressed love for Deutschland as well as belief in the opportunities of America (*New York Clipper,* 24 May 1873, p. 60). See also "The Irish Heart," "Two Flowers from Paddy's Land," and especially "Dublin."

86. *New York Clipper,* 2 August 1873.

87. Karl Buchele, *Land und Volk der Vereinigten Staaten von Nord Amerika* (Stuttgart, 1865), quoted by O'Connor, pp. 113-115. Irish writers also lamented that "we meet every day the apostate children of Irish parents, sons of emigrants, and themselves the

worst enemies of emigrants" (Robert Ernst, *Immigrant Life in New York City, 1825-1863* [N.Y.: King's Crown Press, 1949], p. 180).

88. *New York Clipper,* 26 September 1874, p. 204.
89. See "Dutch as Sauerkraut."
90. Carl Wittke, *We Who Built America: The Saga of the Immigrant,* rev. ed. ([Cleveland]: Case Western Reserve Univ., 1964), pp. 186-189; O'Connor, p. 7; Kathleen Neils Conzen, *Immigrant Milwaukee, 1836-1860: Accommodation and Community in A Frontier City* (Cambridge, Ma.: Harvard Univ. Press, 1976), p. 67; Browne, p. 166.
91. *New York Clipper,* 22 November 1873, p. 268; 14 February 1874, p. 364. *See also* "The Two Emigrants."
92. *New York Clipper,* 30 August 1873. Another Dutch double song called "I Vonder Vat's Her Name," was virtually identical (*New York Clipper,* 28 March 1874, p. 412).
93. *New York Clipper,* 28 March 1874, p. 412.
94. Certainly German audiences enjoyed farces about courtship; a contemporary drawing of a play in progress at the Stadt Theatre showed a man and woman onstage in German dress, in what is obviously an elopement scene, with the man helping the woman down a ladder (Odell, VIII, opp. 606).
95. Ernst, p. 180; Wittke, *We Who Built America,* p. 155.
96. *New York Clipper,* 26 September 1874, p. 412.
97. *New York Clipper,* 10 January 1874, p. 325.
98. *New York Clipper,* 9 January 1875, p. 323; 26 September 1874, p. 207; 12 September 1874, p. 191. Others were Tommie and Annie Dayton, Nat and Bernetta Blossom, and Billy and Sadie Hasson (*New York Clipper,* 8 January 1876, p. 327; 22 January 1876, p. 343; Al Fostelle, "The Days of Tony Pastor," *New York Clipper,* 19 December 1914).
99. *New York Clipper,* 9 January 1875.
100. Shannon, pp. 54-56.
101. *New York Clipper,* 6 March 1875.
102. *New York Clipper,* 2 October 1869, p. 207.
103. E.g., *see* the Bennetts, the Fieldings, and the Morrises (*New York Clipper,* 8 October 1870, p. 215; 15 October 1870, p 223; 10 September 1870, p. 182).
104. *Sporting Times and Theatrical News,* 13 May 1871, p. 6; *New York Clipper,* 12 April 1873, p. 15.
105. *New York Clipper,* 5 April 1873, p. 6; 22 January 1870, p. 335; 12 September 1874, p. 191.
106. *New York Clipper,* 8 January 1876, p. 328.
107. Metropolitan Theatre (Wash., D.C.), *New York Clipper,* 12 April 1873, p. 15; Metropolitan Theatre (N.Y.C.), Odell, IX, 603-605; Parisian Varieties (N.Y.C.), Odell, X, 92-93; Leavitt, p. 162; Odell, X, 456, 648; XI, 318.
108. "Life of Tony Pastor," *Tony Pastor's Songs* (N.Y., 1891), quoted by Zellers, "Tony Pastor," p. 85.

Notes for Chapter 3

109. Playbill, Tony Pastor's Opera House, 4 August 1865, Tony Pastor file, N.Y.P.L.-L.C.
110. *New York Herald,* 26 August 1865, p. 71.
111. McCabe, *Lights and Shadows of New York Life,* p. 550.
112. "Tony Pastor Records the Origin of American Vaudeville," *Variety,* 15 December 1906, p. 17; *New York Clipper,* 18 October 1873, p. 231.
113. "Tally One More Birthday for 'Tony' Pastor as a Manager," *New York Morning Telegraph,* 23 March 1904.

Chapter 3

1. Odell, XIII, 82-115.
2. *New York Dramatic Mirror,* 13 December 1884, p. 8; 18 December 1886, p. 11; 20 December 1884, p. 11; 25 October 1884, p. 8; 3 January 1885, p. 11.
3. Browne, p. 327; Josiah Strong, "Why the City Grows," in *The Twentieth Century City* (N.Y., 1898), repr. in *City Life, 1865-1900: Views of Urban America,* eds. Ann Cook, Marilyn Gittell, and Herb Mack (N.Y.: Praeger, 1973), p. 15.
4. *Spirit of the Times,* 23 September 1871, p. 96; *New York Clipper,* 14 December 1872, p. 294.
5. *New York Clipper,* 8 June 1878. *See also* the Prospect Concert Hall's blurb, *New York Dramatic News,* 12 July 1884, p. 11.
6. *New York Clipper,* 2 January 1875, p. 318.
7. *New York Clipper,* 13 February 1875, p. 363; 13 March 1875, p. 398; 30 January 1875, p. 350; 9 October 1875, p. 223. *See also* "Tony Pastor Records the Origin of American 'Vaudeville'."
8. *New York Figaro,* October 1876, p. 3. *See also New York Clipper,* 1 February 1879, p. 335.
9. *The Ladies Guide and City Directory for Shopping, Travel, Amusements, Etc. in the City of New York* (N.Y.: G. P. Putnam's Sons, 1885), pp. 111, 115, 42-43; [James Dabney] McCabe, [Jr.], *New York by Sunlight and Gaslight* (n.p.: 1882), p. 427. (A copy of McCabe is in the N.Y.P.L.-Local History Division; it lacks a title page.)
10. *New York Dramatic News,* 14 November 1882, p. 2; 31 December 1881, p. 9. *See also New York Dramatic News,* 14 January 1882, p. 2; 29 October 1881, p. 2; 10 April 1883, p. 10; *The Theatre: A Weekly Journal of the Stage,* 28 October 1882, p. 10; 18 November 1882, p. 11.
11. The true Victorian lady was worlds apart from the variety house, in a secluded world where "a man usually does not smoke in the presence of a virtuous woman" (F.C. Valentine [Heinrich Oscar von Karlstein], *Gotham and the Gothamites* [London: Field and Tuer, 1887], p. 44); for such a one, the variety house would be off-limits. Middle-class guides to New York such as *The Ladies' Guide and City Directory for Shopping, Travel, Amusement, Etc. in the City of New York* and *The Sun's Guide to New York* (N.Y.: R. Wayne Wilson, 1892) do not list variety houses; the latter warns that "Lower Broadway is not a place for promenading in the day-time" (p. 11). The memoirs of Mabel Osgood Wright—daughter of a Harvard-educated clergyman, and a typical middle-class lady of the day—mention private sociables and performances of Edwin Booth, but not one variety house (*My New York* [N.Y.: Macmillan, 1926]).

12. *See* McCabe, *New York by Sunlight and Gaslight,* p. 489; for comments on Koster and Bial's, *New York Dramatic News,* 16 April 1881, p. 7.
13. *New York Dramatic News,* 25 April 1885, p. 11.
14. *New York Dramatic News,* 20 February 1886, p. 11; 24 October 1885, p. 11.
15. *New York Dramatic News,* 17 October 1885, p. 11; 30 January 1886, p. 11.
16. Gilbert, pp. 114-115.
17. The intense rivalry between Miner's Theatre and the London Theatre in the eighties is described in "Pat Rooney the First," *Variety,* 25 December 1912.
18. Odell, passim.
19. Nevins, pp. 75, 92.
20. Odell, X, 441-477.
21. E.g., the Sheerans, "America, Ireland, Germany" (Odell, XI, 562); the Maras, "Leaving Thee Erin" (Odell, X, 667); Kurtz and Brooks, "The Emigrant's Lament" (Odell, XI, 126); Henshaw and Ten Broeck, "Farewell to the Faderland" (*New York Clipper,* 21 October 1876, p. 235); the "Dutch" Mendels, "Off to America" (Ibid., p. 239); the Peasleys, "Teddy's Departure" (Odell, X, 666); the Murphys, "Just from Ireland" (Odell, XI, 530); Hodges and DeVere, "Just Over" (*New York Dramatic News,* 10 October 1885, p. 11); Ransome and Bordeaux, "Across the Atlantic" (Odell, XII, 314); Coleman and McCarthy, "The Pair from Castlebar" (Odell, XI, 576); the Ringlers, "The Little Shamrocks" (Odell, XI, 563); Carr and Wentworth, "The Happy Pair" (Odell, XI, 111); and the Peasleys, "The Galway Pair" (Odell, X, 474).
22. Odell, X, 282; *New York Clipper,* 23 October 1880, p. 243; Odell, X, 461.
23. *New York Clipper,* 17 March 1877, p. 407; Odell, XI, 342; X, 281; *New York Clipper,* 2 December 1876, p. 286; Odell, XII, 112.
24. Gilbert, p. 74.
25. E.g., A. H. and Nellie LeClair, "Shakespeare in the Kitchen" (Odell, XI, 548); Gibson and Davis, "Actors in the Kitchen" (Odell, XI, 556); the Burgesses, "Trouble in the Kitchen" (Odell, XI, 112); the Conways, "The Kitchen Actress" (Odell, X, 284); and the Daileys, "Kitchen Domestics" (Odell, X, 463).
26. Odell, VIII, 639; IX, 468; Gerald Bordman, *American Musical Theatre: A Chronicle* (N.Y.: Oxford Univ. Press, 1978), pp. 28, 43-46.
27. *New York Dramatic News,* 19 November 1887, p. 11; Odell, XII, 319; XIII, 526, 102, 108; *New York Clipper,* 7 December 1889, p. 656.
28. Odell, XII, 120, 323, 116; XI, 130; XII, 120, 327. *See also* Paddy and Ella Murphy, Odell, XII, 316, 512.
29. E.g., Osborne and Wentworth, "Mollie's Troubles and Sun Shine" (*New York Clipper,* 20 January 1877, p. 343); James and Kate Edwards, "Everyday Life" (*New York Clipper,* 21 October 1876, p. 239); Morosco and Gardner, "Lena's Birthday" (Odell, XII, 524) and "Schlum Family" (Odell, XII, 114-115, 312, 512; XIII, 84, 333; *New York Dramatic News,* 18 December 1886, p. 11); Frank and Fanny Davis, "Mahoney the Masher" (Odell, XII, 315), "The Old Veteran" (Odell, XIII, 87, 511), "Four O'Clock in the Morning" (*New York Dramatic News,* 25 February 1888, p. 8), and "Maloney's Night On" (Odell, XIII, 96, 333); Max and Martha Miller, "Going to the Picnic" (Odell, XI, 321).

30. Unidentified clipping, Maggie Vickers file, N.Y.P.L.-L.C.; *Dramatic Magazine*, 26 December 1891; Odell, X, 450, 675; XI, 138; XII, 124, 132-134.
31. Maldwyn A. Jones, *Destination American* (N.Y.: Holt, Rinehart, and Winston, 1976), pp. 11, 17, 144.
32. Jones, pp. 168, 171, 196, 214-215.
33. La Vern J. Rippley, *The German Americans* (Boston: Twayne, 1976), pp. 82, 88; Robert Henry Billigmeier, *Americans from Germany: A Study in Cultural Diversity*, Minorities in American Life Series (Belmont, Calif.: Wadsworth, 1974), p. 97; Wittke, *We Who Built America*, p. 245.
34. Jones, pp. 75-78, 81, 87, 114-115, 127, 132.
35. *The Sun's Guide to New York*, p. 2; *Illustrated New York: The Metropolis of To-Day* (N.Y.: International Publishing Co., 1888), pp. 46-47; Harry H. Marks, *Small Change; or, Lights and Shades of New York* (N.Y.: Standard Publishing Co., 1882), pp. 29-30; Mary R. Henderson, *The City and the Theatre: New York Playhouses from Bowling Green to Times Square* (Clifton, N.J.: James T. White, 1973), p. 129.
36. Matthew Hale Smith, Henry L. Williams, and Ralph Bayard, eds., *Wonders of a Great City: or the Sights, Secrets and Sins of New York* (Chicago: People's Publishing Co., 1887), p. 233; *Illustrated New York*, pp. 74, 55.
37. *The Sun's Guide to New York*, pp. 16, 19, 22, 24; Odell, X, 282, 671; XI, 104, 334, 568; *The Sun's Guide to New York*, p. 43.
38. See the reconstruction of Harrigan's similar audience in E. J. Kahn, Jr., *The Merry Partners: The Age and Stage of Harrigan and Hart* (N.Y.: Random House, 1955), pp. 14-25.
39. Marks, pp. 29-30, 62.
40. Wittke, *The Irish in America*, p. 258.
41. Kahn, p. 63.
42. *New York Clipper*, 11 September 1886, p. 415.
43. E.g., the Morrisseys, "Flirtation" (*New York Clipper*, 11 November 1876, p. 259); the Winnetts, "Love in Broken Dutch" (*New York Clipper*, 20 January 1877, p. 343); Sheridan and Jourdan, "A Moonlight Flirtation" (*New York Clipper*, 8 February 1879, p. 366).
44. Odell, XII, 315, 116; XI, 345, 548, 337. *See also* Frank and Fanny Davis, "Fogarty's Night Out, or Love in Ireland" (Odell, XI, 326); John Russell and Lulu Arlington, "Mulcahey's Flirtation" (Odell, XII, 329); Joe Redmond and Ada Clifton, "A Modern Flirtation" (Odell, XII, 520); Bruns and Monroe, "Conductor and German Sweetheart" (*New York Dramatic News*, 5 March 1887, p. 11); Larry and Lizzie Smith, "Love Letters" (Odell, XII, 531).
45. Odell, XI, 114, 572. *See also* Wills and Adams, "The German Mashers" (Odell, XI, 339).
46. *New York Clipper*, 8 February 1879, p. 364.
47. Gilbert, p. 11.
48. Odell, XI, 131-132; XII, 533; *New York Dramatic News*, 3 January 1885, p. 11; Odell, XI, 328.

49. *New York Clipper,* 22 December 1877, p. 307.
50. Marks, pp. 95-96.
51. Jeppe Delano, "Reminiscences of Jeppe and Fanny Delano," *New York Clipper,* n.d., Jeppe Delano file, N.Y.P.L.-L.C. Jeppe, while employed at Guild and Delano, made a stage crown for Edwin Booth, on view today at the Player's Club in New York.
52. Ibid.
53. Ibid.
54. *New York Clipper,* 21 October 1876, p. 239.
55. Delano, "Reminiscences."
56. *New York Clipper,* 3 April 1875, p. 4.
57. *New York Clipper,* 27 April 1875, p. 380.
58. *New York Clipper,* 13 March 1875.
59. *New York Clipper,* 17 March 1877, pp. 406, 403. Jeppe was known as the "originator of his peculiar style of doffing the chapeau" (Odell, XII, 122).
60. *New York Clipper,* 1 February 1879, p. 358.
61. Fostelle, "The Days of Tony Pastor."
62. *New York Dramatic News,* 12 December 1885, p. 11.
63. E.g., the 1878-79 season brought Fields and Thornton to New York City in "Dodging for a Wife"; Alice and Oliver Wren in "Love at First Sight"; and Newcomb and Mayo, in "Sweethearts" (*New York Clipper,* 28 September 1878, p. 215; Odell, X, 676, 679). Adams and Linton, an early team performing together since 1873 with a sketch called "Quakers," were billed as "Neat and Refined" in the 1877-78 season, and in an act called "Jealousy" the following season—also titled "I've Only Been Down to the Wigwam; or, Dibdin's Jealousy" (*New York Clipper,* 13 October 1877, p. 227; Odell, X, 685; XI, 340).
64. Odell, X, 657; *New York Dramatic News,* 22 August 1885, p. 7; playbill, Tony Pastor's Troupe, n.p., n.d., Tony Pastor file, N.Y.P.L.-L.C.; Odell, XIII, 108; XI, 561, 563; XIII, 87; XV, 141.
65. *New York Clipper,* 28 August 1880, p. 183.
66. Billy Wylie, Gagbook, N.Y.P.L.-L.C.
67. E.g., Rose and Harry Franklin, "Fighting for a Wife" (Odell, XI, 319); Elmer Grandin and Josephine Shanley, "Won at Last" (Odell, XI, 320): Edith Sinclair and Ed Barnes, "Faint Heart Never Won Fair Lady" (Odell, XI, 347); Emily and Tommie Harris, "Hymenial Happiness Happily Handled" (*New York Clipper,* 18 September 1880, p. 207); John Hogan and Lizzie Mowbray, "Flirtations" (Odell, XI, 533); Den and Ella Howe, "Flirtation" (Odell, XI, 544); Dolph Levino and Susie Dillion, "Love vs. Music" (Odell, XI, 556); Jennie Leland and Tony Farrell, "Love in a Hammock" (Odell, XII, 109, 325; *New York Dramatic News,* 13 December 1884, p. 8); James Dilks and Nellie Gray, "Something Else Outside" (Odell, XII, 113) and "Somebody Kissing Outside" (*New York Dramatic News,* 5 September 1888, p. 9); Beane and Gilday, "Love Letters" (Odell, XIII, 113); Lew Roseland and Millie May, "The Lover's Post Office" (Odell, XII, 532); Charles Phillips and Gracie Sherwood, "Fun in a Parlor" (Odell, XII, 515); Frank Jones and Alice Montague, "His First Visit" (Odell, XII, 333); William and

Fanny Everett, "A Husband Wanted" (Odell, XIII, 88); and Phil and Chrissie Sheridan, "Linda's Wedding Day" (*New York Dramatic News,* 7 January 1888, p. 8).

68. Aileen S. Kraditor, *The Ideas of the Woman Suffrage Movement, 1890-1920* (1965; repr. N.Y.: Anchor Books, 1971), p. 1; Eleanor Flexnor, *Century of Struggle: The Woman's Rights Movement in the United States,* Rev. ed. (Cambridge, Ma.: Belknap Press of Harvard Univ. Press, 1975), p. 167; *New York Times,* 12 October 1881, p. 5; 4 November 1885, p. 4; 12 October 1887, p. 3; 9 January 1880, p. 2; 11 May 1881, p. 1; 24 April 1881, p. 9; 16 December 1883, p. 1; 13 April 1882, p. 1; 21 February 1882, p. 3; 22 February 1882, p. 3; 24 February 1882, p. 8.

69. E.g., *New York Times,* 2 February 1882, p. 3; 3 February 1882, p. 8; 20 May 1882, p. 5; 11 January 1882, p. 1; 31 May 1882, p. 1; 14 December 1882, p. 4; 3 August 1882, p. 2; 30 September 1882, p. 5; 19 April 1883, p. 1; 20 April 1883, p. 2; 14 March 1884, p. 3; 4 September 1884, p. 1; 13 February 1885, p. 8; 14 February 1885, p. 3; 24 March 1886, p. 2; 25 March 1886, p. 8; 24 October 1886, p. 6; 26 October 1886, p. 10; 22 April 1887, p. 5; 4 March 1887, p. 5; 8 June 1888, p. 6; 23 March 1888, p. 2; 17 August 1888, p. 4; 26 Arpil 1889, p. 5; 27 April 1889, p. 8.

70. *New York Times,* 18 May 1880, p. 4; 13 April 1882, p. 10; 16 October 1887, p. 4; 20 June 1888, p. 6; 17 September 1882, p. 8.

71. Wittke, *We Who Built America,* p. 244; Ernst, pp. 178, 152, 179; Susan B. Anthony and Ida Husted Harper, *The History of Woman Suffrage* (Rochester, N.Y.: Susan B. Anthony, 1902), IV, xxiii.

72. *New York Times,* 12 October 1881, p. 4; 12 August 1882, p. 3; 23 May 1886, p. 5; 12 August 1886, p. 4.

73. E.g., *New York Clipper,* 1 January 1870, p. 310; *Sporting Times and Theatrical News,* 10 February 1872, p. 9; 2 March 1872, p. 7; Gilbert, p. 81; Billy Wylie, Gagbook.

74. Jerry Cohan, Cohan Family Repertoire-Book, Harvard Theatre Collection. For a discussion of Cohan's gagbook as representative of the process of refinement in variety humor, *see* Laurence Senelick, "Variety into Vaudeville, the Process Observed in Two Manuscript Gagbooks," *Theatre Survey,* 19 (May 1978), pp. 1-15.

75. June Sochen, *Herstory: A Woman's View of American History* (N.Y.: Alfred Publishing, 1974), pp. 181-183; Robert Riegel, *American Women: A Story of Social Change* (Cranbury, N.J.: Fairleigh-Dickinson Univ. Press, 1970), pp. 147-149; Schlesinger, *The Rise of the City,* p. 142; Marks, pp. 29, 46.

76. *New York Dramatic News,* 23 April 1888, p. 8; *New York Clipper,* 29 March 1879, p. 6; Odell, X, 674; XI, 127; *New York Clipper,* 9 November 1889, p. 590; *New York Dramatic News,* 11 April 1885, p. 11; Odell, XIII, 104.

77. Odell, XIII, 85; *New York Dramatic News,* 9 July 1888, p. 8; Odell, XIV, 115, 358, 114.

78. Odell, X, 459; *New York Clipper,* 2 March 1878, p. 391; Odell, X, 462; *New York Clipper,* 8 February 1879, p. 366.

79. *New York Clipper,* 28 February 1880, p. 390; Odell, XII, 111-112, 318, 321, 519; *New York Dramatic News,* 28 March 1885, p. 8.

80. *New York Dramatic News,* 12 July 1884, p. 11; 28 March 1885, p. 11; 24 October 1885, p. 11. The composition of the company changed somewhat over a season, with the

exception of Hallen and Hart, but the entertainment presented at Harry Miner's Eighth Avenue Theatre in October 1886 was probably a typical Hallen and Hart bill. See *New York Dramatic News*, 16 October 1886, p. 7.

81. *New York Dramatic News*, 16 October 1886, p. 7.
82. *New York Dramatic News*, 6 March 1886, p. 11.
83. *New York Dramatic News*, 3 December 1887, p. 11; 6 March 1886, p. 11.
84. *New York Dramatic News*, 10 December 1887, p. 11.
85. *New York Dramatic News*, 9 June 1888, p. 8; unidentified clipping, Joe Hart file, N.Y.P.L.-L.C.
86. Odell, passim; *New York Dramatic News*, 25 December 1886, p. 11.
87. E.g., Billy and Maggie Ray were performing in "Uncle Eph's Birthday" and "Home Again" in 1877; Emile and Pauline Ames in "The Return from the War." Lew and Pauline Parker did blackface work in "South," surely a plantation number (*New York Clipper*, 20 October 1877, p. 239; 13 January 1877, p. 334; 16 November 1878, p. 270; 22 February 1879, p. 382). Harry Woodson had played an old Negro man alone in the seventies, and from 1883 to 1891 or so, he was performing his well-known character alongside his wife Laura Bennett in "Patchwork" and "Pleasant Moments"; her contribution was her singing and xylophone playing (*New York Dramatic News*, 10 May 1884, p. 11; Odell, XII, 530; *New York Dramatic News*, 23 July 1887, p. 7; 19 September 1885, p. 11; 19 May 1888, p. 8). John and Lottie Burton's act, "At the Depot," from 1883-84 and 1884-85 bills, was also a "plantation act" (*New York Dramatic News*, 28 November 1885, p. 11; Odell, XII, 317, 528).
88. *New York Dramatic News*, 10 October 1885, p. 11; 18 July 1885, p. 7; 6 March 1886, p. 11; 30 January 1886, p. 11; 17 October 1885, p. 11; Odell, XIII, 101; unidentified clipping dated 28 February 1906, John Healey file, N.Y.P.L.-L.C.
89. *New York Clipper*, 16 November 1878, p. 270.
90. *New York Clipper*, 22 February 1879, p. 382; 25 September 1880, p. 215.
91. *New York Clipper*, 15 December 1877, p. 299; 2 March 1878, p. 391; 30 November 1878, p. 286; *New York Morning Telegraph*, 20 December 1906.
92. "Divorced Carrie Swain," unidentified clipping, Carrie Swain file, N.Y.P.L.-L.C.; "$5,000,000 for Carrie Swain," unidentified clipping dated 1904, Carrie Swain file, N.Y.P.L.-L.C.; "Carrie Swain is Not the Wife of Frank Gardiner," unidentified clipping dated 18 March 1905, Carrie Swain file, N.Y.P.L.-L.C.; *New York Morning Telegraph*, 20 December 1906.
93. "$5,000,000 for Carrie Swain."
94. *New York Clipper*, 15 December 1877, p. 299.
95. "Carrie Swain," unidentified clipping, Carrie Swain file, N.Y.P.L.-L.C.
96. Gilbert, p. 84; Kahn, p. 144.
97. Odell, XIII, 108; XII, 322; *New York Dramatic News*, 12 December 1885, p. 11.
98. *New York Dramatic News*, 18 July 1885, p. 7; Odell, XII, 119, 304. Other routines by the Whites were "Blockaded," "A Big Mistake," "On the Frontier," "Past, Present, Future," and "Papa's New Coachman" (Odell, XII, 116, 117, 135, 325; XIII, 106).
99. Odell, XIV, 354-374; *New York Dramatic News*, 25 December 1886, p. 11; Odell, XII,

Notes for Chapter 3

132, 324, 329; *New York Dramatic News,* 12 July 1884, p. 11; 25 December 1886, p. 11.

100. Odell, XIII, 93.

101. Odell, XI, 522; *New York Dramatic News,* 10 April 1886, p. 11; 5 March 1887, p. 11.

102. Odell, XI, 138, 532; XII, 132, 514, XIII, 95; XII, 522, 99. Others were Redmond and Blake, "Theatrical Tramps" (Odell, XI, 557); the Chamberlains, "The O'Donovan's Rehearsal" (Odell, XI, 340); the Sheerans, "Theatrical Engagements" (Odell, XII, 518); Kurtz and Brooks, "Booked" (Odell, XI, 326); the Vidocqs, "A Rehearsal" (Odell, XII, 119; XIII, 114); the Werners, "After the Opera" (Odell, XII, 122); the Forresters, "A Rehearsal" (*New York Dramatic News,* 25 April 1885, p. 11); Phillips and Bach, "I'm Bound to be an Actor" (Odell, XII, 528); Byron and Blanch, "Stagestruck" (Odell, XIII, 106); Matthews and Harris, "An Actor in Trouble" (Odell, XII, 329); Hume and Lindsay, "Clipper Ads" (Odell, XII, 128); Hallen and Hart, "I'm an Actor" (Odell, XI, 555); Lloyd and Newton, "An Actor's Nerve" (*New York Dramatic News,* 19 September 1885, p. 11).

103. Ernst, p. 130; Marks, pp. 94–96.

104. *New York Dramatic News,* 10 October 1885, p. 11; Odell, XI, 113; *New York Clipper,* 28 February 1880, p. 390; Odell, XI, 556, 340; Bordman, pp. 51–52.

105. Laurie, *Vaudeville,* p. 47.

106. "John E. Henshaw," obit., *New York Times,* 6 September 1939; *Cleveland News,* 23 January 1908; *New York Clipper,* 21 October 1876, p. 235; Odell, XIII, 93, 95, 97, 333.

107. Gilbert, p. 126.

108. Gilbert, p. 127.

109. *New York Dramatic News,* 31 January 1885, p. 11.

110. E.g., *see Sporting Times and Theatrical News,* 4 February 1871, p. 6; *New York Clipper,* 15 January 1876, p. 331; 5 February 1876, p. 358; 9 January 1875, p. 328; 26 September 1874, p. 206; 8 January 1876, p. 327.

111. *New York Dramatic News,* 3 May 1884, p. 11; 6 March 1886, p. 11. *See also* Morosco and Gardner, *New York Dramatic News,* 11 April 1885, p. 8; Sully and Germon, *New York Dramatic News,* 18 April 1885, p. 11; Ed and Alice Clark, *New York Dramatic News,* 18 April 1885, p. 11; Stanley and Conway, *New York Dramatic News,* 10 October 1885, p. 11.

112. *See* Wills and Adams, *New York Dramatic News,* 21 November 1885, p. 11; Richmond and Glenroy, *New York Dramatic News,* 24 March 1888, p. 8; Ross and Connelly, *New York Dramatic News,* 27 March 1886, p. 11; Frank and Fanny Davis, *New York Dramatic News,* 12 April 1884, p. 11.

113. E.g., the Conways, *New York Dramatic News,* 19 September 1885, p. 11; the Davises, *New York Dramatic News,* 30 January 1886, p. 11; Beane and Gilday, *New York Dramatic News,* 26 November 1887, p. 11.

114. *New York Dramatic News,* 27 December 1884, p. 11. *See also* Stanley and Conway, *New York Dramatic News,* 20 December 1884, p. 11; Ellis and Moore, *New York Dramatic News,* 19 February 1884, p. 10; Beane and Gilday, *New York Dramatic News,* 3 May 1884, p. 11; Watson and Hutchings, *New York Dramatic News,* 3 January 1885, p. 11.

115. "Memories of a Veteran," unidentified clipping dated 11 May 1913, Jerry Cohan file, N.Y.P.L.-L.C.
116. Jones, p. 87.
117. Odell, XI, 542–543.
118. "Bright Gossip of Stage and Stars," *Baltimore Star,* 11 March 1909.
119. "Jerry Cohan, Loved Stage Veteran Dies," unidentified clipping dated 2 August 1917, Jerry Cohan file, N.Y.P.L.-L.C.; "Memories of a Veteran."
120. Ward Morehouse, *George M. Cohan: Prince of the American Theatre* (N.Y.: J. B. Lippincott, 1943), pp. 24–25; Odell, XI, 570; "Bright Gossip of Stage and Stars."
121. "Memories of a Veteran."
122. Cohan Family Repertoire-Book; *New York Dramatic News,* 30 June 1888, p. 1; 19 May 1888, p. 8.
123. Transcribed by Senelick, "Variety into Vaudeville," p. 12.
124. Senelick, "Variety into Vaudeville," p. 13.
125. Cohan Family Repertoire-Book.
126. "Memories of a Veteran."
127. "Jerry Cohan, Loved Stage Veteran Dies."
128. *New York Dramatic News,* 9 July 1887, p. 7; Odell, XII, 325; *New York Dramatic News,* 13 June 1885, p. 11.
129. Odell, XII, 328; *New York Dramatic News,* 6 December 1884, p. 8.
130. Odell, XII, 113; *New York Clipper,* 2 October 1886, p. 460.
131. *New York Clipper,* 12 October 1889, p. 518; Odell, XII, 512.
132. *New York Dramatic News,* 20 August 1887, p. 7; 1 November 1884, p. 11; *New York Clipper,* 9 November 1889, p. 591. See also Frank and Lillian White, *New York Dramatic News,* 17 December 1887, p. 8; Lang and Rosa, *New York Dramatic News,* 22 November 1884, p. 11.
133. E.g., Conways, *New York Dramatic News,* 31 January 1885, p. 11; Vidocqs, *New York Dramatic News,* 21 January 1888, p. 9; Wylie and Sanford, Jones and Montague, and Farrell and Leland, *New York Dramatic News,* 1 November 1884, p. 11.
134. *New York Dramatic News,* 29 November 1884, p. 11; 5 December 1885, p. 11; 12 April 1884, p. 11.
135. Odell, XIII, 93. See also review of Alice Hutchings, *New York Dramatic News,* 14 March 1885, p. 11.
136. Unidentified clipping, Fanny Beane file, N.Y.P.L.-L.C.
137. *New York Clipper,* 3 February 1877, p. 35
138. Ibid.
139. *New York Clipper,* 28 September 1878, p. 215; 30 November 1878, p. 183.
140. *New York Dramatic News,* 23 June 1888, p. 9; Odell, XIV, 374; "Fanny Beane Destitute," *New York Dramatic Mirror,* 17 February 1906.
141. *New York Clipper,* 20 March 1880, p. 415; Odell, XI, 564, 565; XII, 135, 325, 533;

New York Clipper, 7 December 1878, p. 294; Odell, XIII, 113; *New York Dramatic News,* 28 March 1885, p. 8.

142. *New York Dramatic News,* 28 March 1885, p. 8; 31 December 1887, p. 8.
143. "Old Friends Make Fanny Beane Happy," *New York Commercial,* 13 February 1906.
144. *New York Clipper,* 20 March 1880, p. 415; *New York Dramatic News,* 23 May 1885, p. 11.
145. "Fanny Beane, Famous Dancer, Now a Wreck," unidentified clipping dated 7 February 1906, Fanny Beane file, N.Y.P.L.-L.C.
146. "Old Friends Make Fanny Beane Happy."
147. Ibid.
148. *New York Dramatic News,* 20 June 1885, p. 7; *New York Dramatic News,* 23 May 1896.
149. *New York Dramatic Mirror,* 11 May 1895, p. 20; 16 January 1897, p. 20; *New York Dramatic News,* 1 May 1884, p. 3; 19 December 1885, p. 11; 8 August 1885, p. 11; 9 July 1887, p. 7; 18 December 1886, p. 11; 12 March 1887, p. 11; 28 October 1886, p. 11; 27 February 1886, p. 11; 28 January 1888, p. 8.
150. "John E. Henshaw," [*New York*] *Dramatic Mirror,* n.d., John E. Henshaw file, N.Y.P.L.-L.C.; *Cleveland News,* 23 January 1908; "John E. Henshaw," obit., *New York Times,* 6 September 1939; *Cleveland Morning Telegraph,* clipping dated February 1908, John Henshaw file, N.Y.P.L.-L.C.
151. "May Ten Broeck," photograph (cigarette card), May Ten Broeck file, N.Y.P.L.-L.C.
152. *New York Clipper,* 23 November 1889, p. 623.
153. *New York Clipper,* 28 September 1889, p. 491.

Chapter 4

1. "Memories of a Veteran."
2. Gilbert, p. 198.
3. Ibid., p. 202.
4. John Kasson, *Amusing the Million: Coney Island at the Turn of the Century* (N.Y.: Hill and Wang, 1978), pp. 4–6. See also John Tomsich, *A Genteel Endeavor: American Culture and Politics in the Gilded Age* (Stanford, Calif.: Stanford Univ. Press, 1971).
5. Gilbert, pp. 204–205.
6. Robert Grau, *Forty Years of Observations of Music and the Drama* (N.Y.: Broadway Publishng Co., 1909), p. 4; Gilbert, pp. 205–206.
7. Martin Beck and Alexander Pantages had been waiters; Percy Williams had sold liver pads in a medicine show, and Fred Mozart had been a circus fire-eater. E. F. Albee was sensitive about his social advancement, and studiously avoided any mention of his circus days (Gilbert, pp. 210, 219, 215, 220; Laurie, *Vaudeville,* p. 344).
8. Laurie, *Vaudeville,* p. 362.
9. *New York Dramatic Mirror,* 1 April 1899, p. 18.

10. *New York Dramatic Mirror,* 23 November 1901, p. 18. See also *New York Dramatic Mirror,* 5 November 1898, p. 18; 25 February 1899, p. 18.
11. *Chicago Record-Herald,* quoted by *New York Dramatic Mirror,* 23 May 1903, p. 19.
12. *New York Dramatic Mirror,* 17 August 1895, p. 17.
13. *New York Dramatic Mirror,* 14 September 1895. See also Blair and Murilla, *New York Dramatic Mirror,* 13 July 1895, p. 18.
14. *New York Dramatic Mirror,* 31 October 1896, p. 19; 15 October 1898, p. 19. See also Signor Alberti and Madame Orlandi, *New York Dramatic Mirror,* 6 February 1897, p. 19; McKee Rankin and Nance O'Neil, *New York Dramatic Mirror,* 15 January 1898, p. 18.
15. In contrast, the entire U.S. population increased only 2⅓ times, and the working-class population grew tenfold (Robert Wiebe, *The Search for Order, 1877-1920* [N.Y.: Hill and Wang, 1967], 111ff.; Richard Hofstadter, *The Age of Reform: From Bryan to F.D.R.* [N.Y.: Knopf, 1968], pp. 215-216).
16. *New York Dramatic Mirror,* 18 April 1896, p. 19.
17. Charles Funnell, *By the Beautiful Sea: The Rise and the High Times of that Great American Resort, Atlantic City* (N.Y.: Knopf, 1975), pp. 47-51.
18. Louise B. More, *Wage-Earners' Budgets: A Study of Standards and Cost of Living in New York City* (N.Y.: Henry Holt, 1907), p. 95.
19. More, pp. 142-143.
20. Ibid., pp. 104, 167-181.
21. John Van Dyke, *The New New York* (N.Y.: Macmillan, 1909), pp. 118, 193-194; Jessie Lynch Williams, *New York Sketches* (N.Y.: Charles Scribner's Sons, 1902), pp. 71-80, 102.
22. *New York Dramatic Mirror,* 7 November 1896, p. 19; 26 December 1896, p. 19; 31 October 1896, p. 19. For billings, see McAvoy and Rogers, *New York Dramatic Mirror,* 19 October 1895, p. 20; Redding and Stanton, *New York Dramatic Mirror,* 26 October 1895, p. 19; Romer and Collette, *New York Dramatic Mirror,* 26 December 1896, p. 20; Stanley and Jackson, *New York Dramatic Mirror,* 25 February 1899, p. 18; the Gleesons, *New York Dramatic Mirror,* 29 October 1898, p. 20; Mr. and Mrs. F. K. Tobin, *New York Dramatic Mirror,* 21 January 1899, p. 18; Smith and Fuller, *New York Dramatic Mirror,* 4 February 1899, p. 18; Kelly and Violette, *The Cast,* 3 December 1900; Williams and Melburn, *The Cast,* 19 March 1900; White and Stuart, *The Cast,* 14 January 1901; the Barrows, *The Cast,* 1 April 1901.
23. Schlesinger, *The Rise of the City,* p. 41; Harold Faulkner, *The Quest for Social Justine, 1898-1914,* A History of American Life, vol. 11 (N.Y.: Macmillan, 1931), pp. 155-157; Andrew Sinclair, *The Better Half: The Emancipation of the American Woman* (N.Y.: Harper Torchbooks, 1975), p. 117; Flexnor, p. 182; Peter Filene, *Him/Her/Self* (N.Y.: New American Library, 1976), pp. 8-10; David Kennedy, *Birth Control in America: The Career of Margaret Sanger* (New Haven: Yale Univ. Press, 1970), pp. 42, 45-46.
24. Filene, p. 8; *New York Dramatic Mirror,* 21 January 1893, p. 3.
25. *New York Dramatic Mirror,* 24 October 1896, p. 17; 26 January 1901. See also *New York Dramatic Mirror,* 19 February 1898, p. 16; 29 January 1898, p. 18; 25 February 1899, p. 18.

270   Notes for Chapter 4

26. *New York Dramatic Mirror,* 14 January 1899, p. 18; 18 February 1899, p. 18.
27. *New York Dramatic Mirror,* 31 October 1896, p. 19. For descriptions of acts as "cute," etc., see Cressy and Dayne, *New York Dramatic Mirror,* 5 October 1901, p. 18; Cushman and Holcombe, *New York Dramatic Mirror,* 9 November 1895, p. 17; the Winters, *The Cast,* 24 September 1900; the Drews, *New York Dramatic Mirror,* 29 February 1896, p. 19; the Kelceys, *The Cast,* 4 February 1901; Condit and Morey, *The Cast,* 3 March 1902; Murray and Lane, *The Cast,* 8 October 1900.
28. *Toledo Blade,* 1 March 1906. *See also* Gilbert, p. 156; Laurie, *Vaudeville,* p. 50; *New York Dramatic Mirror,* 6 March 1897, p. 18.
29. Gilbert, p. 156; *New York Dramatic Mirror,* 26 October 1895, p. 19.
30. Gilbert, pp. 156–157.
31. *New York Dramatic Mirror,* 8 February 1896, p. 19; 22 February 1896, p. 19; 31 October 1896, p. 23; 29 February 1896, p. 19.
32. *New York Dramatic Mirror,* 22 February 1896, p. 19.
33. Miscellaneous playbills, Johnstone Bennett file, Player's Col., N.Y.P.L.-L.C.; unidentified clipping dated 16 April 1906, Johnstone Bennett file, N.Y.P.L.-L.C.; *Indianapolis Star,* 2 September 1907; "'Jane' In a New Field," *New York Dramatic Mirror,* 7 November 1896.
34. The Drews, for example, were performing farce-comedies of little consequence before vaudeville. Some years later, asked the difference between John and Sidney Drew, a theatre manager quipped, "John Drew, but Sidney didn't" (*Advertiser,* 22 October 1895; *Spirit of the Times,* 4 October 1890; *Los Angeles Examiner,* 29 March 1912); John Mason's reputation had suffered in the nineties from debts and uncreditable desertion of the Boston Museum company. After two years in vaudeville he declared, "This season is my last in that kind of work, I can assure you. Next year I will return to the legitimate for good and for all" (*Boston Globe,* 21 October 1890; unidentified clipping, John and Marion Mason file, Locke Col. [NAFR+, 339], N.Y.P.L.-L.C.; *New York Mirror,* 16 April 1898).
35. "Tony Pastor," *Variety,* 29 December 1931.
36. *New York Dramatic Mirror,* 10 October 1896, p. 17; 20 February 1897, p. 17; 17 April 1897, p. 17; "A Clever Comedy Duo," *New York Dramatic Mirror,* 1 January 1898.
37. *New York Dramatic Mirror,* 1 October 1898, p. 18.
38. Unidentified clipping dated 18 December 1904, Milton and Dolly Nobles file, Locke Col., N.Y.P.L.-L.C.
39. *New York Dramatic Mirror,* 12 November 1898, p. 20.
40. *New York Dramatic Mirror,* 26 December 1896, p. 19; 7 January 1899, p. 18. *See also* Barry and Thomas, *New York Dramatic Mirror,* 7 March 1896, p. 20; Stanley and Jackson, *New York Dramatic Mirror,* 25 February 1899, p. 19; the Sidmans, *New York Dramatic Mirror,* 22 October 1898, p. 19.
41. *The Cast,* 14 October 1901; "Fifteen Lively Acts at Pastor's," *New York Telegraph,* 31 January 1907. Formerly of the Four Shamrocks, Jack Daly had teamed up with wife Annie Devere in 1886 (*New York Dramatic News,* 6 November 1886, p. 11; 11 December 1886, p. 11).
42. E.g., Favor and Sinclair, "The Maguires" (Odell, XIV, 362; *New York Dramatic Mir-*

ror, 31 October 1896, p. 19); Ricci and Chandler, "O'Brody's Election" (*The Cast*, 29 October 1900); Casey and LeClair, "The Irish Tenants" (*The Cast*, 27 February 1909); John and Emma Ray, "Casey the Fireman" (*The Cast*, 18 April 1904); Nelson and Milledge, "Officer Hogan" (*New York Dramatic Mirror*, 7 November 1903, p. 18); Barret and Belle, "Dooley's Tavern" (*Variety*, 26 September 1908, p. 14).

43. Odell, XIV, XV, passim.
44. *The Cast*, 9 November 1903; *Variety*, 10 October 1908, p. 13.
45. Odell, XV, 411; *The Cast*, 19 March 1910; *New York Dramatic Mirror*, 18 January 1896, p. 19; 17 September 1898.
46. *New York Dramatic Mirror*, 31 October 1896, p. 19.
47. *New York Dramatic Mirror*, 17 September 1898; 10 August 1895, p. 17. Others who claimed these virtues for their acts were Louise Arnott and Tom Gunn, with "A Natural Irish Comedy" (*The Cast*, 19 December 1904), and Casey and LeClair, with a "True-to-Nature Depiction of Celtic Tenement Life" (*The Cast*, 27 February 1909).
48. Shannon, pp. 131-132.
49. Ibid., p. 142.
50. Kahn, pp. 273-274; Shannon, p. 143.
51. Distler, p. 192.
52. "Mark Murphy, Comedian, Dies," *New York Telegraph*, 11 January 1917; *Duluth Herald*, 15 November 1911; unidentified clipping dated 25 December 1891, Mark Murphy file, Locke Col., N.Y.P.L.-L.C.; *The Cast*, 24 September 1900; *New York Dramatic Mirror*, 24 January 1903, p. 18; *Variety*, 8 December 1906, p. 9; *Pittsburgh Leader*, 19 February 1915; *Vancouver News*, 28 December 1911.
53. *New York Dramatic Mirror*, 24 January 1903, p. 18; *Variety*, 13 January 1906, p. 10.
54. *New York Dramatic Mirror*, 7 December 1895, p. 19; *The Cast*, 11 November 1901; 30 November 1903; 20 November 1909; *Variety*, 19 December 1908, p. 14; 2 January 1909, p. 16. *See also* Girard and Gardner, *New York Dramatic Mirror*, 6 April 1901, p. 18; *The Cast*, 25 April 1904; 2 January 1909; *Variety*, 13 October 1906. Girard and Gardner were featured on the cover of the 20 October 1906 *Variety*.
55. *The Cast*, 9 January 1905; *New York Dramatic Mirror*, 16 February 1901, p. 18.
56. *New York Dramatic Mirror*, 16 February 1901, p. 18.
57. E.g., Carroll and Doyle, *Variety*, 13 October 1906; Earle and Bartlett, *Variety*, 22 December 1906, p. 12; Casey and LeClair, *Variety*, 19 September 1908, p. 25; Van Leer and Duke, *New York Dramatic Mirror*, 21 November 1903, p. 18; Louise Arnott & Co., *New York Dramatic Mirror*, 7 January 1905, p. 17.
58. *New York Dramatic Mirror*, 22 October 1898, p. 19; 16 February 1901, p. 18.
59. *New York Dramatic News*, 9 July 1887, p. 7; "Mary Richfield of Ryan & Richfield Retires from Stage," unidentified clipping dated 6 May 1911, Ryan and Richfield file, Locke Col., N.Y.P.L.-L.C.; *New York Dramatic Mirror*, 29 January 1898, p. 18; *The Cast*, 14 May 1900; 16 April 1900.
60. *New York Dramatic Mirror*, 16 November 1901, p. 18; *Pittsburgh Leader*, 28 February 1915; 4 March 1915; *New York Journal*, 13 March 1913; *The Cast*, 28 November 1904; *New York Morning Telegraph*, 25 March 1906.

61. *Brooklyn Eagle,* 23 May 1915; unidentified clipping, Ryan and Richfield file, Locke Col., N.Y.P.L.-L.C.
62. *The Cast,* 2 October 1909; *Cleveland Plain Dealer,* 7 January 1912.
63. See *Hartford Courant,* 21 November, n.y., Ryan and Richfield file, Locke Col., N.Y.P.L.-L.C; *Brooklyn Eagle,* 23 March 1915; *Pittsburgh Leader,* 28 February 1915; *New York Mirror,* 19 January 1902; *Variety,* 25 March 1911.
64. *Toledo Blade,* 12 January 1912.
65. *New York Journal,* 13 March 1913; *Minneapolis Journal,* 1 September 1914; *New York Mirror,* 19 January 1902; 3 December 1906; *New York Daily Telegraph,* 24 July 1910.
66. *New York Mirror,* 8 December 1906; 2 December 1909.
67. *New York Star,* 3 October 1909.
68. Shannon, pp. 144-145; Maurice Horn, ed., *The World Encyclopedia of Comics* (N.Y.: Chelsea House, 1976), p. 132. "Bringing Up Father" was said to be inspired by a popular 1893 play on the subject, *The Rising Generation,* by William Gill (Horn, p. 132). Irish social mobility was also the theme of a short-lived series by F. P. Dunne that appeared in *Ladies' Home Journal* at the turn of the century. In the opening piece, wife Molly Donahue is the resented agent of Americanization to husband Malachi, who is forced to wear a starched collar as he sits on his porch stoop, and to agree to buy a piano—only to learn his wife has already arranged its purchase (Finley Peter Dunne, "Molly Donahue, Who Lives Across the Street from Mr. Dooley," *Ladies' Home Journal,* December 1899, p. 6).
69. *New York Star,* 3 October 1909.
70. *New York Mirror,* 8 December 1906; 2 December 1909. See also *New York Dramatic Mirror,* 28 September 1895, p. 17.
71. *New York Dramatic Mirror,* 14 January 1905, p. 18; *New York Mirror,* 12 December 1908.
72. LeRoy and Clayton added a new sketch called "Hogan's Millions" to their repertoire in the fall of 1908. In the new sketch, LeRoy's old persona, cab-driver Hogan, strikes it rich and tries to enter society. LeRoy moved "a step away from the usual Irish comedian," dressing his character "stylishly and in perfect taste" (*Variety,* 19 December 1908). The end of the decade found James F. Leonard and Clara Whitney doing "Duffy's Rise," which showed an Irish bricklayer just come into money whose wife wants to emulate high society. Following Mag Haggerty's example, the wife changes their name to "Dufae" (*New York Telegraph,* 31 October 1909; 26 December 1909). See review in *Variety,* 27 June 1913.
73. Statistics are derived from a thorough sampling of the *New York Dramatic Mirror,* for the 1894-1904 period, and of *Variety,* 1904-1913.

    Most Dutch acts still featured unabashed funmaking—"the usual singing, yodeling, dancing and love-making which is a feature of all German plays" (Reilly and Templeton, *New York Dramatic Mirror,* 20 February 1897; *see also* the Winnings, *Variety,* 5 February 1910). Nonetheless, sketch titles suggest that, like Irish sketches, German sketches were less concerned with nationalistic concerns (e.g., Grapewin and Chance, *New York Dramatic Mirror,* 25 February 1899; Rae and Brosche, *The Cast,* 26 February 1900; 24 March 1902; *New York Dramatic Mirror,* 7 March 1903). And like the Irish brogue, the German dialect had become a stage skill, rare enough to be admired when it was sustained (e.g., Evans and Mills, *New York Dramatic Mirror,* 10 December 1898; Teed and Lazelle, *Variety,* 26 October 1907). Indicative of the changes are Watson and Hutchings, an old-time variety team still popular at the turn of the century (*see New York Dramatic Mirror,* 13 July 1895; 9 November 1895; 8 October 1898; 19 November 1898), who felt the need to bolster their act with new appeals to hold the new vaudeville clientele. By 1896 they had added a third partner to their act, a tramp comedian; Alice Hutchings had begun playing "Mrs. A. M. Bloomer" by 1898; and a monkey was incorporated into the team before 1903 (*New York Dramatic Mirror,* 18 April 1896; 19 November 1898; *The Cast,* 9 November 1903). By 1906 their humor was reviewed by *Variety* as "rough and crude," and they were henceforth relegated to the small-time circuits (*Variety,* 8 December 1906).

By the teens German acts were rarely seen in New York (and by the war were taboo), and barely resembled themselves when they appeared (*see* Frey and Field, *Variety,* 26 February 1910; Stanley and Wilson, *Variety,* 22 September 1906; Gramlich and Hall, *Variety,* 28 October 1911).

74. Jones, p. 202; Frank Coppa and Thomas Curran, *The Immigrant Experience in America* (Boston: Twayne, 1976), p. 149.

75. *New York Dramatic Mirror,* 31 October 1903, p. 18.

76. For a discussion of leading male stage Hebrews, *see* Distler, pp. 161–176.

77. Odell, XII, 112; XII–XV, passim; *New York Dramatic Mirror,* 17 December 1898, p. 18; 7 February 1903, p. 18.

78. *New York Dramatic Mirror,* 4 March 1899, p. 18; 9 December 1893, p. 3; 1 June 1895, p. 3; unidentified clipping dated 18 December 1904, William E. Hines file, N.Y.P.L.-L.C.

79. *Variety,* 29 September 1906; *see also Variety,* 6 April 1907, p. 12. Some others were Harry and Sadie Fields, *New York Dramatic Mirror,* 19 November 1898, p. 20; *The Cast,* 21 May 1900; Mildred Franklin and Joe Hayman, *New York Dramatic Mirror,* 23 September 1905, p. 16; Gilbert and Shaw, *The Cast,* 2 January 1905; and Watson and Hanlon, *Variety,* 5 December 1908, p. 15.

80. Al Green and Joe Laurie, Jr., *Show Biz from Vaude to Video* (N.Y.: Henry Holt, 1951), p. 7.

81. Thomas Kessner, *The Golden Door: Italian and Jewish Immigrant Mobility in New York City, 1880–1915* (N.Y.; Oxford Univ. Press, 1977), pp. 154, 168, 173.

82. *Variety,* 7 October 1911, p. 20.

83. *See New York Star,* 25 July 1914; *Chicago Record-Herald,* 23 March 1913; 14 August 1913.

84. Between 1898 and 1906, Idalene Cotton and Nick Long's vehicle was "Managerial Troubles," in which Long played an Italian character. But the real appeal of the act was Cotton's mimicry of various female legitimate stars, one of which was Duse as a denizen of "The Bend." In 1908–09 Cotton and Long debuted a new sketch solely concerned with husband-wife relations and dropped the Italian impersonations entirely (*New York Telegraph,* 7 August 1898; unidentified clipping dated 4 June 1899, Cotton and Long file, Locke Col., N.Y.P.L.-L.C.; *Toledo Blade,* 2 March 1906; *New York Dramatic Mirror,* 27 April 1901; *Variety,* 21 November 1908, p. 15; "Idalene Cotton Makes Hit as Mimic Artist," *Sunday Examiner Magazine,* n.d., Idalene Cotton file, N.Y.P.L.-L.C.; *St. Paul Dispatch,* 7 January 1907). *See also* Nibbe and Bordeaux,

Variety, 3 November 1906, p. 12; 4 May 1907, p. 10. The Allisons performed "Minnie from Minnesota" in New York between 1903 and 1906 (e.g., *The Cast,* 4 January 1904; 20 March 1905; *Variety,* 29 September 1906). For a description of Hall and Coburn's act, see *New York Dramatic Mirror,* 23 May 1980, p. 16.

85. Arthur Meier Schlesinger, *The Rise of Modern America, 1865-1951* (N.Y.; Macmillan, 1951), p. 169.

86. Richard Moody, *America Takes the Stage: Romanticism in American Drama and Theatre, 1750-1900* (Bloomington: Indiana Univ. Press, 1955), p. 49; statistics derived from *New York Dramatic Mirror,* sampling, 1895-1905, and *Variety,* 1905-1913. For example of new blackface themes, see Green and Werner, *New York Dramatic Mirror,* 23 September 1905, p. 16.

87. Robert C. Toll, *On With the Show: The First Century of American Show Business* (N.Y.: Oxford Univ. Press, 1976), pp. 113-115.

88. *New York Dramatic News,* 26 May 1888, p. 8; 18 July 1888, p. 9; James Weldon Johnson, *Black Manhattan* (N.Y.: Atheneum, 1968), pp. 94-104.

89. E.g., see Johnson and Dean, clipping file, N.Y.P.L.-L.C.; *The Cast,* 28 May 1900; Hogan and Wilkes, *The Cast,* 14 September 1903; *New York Dramatic Mirror,* 17 October 1903, p. 18; Johnson, *Black Manhattan,* pp. 102-103; Billy and Madrid Jackson, *The Cast,* 5 March 1900; 7 May 1900; Al and Mamie Anderson, *The Cast,* 22 October 1900; Fagan and Byron, *New York Dramatic Mirror,* 31 October 1903, p. 18; Murphy and Francis, *The Cast,* 15 February 1904; *Variety,* 17 October 1908, p. 16; Raustus and Banks, *New York Dramatic Mirror,* 26 September 1903, p. 21; the Woodwards, *The Cast,* 19 December 1904; Johnson and Wells, *New York Dramatic Mirror,* 7 January 1905, p. 17; the McCarvers, *Variety,* 19 October 1907, p. 12; Maceo and Fox, *Variety,* 19 January 1907, p. 11; the Jalvans, *Variety,* 22 December 1906, p. 10; the Kratons, *Variety,* 15 December 1906, p. 10.

90. *The Cast,* 24 September 1900; 22 October 1900; Dewey and Thornton, *Variety,* 24 November 1906, p. 10; Laurie, *Vaudeville,* p. 203; *The Cast,* 3 April 1905.

91. Donald Bogle, *Toms, Coons, Mulattoes, Mammies and Bucks: An Interpretive History of Blacks in American Films* (N.Y.: Viking, 1973), p. 8.

92. Laurie, *Vaudeville,* p. 201; *The Cast,* 4 March 1901; *New York Dramatic Mirror,* 25 March 1899, p. 18. On Genaro and Bailey, and Howard and Bland, see Dave Genaro file, N.Y.P.L.-L.C.; Bert Howard file, N.Y.P.L.-L.C. See also Carroll and Crawford, *New York Dramatic Mirror,* 26 November 1898, p. 18; the Macks, *The Cast,* 12 December 1904; Hill and Whittaker, *New York Dramatic Mirror,* 25 April 1903, p. 18; Maddox and Melvin, *New York Dramatic Mirror,* 28 October 1905, p. 17; Tom and Stacie Moore, *Variety,* 9 April 1910, p. 20. On black vaudevillians, see Helen Armstead-Johnson, "Blacks in Vaudeville: Broadway and Beyond," in *American Popular Entertainment,* pp. 77-86.

93. *Variety,* 16 February 1907, p. 11; 20 April 1907, p. 13.

94. *New York Dramatic Mirror,* 12 November 1898. See also discriminatory review of Johnson and Dean in *Variety,* 2 October 1909.

95. *See* Bogle, p. 17; Johnson, *Black Manhattan,* pp. 109-110, 126-128.

96. Odell, XIV, 118; *The Cast,* 16 September 1901; *New York Dramatic Mirror,* 2 November 1895, p. 19; 1 February 1896, p. 19; 29 February 1896, p. 19; 2 May 1903, p. 18.

97. Odell, XIV, 356; *New York Dramatic Mirror,* 25 February 1899, p. 18; *The Cast,* 19 March 1900; 3 December 1900; 16 September 1901; 12 September 1904; 24 October 1904.
98. *Cincinnati Commercial,* 14 March 1910; *Louisville Herald,* 11 January 1909; *New York Dramatic Mirror,* 3 October 1896, p. 19.
99. *Louisville Herald,* 11 January 1909; *Cincinnati Commercial,* 14 March 1910; *The Cast,* 11 September 1909; 19 March 1910.
100. *New York Dramatic Mirror,* 15 April 1905.
101. Others were Rado and Bertram, *The Cast,* 18 April 1904; Gorman and West, *The Cast,* 8 June 1903; Tanner and Gilbert, *The Cast,* 22 February 1904; Waller and McGill, *The Cast,* 29 February 1904; the Fansons, *New York Dramatic Mirror,* 1 February 1896, p. 19; Sisson and Wallace, *The Cast,* 22 October 1900; Rawson and Clare, *Variety,* 9 February 1907.
102. See Van Wyck Brooks, *The Confident Years: 1895-1915* (N.Y.: E. P. Dutton, 1955), 116ff.
103. On the Yellow Kid, *see* Horn, p. 711.
104. Kahn, p. 275.
105. *New York Dramatic Mirror,* 26 May 1894, p. 6; 28 March 1896, p. 19; 8 February 1896, p. 19; *The Cast,* 9 December 1901.
106. *New York Dramatic Mirror,* 7 September 1895; 26 February 1898, p. 16; 14 January 1899, p. 18.
107. *New York Sun,* 6 November 1901. See also *New York Dramatic Mirror,* 24 September 1898; unidentified clipping, Eva Williams file, N.Y.P.L.-L.C.
108. Ibid.
109. *New York Dramatic Mirror,* 28 December 1901, p. 18; *The Cast,* 7 March 1904.
110. *New York Dramatic Mirror,* 1 February 1902.
111. *New York Star,* 24 April 1909.
112. *Cincinnati Enquirer,* 17 December 1900.
113. *New York Dramatic Mirror,* 4 March 1899, p. 18; 8 April 1899, p. 18. See also *New York Dramatic Mirror,* 24 September 1898.
114. *New York Commercial Advertiser,* 26 May 1900.
115. *New York Dramatic Mirror,* 15 April 1905.
116. Unidentified clipping dated 26 May 1900, Eva Williams file, N.Y.P.L.-L.C.; *New York Dramatic Mirror,* 15 April 1905.
117. *New York Dramatic Mirror,* 15 April 1905.
118. *See* M. A. Wolff, *Sketches of Lowly Life in a Great City,* ed. Joseph Henius (N.Y.: G. P. Putnam's Sons, 1899).
119. James D. Hart, *The Popular Book: A History of America's Literary Taste* (N.Y.: Oxford Univ. Press, 1950), p. 209.
120. Moody, p. 128; on genesis of *The Old Homestead, see James Madison's Weekly Radio Service,* 21 December 1935, pp. 7-9. Teams from the eighties were the Fieldings, with "Josh Z. Beck"; Carter and Anderson in "The Old Rustic Bridge" and "The Old Farm

276   Notes for Chapter 4

Gate"; Mayo and Sutherland in "Country Cousins"; and Adair and Thatcher in "The Countryman's Visit" (Odell, XII, 512, 124, 129, 529, 530). Teams from the late nineties were Thorne and Carleton in "A Country Politician" (*New York Dramatic Mirror,* 22 February 1896); Murphy and Kursale in "Down on the Farm" (*New York Dramatic Mirror,* 11 January 1896); Stewart and Morton in "Uncle Josh's Visit" (*New York Dramatic Mirror,* 16 January 1897); Mr. and Mrs. Byron Spaun in a "Rube Sketch" (*New York Dramatic Mirror,* 15 October 1898); and Boyle and Graham in a sketch featuring "Sal Skinner" (*New York Dramatic Mirror,* 18 February 1899).

121. *New York Dramatic Mirror,* 18 March 1899, p. 18; 19 September 1896, p. 17. See also *New York Dramatic Mirror,* 22 October 1898, p. 19; 10 September 1898.

122. *New York Dramatic Mirror,* 18 March 1899, p. 18; "Success then Death," *Kansas Journal,* 22 March 1903.

123. Others were Hanson and Drew as "Yankee Farmer" and a "City Girl" (*The Cast,* 12 March 1900); Dan and Dolly Mann in "Mandy Hawkins" (*New York Dramatic Mirror,* 5 January 1901; 13 April 1901); Ted and Laura Harris in "A Country Lawyer" (*The Cast,* 11 March 1901); Nugent and Fertig in a "Pastoral Gem" (*The Cast,* 22 October 1900); Henderson and Ross in "Fun at Grigg's Corner" (*The Cast,* 17 December 1900); Sam and Ida Kelley as "Si and Mandy" (*The Cast,* 12 May 1902); the Litchfields in "Down Home at the Farm" (*The Cast,* 27 May 1901); and Perkins Fisher and wife in "The Half-Way House" (*The Cast,* 22 February 1904; *Variety,* 22 September 1906).

124. Peter Schmitt, *Back to Nature: The Arcadian Myth in Urban America* (N.Y.: Oxford Univ. Press, 1969), passim.

125. Schmitt, xvi–xvii.

126. Wright, p. 54.

127. Hart, p. 206.

128. Ibid., pp. 205–208.

129. *Cincinnati Commercial,* 14 March 1910; *New York Dramatic Mirror,* 5 January 1901.

130. *New York Dramatic Mirror,* 18 March 1899, p. 18.

131. *New York Dramatic Mirror,* 24 September 1898; 29 October 1898, p. 20; 24 August 1895. See also the Litchfields, *New York Dramatic Mirror,* 7 January 1905, p. 17; the Manns, *New York Dramatic Mirror,* 13 April 1901, p. 18.

132. *New York Dramatic Mirror,* 24 August 1895.

133. *New York Dramatic Mirror,* 18 March 1899, p. 18. See also *New York Dramatic Mirror,* 12 December 1896, p. 19.

134. *New York Dramatic Mirror,* 5 January 1901; 13 April 1901, p. 18.

135. "Arthur Sidman's Humor," unidentified clipping, Arthur Sidman file, N.Y.P.L.-L.C.

136. *New York Morning Telegraph,* 15 March 1908; *Buffalo Times,* 12 April 1914.

137. *New York Dramatic Mirror,* 31 December 1898, p. 18.

138. *The Cast,* 30 April 1900; 20 May 1901; 23 September 1901; 9 November 1903; 21 September 1903; 8 May 1905.

139. *New York Dramatic Mirror,* 5 October 1901, p. 18.

140. Ibid.

141. "Continuous Vaudeville," unidentified clipping dated 30 October 1910, Cressy and Dayne file, Locke Col., N.Y.P.L.-L.C.
142. *New York Dramatic Mirror,* 29 October 1901, p. 18.
143. Elbert Hubbard, *The Philistine,* quoted by *New York Star,* 24 December 1910.
144. The Rev. Dr. S. C. Clair, *The Caste* (Columbus, Ohio), quoted by *New York Dramatic Mirror,* 23 May 1903, p. 19.
145. Unidentified clipping, Cressy and Dayne file, N.Y.P.L.-L.C.
146. E.g., the virtues of realism and absence of exaggeration were claimed for Bloom and Cooper's tramp act by both critics and Lew Bloom himself (*New York Telegraph,* 23 June 1907; 3 October 1907). Critics even praised Bloom's "acting" and compared his characterization favorably to Booth's "Hamlet" and Joseph Jefferson's "Rip" (*[Kansa]s City Journal,* n.d., Lew Bloom file, N.Y.P.L.-L.C.). On Bloom and Cooper's tramp act, see also *New York Dramatic Mirror,* 6 March 1897, p. 17; 29 October 1898; *Rochester Times,* 7 November 1906; *Variety,* 16 March 1907, p. 11; and Lew Bloom file, N.Y.P.L.-L.C.
147. Other mixed tramp acts were William Kaye and Ada Henry in "A Morning Call" (Odell, XIV, 354; *New York Dramatic Mirror,* 14 September 1895; 28 September 1895, p. 17; 30 November 1895, p. 19); Frey and Fields, with "A Tramp's Reception" (*New York Dramatic Mirror,* 6 February 1897); Nat Wills and Mlle. Lorretta as "Tramp and Gay Soubrette" (*New York Dramatic Mirror,* 26 November 1898); Fredo and Forrest, the "Musical Tramp and Elastic Soubrette" (*The Cast,* 2 April 1900); Cogan and Bacon in "The Tramp's Visit" (*The Cast,* 12 November 1900); the Brownings in "A Merry Tramp" (*The Cast,* 29 October 1900); Cook and Sonora as "The Merry Tramp and the Singing Maid" (*The Cast,* 21 October 1901); Mazur and Mazette, "The Hobo and the Maid" (*The Cast,* 19 September 1904); and the Latonas as "Tramp Musician and Soubrette" (*The Cast,* 24 April 1905).

Some teams playing burglars were Deltwyn and Adams (*New York Dramatic Mirror,* 3 October 1896); Dolan and Lenhaar (*New York Dramatic Mirror,* 1 April 1899); Mason and Keeler (*The Cast,* 24 April 1905); Dixon and Nordstrom (*New York Dramatic Mirror,* 16 September 1905; Kelso and Leighton (*Variety,* 16 March 1907); Macart and Bradford, (*The Cast,* 26 March 1910); Nugent and Fertig (*New York Dramatic Mirror,* 27 April 1901): Lockney and Fletcher (*Variety,* 12 February 1910); and the McCanns (*Variety,* 16 December 1911). Among others, Besnah and Miller, and Bennett and Kent, played Western characters (*The Cast,* 18 March 1901; *New York Dramatic Mirror,* 24 October 1896); and in the hotel servant category were Ford and Dot West (*The Cast,* 11 February 1901), Smirl and Kessner (*The Cast,* 26 September 1904), Dunn and Jerome (*New York Dramatic Mirror,* 8 April 1899), the Farleys (*The Cast,* 15 February 1904), Ross and Lewis (*Variety,* 20 October 1906), Zinell and Boutelle (*Variety,* 29 December 1906), and the Rooneys (see chapter 6, below).
148. Statistics derived from Odell, XII-XIII; *New York Dramatic Mirror,* 1895-1905.
149. *New York Dramatic Mirror,* 22 January 1898, p. 18; 20 February 1897, p. 17; 25 January 1896, p. 19; *Variety,* 16 December 1905, p. 11. See also Maxwell and Dudley, "Love and Billiards" (*The Cast,* 5 November 1900); Rossley and Rostelle, "The Widow's Courtship" (*The Cast,* 12 November 1900); Bellman and Moore, "Love in a Photograph Agency" (*The Cast,* 4 April 1904); Boniface and Waltzinger, "The Woman Who Hesitates is Won" (*The Cast,* 17 March 1902; 8 February 1904); the Riches' "A College Boy's Flirtation" (*Variety,* 20 October 1906); the Woodses' "A Tennis Flirta-

tion" (*The Cast*, 7 November 1908); O'Rourke and Dare, "After the French Ball" (*New York Dramatic Mirror*, 20 February 1897, p. 17.

150. *New York Dramatic Mirror*, 6 February 1897, p. 19.

151. *Variety*, 22 December 1906, p. 10; 2 April 1910, p. 20.

152. E.g., Coombs and Stone, *New York Dramatic Mirror*, 15 February 1908, p. 13; Wilke and Watson, *Variety*, 21 November 1908, p. 15; Ronair and Ward, *Variety*, 11 November 1911, p. 22.

153. *New York Dramatic Mirror*, 23 March 1901, p. 18.

154. Michael Gordon, *The American Family: Past, Present and Future* (N.Y.: Random House, 1978), pp. 169, 174–176.

155. Gordon, p. 177; James McGovern, "The American Woman's Pre-World War I Freedom in Manners and Morals," *Journal of American History*, 55 (September 1968), 319.

156. *Variety*, 16 December 1905, p. 11.

157. *New York Dramatic Mirror*, 18 January 1896, p. 19; 29 January 1898, p. 18; 7 January 1899, p. 18; *The Cast*, 24 December 1900; *New York Dramatic Mirror*, 11 April 1903, p. 20; *The Cast*, 6 February 1909; *New York Dramatic Mirror*, 19 November 1898, p. 18. See also the Wrens, "A Lesson for Husbands" (*New York Dramatic Mirror*, 2 May 1896, p. 19); Emmet and Mortland, "A Honeymoon in a Harlem Flat" (*New York Dramatic Mirror*, 26 February 1898, p. 16); Mr. and Mrs. R. J. Dunstan, "When a Man's Married" (*New York Dramatic Mirror*, 15 January 1898, p. 19); McWade and May, "A Matrimonial Blizzard" (ibid.); Rice and Cohen, "Our Honeymoon" (*New York Dramatic Mirror*, 7 January 1899, p. 18); Gardner and Gilmore, "A Lover's Quarrel" (ibid.); Linton and McIntyre, "An Unloving Lover" (*New York Dramatic Mirror*, 5 October 1901, p. 18); Kingsley and Lewis, "After the Honeymoon" (*New York Dramatic Mirror*, 21 March 1903, p. 18); Lauder and Stanley, "Detained on Business" (*New York Dramatic Mirror*, 25 April 1903, p. 18); Orr and Dorr, "A Domestic Blizzard" (*The Cast*, 8 May 1905); Mr. and Mrs. Fitzsimmons, "A Fight for Love" (*The Cast*, 3 October 1908).

158. *New York Dramatic Mirror*, 24 December 1898, p. 18. See also Stine and Evans, "Wanted a Divorce" (*The Cast*, 8 October 1900); Hanson and Drew, "Breaking Up Housekeeping" (*The Cast*, 15 October 1900); Emmet and Mortland, "South Dakota Divorce" (*The Cast*, 17 October 1904); Seligman and Harcourt, "A Dakota Widow" (*Variety*, 24 November 1906, p. 8).

159. Filene, pp. 35–38; Schlesinger, *The Rise of the City*, p. 154; Gordon, p. 294; Theodore Roosevelt, quoted by David Kennedy, p. 42.

160. Gordon, p. 297; Filene, pp. 77–78.

161. Filene, p. 78; Gordon, pp. 205–210.

162. Filene, pp. 77–80. See also David J. Pivar, *Purity Crusade: Sexual Morality and Social Control, 1868–1900* (Westport, Conn.: Greenwood Press, 1973); Andrew Sinclair, *Era of Excess: A Social History of the Prohibition Movement* (N.Y.: Harper Colophon, 1964).

163. *New York Dramatic Mirror*, 28 January 1899, p. 18; 31 December 1898, p. 18; unidentified clipping, Charles and Mabel Ross file, Locke Col., N.Y.P.L.-L.C.; *The Cast*, 12 September 1908; *Pittsburgh Leader*, 10 September 1911.

164. *New York Dramatic Mirror,* 18 February 1899, p. 18. *See also* Coote and Kingsley, *New York Dramatic Mirror,* 17 April 1897, p. 17; the Blondells, *New York Dramatic Mirror,* 12 March 1898, p. 18; Wayne and Caldwell, *New York Dramatic Mirror,* 4 February 1899, p. 18; the Nobles, unidentified clipping dated 14 December 1907, Milton and Dolly Nobles file, Locke Col., N.Y.P.L.-L.C.

165. E.g., *see* Davis and MacCauley, *New York Dramatic Mirror,* 16 February 1901, p. 18; Gardner and Maddern, *New York Dramatic Mirror,* 19 January 1901.

166. *New York Dramatic Mirror,* 12 December 1896, p. 19; 21 February 1903, p. 18. *See also* "Why Doogan Swore Off," *New York Dramatic Mirror,* 24 January 1903, p. 18.

167. Filene, p. 80; *New York Dramatic Mirror,* 21 February 1903, p. 18.

168. *New York Dramatic Mirror,* 7 January 1899, p. 18.

169. Filene, p. 38.

170. *New York Dramatic Mirror,* 14 September 1895; 25 January 1896, p. 19; 5 October 1895, p. 19; 12 October 1895, p. 17.

171. *New York Dramatic Mirror,* 19 October 1895, p. 19; 7 December 1895, p. 19; *The Cast,* 23 April 1900; 29 October 1898, p. 19; 17 December 1898, p. 18; 11 March 1899, p. 18.

172. *See* Finley Peter Dunne, "On the New Woman," in *Mr. Dooley in Peace and War* (Boston: Small and Maynard, 1899), pp. 136-140.

173. Anthony and Harper, IV, xxii.

174. *See* Sinclair, *The Better Half,* pp. 293-296; William L. O'Neill, *Everyone Was Brave: A History of Feminism in America* (Chicago: Quadrangle Books, 1969), p. 147.

175. *See* Flexnor, pp. 182ff.

176. Sinclair, *The Better Half,* pp. 319-320.

177. Filene, pp. 25-29; Scott, *The American Woman,* p. 16; Sinclair, *The Better Half,* p. 172.

178. *New York Dramatic Mirror,* 22 October 1898, p. 19.

179. *New York Dramatic Mirror,* 21 January 1899, p. 18; 14 January 1899, p. 18.

180. *Toledo Blade,* 1 March 1906.

181. *See* Genaro and Bailey, *Variety,* 30 December 1905, p. 9; Hallen and Fuller, 22 September 1906; 9 February 1907, p. 11.

182. *New York Dramatic Mirror,* 2 March 1901, p. 18. *See also* Clark and St. Clair, "The Female Barber" (*New York Dramatic Mirror,* 21 September 1895, p. 19); Topack and West, "The Female Editor" (*The Cast,* 14 December 1903); Philbrooks and Reynolds, "Miss Steno Stenographer" (*The Cast,* 5 December 1904). Unintentionally condescending, no doubt, was "Gus Edwards' Blonde Typewriters," a chorus-girl act (*The Cast,* 30 October 1909).

183. *New York Dramatic Mirror,* 23 February 1901, p. 18; 11 May 1901, p 18; 21 February 1903, p. 18; 6 March 1897, p. 23.

184. *New York Dramatic Mirror,* 5 November 1898, p. 18; 21 January 1899, p. 18.

185. *New York Dramatic Mirror,* 16 February 1901, p. 18; 5 October 1901, p. 18.

186. *New York Dramatic Mirror,* 1 October 1898; 5 October 1901, p. 18.

187. *See* Barbara Welter, "The Feminization of American Religion, 1800-1860" and Dee Garrison, "The Tender Technicians: The Feminization of Public Librarianship, 1876-1905," in *Clio's Consciousness Raised: New Perspectives on the History of Women,* eds. Mary S. Hartman and Lois Banner (N.Y.: Harper Colophon, 1974), pp. 137-157; 158-178.

Chapter 5

1. *New York Dramatic Mirror,* 16 September 1905, p. 18.
2. *New York Star,* 3 October 1908, p. 29.
3. *New York Star,* 7 November 1908, p. 24; 3 October 1908, p. 29. *See also* B.F. Keith, "The Origin of Continuous Vaudeville," *New York Dramatic Mirror,* 1906, Locke Col., Ser. 2, Paige-Petrova file (NAFR+, 284), N.Y.P.L.-L.C.
4. Frederick Allen, *The Big Change: America Transforms Itself, 1900-1950* (N.Y.: Harper and Bros., 1952), pp. 115-117.
5. On the development of new urban values, *see* Gunther Barth, *City People: The Rise of Modern City Culture in Nineteenth-Century America* (N.Y.: Oxford Univ. Press, 1980), chap. 1.
6. Blanche Gelfant, *American City Novel,* 2nd ed. (Norman, Okla.: Univ. of Oklahoma Press, 1970), 25ff.; Noel P. Gist and L. A. Halbert, *Urban Society,* 4th ed. (N.Y.: Thomas Y. Crowell, 1956), 273ff.; Barth, p. 23.
7. *Variety,* 31 October 1908, p. 15; 19 February 1910, p. 17; 30 December 1911, p. 19; 25 January 1908.
8. E.g., Long and Cotton, "The Banker and the Thief" (*Variety,* 21 November 1908, p. 15); Connelly and Webb, "College Chap's Sweetheart" (*Variety,* 28 November 1908, p. 13); the Rich Duo, "A College Boy's Flirtation" (*Variety,* 20 October 1906); the Nawns, "The College Coach" (*Variety,* 4 October 1912); the Stanfords, "Law Clerk and Soubrette" (*The Cast,* 20 February 1905); Davis and Macauley, "The Unexpected" [law student and fiancee] (*The Cast,* 9 November 1903); Gardner and Maddern, "A Rise in Rye" [stockbroker and widow] (*The Cast,* 17 April 1905).
9. Riverside Theatre, *Variety,* 25 October 1912; Colonial Theatre, *Variety,* 17 April 1909; 28 October 1911, p. 16. For mention of a lawyer in audience, *see* Murphy and Nichols, *New York Mirror,* 10 February 1906.
10. E.g., the Wallaces, *Variety,* 6 October 1906; McConnell and Simpson, *Variety,* 30 December 1911, p. 14; Clark and Hamilton, *Variety,* 9 April 1910, p. 16; Shirley and Kessler, *Variety,* 14 October 1911, p. 18; Caine and Odom, *Variety,* 5 March 1910, p. 16; Mack and Walker, *Variety,* 16 September 1911, p. 19; Duffy and Lorenze, *Variety,* 28 October 1911, p. 16; Harry and Mae Howard, *Variety,* 18 April 1908; Rice and Cohen ("punk"), *Variety,* 26 November 1910; Richards and Kyle, *Variety,* 17 January 1913; Henshaw and Avery, *Variety,* 11 November 1911; Cross and Josephine, *Variety,* 9 September 1911, p. 20.
11. Stanley and Leonard, *Variety,* 15 December 1906, p. 9; *see also* Cartmel and Harris, *Variety,* 1 November 1912.
12. Gist, p. 273; Barth, pp. 19, 56-57; Frederic Thompson, "Amusing the Million," *Everybody's Magazine,* 19 (September 1908), p. 386.

Notes for Chapter 5   281

13. E.g., Ronair and Ward, *Variety*, 11 November 1911, p. 22; the DeMuths, *Variety*, 24 November 1906, p. 9.
14. *Variety*, 9 September 1911, p. 21.
15. E.g., Tom Gray and Fan Bourke, *Variety*, 21 October 1911; Johnny Stanley and Fan Bourke, *Variety*, 10 February 1912, p. 21.
16. Colonial Theatre, *Variety*, 27 January 1912, p. 19; Orpheum Theatre, *Variety*, 9 September 1911, p. 21; Greenpoint Theatre, *Variety*, 6 March 1909; Colonial Theatre, *Variety*, 13 March 1909.
17. *See* Gilbert, 152ff., 373ff.
18. *Variety*, 10 November 1906, p. 12; 30 December 1905, p. 9; 16 December 1905, p. 7; 13 April 1907, p. 12.
19. *Variety*, 10 November 1906, p. 10; 8 December 1906, p. 7; 29 December 1906, p. 10; 12 January 1907, p. 9; 30 March 1907, p. 12; 26 March 1910, p. 12.
20. *Variety*, 18 November 1911, p. 20.
21. *Variety*, 2 December 1911, p. 22; 20 January 1912, p. 16; 28 March 1908, p. 13.
22. *Variety*, 13 January 1906, p. 10; 1 December 1906, p. 11; 31 July 1909. Presumably realizing the old material had lost its following, in 1910 Williams and Tucker were working on a new sketch called "Us Two," in which Tucker would play a burglar (*New York Telegraph*, 24 April 1910). I have found no evidence that they or the sketch appeared in New York City.
23. *Variety*, 6 November 1909, p. 19; 13 January 1912, p. 18.
24. *Variety*, 8 December 1906, p. 9; 23 March 1907, p. 13; 30 December 1905, p. 8.
25. *Variety*, 30 September 1911, p. 19.
26. *Variety*, 14 December 1907; 6 April 1907, p. 6; 26 November 1910.
27. *Variety*, 19 March 1910, p. 16; 30 December 1905, p. 5; *Variety*, 20 November 1909, p. 19.
28. E.g., *see* Melburn, Macdowell, and Pauline Willard in "A Condensed Version of Victorien Sardou's Masterpiece, 'LA TOSCA' " (*The Cast*, 21 March 1904); Dixon and Holmes, in "the Lighthouse Scene" from *Shore Acres* (*The Cast*, 30 January 1905); Mr. and Mrs. William Robyns (*New York Dramatic Mirror*, 28 January 1905); "Juanita" (*New York Dramatic Mirror*, 30 September 1905); Seligman and Bramwell, "Public Opinion vs. Politics" (*Variety*, 10 April 1909).
29. *New York Dramatic Mirror*, 4 April 1908, p. 13.
30. Ibid.
31. *Variety*, 7 November 1908, p. 18; 12 March 1910, p. 16; 3 November 1906, p. 9.
32. E.g., the Healeys, *New York Dramatic Mirror*, 5 January 1895, p. 6; Fletcher and Figman, *New York Dramatic Mirror*, 17 April 1897, p. 17; the Neuvilles, *New York Dramatic Mirror*, 15 January 1898, p. 18; Dolan and Lenharr, *New York Dramatic Mirror*, 29 January 1898, p. 18.
33. *Baltimore American*, 11 October 1907; *New York Dramatic Mirror*, 9 May 1896, p. 18; 20 March 1897, p. 18; "Charles J. Ross Dead," *New York Times*, 16 June 1918; The

Cast, 20 February 1905; *Milwaukee News,* 21 October 1913; *Variety,* 14 November 1913. *See also* extensive Ross and Fenton files, N.Y.P.L.-L.C.

34. *New York Dramatic Mirror,* 20 July 1895, p. 18; 26 December 1896, p. 19; 29 October 1901, p. 18; *The Cast,* 14 December 1903; *New York Dramatic Mirror,* 23 May 1903, p. 18; 21 January 1905, p. 18.

35. Charles J. Ross, "Travesty Then and Now," *Variety,* 23 December 1911.

36. *New York Dramatic Mirror,* 4 May 1901, p. 18; unidentified clipping dated 25 February 1905, Will H. Murphy file, Locke Col., N.Y.P.L.-L.C. Statistics derived from *The Cast,* and *Variety,* 1905–1913, and misc. clippings in Will H. Murphy file, Locke Col., N.Y.P.L.-L.C.

37. *New York Dramatic Mirror,* 7 October 1905, p. 18.

38. *Hartford Courant,* 14 January 1908; unidentified clipping dated 25 February 1905, Will H. Murphy file, Locke Col., N.Y.P.L.-L.C., *Detroit Journal,* clipping dated December 1905, Will H. Murphy file, Locke. Col., N.Y.P.L.-L.C. *See also New York Telegraph,* 15 April 1908; *New York Dramatic Mirror,* 28 October 1905, p. 17.

39. *New York Mirror,* 6 February 1909; 8 April 1909.

40. E.g., *see* Arthur Dunn and partner, *New York Dramatic Mirror,* 10 September 1899; Carr and Jordan, *New York Dramatic Mirror,* 31 August 1895; Post and Clinton, *The Cast,* 29 April 1901; McWatters and Tyson, *New York Dramatic Mirror,* 24 December 1898; Cook and Sonora, *The Cast,* 21 October 1901; McRae and Wyatt, *The Cast,* 14 September 1903; Felix and Barry, *The Cast,* 3 February 1902; Findlay and Burke, *The Cast,* 3 October 1904; McIntyre and Rice, *The Cast,* 28 November 1904; Keogh and Ballard, *The Cast,* 5 December 1904; Howard and Bland, *The Cast,* 16 January 1905; Moore and Littlefield, *The Cast,* 5 December 1904; Bellman and Moore, *The Cast,* 12 December 1904.

41. Routines concerned with vaudeville were performed by Gray and Bourke, *Variety,* 21 October 1911; Deane and Sibley, *Variety,* 11 November 1911; Gardner and Stoddard, *The Cast,* 23 October 1909; Findlay and Burke, *The Cast,* 3 October 1904; Bellman and Moore, *The Cast,* 12 December 1904; Moore and Littlefield, unidentified clipping, Victor Moore file, Locke Col., N.Y.P.L.-L.C.; Post and Clinton, *The Cast,* 29 April 1901; Keogh and Ballard, *The Cast,* 5 December 1904; Cook and Sonora, *The Cast,* 21 October 1901; Rado and Bertram, *New York Dramatic Mirror,* 14 October 1905; Maddox and Melvin, *New York Dramatic Mirror,* 28 October 1905; Barry and Hughes, *Variety,* 21 March 1908; and Sullivan and Pasquelina, *Variety,* 31 October 1908.

42. *The Cast,* 3 April 1905; *New York Dramatic Mirror,* 14 October 1905, p. 15; *Variety,* 3 November 1906, p. 9; Green and Laurie, pp. 29, 66; *Variety,* 16 September 1911, p. 18; 18 November 1911, p. 18; 20 January 1912, p. 2.

43. E.g., Barry and Halvers, *Variety,* 10 November 1906, p. 12; Felix and Caire, *Variety,* 19 December 1908, p. 18; Stanley and Russell, *Variety,* 5 December 1908, p. 15; Maddox and Melvin, *New York Dramatic Mirror,* 28 October 1905, p. 17; McWatters and Tyson, *Variety,* 20 February 1909; the Barrys, *Variety,* 13 October 1906.

44. *See* Marquard and Seeley, *Variety,* 1 November 1912; Marquard and Kent, *Variety,* 16 December 1911, p. 16; Hite and Donlin, *Variety,* 31 October 1908, p. 12.

45. *New York Dramatic Mirror,* 28 January 1905, p. 18; *Variety,* 17 October 1908, p. 16.

46. *The Cast,* 11 January 1904; *Variety,* 26 January 1907, p. 10.

47. *The Cast,* 4 November 1911; *Variety,* 30 September 1912.
48. E.g., Whitman and Davis, *New York Dramatic Mirror,* 20 July 1895, p. 18; Huth and Clifford, *New York Dramatic Mirror,* 3 August 1895, p. 17; Flynn and Waltzer, *New York Dramatic Mirror,* 19 October 1895, p. 19.
49. E.g., see Agnes Proctor, *New York Dramatic Mirror,* 29 January 1898, p. 18; the DeMars, *New York Dramatic Mirror,* 19 February 1898, p. 16; the Blondells, *New York Dramatic Mirror,* 12 March 1898, p. 18; the Sidmans, *New York Dramatic Mirror,* 24 September 1898; Burke and Urquhart, *New York Dramatic Mirror,* 4 March 1899, p. 18; Bryton and Filkins, *New York Dramatic Mirror,* 3 April 1897, p. 17.
50. E.g., Green and Friend, *New York Dramatic Mirror,* 3 December 1898, p. 18; the Marshes, *New York Dramatic Mirror,* 25 January 1896, p. 19.
51. E.g., Murphy and Willard, *New York Dramatic Mirror,* 14 November 1903, p. 20; Kelly and Violette, *The Cast,* 7 October 1901; Ekert and Berg, *The Cast,* 3 October 1904; Carter and Bluford, *The Cast,* 5 December 1904; Libby and Trayer, *The Cast,* 6 February 1905; Marion and Deane, ibid.; Ryan and Innes, *New York Dramatic Mirror,* 21 October 1905, p. 18; the DeMuths, *Variety,* 13 October 1906; Fagon and Byron, *New York Dramatic Mirror,* 21 January 1905, p. 18; Newell and Niblo, *New York Dramatic Mirror,* 31 October 1903, p. 18.
52. *Variety,* 23 December 1905, p. 6; 26 September 1908, p. 18.
53. Sophie Tucker, *Some of These Days: An Autobiography* (London: Hammond, 1948), pp. 31-32.
54. *Variety,* 3 November 1906, p. 18; *New York Dramatic Mirror,* 24 January 1903, p. 18; Jane Addams, "The Subtle Problems of Charity," *Atlantic Monthly* (1899), quoted by Barth, p. 141.
55. Anna Marble, "The Woman in Variety," *Variety,* 13 October 1906.
56. Unidentified clipping dated 11 January 1912, Valeska Suratt file, Locke Col., N.Y.P.L.-L.C.; "Is Particular As to Dresses," *Rochester Times,* 2 August 1912.
57. *San Francisco Chronicle,* 12 June 1905; *Variety,* 24 April 1909; unidentified clipping dated 4 January 1911, Valeska Suratt file, Locke Col., N.Y.P.L.-L.C.
58. *Variety,* 27 April 1907, p. 12. See also Truax and Campbell, *Variety,* 14 October 1911, p. 23; Kelly and Violette, *Variety,* 17 November 1906, p. 11; Hagan and Wescott, *Variety,* 6 October 1906; Mora and Richards, *Variety,* 5 February 1910, p. 17; Farrell and LeRoy, *Variety,* 17 November 1906, p. 11; Gorman and West, *Variety,* 30 December 1905, p. 9; Flemen and Miller, *Variety,* 27 October 1906, p 8.
59. *Variety,* 9 September 1911, p. 16; Raymond and Smith, *Variety,* 27 January 1912, p. 17; 14 March 1913; *The Cast,* 28 October 1911.
60. Gilbert, pp. 27-31.
61. *New York Dramatic Mirror,* 24 October 1896, p. 17; *The Cast,* 21 March 1904. B. F. Keith noted in 1906 that audiences expect "to find every act presented with an appropriate stage setting, which was unnecessary in the early days of the varieties" (B. F. Keith, "The Origin of Continuous Vaudeville").
62. *The Cast,* 20 February 1905; *New York Dramatic Mirror,* 21 January 1905, p. 18.
63. *New York Dramatic Mirror,* 28 January 1905, p. 18.
64. *New York Telegraph,* 26 September 1911; *Variety,* 30 September 1911, p. 18. For typi-

cal mechanical effects, *see* Connelly and Webb, *Variety,* 19 March 1910, p. 14; Lopez and Lopez, *Variety,* 12 March 1910, p. 17.

65. *Variety,* 2 April 1910, p. 20. In Gardiner and Vincent's sketch "The Flying Horse," with two full-stage sets, a "magic horse" took the couple from Arabia to America, and they were said to "fly" before a moving-picture panorama view of the country (*Variety,* 2 December 1911).

66. *Variety,* 20 January 1912, p. 16; 9 September 1911, p. 16.

67. Lary May, *Screening Out the Past: The Birth of Mass Culture and the Motion Picture Industry* (N.Y.: Oxford Univ. Press, 1980), pp. 20-38; Green and Laurie, pp. 5, 56; Marjorie Rosen, *Popcorn Venus: Women, Movies and the American Dream* (N.Y.: Avon, 1974), p. 20.

68. See Bordman, chaps. 4 and 5.

69. *Boston Herald,* 26 March 1904.

70. From seven vaudeville houses in 1896, New York City had thirty-one in 1910; Chicago houses increased from six to twenty-two in the same period, Philadelphia houses from twelve to thirty (Toll, *On With the Show,* p. 272).

71. *Variety,* 19 June 1909.

72. Playbill, Tivoli Theatre, South Africa, 2 January 1905; unidentified clippings dated 1904 and 1905, Valeska Suratt scrapbook (MWEZ, n.c. 1906), N.Y.P.L.-L.C.

73. *New York Morning Telegraph,* 28 March 1905.

74. *San Francisco Call,* 12 June 1905; *Los Angeles Daily Times,* 27 June 1905; *Cincinnati Enquirer,* 15 May 1905.

75. *Indianapolis Sun,* 20 February 1906.

76. *Indianapolis Morning Star,* 20 February 1906.

77. Mark Sullivan, *Our Times: The United States, 1900-1925* (N.Y.: Charles Scribner's Sons, 1930), III, 341.

78. *Cleveland World,* 9 May 1905.

79. *Indianapolis Sun,* 20 February 1906; *San Francisco Chronicle,* 12 June 1905; *Cleveland Town Topics,* 13 May 1905; *Indianapolis Sentinel,* 20 February 1906; *Indianapolis Morning Star,* 20 February 1906; *Detroit Free Press,* 27 March 1906; Sullivan, III, 547.

80. *Portland Daily Press,* 1 May 1906; *Daily Press Knickerbocker and Albany Morning Express,* 12 September [1905]; *Cleveland Town Topics,* 13 May 1905; *Variety,* 23 December 1905; *Boston Journal,* 17 November 1906. See also *The Stage,* 2 December 1905, p. 9.

81. "No Petticoats is Secret of Style," *Indianapolis Morning Star,* 23 February 1906.

82. *The Stage,* 2 December 1905, p. 9; "Miscreant Ruins Valeska's Frock," *New York Morning Telegraph,* 18 January 1906. See also *New York World,* 18 January 1906; *New York Times,* 18 January 1906.

83. *Detroit News,* 28 March 1906.

84. *The Cast,* 4 December 1909; "Female Stars Outnumbered Sheiks in Old Days," *New York News,* 22 July 1923.

85. *Cleveland Town Topics,* 13 May 1905.

86. *Indianapolis Star,* 5 January 1908; *New York Telegraph,* 29 August 1907.
87. Unidentified clipping dated 4 April 1908, Nora Bayes file, Locke Col. (NAFR+, 46), N.Y.P.L.-L.C.; Gilbert, p. 334.
88. Carolyn Wilson, "Clothes Worn on the Chicago Stage," *Philadelphia Tribune Journal,* 19 May 1913; *Variety,* 28 August 1910.
89. *Chicago News,* 31 January 1912.
90. *Pittsburgh Leader,* 4 February 1912; *Erie Herald,* 6 January 1912.
91. *Variety,* 14 August 1909; "Nora Bayes Tells How to be Happy Even Though Married," *Philadelphia Times,* 19 September 1910; *Vanity Fair,* 12 August 1911.
92. Wilson, "Clothes Worn on the Chicago Stage."
93. *Pittsburgh Leader,* 6 February 1912; *Syracuse Post,* 21 December 1911; *Buffalo Commercial,* 4 October 1910; *Baltimore American,* 7 November 1911; *Chicago Record,* 2 February 1912; "Bayes-Norworth at Best in Vaudeville," *Chicago Examiner,* 31 January 1912.
94. See *New York Telegraph,* 21 September 1909; 7 November 1909; 5 May 1910; 5 November 1910; *New York Evening Sun,* 1 December 1909; *New York Sun,* 27 April 1910.
95. *New York Times,* 7 January 1910; *Philadelphia Inquirer,* 21 March 1911; *Harper's Weekly,* 7 December 1912; *Chicago Journal,* 23 November 1908; *New York Review,* 20 January 1912.
96. *Variety,* 14 August 1909. Similarly, in Boston, Bayes and Norworth "gave a jaded audience a bit of real recreation" (*Boston Transcript,* 20 April 1909); to a Chicago critic, the team exhibited a "brave departure" from the usual, "independence and brilliant originality" (*Chicago News,* 31 January 1912).
97. *Chicago News,* 8 February 1909; *Cincinnati Commercial,* 10 September 1911; *Syracuse Post,* 21 December 1911; *Cleveland Leader,* 26 September 1911; *Chicago Examiner,* 31 January 1912; *Chicago News,* 31 January 1912.
98. *New York Telegraph,* 15 May 1910; *Los Angeles Examiner,* 19 September 1916; *Chicago Journal,* 7 June 1910; *New York Mirror,* 11 April 1912. These descriptions were used in reference to Elizabeth Brice and Charles King, together in vaudeville (and musical comedy) from 1910 until 1918 (*Newark Eagle,* 20 February 1918), and thought to "sing a certain sort of sentimental, semi-humorous and syncopated song, so much better than any 'team' since Nora Bayes and Jack Norworth split up" (*Kansas City Star* 16 August 1914). Other teams prominent in this line were Gladys Clark and Henry Bergman, William Rock and Maude Fulton, and Mr. and Mrs. Carter DeHaven; *see* clipping files on each in N.Y.P.L.-L.C.
99. Sam Morton, "When Women Were Prey"; unidentified clipping dated 27 July 1905, Sam and Kitty Morton file, Locke col., N.Y.P.L.-L.C.
100. Unidentified clipping dated 2 April 1912, Sam and Kitty Morton file, Locke col., N.Y.P.L.-L.C.; *Variety,* 28 March 1913; *New York Times,* 14 November 1916.
101. *Variety,* 16 January 1914; *Brooklyn Daily Eagle,* 6 July 1916; *Boston Transcript,* 13 May 1919.
102. *Variety,* 17 June 1911; *New York Telegraph,* 13 June 1911; *Toledo Blade,* 16 September 1918; *Theatre World,* 20 March 1920. One reviewer suggested that "some of the

song and dance teams who work in one and for that reason feel justified in calling themselves entertainers ought to watch Jim and Bonnie's act some time and learn how experts do it" (*New York Telegraph,* 29 October 1913). *See also* extensive N.Y.P.L.-L.C. files.

103. See above, chapter three; *New York Dramatic Mirror,* 15 January 1898; 4 March 1899, p. 18; *The Cast,* 26 November 1900; 20 January 1902; *New York Dramatic Mirror,* 9 May 1903, p. 18; *Variety,* 6 March 1909; *New York Telegraph,* 5 September 1909; 7 November 1909. In 1913, they could be found at an out-of-the-way small-time New York house, the Greeley Square (*New York Clipper,* 25 January 1913); "Molly Fuller Having Revival," *Variety,* 7 May 1915.

104. *New York Telegraph,* 12 March 1915.

105. *Variety,* 14 May 1915; *New York Telegraph,* 12 May 1915; *New York Star,* 15 September 1915; *New York Dramatic Mirror,* 15 April 1916.

106. Barth, p. 109.

107. *Variety,* 19 March 1910, p. 18.

108. E.g., Sampson and Douglas, *Variety,* 2 November 1907, p. 10; Hines and Remington, *New York Dramatic Mirror,* 11 April 1908, p. 17.

109. *Variety,* 4 November 1911, p. 17; 5 March 1910, p. 16. *See also* Early and Late, *Variety,* 26 September 1908, p. 14; Howard and Barrison, *Variety,* 14 November 1908, p. 15; Flemen and Roth, *Variety,* 5 December 1908, p. 16; Caulfield and Dunn, *Variety,* 18 December 1909, p. 17; McDermott and Raymond, *Variety,* 21 November 1908, p. 15; Lester and Kellett, *Variety,* 30 October 1909, p. 12.

110. *Variety,* 18 October 1912; 27 September 1912.

111. *Variety,* 16 January 1909; 16 September 1911, p. 19; 21 January 1916; *Billboard,* 22 September 1917.

112. *Variety,* 20 March 1909; 21 January 1916; *The Cast,* 27 January 1912.

113. Laurie, Vaudeville, p. 225; *Variety,* 10 December 1910; 16 September 1911, p. 19.

114. *Variety,* 9 February 1917; 21 January 1916; 9 January 1920. *See also Variety,* 27 September 1923.

115. *Variety,* 26 February 1910, p. 12; 10 December 1910; Laurie, *Vaudeville,* p. 228.

116. E.g., Redway and Lawrence, *Variety,* 29 November 1912; Newhoff and Phelps, *Variety,* 20 June 1913; Wood and Wyde, *Variety,* 13 December 1912; Anna Laughlin and William Gaxton, *Variety,* 31 December 1915; Sully and Houghton, *Variety,* 19 September 1919; *New York Dramatic Mirror,* 17 June 1919; Morton and Glass, *New York Tribune,* 17 June 1913; Ames and Winthrop, *Variety,* 22 September 1916; Clark and Bergman, *Philadelphia Inquirer,* 6 February 1912; McCarty and Faye, *Variety,* 5 January 1917.

117. Brett Page, *Writing for Vaudeville* (Springfield Ma.: The Home Correspondence School, 1915), p. 134.

118. Ibid., p. 136.

119. *Variety,* 11 September 1909; *The Cast,* 14 September 1912.

120. Page, pp. 461-474.

121. *Variety,* 11 September 1909.

122. *Variety*, 8 March 1918; 5 March 1920; 22 October 1920. See also Faber and Taylor, *Variety*, 12 April 1918; Lynn and LaRue, *Variety*, 22 February 1918; Walzer and Dyer, *Variety*, 14 November 1919; Allen and Francis, *Variety*, 19 November 1920.

123. *The Cast*, 3 April 1909. E.g., see *Variety*, 9 January 1915; *New York Star*, 28 July 1918; *Brooklyn Eagle*, 12 October 1916. see also extensive Barnes and Crawford files and scrapbooks, N.Y.P.L.-L.C.

124. *New York Telegraph*, 1 February 1920.

125. *Los Angeles Examiner*, 15 June 1913.

126. *Variety*, clipping dated 1919, T. Roy Barnes file (MWEZ, n.c. 4495), N.Y.P.L.-L.C.; *Toledo Blade*, 24 October 1911; *New York Dramatic Mirror*, 16 October 1915.

127. Unidentified clipping dated January 1915, T. Roy Barnes file (MWEZ, n.c. 4495), N.Y.P.L.-L.C.

128. *Variety*, 10 May 1918; *Indianapolis Star*, 26 December 1911; *Chicago Examiner*, 26 October 1913.

129. *Detroit News*, 31 October 1916; unidentified clippings, T. Roy Barnes scrapbook (MWEZ, n.c. 23, 036), N.Y.P.L.-L.C.; *Indianapolis Star*, 26 December 1911; *Chicago Examiner*, 26 October 1913; *Chicago Inter-Ocean*, 21 October 1913.

130. Donald Meyer, *The Positive Thinkers: A Study of the American Quest for Health, Wealth and Personal Power from Mary Baker Eddy to Norman Vincent Peale* (N.Y.: Doubleday, 1965), pp. 162-167; C. Wright Mills, *White Collar: The American Middle Class* (N.Y.: Oxford Univ. Press, 1951), xvii, 63ff., 167ff.

131. *Variety*, 14 January 1925; 6 December 1923.

132. *Variety*, 28 May 1924; George Burns, *I Love Her, That's Why!* (N.Y.: Simon and Schuster, 1955), p. 87.

133. *Variety*, 12 July 1918; *Billboard*, 5 February 1916; *Variety*, 24 September 1920.

134. E.g., McWatters and Tyson, *New York Dramatic Mirror*, 15 October 1898, p. 19; Wills and Loretta, *New York Dramatic Mirror*, 7 January 1899, p. 18; Foy and Clark, *New York Dramatic Mirror*, 29 January 1898, p. 18; the Doners, *New York Dramatic Mirror*, 19 October 1901, p. 18; Tredenick and Farm, *Variety*, 20 January 1906; Franklyn and Eva Wallace, *Variety*, 31 March 1906; Stanley and Wilson, *Variety*, 22 September 1906; Barry and Felix, *Variety*, 23 March 1907, p. 13; Dooley and Sales, *Variety*, 21 November 1908, p. 17; Howard and Linder, *Variety*, 29 September 1906; Kennedy and Rooney, *Variety*, 18 January 1908; Hill and Silviany, *Variety*, 28 December 1907; Tom and Stacie Moore, *Variety*, 9 April 1910, p. 20.

135. *Variety*, 22 January 1910, p. 17. See also Sampsel and Reilly, *Variety*, 16 September 1911, p. 19.

136. *New York Dramatic Mirror*, 28 January 1899, p. 18.

137. E.g., McAvoy and May, *New York Dramatic Mirror*, 11 April 1896, p. 19; Gardner and Simon, *New York Dramatic Mirror*, 30 November 1901, p. 18; Fields and Stewart, *New York Dramatic Mirror*, 26 February 1898, p. 16.

138. Unidentified clipping dated 16 June 1907; unidentified clipping (Milwaukee, Wisc.), Mae Melville file, Locke Col., N.Y.P.L.-L.C.

139. *Boston Traveller*, 6 May 1909.

140. *Duluth Herald*, 29 January 1913; *Louisville Times*, 1 December 1910; *Rochester*

288   Notes for Chapter 5

        Times, 15 April 1913; *Brooklyn Eagle,* 18 August 1914; unidentified clipping dated 3 September 1913, Mae Melville file, Locke Col., N.Y.P.L.-L.C.

141. *Boston Traveller,* 6 May 1909.

142. *Cincinnati Commercial,* n.d., Mae Melville file, Locke Col., N.Y.P.L.-L.C.; *Cincinnati Commercial,* 16 January 1912; *New York Telegraph,* 1 April 1910.

143. Unidentified clipping (Milwaukee, Wisc.); *Variety,* 17 July 1909; 14 August 1909; *Boston Traveller,* 6 May 1909; unidentified clipping dated 3 September 1913; Mae Melville file, Locke Col., N.Y.P.L.-L.C.

144. *Rochester Times,* 15 April 1913; *Variety,* 29 August 1913; *New York Tribune,* 9 June 1914.

145. *Chicago News,* 26 May 1914; *New York Star,* 8 March 1916; *New York Star,* 2 May 1916.

146. *Variety,* clipping dated December 1908, Montgomery and Moore file, N.Y.P.L.-L.C.; "Montgomery and Moore Separate," *New York Review,* 5 June 1915; *Kansas City Times,* 15 October 1915; *New York Dramatic Mirror,* 20 May 1914; *Philadelphia North American,* 26 May 1914.

147. *Toledo Blade,* 17 April 1915.

148. *Philadelphia North American,* 26 May 1914; *Philadelphia Telegraph,* 26 May 1914; *St. Louis Globe Democrat,* 13 April 1915; *Detroit Journal,* 30 March 1915; *Variety,* 23 January 1909.

149. *Toledo Blade,* 17 April 1915.

150. *Chicago News,* 17 March 1915; *Detroit News,* 30 March 1915.

151. "Florence Moore Made Faces at Audience and 'Found Herself,' " *Evening Wisconsin,* 8 September 1915.

152. *New York Times,* 14 April 1918; *Philadelphia North American,* 26 May 1914. Similarly, comedienne Mabel Hite entertained with "her queer poses, staccato form of speech, tricks of face" and "burlesque makeup." "Why don't I ever try to play a part in swell dresses and try to look like Ethel Barrymore?" asked Mabel Hite, and answered herself, "It's because I'd make about 30 cents a week...." (unidentified clipping dated 28 April 1906, Mabel Hite file [711], Locke Col., N.Y.P.L.-L.C.; *New York Telegraph,* 2 November 1906; "The Romance of Mabel and Mike," unidentified clipping dated 14 April 1907, Mabel Hite file, Locke Col. [ser. 2, NAFR+, 245] N.Y.P.L.-L.C.).

153. *Chicago News,* 17 March 1915.

154. *Chicago News,* 17 March 1915; *Philadelphia Ledger,* 22 May 1917.

155. *Variety,* 14 November 1908, p. 15. Mabel Hite pointed out to a reviewer that although women were presumed not to have a sense of humor, this misconception was blatantly untrue ("The 'Make-up' Half Hour With Mabel Hite," *Theatre,* July 1911). *See also* Richards and Grovers, *Variety,* 19 September 1908, p. 18; Spink and Welsh, *Variety,* 6 January 1912, p. 18; Verdin and Dunlop, *Variety,* 30 December 1911, p. 15; Deane and Sibley, *Variety,* 11 November 1911, p. 23; Elinore and Williams, *Variety,* 18 November 1911, p. 23; *Billboard,* 8 January 1916; 15 January 1916. Like Florence Moore and Mabel Hite, Kate Elinore wore the "most grotesque" of costumes and conducted herself in a manner "quite insane"; not until spring, 1917 would she begin performing

her comedy in straight costume (*Milwaukee News*, 14 January 1913; *Variety*, 6 April 1917).

156. *Variety*, 14 October 1911, pp. 18-19.
157. *Variety*, 14 October 1911, pp. 18-19; 2 November 1907, p. 10; 30 December 1911, p. 15.
158. *Variety*, 11 November 1911, p. 23; 25 November 1911, p. 22; 2 November 1907, p. 10; 28 October 1911, p. 16. Lee White, the comedienne in Perry and White, also had "a good idea of comedy," but was thought "too classy to resort to some of the things she is now indulging in" (*Variety*, 31 January 1913).
159. *Variety*, 28 October 1911, p. 16. Similarly, it was said of Mabel Hite that "every inch of her small body is a dynamic force which brings forth laughter. Doing fearful stunts with her agile and supple body she brings down the house with every move.... It is sui generis. She may be imitated, but her imitators lack that personality which is a part of Mabel Hite that can not be appropriated." Nonetheless, original as her talent was, one reviewer wondered "if she'll show up so well when there's no comedian to show the contrast" (*Milwaukee Sentinel*, 7 May 1906; unidentified clipping dated 25 November 1906, Mabel Hite file [711], Locke Col., N.Y.P.L.-L.C.).
160. *Variety*, 7 November 1908, p. 9.
161. Flexnor, pp. 257-261.
162. Kraditor, pp. 4-5.
163. Flexnor, pp. 263-265.
264. *Variety*, 13 January 1912, p. 18; *New York Mirror*, 1 November 1911; *Variety*, 12 July 1912. See also Miss Ray Cox, *Variety*, 26 September 1908, p. 17; "When Women Rule," *Variety*, 2 May 1913; "The Suffragette," *Variety*, 25 April 1913; "The Last of the Suffragettes," *Variety*, 28 August 1909; "In 1999," *New York Telegraph*, 22 March 1912; Whittier and Ince, *Variety*, 30 December 1911, p. 17.
165. *Baltimore American*, 15 April 1912, quoted by Flexnor, pp. 267-268.
166. Filene, pp. 30-31; Sinclair, *The Better Half*, pp. 318, 321.
167. Kraditor, pp. 116-128.
168. Sullivan, III, 342-343.
169. Filene, pp. 7-10, 12.
170. *Variety*, 1 January 1910, p. 15; 22 January 1910, p. 19; 14 October 1911, p. 18; 16 September 1911, p. 19.
171. *Variety*, 12 February 1910, p. 19.
172. *Variety*, 28 November 1908, p. 15; 26 December 1908, p. 11.
173. *Variety*, 12 February 1910, p. 20.
174. *New York Dramatic Mirror*, 18 September 1912, p. 23.
175. *Variety*, 20 January 1912, p. 16.
176. *Variety*, 24 February 1912, p. 17. Similarly, in an act by Hayward and Stafford called "The Devil Outwitted," when the husband and wife argued about the behavior expected of a spouse, "the applause fluctuates between the sexes in the audience — except the hen-pecked and the rooster-ruled ones" (*New York Telegraph*, 21 January 1914).

177. May, pp. 37, 107–108.
178. O'Neill, p. 129; Henry Finck, "Are Womanly Women Doomed," *The Independent,* 53 (January 1901), 270. Two other incidences of physical opposition by men to suffragists are described in Ronald Schaffer, "The New York City Woman Suffrage Party, 1909–1919," *New York History,* 43 (July 1962), 271–272.
179. *Variety,* 10 October 1908, p. 12.
180. *New York Telegraph,* 20 October 1908; *Variety,* 2 January 1909; *New York Mirror,* 9 January 1909.
181. *Variety,* 24 October 1909, p. 15.
182. *Variety,* 10 October 1908, p. 12; 2 January 1909.
183. *Variety,* 9 January 1909, p. 14.
184. *Variety,* 9 January 1909, p. 14; 31 July 1909. See also French and Eis, "Dance of Fortune" (*Variety,* 17 January 1913); Smith and Donaldson, "Vampire Dance" (*Variety,* 28 August 1909); Coccio and Amato, "Slums of Paris" (*Variety,* 3 December 1910); Rock and Fulton, "The Dance with the Devil" (*Variety,* 19 September 1908; *Memphis Commercial,* 19 December 1912).
185. May, pp. 30–35. See also Lewis Allen Erenberg, "Urban Nightlife and the Decline of Victorianism: New York's Restaurants and Cabarets, 1890–1918" (Ph.D. diss., Univ. of Michigan, 1974).
186. E.g., Vesta Tilley (*Variety,* 19 April 1909); Adelaide and Hughes ("Society Flocks to Watch Adelaide and Hughes Dancing," *New York Evening Journal,* 10 February 1914).
187. May, pp. 32–33.
188. Barth, pp. 174–175.
189. *Variety,* 9 April 1910, p. 16; 9 September 1911, p. 20; 22 October 1910.

Chapter 6

1. Laurie, *Vaudeville,* p. 246; Bill Smith, *The Vaudevillians* (N.Y.: Macmillan, 1976), p. 83.
2. Nick Grinde, "Where's Vaudeville At," *Saturday Evening Post,* 11 January 1930, p. 44; *Variety,* 29 December 1916.
3. Laurie, *Vaudeville,* p. 3.
4. DiMeglio, p. 119; Tucker, p. 131. See also Laurie, *Vaudeville,* pp. 481–482.
5. Jack Haley, quoted by Smith, p. 132.
6. Marian Spitzer, *The Palace* (N.Y.: Atheneum, 1969), pp. 3–6; Laurie, *Vaudeville,* p. 487.
7. Spitzer, *The Palace,* pp. 18–22; Laurie, *Vaudeville,* p. 482.
8. Spitzer, *The Palace,* 26ff.
9. *Variety,* 4 September 1914; 25 December 1914; Laurie, *Vaudeville,* p. 491.
10. E.g., *see* Majestic Theatre, *Billboard,* 1 January 1916; Palace Theatre, *Variety,* 19 September 1919; 9 January 1915; 5 March 1915; Colonial Theatre, *Variety,* 11

September 1914; Columbia Theatre, St. Louis, *Billboard,* 4 December 1915; Chicago Palace, *Billboard,* 8 January 1916; Colonial Theatre, *Billboard,* 29 January 1916; 3 November 1916; Riverside Theatre, *Variety,* 26 January 1917; Colonial Theatre, *Variety,* 2 February 1917; 16 February 1917; Royal Theatre, *Variety,* 30 March 1917; Palace Theatre, *Variety,* 13 April 1917.

11. *Variety,* 20 April 1917; 27 February 1920; Laurie, *Vaudeville,* p. 491.

12. Smith, pp. 132, 55, 83; *Variety,* 11 October 1923; 26 January 1917; 20 December 1923. See also Larry Wilde, *The Great Comedians Talk about Comedy* (N.Y.: Citadel Press, 1968), pp. 145-146.

13. *Billboard,* 5 February 1916; 8 December 1917; DeMeglio, p. 162.

14. Smith, p. 1. See also Prospect Theatre, *Variety,* 17 October 1914; John Lahr, *Notes of a Cowardly Lion: the Biography of Bert Lahr* (N.Y.: Knopf, 1969), p. 19.

15. DiMeglio, p. 40; *Variety,* 2 January 1920.

16. Marian Spitzer, "The Business of Vaudeville," *Saturday Evening Post,* 24 May 1924, p. 18; Smith, pp. 10, 132.

17. *Variety,* 24 October 1914.

18. *Billboard,* 1 January 1916; 1 September 1917. See also Chicago Palace, *Billboard,* 15 January 1916; Colonial Theatre, *Billboard,* 12 February 1916; Bushwick Theatre, *Variety,* 1 December 1916; Palace Theatre, *Variety,* 12 January 1917; Colonial Theatre, *Variety,* 23 March 1917; Chicago Palace, *Billboard,* 17 November 1917.

19. Jack Haley, quoted by Smith, p. 131.

20. Gilbert Seldes, *The 7 Lively Arts,* 2nd ed. (N.Y.: Sagamore Press, 1957), p. 223.

21. *Variety,* 3 November 1916. See Albert F. McLean, Jr., *American Vaudeville as Ritual* (Lexington, Ky.: Univ. of Kentucky Press, 1965), pp. 91-105, for a detailed discussion of the "carefully contrived" "series of controlled accelerations toward climaxes of excitement" in the vaudeville show.

22. These statistics and conclusions are based on a careful sampling of the vaudeville sections in *Variety* and *Billboard* for these years.

23. George Gottlieb, quoted by Page, p. 7.

24. *Variety,* 10 October 1914; *Billboard,* 25 December 1915; *Variety,* 23 January 1914; 17 February 1922; 27 February 1914; *Billboard,* 25 December 1915; 24 November 1917; *Variety,* 17 September 1924; 10 September 1915; *Billboard,* 11 December 1915; *Variety,* 26 January 1917; Laurie, *Vaudeville,* p. 31; *Variety,* 19 September 1919. Mixed juggling acts were the Royal Gascoignes (*Variety,* 25 February 1925), the Hennings (*Variety,* 11 February 1925), Bagget and Sheldon (*Variety,* 5 January 1923), and Pielert and Scofield (*Billboard,* 5 February 1916); acrobatic teams were Les Grohs (*Variety,* 5 November 1915), the Brads (*Variety,* 3 April 1914), Samsted and Marion (*Variety,* 28 January 1921), Bradley and Ardine (*Variety,* 4 February 1921), and Archie and Gertie Falls (*Variety,* 22 September 1922; 6 October 1922).

25. *Minneapolis Journal,* 21 April 1912; *Hartford Courant,* 20 January 1909; unidentified clipping dated 24 February 1906, Reynolds and Donegan file, N.Y.P.L.-L.C.; unidentified clipping dated 20 November 1906, Reynolds and Donegan file, N.Y.P.L.-L.C.; *Vanity Fair,* 9 August 1909.

26. *Variety,* 25 July 1908; unidentified clipping dated 28 August 1919, Reynolds and

Donegan file, N.Y.P.L.-L.C.; *New York Mirror,* 1 August 1908; *New York Star,* 30 May 1915.

27. *New York World,* 9 November 1910; *Variety,* 25 July 1908; 15 November 1918.
28. *Variety,* 14 August 1909; *New York World,* 9 November 1910; *New York Telegraph,* 1 January 1915; *Buffalo Enquirer,* 11 July 1916.
29. *Cleveland Leader,* 2 July 1916; *see* newspaper photographs in Reynolds and Donegan file, N.Y.P.L.-L.C.
30. *See* Page, pp. 7-8; Spitzer, "The Business of Vaudeville," p. 130.
31. For representative bills with male-female song and dance teams in number two position, *see* Palace Theatre, *Variety,* 19 November 1915; Alhambra Theatre, unidentified clipping, T. Roy Barnes Scrapbook (MWEZ, n.c. 23, 030), N.Y.P.L.-L.C.; Colonial Theatre, *New York Telegraph,* 22 October 1913; Riverside Theatre, *New York Star,* 22 June 1919; Bronx Theatre, *New York Telegraph,* 27 December 1911; Colonial Theatre, *New York Star,* 6 October 1918.
32. Laurie, *Vaudeville,* p. 38.
33. For a straight song and dance team, *see* Norton and Lee file, Locke Col., N.Y.P.L.-L.C.; abundant information on the important "musical comedy" teams can be found in Paul Morton file, N.Y.P.L.-L.C., Armand Kalisz file, Locke Col., N.Y.P.L.-L.C., Kalmar and Brown file, Locke Col., N.Y.P.L.-L.C., and Chip and Marble, Locke Col. (Ser. 2, NAFR+); *see* clippings on Dooley and Rugel in Dooley family file, N.Y.P.L.-L.C., for a burlesque song and dance act.
34. *New York Times,* 31 October 1939; unidentified clipping dated 6 July 1952, Pat Rooney II file, N.Y.P.L.-L.C.
35. *New York Dramatic Mirror,* 24 September 1898; *The Cast,* 29 February 1904; Jimmy Lyons and Sam Carlton, "The Rooneys," unpublished TS, Theatre Collection, Humanities Research Center, Univ. of Texas at Austin, pp. 16-24.
36. "Pat Rooney is 70 Today," *New York Herald-Tribune,* 4 July 1949; Lyons and Carlton, pp. 24-25.
37. *Philadelphia Times,* 13 October 1908; unidentified clipping, Rooney and Bent file, N.Y.P.L.-L.C.
38. *New York Mirror,* 25 September 1909; Lyons and Carlton, pp. 37-38.
39. Lyons and Carlton, p. 38.
40. *Variety,* 12 February 1910; *New York Telegraph,* 19 December 1910; Lyons and Carlton, p. 38.
41. "Ol' Man Rooney...He Just Keeps Rolling Along," *Cue,* 14 July 1951.
42. *Variety,* 3 April 1914; Lyons and Carlton, p. 42.
43. *Variety,* 3 April 1914; *New York Dramatic Mirror,* 8 April 1914.
44. *Los Angeles Examiner,* 14 August 1913; unidentified clipping Pat Rooney, Jr. (II) file, N.Y.P.L.-L.C., *Milwaukee News,* 5 March 1912; *Variety,* 9 May 1908.
45. Unidentified clipping, Rooney and Bent file, Locke Col., N.Y.P.L.-L.C.; *Variety,* 28 November 1908.
46. *Brooklyn Daily Eagle,* 13 September 1944.

47. *New York Herald-Tribune*, 27 July 1951; *New York Telegraph*, 22 April 1914; *Variety*, 16 December 1925. They were praised in the 6 February 1927 *Congressional Record* by Congressman T. Weber Wilson of Mississippi ("Pat Rooney Autobiography," unpublished TS, Theatre Collection, Humanities Research Center, Univ. of Texas at Austin).
48. Fred Astaire, *Steps In Time* (N.Y.: Harper and Brothers, 1959), p. 47.
49. For male-female dance teams in the next-to-last position, *see* the Rooneys, *New York Star*, 22 June 1919; Dooley and Rugel, *Variety*, 19 November 1915; McKay and Ardine, *Billboard*, 20 October 1917.
50. Mason and Keeler, *Variety*, 5 November 1915. For examples, *see* Cressy and Dayne, *New York Star*, 23 February 1916; McConnell and Simpson, *Billboard*, 20 October 1917; the Vans, *Billboard*, 25 December 1915.
51. Page, p. 8.
52. E.g., *see New York Star*, 3 October 1915; 9 June 1920.
53. *New York Dramatic Mirror*, 1 April 1899; *Billboard*, 25 December 1915; *New York Dramatic Mirror*, 18 April 1903; *Variety*, 28 October 1911; 7 February 1924. See files on Dolan and Lenhaar, and Moore and Littlefield, N.Y.P.L.-L.C. *See also* the Ushers, *The Cast*, 21 October 1911; *The Cast*, 7 March 1904; *Billboard*, 11 December 1915.
54. *New York Dramatic Mirror*, 21 October 1905; *Variety*, 7 November 1908; 30 January 1914; 12 November 1920. See also Hyams and McIntyre file, N.Y.P.L.-L.C.
55. *Billboard*, 1 January 1916; *Variety*, 20 February 1920; Spitzer, *The Palace*, p. 133. See extensive files on the Barrys, N.Y.P.L.-L.C.
56. *Variety*, 7 November 1914; 1 January 1915.
57. E.g., Norton and Lee, *Billboard*, 11 December 1915; Kalmar and Brown, *New York Star*, 28 July 1918.
58. *Variety*, n.d., Dolly Connolly file, Locke Col. (Ser. 3, vol. 317), N.Y.P.L.-L.C.; *Providence Journal*, 31 December 1912; *Newark Eagle*, n.d., Dolly Connolly file, Locke Col. (Ser. 3, vol. 317), N.Y.P.L.-L.C.
59. *Los Angeles Examiner*, 9 March 1909; *Kansas City Post*, 4 December 1910; *Dayton News*, 17 February 1920; unidentified clipping dated 20 March 1917, Stella Mayhew file, Locke Col. (MWEZ, n.c. 23,037), N.Y.P.L.-L.C.
60. "'Yumpin Yimminy' Brendel, The Swede Who Wasn't, Dies," *New York Herald-Tribune*, 10 April 1964; "El Brendel, 73, Dies on Coast; Film Comedian in 20's and 30's," unidentified obit. dated 10 April 1964, El Brendel file, N.Y.P.L.-L.C.; unidentified clipping dated 22 March 1915, El Brendel file, N.Y.P.L.-L.C.
61. *Variety*, 10 May 1918; 21 October 1925; *Billboard*, 27 October 1917.
62. *Variety*, 31 May 1918; 10 February 1922.
63. *New York Star*, 7 September 1919; *Variety*, 17 October 1919; 21 January 1925.
64. "Herbert Williams," obit., *New York World-Telegraph*, 2 October 1936; "Herbert Williams," obit., *Variety*, 7 October 1936; *New York World-Telegram*, 22 April 1935; Charles and Louise Samuels, *Once Upon a Stage: The Merry World of Vaudeville* (N.Y.: Dodd, Mead, 1974), p. 159. In its obituary, *Variety* maintained none of Herb's friends knew why he turned to comedy.
65. Samuels, p. 160; *Duluth Herald*, 26 October 1914; *Detroit Journal*, 14 March 1918.

Notes for Chapter 6

66. Samuels, pp. 159-160.
67. Samuels, p. 160; *New York Clipper,* 10 December 1919; *Variety,* 26 June 1914; "Herbert Williams of the Cat and Bells," *Brooklyn Daily Eagle,* 15 September 1935. See also Herbert Williams files, N.Y.P.L.-L.C.
68. Page, p. 9. When Hunting and Francis opened the second part of their bill at the Palace in October 1919, it was said their talk went right out the door (*Variety,* 10 October 1919). See also Hampton and Blake, *Variety,* 10 February 1922.
69. E.g., *see* Wright and Dietrich, Riverside Theatre, *New York Star,* 9 June 1920; Whiting and Burt, Palace Theatre, *Billboard,* 6 October 1917.
70. Sadie Burt, memoir of George Whiting, unpublished TS, N.Y.P.L.-L.C., pp. 2-5; Green and Laurie, pp. 79, 101.
71. *Variety,* 26 September 1914; 31 October 1914; *Billboard,* 6 October 1917; *Variety,* 1 October 1920.
72. *Variety,* 17 October 1919; "George Whiting, 61, Song Writer, Dead," *New York Times,* 20 December 1943; "George Whiting Dies; Lyricist, Vaudeville Star," *New York Herald-Tribune,* 20 December 1943.
73. *Variety,* 27 February 1920; 1 October 1920; Burt, p. 8.
74. Burt, p. 8.
75. Ibid., p. 9.
76. E.g., *see New York Clipper,* 20 October 1920; *New York Star,* 24 November 1918; *Billboard,* 1 January 1915; playbill, B. F. Keith's Theatre, n.p., 13 March 1916.
77. *See* Kerr and Weston, *Variety,* 26 November 1915.
78. Page, p. 9.
79. Frances Rust, *Dance in Society* (London: Routledge and Kegan Paul, 1969), pp. 80-82; Joseph and June Csida, *American Entertainment: A Unique History of Popular Show Business* (N.Y.: Watson-Guptill, 1978), p. 159; Albert McCarthy, *The Dance Band Era: The Dancing Decades from Ragtime to Swing, 1910-1950* (Phila.: Chilton Book, 1971), p. 10.
80. Rust, p. 83.
81. Ibid., pp. 83-84.
82. Anatole Chujoy, "The Castles," *The Dance Encyclopedia* (N.Y.: Barnes, 1949), p. 87. Laurie, *Vaudeville,* p. 44; Csida, p. 212; Vernon and Irene Castle, *Modern Dancing* (N.Y.: Harper and Bros., 1914).
83. For appearances by these teams, *see Variety,* 3 December 1915; 16 January 1915; 24 October 1914; 30 January 1915; 9 July 1924: 22 October 1920; 24 January 1924; 9 January 1920; 10 August 1921; *Billboard,* 22 January 1916; 11 December 1915; 8 January 1916; 10 November 1917. *See also* chapter on "hoofers" in Laurie, *Vaudeville,* pp. 38-47; interview with Sammy Berk in Smith, pp. 63-67; coverage of the dance craze in *Variety,* 24 December 1915; 26 December 1919; Erenberg, passim.; and extensive files in N.Y.P.L.-L.C. on the Astaires, the Castles, and Maurice and Walton.
84. *Boston Transcript,* 13 October 1914; unidentified clipping dated July 1900, Adelaide and Hughes file, N.Y.P.L.-L.C.; *New York Mirror,* 5 February 1910; *New York Telegraph,* 4 June 1913.

85. *Billboard,* 25 December 1915; 8 September 1917; *New York Review,* 10 October 1914; "Adelaide-Hughes Triumph at the Palace Grows," *New York Dramatic Mirror,* 14 December 1918; Laurie, *Vaudeville,* p. 45; "Society Flocks to Watch Adelaide and Hughes Dancing."

86. *Louisville Courier Journal,* 6 April 1916; *New York Dramatic Mirror,* 1 July, n.y., Adelaide and Hughes file, N.Y.P.L.-L.C.; *Washington Star,* 27 January 1914; unidentified clipping dated 15 August 1914, Adelaide and Hughes scrapbook (MWEZ, n.c. 4423), N.Y.P.L.-L.C.; *Variety,* 25 August 1916.

87. *Variety,* 15 October 1920.

88. Laurie, *Vaudeville,* pp. 228–229.

89. With the exception of Laurie's *Vaudeville,* Ryan and Lee are unmentioned in studies of vaudeville; even Ben Ryan's obituary in the 10 July 1968 *Variety* mistakenly identified him as "long of Ryan & (Sammy) Lee" in vaudeville.

90. *Toledo Blade,* 19 November 1914; unidentified clipping, Ryan and Lee file, N.Y.P.L.-L.C.; Laurie, *Vaudeville,* p. 228. The 27 June 1913 *Variety* complained, "A 'two-act.' 'Tis hard to restrain from a long dissertation on 'two-acts,' this boy and girl affair people in and out of vaudeville appear to think is all sufficient. A girl, a boy, some clothes, some songs and a dance. Well, it has been overdone.... 'Mixed two-acts' are too similar."

91. *Variety,* 29 March 1918; 4 February 1925.

92. *Variety,* 8 December 1916. One influence—although there is little supporting evidence—may have been the rube act, which was apparently getting broader. Even the straight women in some of these acts were almost "boobs"; e.g., in Mr. and Mrs. Jack McGreevy's act, she played "an 'overgrown' village girl who gapes wide-eyed and opened mouth at the simplest things told her." He carried the act, and she said little, but when she did talk, laughs followed (*Variety,* 28 January 1911). In her act with "Pop" Chadwick, Ida May Chadwick played a "rube kid," a piece of evidence showing kid work could also be done in rube acts (*Variety,* 22 October 1910).

93. *Variety,* 24 September 1924.

94. *Chicago Tribune,* 17 October 1915; *Variety,* 4 February 1925; *Detroit Journal,* 24 November 1914.

95. *Louisville Times,* 27 October 1914; *New York Journal,* 3 February 1914. Similarly, the *Detroit Journal* claimed it was "put over with a difference" (24 November 1914).

96. *Toledo Blade,* 15 September 1915.

97. *Chicago Tribune,* 17 October 1915.

98. *Variety,* 24 September 1924; *New York Star,* 31 March 1918.

99. *Variety,* 8 December 1916; *see also Detroit Journal,* 24 November 1914.

100. *New York Journal,* 3 February 1914; two extant pictures also testify to Lee's pretty face; in one, she is in the pose of her character and wears street clothes (Ryan and Lee file [MWEZ+, n.c. 9109], N.Y.P.L.-L.C.).

101. *Variety,* 12 March 1924.

102. Smith, p. 173. This will be discussed further in Chapter 8.

103. *Variety,* 3 February 1922; 10 October 1919.

Notes for Chapter 6

104. *Variety*, 22 October 1924; *Billboard*, 11 October 1924; *Variety*, 29 March 1923.
105. *Billboard*, 5 December 1925; *Variety*, 27 February 1920; 26 September 1919; 19 September 1919; 5 January 1923; 14 October 1925. A vamp of the "baby" species was described by a writer of the day as having bobbed locks, scarlet lips, dangerous eyes, and coquettish glances (Howard Greer, "In Real Bohemia," *Theatre Magazine*, January 1920, pp. 22, 24).
106. *Variety*, 11 February 1916; 17 November 1917; *Billboard*, 8 September 1917.
107. *Billboard*, 8 September 1917.
108. *New York Telegraph*, 4 September 1917.
109. Unidentified clipping dated 13 January 1919, Aileen Bronson file, N.Y.P.L.-L.C.; *Toledo Blade*, 16 October 1922. "Laurie Divorce Off," *Variety*, 14 July 1920; "Stage 'Kid' Lets Out Secret of Her Marriage," *Toledo Blade*, 20 April 1921.
110. *Variety*, 24 September 1924.
111. Laurie, *Vaudeville*, pp. 228–229.
112. *New York World-Telegram*, 1 April 1937.
113. Laurie, *Vaudeville*, p. 228.
114. *Variety*, 5 November 1915.
115. Horn, pp. 40, 662, 225–226, 118.
116. Stephen Becker, *Comic Art in America* (N.Y.; Simon and Schuster, 1959), p. 182.
117. *Variety*, 24 September 1924; 18 March 1925.
118. *Billboard*, 24 October 1925; *Variety*, 9 September 1925; 25 February 1925; *Billboard*, 29 October 1927; 23 November 1929; "Helen Broderick," obit., *Variety*, 30 September 1959; *Variety*, 9 February 1917; 24 December 1924.
119. *Variety*, 26 April 1923; *Opinion*, 30 July 1941; *Variety*, 17 August 1927.
120. *New York American*, 1 June 1935; *Variety*, 22 September 1937; *Opinion*, 30 July 1941.
121. *Variety*, 17 August 1927.
122. Unidentified clipping dated January 1915, T. Roy Barnes file (MWEZ, n.c. 4495), N.Y.P.L.-L.C. See also *Los Angeles Examiner*, 15 June 1913.
123. *Variety*, 18 April 1906; 27 March 1909; *Winnipeg Telegram*, 14 October 1911; *Variety*, 11 October 1912; *New York Dramatic Mirror*, 27 August 1913; *Los Angeles Examiner*, 25 March 1913.
124. *Chicago Herald*, 20 December 1914.
125. *New York Dramatic Mirror*, 10 December 1913; *San Antonio Light*, 29 March 1917; *New York Dramatic Mirror*, 27 August 1913.
126. *Variety*, 27 March 1909.
127. *Variety*, 10 February 1922; 24 March 1922.
128. *Variety*, 9 September 1921; 27 September 1923; 7 January 1925.
129. *Variety*, 8 April 1925; 22 December 1922; 24 June 1924.
130. *Variety*, 4 March 1925; 12 April 1923; Kate Davy, "An Interview with George Burns," *Educational Theatre Journal*, 27 (October 1975), pp. 348–349.

131. James Madison, *James Madison's Weekly Service,* no. 1 [1922].
132. Laurie, *Vaudeville,* pp. 423-427. *See also* James Madison, *Madison's Budget,* no. 19 [1926], pp. 20-21; William McNally, *McNally's Bulletin No. 11* (N.Y.: William McNally, 1925), pp. 77-81, 81-83, 83-85, 85-87, 91-93, 93-95, 99-103.
133. *Variety,* 5 January 1923.
134. *New York Clipper,* 26 January 1921; *Variety,* 28 January 1921.
135. *Variety,* 26 March 1920; 11 February 1921.
136. *New York Telegraph,* 13 January 1920; *Variety,* 28 January 1925; "Good Bill at Shea's," unidentified clipping, William Gibson file, N.Y.P.L.-L.C.
137. Rosen, p. 121.
138. *Variety,* 6 October 1922.
139. *Variety,* 28 January 1925.
140. Horn, pp. 512, 178, 126; Rosen 64ff., 77ff., 86ff.
141. William E. Leuchtenburg, *The Perils of Prosperity, 1914-1932,* Chicago History of American Civilization Series (Chicago: Univ. of Chicago Press, 1958), p. 159; Filene, p. 106.
142. Leuchtenburg, p. 160; Filene, pp. 107-115.
143. Filene, pp. 134-135; Leuchtenburg, pp. 168-171.
144. For a provocative and scholarly social history of the twenties, approached not as an era of superficial excitements and meaningless escape, but as a decade of cultural accommodation and often painful social reconstruction—focusing on youth as the agents of change—*see* Paula S. Fass, *The Damned and the Beautiful: American Youth in the 1920s* (N.Y.: Oxford Univ. Press, 1977).
145. See Filene, pp. 118ff., 133-136, 142-148; Fass, pp. 23-25. Filene offers the only detailed account—and an excellent one—of the decline of "manliness" as defined by Victorians and the threat posed by the New Woman to men.
146. As Fass puts it, "The young rake or flapper, strutting defiantly in the pages of the *Atlantic* or the *Ladies' Home Journal* or even the *New Republic,* had about as much to do with the average high school or college youth as Jay Gatsby did with the average bootlegger. They were not real but fictionalized, emotion-packed distortions of a type that was meant to evoke rather than to describe and finally to comfort through rebuke (pp. 17-18).
147. *Variety,* 17 December 1915; 5 March 1920; *Kansas City Times,* 8 December 1919; *Variety,* 28 January 1925; Will Durant, "The Modern Woman," *Century Magazine,* 113 (February 1927), p. 422. Similar male-female routines were Morton and Glass's "1917-50," performed between 1917 and 1921 (with the title changing yearly); Ray Raymond and Florrie Millership's act contrasting an 1840 girl's behavior—she rejects a wealthy suitor to marry the poor artist she loves—with a 1925 girl's, who rejects her young lover for a senile person in a Rolls Royce; Keating and Ross's act, contrasting old-fashioned love-making with modern courtship; and Murray and Oakland's impersonation of an 1862 couple, with a statement on modern couples naturally implied (*New York Post,* 27 November 1917; *Variety,* 11 February 1921; 28 January 1925; 19 January 1923; 12 January 1923). An interesting act was "Cave Man Love," done by a small cast: a young man who proposes is turned down, until he dreams about cavemen

Notes for Chapter 7

days and learns how cavemen handled women—new tactics which bring his modern girlfriend around (*Variety*, 12 March 1920). Filmmakers were also fond of tracing women backward and forward through time; King Vidor's 1924 *Wine of Youth,* for example, contrasted the girls of the twenties with their mothers and daughters (Rosen, p. 79).

Chapter 7

1. *New York Clipper,* 20 July 1921.
2. *Variety,* 14 October 1921; 9 January 1920; 12 November 1920; 11 October 1923; 30 July 1924.
3. *Variety,* 4 October 1923; 11 October 1923; 18 October 1923; 25 October 1923.
4. *Variety,* 31 October 1919, p. 14.
5. Toll, *On With the Show,* pp. 198-202; David Ewen, *The Story of America's Musical Theatre* (Phila.: Chilton Book, 1961), 29ff.; Ethan Mordden, *Better Foot Forward: The History of American Musical Theatre* (N.Y.: Crossman, 1976), pp. 59-62, 73-74.
6. Toll, *On With the Show,* pp. 313-316.
7. Ibid., p. 315.
8. Ewen, pp. 87, 94; Toll, *On With the Show,* p. 326.
9. Ewen, 51ff.
10. Csida, p. 234.
11. George E. Mowry, ed., *The Twenties: Fords, Flappers and Fanatics* (Englewood Cliffs, N.J.: Prentice-Hall, 1963), pp. 3, 43.
12. *Variety,* 23 January 1909; *New York Dramatic Mirror,* 10 April 1909; *New York Mirror,* 6 June 1909.
13. *Variety,* 7 November 1919; *New York Star,* 11 November 1919; unidentified clipping, Rooney and Bent file, Locke Col., N.Y.P.L.-L.C.
14. *Variety,* 14 November 1919.
15. *Variety,* 2 January 1920; *Variety,* clipping dated 1920, Rooney and Bent file, Locke Col., N.Y.P.L.-L.C.; *Seattle Daily Times,* 20 February [1922] *Montreal Gazette,* 10 October 1922.
16. *New York Star,* 12 July 1920; *Times Square Daily,* 2 October 1923; *New York Times,* 23 December 1923; *Brooklyn Citizen,* 23 December 1923.
17. *New York Telegraph,* 22 September 1923; 4 January 1924.
18. *New York Mirror,* 3 March 1917; *Variety,* 2 March 1917; 7 November 1919; *New York Dramatic Mirror,* 24 July 1920.
19. *Variety,* 24 September 1920; *New York Post,* 13 February 1939; *Variety,* 15 July 1921; *Detroit Free Press,* 17 April 1923.
20. *Variety,* 6 September 1923; 9 September 1925.
21. E.g., see Cunningham and Bennett, *Variety,* 13 October 1922; Clinton and Rooney, *Variety,* 15 March 1923; Jim and Betty Morgan, *Variety,* 14 June 1923; Tracey and

Notes for Chapter 7   299

McBride, *Variety,* 7 February 1924; Newhoff and Phelps, *Variety,* 17 June 1925; LeVoie and Lane, *Variety,* 14 February 1924; Bryan and Broderick, *Variety,* 14 February 1924; Roye and Maye, *Variety,* 25 March 1925; Ails and Pullman, *Variety,* 10 March 1926.

22. *Variety,* 3 October 1919; "Vaude Vogue for Operettas Appears," *Variety,* 4 February 1925.
23. E.g., Hammerstein's, *Variety,* 18 September 1914; Alhambra, *Variety,* 6 February 1920; Colonial, *Variety,* 5 November 1915; Alhambra, *Variety,* 7 November 1919; Columbia, St. Louis, *Billboard,* 15 January 1916; Keith's, Cincinnati, *Billboard,* 8 January 1916.
24. *Billboard,* 26 October 1918.
25. *Variety,* 17 October 1919; 14 November 1919; 3 October 1919.
26. *Variety,* 10 October 1919.
27. E.g., Colonial, *Variety,* 20 February 1915; Riverside, *Variety,* 7 November 1919; Palace, *Variety,* 19 September 1919; Hippodrome, *Variety,* 14 January 1925; Palace, *Variety,* 10 September 1924; Palace, *Billboard,* 27 February 1926.
28. *Variety,* 3 February 1922.
29. E.g., Palace, *New York Telegraph,* 28 March 1926; Palace, *New York Star,* 8 February 1920; Palace, *New York Tribune,* 4 June 1922; Riverside, *New York Star,* 22 June 1919.
30. *Billboard,* 21 December 1918.
31. *Variety,* 4 October 1923.
32. *Variety,* 21 January 1925; 1 October 1924.
33. *Billboard,* 17 November 1917; *Variety,* 7 January 1925.
34. In 1917 alone, one hundred standard vaudeville acts left vaudeville for revue or musical comedy (*Variety,* 6 July 1917).
35. E.g., Palace Cincinnati, *Billboard,* 5 December 1925; Riverside, *Variety,* 15 September 1922; Hippodrome, *Billboard,* 19 September 1925.
36. *Variety,* 10 February 1922.
37. Palace, *Variety,* 11 November 1925; 20 January 1922, p. 7.
38. *Variety,* 3 September 1920; 8 October 1920; 17 December 1924. See also Chicago Palace, *Variety,* 15 October 1920; Orpheum Road Show, *Variety,* 24 September 1924.
39. Powers and Wallace, Fifth Avenue Theatre, *Variety,* 13 January 1922; Rugel and Dooley, Palace, *Variety,* 11 February 1921.
40. E.g., see Hippodrome, *Variety,* 23 December 1925; 18 November 1925; "Freak Stage Turns Come Along Strong," *Billboard,* 26 November 1927; "Circus Offerings Trek to Vaude.," *Billboard,* 14 November 1925.
41. *Variety,* 15 September 1922.
42. Lahr, pp. 27-42; *Providence News,* clipping dated 14 October [1921?], Bert Lahr scrapbook (MWEZ, n.c. 22530), N.Y.P.L.-L.C.; *New York Journal,* 30 November 1920; *Rochester Times,* 26 October 1920; *New York Telegraph,* 2 November 1921; *Variety,* 3 December 1920; *New York Telegraph,* 30 November 1920.

43. *Variety,* 26 May 1922; 17 May 1923; *New York Telegraph,* 23 December 1924.
44. *Brooklyn Citizen,* 4 April 1926; *Variety,* 26 May 1922; 17 May 1923; *Billboard,* 4 October 1924; Lahr, p. 66. Jack Pearl recalled Mercedes: "She was the most beautiful Spanish woman you have ever seen in your life. Beautiful, beautiful, God...." (Lahr, p. 51). When Mercedes put on some weight, Lahr complained about it; "She had to look sexy and nice out there as the straight for my jokes" (Lahr, p. 86).
45. *New York Graphic,* 24 March 1926; 3 March 1925; 29 January 1925; *Variety,* 4 March 1925.
46. *Variety,* 8 April 1925; Lahr, p. 78.
47. *New York Daily Mirror,* 22 November 1937; playbill, B. F. Keith's Theatre (Washington, D.C.), 25 January 1925.
48. *New York Times,* 10 March 1925; *New York Graphic,* 10 March 1925; *New York Telegraph,* 14 April 1925; *Rocky Mt. News,* undated clipping, Ted and Betty Healey file (MWEZ, n.c. 22,440), N.Y.P.L.-L.C.; *see also* unidentified clipping dated 22 January 1924 (Wichita), Ted and Betty Healey file, N.Y.P.L.-L.C.
49. Unidentified clipping, Ted Healey file, N.Y.P.L.-L.C.; "Healey and His Holligans," *Shadoplay Magazine,* March 1934; Robert Fender, "What's a Stooge? Ted Healey Tells You!," unidentified clipping, Ted Healey file, N.Y.P.L.-L.C.; *New York Times,* 22 December 1937.
50. The male partner and probably the female of Leavitt and Lockwood were burlesque graduates, and their "Before and After Marriage" lyric, said to be reminiscent of burlesque, went over strong at the Riverside; *Variety* thought they would have no trouble on the big time (13 January 1922). Mayo and Devine's work was thought suggestive of the burlesque prima donna and comedian (*Variety,* 1 October 1924); a flirtation bit by Billy Arlington—straight from burlesque—was a big hit at the Palace in 1922 (*Variety,* 15 September 1922). *See also* Joe Marks and Mae Leonard, *Variety,* 23 June 1922, and Hamilton and Hayes, *Variety,* 14 October 1925.
51. "Bert Wheeler, 73, Always a Pixie," *Variety,* 24 January 1968; *Variety,* 19 March 1915.
52. *Billboard,* 4 October 1924; *Variety,* 3 September 1924; 17 September 1924; 13 January 1926; 16 December 1925.
53. *Billboard,* 19 December 1925; *New York Telegraph,* 10 March 1926; "Bert Wheeler, 73, Always a Pixie." *See also* Bert Wheeler file, N.Y.P.L.-L.C.
54. *Variety,* 11 October 1923; 22 July 1925; 3 September 1924; 25 February 1925; 19 August 1925. Yorke and King were a popular low comedy act. Little seems to be recorded about their stage work, but "hoke" was "liberally sprinkled" in their routine, "Old Family Tintypes." They continued performing after big-time vaudeville disappeared; by 1937 they had played the Palace thirty-seven times, a record for nonconsecutive performances (*Billboard,* 19 December 1925; *Variety,* 18 August 1937; *see also* Yorke and King file, N.Y.P.L.-L.C.). *See also* Van and Vernon, *Billboard,* 12 November 1927).
55. *Billboard,* 12 December 1925.
56. *Hartford Courant,* 21 December 1911; *Variety,* 3 August 1917; 5 January 1923; 30 April 1924; *Billboard,* 16 January 1926.
57. *Variety,* 1 December 1922; 25 February 1925.

58. *Variety*, 8 October 1924; 29 October 1924.
59. *Billboard*, 23 January 1926; "Frank Orth, Played in Boston Blackie," unidentified clipping, Frank Orth obit. file, N.Y.P.L.-L.C.; unidentified clipping dated 7 January 1908, Frank Orth file, N.Y.P.L.-L.C.; *Pittsburgh Post*, 31 August 1914; *New York Star*, 6 February 1918; *Variety*, 9 September 1925.
60. *Variety*, 23 September 1925.
61. *Variety*, 23 December 1921. See also William Demarest and Collete, *Variety*, 30 September 1925; O'Donnell and Blair, *Variety*, 17 December 1924.
62. *Variety*, 3 Decmeber 1924.
63. James Madison, *The Comedian*, no. 6 [1930].
64. *Variety*, 15 September 1922.
65. *Variety*, 22 September 1922; *New York Clipper*, 22 December 1920; *Variety*, 1 November 1923. See also Kimberly and Page, *Variety*, 1 April 1925.
66. *Variety*, 15 September 1922; 10 December 1920.
67. James Madison, *The Comedian*, no. 6 [1930].
68. " 'Cuts' All Over East in Keith Acts' Material," *Variety*, 4 February 1925; DiMeglio, p. 51.
69. Csida, p. 217; Laurie, *Vaudeville*, p. 251.
70. Csida, pp. 219–220, 222; *Variety*, 18 November 1925; 11 March 1925.
71. Csida, pp. 213, 156; *Variety*, 12 January 1917.
72. *Moving Picture World*, 15 May 1915; 22 July 1916; "Feature Acts Take Chances Playing in Motion Pictures," *Variety*, 12 February 1915.
73. Spitzer, *The Palace*, pp. 138–139; Lloyd Lewis, "The Deluxe Picture Palace," *New Republic*, 27 March 1929, p. 175; Mowry, p. 55.
74. *Variety*, 16 September 1925.
75. *Variety*, 17 December 1924. The reviewer of a bill at the small-time Broadway Theatre in New York thought the vaudeville acts' difficulty getting applause indicated that the audience was a film crowd (*Variety*, 4 February 1921); another reviewer noted that a crowd at Loew's State—a vaude-film house—came to see the Gloria Swanson film (*Billboard*, 19 September 1925).
76. "Acts Lose Prestige in Neighborhood Stands as Films Gain Firmer Foothold," *Billboard*, 19 September 1925; "Film-Vaude. Policy 'Scrambling' Routes," *Billboard*, 8 October 1927. After purchasing *The Ten Commandments, Don Quixote*, and Chaplin's *Gold Rush*, vaudeville manager Poli announced he was cutting the number of vaudeville acts to accommodate the length and expense of the feature film (*Billboard*, 10 October 1925). That fall a certain group of Keith-Albee vaude-film houses broke all records for gross receipts: all theatres playing the film of *The Ten Commandments* (*Billboard*, 3 October 1925).
77. "Pictures and Vode [sic] Season's New Policy," *Variety*, 3 September 1920; "Supplying Acts to Picture Houses Planned by Agents," *Variety*, 24 September 1920; "Chicago Film House Increasing Vaudeville," *Variety*, 22 September 1922; "Vaudeville Hit By Film Presentations," *Billboard*, 16 January 1926. That same season *Variety* moved the

vaudeville section to the back of the weekly and gave the film houses a slot in the front pages (Spitzer, *The Palace*, p. 132).

78. *Billboard*, 26 December 1925; *Variety*, 18 October 1923; *Billboard*, 30 January 1926; 19 September 1925; *Variety*, 11 November 1925; *Billboard*, 1 October 1927; *Variety*, 2 December 1925; 18 February 1925.

79. E.g., the Palace Theatre in Cleveland in 1922, the Hippodrome conversion in 1923, and the E. F. Albee Theatre in Brooklyn in 1925 with a seating capacity of 3100 (Spitzer, "The Business of Vaudeville," p. 131; *Variety*, 21 January 1925).

80. *Variety*, 28 January 1925. For half-capacity houses, *see* Riverside, *Variety*, 22 September 1922; 29 September 1922; Palace, *Variety*, 7 January 1925; 14 January 1925; Riverside, *Variety*, 10 September 1924.

81. By 1922 the Majestic in Chicago had a five-a-day policy with eight acts and a film (*Variety*, 22 September 1922); in 1923 the Colonial Theatre became a musical comedy house (*Variety*, 25 October 1923). In 1925, Keith's Syracuse, the Albee in Providence, and Keith's Rochester became three-a-day houses; Keith's 105th Street Cleveland, Keith's Columbus, the Royal and the Alhambra in New York became small-time houses with pictures and acts; the Pantages' San Francisco had six acts and film; and the Cincinnati Palace and the St. Louis Opera House also had films (*Variety*, 15 April 1925; 30 September 1925; 14 January 1925; *Billboard*, 19 September 1925; 10 October 1925).

82. *Billboard*, 13 February 1926.

83. *Variety*, 23 December 1925; 28 January 1925; W. A. S. Douglas, "The Passing of Vaudeville," *American Mercury*, 12 (October 1927), p. 191; *Billboard*, 26 December 1925; *Variety*, 18 November 1925.

84. Spitzer, *The Palace*, pp. 143–144.

85. *Billboard*, 10 September 1927. The brand new Albee Theatre in Brooklyn began a three-a-day policy with films; by November 1927 the Orpheum time was down to three weeks, with the Los Angeles and San Francisco Orpheums and the Palace Chicago left. Two weeks later the San Francisco and Los Angeles houses announced they were installing film equipment and would begin a small-time policy soon (*Billboard*, 10 September 1927; 12 November 1927; 10 December 1927).

86. *Billboard*, 10 September 1927; 1 October 1927.

87. *Billboard*, 8 October 1927. The film industry had completely "scrambled" vaudeville routes, bookers reported; the clear preference for feature films over live acts made it impossible to lay out a route.

88. *Variety*, 25 January 1928.

89. Csida, pp. 228–230.

90. Spitzer, *The Palace*, p. 166.

91. Ibid., pp. 194–198, 204–207. On 24 September 1980, Ms. Spitzer graciously shared with me her vaudeville memories, which were useful in preparing this chapter.

Chapter 8

1. *Variety*, 30 March 1927.
2. On various occasions, Burns has given his age at the time of his street corner debut as

three, seven, twelve, and fourteen. On George Burns's early years, *see* George Burns, *Living It Up; or, They Still Love Me in Altoona* (N.Y.: Berkeley, 1978), 17ff., 28ff.; Burns, *I Love Her,* passim,; "Straight Man," *Time* 42 (13 December 1943), 58, 60; *Current Biography 1951,* s.v. "Burns, George; Allen, Gracie"; Davy, pp. 346-348.

3. Leonard Maltin, *Movie Comedy Teams* (N.Y.: New American Library, 1970), p. 163; Davy, p. 347; George Burns, interview with Barbara Walters, televised on "The Barbara Walters Special," 29 May 1979; Wilde, pp. 135-136.

4. *Variety,* 6 October 1922; Burns, *I Love Her,* p. 74; Davy, p. 347.

5. On Gracie Allen's early life, *see* Katharine Best, "Nitwits of the Networks," *Stage,* 1 May 1939, pp. 35-36; "Gracie Allen's Own Story: 'Inside Me' as Told to Jane Kesner Morris," *Woman's Home Companion,* March 1953, passim.; *Current Biography 1951;* Laurence Senelick, "Gracie Allen," in *Notable American Women: A Biographical Dictionary,* eds. Barbara Sicherman, et al. (Cambridge, Ma.: The Belknap Press of Harvard Univ. Press, 1980), pp. 13-14. Senelick's findings reveal Gracie was several years older than she claimed.

6. Davy, p. 354; Best, p. 35; "Gracie Allen's Own Story," p. 112; Burns, *I Love Her,* p. 86; Louella Parsons, "She Talked Her Way into George's Act," *New York Journal-American,* 3 March 1958; unidentified clipping dated 30 August 1932, Burns and Allen file, N.Y.P.L.-L.C.; unidentified clipping dated 25 June 1933, Burns and Allen file, N.Y.P.L.-L.C.

7. Davy, p. 350.

8. *Variety,* 12 April 1923; Davy, p. 350; Burns, *I Love Her,* p. 88.

9. "Gracie Allen's Own Story," p. 112; ABC Biography of George Burns, [1964-65], mimeographed TS., George Burns file, N.Y.P.L.-L.C.; Ed Sullivan, "Hollywood," unidentified clipping dated 4 January 1938, Burns and Allen file, N.Y.P.L.-L.C.

10. *Variety,* 12 April 1923. On Matthews and Ayres, *see Variety,* 4 March 1925.

11. *Variety,* 12 April 1923; 28 June 1923; Davy, p. 349.

12. *Variety,* 1 November 1923; George Burns, "Gracie Allen as I Know Her," *Independent Woman,* 19 (July 1940), 214; Wilde, p. 137; "Gracie Allen's Own Story," p. 112.

13. Wilde, p. 137; Davy, p. 350.

14. *Variety,* 12 April 1923. George said that Gracie was so cute and so petite that from childhood people had always wanted to take care of her (Burns, *I Love Her,* p. 157).

15. Burns, *I Love Her,* p. 89; "Gracie Allen's Own Story," p. 116; Burns, "Gracie Allen As I Know Her," p. 214.

16. Davy, p. 350; "Gracie Allen's Own Story," p. 112; Best, p. 35.

17. Smith, *The Vaudevillians,* p. 173. While Rubin's account does not match Burns and Allen's account of their beginnings (certainly the latter never mentioned Ben Ryan's wife), it is another piece of evidence linking Gracie with the same Ryan who created Harriette Lee's dumbbell. Likewise, *Variety* noted that Burns and Allen had "a gagging routine worked out along the lines popularized by Ryan and Lee" (30 March 1927).

18. On various occasions George claimed the title looked good on lobby posters (Sullivan, "Hollywood," 4 January 1938): that he was paid sixty per cent, Gracie forty per cent (James Street, "The Wizards of Farce," *Movie and Radio Guide,* undated clipping,

George Burns file, N.Y.P.L.-L.C.); and that "nobody knew what that meant, but I did — Gracie was sixty per cent of the act and I was forty per cent" (Wilde, p. 145).

19. Playbill, Fordham Theatre, December 1923, Burns and Allen file, N.Y.P.L.-L.C.; *Brooklyn Eagle,* clipping dated December 1923, Burns and Allen file, N.Y.P.L.-L.C.; Burns, *I Love Her,* p. 93. See Burns, *I Love Her,* p. 96, for another bit in the act.
20. Wilde, p. 136; Davy, p. 346.
21. Burns, *I Love Her,* pp. 93-94; Sullivan, "Hollywood," 4 January 1938.
22. *T.V. Guide,* undated clipping (November), George Burns file, N.Y.P.L.-L.C.
23. Burns, *I Love Her,* pp. 93-94; "Gracie Allen's Own Story," p. 116. On their early lack of success, *see Variety,* 16 November 1938 for quote from a November 1923 review: "Burns and Allen at the Riverside, New York, and not getting very far with their patter."
24. Burns, *I Love Her,* pp. 103-104; *Variety,* 18 March 1925; 25 March 1925.
25. Burns, *I Love Her,* pp. 103-104.
26. Burns, *I Love Her,* p. 106; Wilde, p. 139.
27. Burns, *I Love Her,* p. 103.
28. Burns, *Living It Up,* p. 43; "Gracie Allen's Own Story," p. 116.
29. Burns, *Living It Up,* pp. 43-45; *I Love Her,* pp. 113-116; Davy, p. 345.
30. "Gracie Allen's Own Story," pp. 119, 122; Burns, *Living It Up,* pp. 165-166.
31. "Gracie Allen's Own Story," p. 123; Burns, *I Love Her,* pp. 122-123.
32. *Variety,* 25 August 1926.
33. Burns, *Living It Up,* pp. 46-51.
34. Davy, p. 349.
35. Burns, *Living It Up,* pp. 52-53.
36. Burns, *I Love Her,* p. 147. See also *Variety,* 25 August 1926.
37. *Variety,* 30 March 1927; Burns, *I Love Her,* pp. 128, 134; *Variety,* 25 March 1931.
38. Burns, *I Love Her,* pp. 120-121, 137. A 1932 routine was observed to be brand new material mixed with old (unidentified clipping dated 30 August 1932, Burns and Allen file, N.Y.P.L.-L.C.).
39. George Burns and Gracie Allen (Columbia DB 286-1930), recorded on *A Nostalgia Trip to the Stars, 1920-50,* Monmouth Evergreen 7030, [1973].
40. George Burns and Gracie Allen (1933), recorded on *Great Moments in Show Business,* Epic FLS 15105, 1966.
41. *New York Sun,* 15 May 1933; Burns and Allen, recorded on *Great Moments in Show Business.*
42. E.g., *see New York Evening Post,* 14 July 1933; *New York Times,* 17 June 1934; *New York Evening Post,* 21 January 1935; *New York Herald-Tribune,* 25 January 1936.
43. *Variety,* 25 August 1926; 25 March 1931.
44. "Gracie Allen's Own Story," p. 116.

45. Ibid., p. 123.
46. Unidentified clipping dated 30 August 1932, Burns and Allen file, N.Y.P.L.-L.C. *See* photographs in same file.
47. *See* Gracie's ideas for going into the department store business, and for solving the unemployment of the depression, in Arthur Frank Wertheim, *Radio Comedy* (N.Y.: Oxford Univ. Press, 1979), pp. 204, 206.
48. *Billboard,* 9 April 1927.
49. E.g., the 1933 recording: "Well, Gracie, I'm sorry to hear about your missing brother," says George; "Oh, that's too bad, George, because my brother's missing too," replies Gracie, with all the sympathy anyone could muster.
50. "Gracie Allen Dead; Comedienne Was 58," *New York Times,* 29 August 1964; Wilde, p. 138; Burns, *Living It Up,* p. 58.
51. Davy, p. 353.
52. "Gracie Allen Dead; Comedienne Was 58."
53. Tony Vellela, "George Burns Concert—Shades of Old Vaudeville," *Christian Science Monitor,* 12 March 1973.
54. Wilde, p. 140.
55. E.g., Davy, p. 345; Vellela, "George Burns Concert"; Burns, *I Love Her,* p. 106; Wilde, p. 138; George Burns, interview with Barbara Walters.
56. "Gracie Allen Dead; Comedienne Was 58"; "Gracie Allen's Own Story," pp. 116, 124. "I hear George as if I'd never heard him before," continued Gracie ("Gracie Allen's Own Story," p. 116). Her readings were "instinctive," wrote Burns in *I Love Her* (p. 198).
57. "Gracie's Wit Lives On," *New York World-Telegraph and Sun,* 2 September 1964; Wilde, pp. 143-144; Burns, *I Love Her,* p. 198. *See also* unidentified clipping dated 30 August 1932, Burns and Allen file, N.Y.P.L.-L.C.
58. Like much of Burns and Allen's self-analysis, their discussion of Gracie's reaction to the audience is contradictory. During their early radio days they worked with the lights off, because "if I saw an audience I'd be through. Because there's no audience for me," claimed Gracie ("Gracie Allen's Own Story," p. 123). "Applause meant nothing to Gracie," explained George; "There was a curtain between her and the audience" ("Gracie Allen Dead; Comedienne was 58"). If there were a "curtain" between Gracie and the audience, there'd be no danger of them distracting her; presumably, she worked without taking notice of the audience—but if she did notice them, it made her self-conscious.
59. Burns, *I Love Her,* pp. 88-89.
60. "Gracie Allen Dead; Comedienne was 58"; "Gracie Allen's Own Story," p. 116. Gracie claimed that in real life she bungled things just as she did on the air (Inez Whiteley Foster, "Gracie Isn't So Dumb Off the Air," *Independent Woman,* 26 [October 1947], 293).
61. Davy, p. 354; "George Burns has Starring Role at 79," *Boston Sunday Globe,* 12 May 1975.
62. "Miss Allen and Mr. Burns at Home," *New York Times,* 6 May 1934. "Nobody

believes Gracie is a comedienne," George declared; "They're convinced she's as nutty as a fruitcake" (ibid.). *See also* "Gracie Allen's Own Story," p. 124; Burns, *I Love Her,* p. 133.

63. Davy, p. 345; "Miss Allen and Mr. Burns at Home."
64. "George Burns has Starring Role at 79."
65. Orrin E. Dunlap, Jr., "George Burns and Gracie Allen Discuss the Production of their Broadcast," *New York Times,* 26 January 1936.
66. Burns, *I Love Her,* pp. 154-156; John Maynard, "The Gal Who Knows When to Say No," *Pictorial Review,* 1 November 1953, p. 4.
67. Burns and Allen's public statements reveal only basic facts about the private Gracie: she loved clothes and parties, playing canasta, her children and George. She was extremely shy and modest, insisted George: "She honestly believes she is not an interesting person.... For a woman who likes to be alone, Gracie has landed in a great spot—she never can be" ("Gracie Allen's Own Story," p. 127; Burns, *I Love Her,* pp. 154, 85).
68. When Gracie met fans in public, they always asked her if she was "really like that?" and she always said "of course" and went along with them (Burns, *I Love Her,* p. 155).
69. Filene, pp. 154-158. For typical Dumb Dora scripts of the day (all very imitative of Burns and Allen) *see* the "Luke and Lizzie" and "Sam and Sally" routines in James Madison, *The Radio Humorist,* 1, no. 7 (April 1936), pp. 13-20; no. 8 (May 1936), pp. 15-21; no. 9 (June 1936), pp. 18-20.
70. Ibid., pp. 160-161.
71. Rosen, pp. 173-197.
72. Foster, p. 294; Marie Torre, "Gracie to Turn Intelligent," *New York Herald-Tribune,* 11 February 1958.
73. "Gracie Allen Dead," *New York Journal-American,* 28 August 1964.
74. Burns, "Gracie Allen as I Know Her," p. 214.
75. Burns, "Gracie Allen as I Know Her," p. 198; *New York Evening Post,* 6 February 1936; "Gracie Allen's Own Story," p. 126.
76. See "Candidette," *Time,* 35 (18 March 1940), 36; "Gracie Allen Sure Realist Art Needs Dark Room Technique," *New York World-Tribune,* 24 September 1938.
77. "Gracie Allen's Own Story," p. 123. *See also* Burns, *Living It Up,* p. 57.
78. Maynard, p. 5.
79. Wilde, p. 135.
80. Burns, *Living It Up,* p. 57.
81. Paul Gardner, "Burns and Channing—What Do They See in Each Other," *New York Times,* 15 August 1976.
82. Ibid.
83. Wilde, p. 136.
84. *Variety,* 25 September 1934.
85. George Burns and Gracie Allen, vaudeville routine, performed by George Burns and

Madeline Kahn and televised on "Texaco Presents Bob Hope's All-Star Vaudeville Tribute to the Palace Theatre," 8 January 1978.

86. Davy, p. 354.
87. Maltin, pp. 165, 179; Davy, p. 351; "Gracie Allen Dead; Comedienne Was 58." *See also* unidentified clipping dated 25 June 1933, Burns and Allen file, N.Y.P.L.-L.C.
88. Street, "The Wizards of Farce"; *Current Biography 1951*.
89. "Candidette"; ABC Biography of George Burns; Wilde, p. 131; Burns, *I Love Her*, pp. 147-148; "Gracie Allen's Own Story," pp. 124-126.
90. Maltin, p. 166; Davy, pp. 345, 351; Clara Beranger, "How Dumb is Gracie Allen," *Liberty Magazine*, 1 September 1934; *Variety*, 17 May 1939.
91. Davy, p. 351; Burns, *I Love Her*, p. 144.
92. Maltin, p. 166; Davy, p. 352. *See* Maltin, pp. 166-168, for a sample of the classic Burns and Allen bit in *International House*.
93. *New York American*, 9 November 1935; *Variety*, 25 September 1934; 5 October 1938; George Burns and Gracie Allen, recorded radio script, 26 September 1934, Museum of Broadcasting, New York City; *New York Herald-Tribune*, 11 April 1937.
94. *New York Post*, 25 May 1937; 13 April 1937; *Variety*, 5 October 1938. *See also Variety*, 14 April 1937; *New York Evening Post*, 6 February 1936.
95. *New York Post*, 13 April 1937; *New York Daily News*, 16 July 1936; *New York Post*, 3 May 1938; *Variety*, 3 May 1939.
96. Wertheim, p. 208; Burns, *I Love Her*, pp. 173-174; Wilde, p. 147; *Variety*, 8 September 1943.
97. Burns, *I Love Her*, pp. 173-174. They had dropped the "kissing bit" in 1938 (*New York Post*, 15 February 1938).
98. Wilde, p. 147; *Variety*, 8 September 1943; "Straight Man." George Burns and Gracie Allen (1940), recorded on *When Radio Was King*, Memorabilia MLP-722, 1974, preserves a show featuring Bing Crosby.
99. *Variety*, 14 October 1942.
100. E.g., during the presidential election of 1944, Burns and Allen excitedly entertained a supposed GOP presidential candidate—only to discover he was just a butcher (*Variety*, 23 August 1944). In 1947, with the much-publicized return to long dresses, one script featured Gracie's campaign to keep short dresses around, with George's wholehearted assistance—since he was too tight to buy Gracie a new wardrobe. George masqueraded as a French designer, and echoed in pidgin French Gracie's arguments for short skirts with guest star Edith Head (George Burns and Gracie Allen, recorded radio script, 18 September 1947, Museum of Broadcasting, New York City).
101. The routine was from a 1947 radio program (Charles McHarry, "Curtain Without Tears—She'll Exit Laughing," *New York Daily News*, 7 May 1958).
102. McHarry, "Curtain Without Tears—She'll Exit Laughing."
103. Burns and Allen, recorded on *When Radio Was King*. The laugh-getting was largely George's responsibility also in the 18 September 1947 script, Museum of Broadcasting.
104. *Variety*, 23 August 1944; "Gen. Foods Axes Burns & Allen," *Variety*, 9 March 1949; 16 March 1949.

105. *Variety*, 11 September 1946.
106. Maynard, p. 5; Gilbert Seldes, "Comical Gentlewomen," *Saturday Review*, 36 (2 May 1953), 37. See "Life's One Long Gag," *Weekend Magazine*, clipping dated 1957, Gracie Allen file, N.Y.P.L.-L.C., for samples of the less sophisticated television dialogue.
107. *New York Times*, 17 July 1955.
108. Maynard, p. 4; "Gracie Allen, 58; Cardiac Victim," *Variety*, 2 September 1964.
109. "George and Gracie Set a Zany Pace," *Cue*, 6 January 1951, p. 26. See Burns, *I Love Her*, p. 200; Davy, pp. 354–355.
110. "Burns and Allen," *Newsweek*, 24 June 1957, p. 94; John Crosby, "Radio and Television," *New York Herald-Tribune*, 2 November 1950. George explained, "We never play for the big laugh. If it comes, it comes incidentally. We aim at the small chuckle, but we try to keep it there. We don't end our scenes on a yuk, we taper it off" (Maynard, p. 5).
111. Gardner, "Burns and Channing."
112. McHarry, "Curtain Without Tears—She'll Exit Laughing."

Conclusion

1. "Fanny Beane Destitute"; [*New York Clipper*], 16 September 1882; *Toledo Times*, 3 September 1911; *New York Mirror*, 8 June 1907.
2. "Ted and Betty Healey Born Funmakers," *Chicago American*, clipping dated 1926, Ted and Betty Healey file, N.Y.P.L.-L.C.
3. *South Bend Tribune*, 15 March 1912; *Terre Haute Tribune*, 6 April 1912; *Pittsburgh Leader*, undated clipping, Dooley and Sales file, N.Y.P.L.-L.C.; *Atlanta Constitution*, undated clipping, Dooley and Sales file, N.Y.P.L.-L.C.; unidentified clipping dated 2 January 1912, Dooley and Sales file, N.Y.P.L.-L.C.
4. *Chicago News*, clipping dated [1906], Paul Morton file, N.Y.P.L.-L.C.
5. *Boston Herald*, 25 November 1913; *Variety*, 2 April 1910; *New York Telegraph*, 31 October 1912 "Paul Morton is Real 'Dandy' on Keith's Bill," *Philadelphia North American*, 9 December 1913.
6. *Variety*, 20 February 1914.
7. *New York Telegraph*, undated clipping, Molly Fuller file, Locke Col., N.Y.P.L.-L.C.
8. *Vanity Fair*, 1 December 1900.
9. "Vaudeville's Thorny Road," unidentified clipping dated August 1906, Mr. and Mrs. Sidney Drew file, Locke Col., N.Y.P.L.-L.C.
10. Unidentified clippings, William L. Gibson file, N.Y.P.L.-L.C.
11. Burns, *Living It Up*, p. 61.
12. *New York Mirror*, 9 October 1909.
13. *Toledo Blade*, 12 March 1917.
14. Madison, *James Madison's Weekly Service*, no. 1 [1922].
15. [*New York Dramatic Mirror*,], 13 June 1903.

16. Charles N. Young, "Nora Bayes, Star of The Follies, Became Comedienne by Accident," *Boston Traveller*, 2 January 1909.
17. *Chicago Examiner*, 14 August 1910; *New York Telegraph*, 9 February 1917; *Toledo Blade*, 13 February 1899.
18. "Jokes for Women," *Philadelphia Telegraph*, 19 May 1917.
19. Frederick North Shorey, "The Romance of Mabel and Mike," unidentified clipping dated 14 April 1907, Mabel Hite file, Locke Col. (Ser. 2, NAFR+, 245), N.Y.P.L.-L.C.; it was said on another occasion of a Hite and Donlin sketch that it was "another sketch that glorifies Mike and Mable" (*Indianapolis Star*, 7 December 1909).
20. *New York Times*, 13 January 1918.
21. *Rochester Post*, undated clipping, Maude Fulton file, Locke Col. (405), N.Y.P.L.-L.C.; *Variety*, 20 September 1912; *Denver Times*, 30 April 1913; *Dayton News*, 5 March 1912; *New York Telegraph*, 17 September 1912; "Maude Fulton," obit., *Variety*, 15 November 1950; "Maude Fulton, 69, Stage Star Dead," *New York Times*, 11 November 1950; *New York Telegraph*, 23 July 1920; *Variety*, 17 August 1921.
22. "Family Teams and Their Finances," *Ohio State Journal*, 30 April 1911.
23. Henry James, *The Notebooks of Henry James*, eds. F. O. Matthiessen and Kenneth B. Murdock (N.Y.: Oxford Univ. Press, 1947), p. 47.
24. Gilbert, p. 347.
25. Madison, *The Comedian*, no. 6 [1930].
26. Smith, p. 82.
27. Ibid., pp. 259, 22.
28. Ibid., p. 82.

Bibliography

Theatrical Sources

Books, Articles, Interviews

Armstead-Johnson, Helen. "Blacks in Vaudeville: Broadway and Beyond." In *American Popular Entertainment: Papers and Proceedings of the Conference on the History of American Popular Entertainment*, pp. 77-86. Edited by Myron Matlaw. Westport, Conn.: Greenwood Press, 1979.

Astaire, Fred. *Steps in Time*. New York: Harper and Brothers, 1959.

Avery, Emmett L., et al. *The London Stage, 1660-1800*. 5 parts in 11 vols. Carbondale: Southern Illinois University Press, 1960-1968.

"The Ballet." *Spirit of the Times*, 27 December 1873. Quoted by Barbara M. Barker, "The Dancer vs. the Management in Post-Civil War America," p. 173. *Dance Chronicle*, II, 3 (1978), 172-187.

Beranger, Clara. "How Dumb is Gracie Allen?" *Liberty Magazine*, 1 September 1934.

Best, Katharine. "Nitwits of the Networks." *Stage*, 1 May 1939, pp. 35-37, 49; 15 May 1939, pp. 29-30, 46.

Bogle, Donald. *Toms, Coons, Mulattoes, Mammies and Bucks: An Interpretive History of Blacks in American Films*. New York: Viking, 1973.

Bordman, Gerald. *American Musical Theatre: A Chronicle*. New York: Oxford University Press, 1978.

Burns, George. "Gracie Allen as I Know Her." *Independent Woman*, 19 (July 1940), pp. 198, 214.

⸻. *I Love Her, That's Why*. New York: Simon and Schuster, 1955.

⸻. Interview with Barbara Walters. Televised on "The Barbara Walters Special," 29 May 1979.

⸻. *Living It Up; or, They Still Love Me in Altoona*. New York: Berkeley, 1978.

"Burns and Allen." *Newsweek*, 24 June 1957, p. 94.

Busby, Roy. *British Music Hall: An Illustrated Who's Who from 1850 to the Present Day*. London: Paul Elek, 1976.

"Candidette." *Time*, 35 (18 March 1940), 36.

Castle, Vernon and Irene. *Modern Dancing*. New York: Harper and Brothers, 1914.

Chujoy, Anatole. "The Castles." *The Dance Encyclopedia*. New York: Barnes, 1949.

Csida, Joseph and June. *American Entertainment: A Unique History of Popular Show Business*. New York: Watson-Guptill, 1978.

Current Biography 1951. S.v. "Burns, George; Allen Gracie."

Darnton, Charles. "Tony Pastor, 39 Years a Manager." *New York World*, 26 March 1904.
Davy, Kate. "An Interview with George Burns." *Educational Theatre Journal*, 27 (October 1975), 345-355.
DiMeglio, John E. *Vaudeville U.S.A.* Bowling Green, Ky.: Bowling Green University Popular Press, 1973.
Disher, M. Willson. *Music Hall Parade.* London: B. T. Batsford, 1938.
Distler, Antonie. "The Rise and Fall of the Racial Comics in American Vaudeville." Ph.D. dissertation, Tulane University, 1963.
Douglas, W. A. S. "The Passing of Vaudeville." *American Mercury*, 12 (October 1927), 188-194.
Dunlap, Orrin E. "George Burns and Gracie Allen Discuss the Production of their Broadcast." *New York Times*, 26 January 1936.
Erenberg, Lewis Allen. "Urban Nightlife and the Decline of Victorianism: New York's Restaurants and Cabarets, 1890-1918." Ph.D. dissertation, University of Michigan. 1974.
Ewen, David. *The Story of America's Musical Theatre.* Philadelphia: Chilton Book, 1961.
"Family Teams and Their Finances." *Ohio State Journal*, 30 April 1911.
Fostelle, Al. "The Days of Tony Pastor." *New York Clipper*, 19 December 1914.
Foster, Inez Whiteley. "Gracie Isn't So Dumb Off the Air." *Independent Woman*, October 1947, pp. 292-294.
Gardner, Paul. "Burns and Channing—What Do They See in Each Other?" *New York Times*, 15 August 1976.
"George and Gracie Set a Zany Pace." *Cue*, 6 January 1951, pp. 13, 26.
Gilbert, Douglas. *American Vaudeville.* 1940. Reprint. New York: Dover, 1963.
"Gracie Allen's Own Story: 'Inside Me' As Told to Jane Kesner Morris." *Woman's Home Companion*, March 1953, pp. 40-41, 100+.
Graham, Philip. *Showboats: The History of an American Institution.* Austin: University of Texas Press, 1951.
Grau, Robert. *Forty Years of Observations of Music and Drama.* New York: Broadway Publishing Co., 1909.
Green, Al, and Laurie, Joe, Jr. *Show Biz from Vaude to Video.* New York: Henry Holt, 1951.
Grimsted, David. *Melodrama Unveiled: American Theatre and Culture, 1800-1850.* Chicago: University of Chicago Press, 1968.
Grinde, Nick. "Where's Vaudeville At?" *Saturday Evening Post*, 11 January 1930, pp. 44-46, 158+.
"Healey and His Hooligans." *Shadoplay Magazine*, March 1934.
Henderson, Mary R. *The City and the Theatre: New York Playhouses from Bowling Green to Times Square.* Clifton, N.J.: James T. White, 1973.
Hewitt, Bernard. *Theatre U.S.A.: 1665-1957.* New York: McGraw-Hill, 1959.
Hodge, Francis. *Yankee Theatre: The Image of America on the Stage, 1825-1850.* Austin: University of Texas Press, 1964.
Johnson, James Weldon. *Black Manhattan.* New York: Atheneum, 1968.
"Jokes for Women." *Philadelphia Telegraph*, 19 May 1917.
Kahn, E. J., Jr. *The Merry Partners: The Age and Stage of Harrigan and Hart.* New York: Random House, 1955.
Lahr, John. *Notes of a Cowardly Lion: The Biography of Bert Lahr.* New York: Knopf, 1969.
Laurie, Joe, Jr. "The Early Days of Vaudeville." *American Mercury*, 47 (February 1946), 232-236.
―――. *Vaudeville: From the Honky-tonks to the Palace.* New York: Henry Holt, 1953.
Lea, K[atherine] M. *Italian Popular Comedy: A Study in the Commedia Dell'Arte, 1560-1620;*

With Special Reference to the English Stage. 2 vols. 1934. Reprint. New York: Russell and Russell, 1962.

Leathers, Victor. *British Entertainers in France.* Toronto: University of Toronto Press, 1959.

Leavitt, Michael B. *Fifty Years in Theatrical Management.* New York: Broadway Publishing Co., 1912.

Leslie, Amy. "Ross." *Some Players,* 1899, p. 589.

Lewis, Lloyd. "The Deluxe Picture Palace." *New Republic,* 27 March 1929, p. 175.

"Life of Tony Pastor." *Tony Pastor's Songs.* New York, 1891. Quoted by Parker R. Zeller, "Tony Pastor: Manager and Impresario of the America Stage," p. 85. Ph.D. dissertation, University of Iowa, 1964.

McAfee, Helen. *Pepys on the Restoration Stage.* 1916. Reprint. New York: Blom, 1966.

McCarthy, Albert. *The Dance Band Era: The Dancing Decades from Ragtime to Swing, 1910-1950.* Philadelphia: Chilton Book, 1971.

McHarry, Charles. "Curtain Without Tears—She'll Exit Laughing." *New York Daily News,* 7 May 1958.

McLean, Albert F., Jr. *American Vaudeville as Ritual.* Lexington, Ky.: University of Kentucky Press, 1965.

MacQueen-Pope, W. *The Melody Lingers On.* London: W. H. Allen, 1950.

Maltin, Leonard. *Movie Comedy Teams.* New York: New American Library, 1970.

Maynard, John. "The Gal Who Knows When to Say No." *Pictorial Review,* 1 November 1953, pp. 4-5.

"Miss Allen and Mr. Burns at Home." *New York Times,* 6 May 1934.

Moody, Richard. *America Takes the Stage: Romanticism in American Drama and Theatre, 1750-1900.* Bloomington: Indiana University Press, 1955.

Mordden, Ethan. *Better Foot Forward: The History of the American Theatre.* New York: Crossman, 1976.

Morehouse, Ward. *George M. Cohan: Prince of the American Theatre.* New York: J. B. Lippincott, 1943.

Morton, Sam. "When Women Were Prey." *Variety,* 12 December 1908, p. 41.

Odell, George C. D. *Annals of the New York Stage.* 15 vols. New York: Columbia University Press, 1927-1945.

"Ol' Man Rooney...He Just Keeps Rolling Along." *Cue,* 14 July 1951.

Page, Brett. *Writing for Vaudeville.* Springfield, Ma.: The Home Correspondence School, 1915.

Parsons, Louella. "She Talked Her Way into George's Act." *New York Journal-American,* 3 March 1958.

Pastor, Tony. "Vaudeville in its Infancy." *Toledo Blade,* 19 February 1898.

Rosenfeld, Sybil. *Strolling Players and Drama in the Provinces, 1660-1765.* Cambridge: Cambridge University Press, 1939.

———. *The Theatre of the London Fairs in the Eighteenth Century.* Cambridge: Cambridge University Press, 1960.

Ross, Charles J. "Travesty Then and Now." *Variety,* 23 December 1911.

———. "The Building and Repairing of Vaudeville Sketches." *New York Dramatic Mirror,* 5 July 1911.

Samuels, Charles and Louise. *Once Upon a Stage: The Merry World of Vaudeville.* New York: Dodd, Mead, 1974.

Schneider, Gretchen. "Gabriel Ravel and the Martinetti Family: The Popularity of Pantomime in 1855." In *American Popular Entertainment: Papers and Proceedings of the Conference on the History of American Popular Entertainment,* pp. 241-58. Edited by Myron Matlaw. Westport, Conn.: Greenwood Press, 1979.

Scott, Harold. *The Early Doors: Origins of the Music Hall.* London: Nicholson and Watson, 1946.

Scott, Virginia. "The Jeu and the Role: Analysis of the Appeals of the Italian Comedy in France in the Time of Arlequin-Dominique." In *Western Popular Theatre,* pp. 1-27. Edited by David Mayer and Kenneth Richards. London: Methuen, 1977.

Seldes, Gilbert. "Comical Gentlewomen." *Saturday Review,* 36 (2 May 1953), p. 37.

―――. *The 7 Lively Arts.* Second edition. New York: Sagamore Press, 1957.

Senelick, Laurence. "George L. Fox and Bowery Pantomime." In *American Popular Entertainment: Papers and Proceedings of the Conference on the History of American Popular Entertainment,* pp. 97-109. Edited by Myron Matlaw. Westport, Conn.: Greenwood Press, 1979.

―――. "Gracie Allen." In *Notable American Women: A Biographical Dictionary,* pp. 13-14. Edited by Barbara Sicherman, et al. Cambridge, Ma.: The Belknap Press of Harvard University Press, 1980.

―――. "Variety into Vaudeville, The Process Observed in Two Manuscript Gagbooks." *Theatre Survey,* 19 (May 1978), 1-15.

Smith, Bill. *The Vaudevillians.* New York: Macmillan, 1976.

Smythe, Charles B. "The Naked Truth." *New York Herald,* 19 November 1866. Quoted by Barbara M. Barker, "The Ballet Girl: Graceful, Ungraceful, or Disgraceful," p. 20. Unpublished paper.

Sobel, Bernard. *A Pictorial History of Burlesque.* New York: Putnam, 1956.

Spitzer, Marian. "The Business of Vaudeville." *Saturday Evening Post,* 24 May 1924, pp. 18-19, 30+.

―――. Interview with author. New York City, 24 September 1980.

―――. *The Palace.* New York: Atheneum, 1969.

"Stage Stories by Late Tony Pastor." *Toledo News Bee,* 28 August 1908.

"Straight Man." *Time,* 42 (13 December 1943), 58, 60.

"Tally One More Birthday for 'Tony' Pastor as a Manager." *New York Morning Telegraph,* 23 March 1904.

Toll, Robert C. *Blacking Up: The Minstrel Show in Nineteenth-Century America.* New York: Oxford University Press, 1974.

―――. *On With the Show: The First Century of American Show Business.* New York: Oxford University Press, 1976.

"Tony Pastor Records the Origin of American 'Vaudeville.'" *Variety,* 15 December 1906, pp. 17, 49.

Torre, Marie. "Gracie to Turn Intelligent." *New York Herald-Tribune,* 11 February 1958.

Truzzi, Marcello. "Circus and Side Shows." In *American Popular Entertainment: Papers and Proceedings of the Conference on History of American Popular Entertainment,* pp. 175-185. Edited by Myron Matlaw. Westport, Conn.: Greenwood Press, 1979.

Tucker, Sophie. *Some of these Days: An Autobiography.* London: Hammond, 1948.

Vellela, Tony. "George Burns Concert—Shades of Old Vaudeville." *Christian Science Monitor,* 12 March 1973.

Wertheim, Arthur Frank. *Radio Comedy.* New York: Oxford University Press, 1979.

Wilde, Larry. *The Great Comedians Talk About Comedy.* New York: Citadel Press, 1968.

W. J. P. "Tony Pastor at 444." *New York Herald,* 26 December 1921.

Zellers, Parker R. "The Cradle of Variety: The Concert Saloon." *Educational Theatre Journal,* 20 (December 1968), 578-85.

―――. "Tony Pastor: Manager and Impresario of the American Stage." Ph.D. dissertation, University of Iowa, 1964.

Songs, Scripts, Recordings

"Because You Vos So Dutch." *New York Clipper,* 26 September 1874, p. 204.
"Boys of the Period." *New York Clipper*, 9 January 1875, p. 324.
Burns, George, and Allen, Gracie. Columbia DB 286–1930. Recorded on *A Nostalgia Trip to the Stars, 1920–50.* Monmouth Evergreen 7030, [1973].
———. 1933. Recorded on *Great Moments in Show Business.* Epic FLS 15105, 1966.
———. 1940. Recorded on *When Radio Was King.* Memorabilia MLP–722, 1974.
———. Recorded Radio Script, 26 September 1934. Museum of Broadcasting, New York City.
———. Recorded Radio Script, 18 September 1947. Museum of Broadcasting, New York City.
———. Vaudeville Routine. Performed by George Burns and Madeline Kahn. Televised on "Texaco Presents Bob Hope's All-Star Vaudeville Tribute to the Palace Theatre," 8 January 1978.
Cohan, Jerry. Cohan Family Repertoire-Book. Harvard Theatre Collection.
"Dere's Somedings de Matter Mit Me." *New York Clipper*, 30 August 1873.
"Deutschland Band." *New York Clipper*, 27 March 1875.
"Don't Go Away, Mollie Darling." *New York Clipper*, 22 November 1873, p. 268.
"Dot Vas Played Ouat." *New York Clipper*, 8 November 1873, p. 252.
"Dublin," *New York Clipper,* 15 August 1874, p. 157.
"Dutch as Sauerkraut." *New York Clipper*, 30 January 1875, p. 348.
"The Elopement." *New York Clipper*, 3 April 1875, p. 4.
"Flirding in the Dark mit Lena." *New York Clipper*, 8 February 1879, p. 364.
"The German Emigrants." *New York Clipper*, 2 August 1873.
Gleason, James. *The Shannons of Broadway.* New York: Samuel French, 1927.
"Goot-pye, Katrina." *New York Clipper*, 14 February 1874, p. 364.
"Hans and Lena." *New York Clipper*, 10 January 1874, p. 325.
"The Irish Heart." *New York Clipper*, 24 May 1873, p. 60.
"I Vonder Vat's Her Name." *New York Clipper*, 28 March 1874, p. 412.
"The King of Song-and-Dance." *New York Clipper*, 8 November 1873, p. 252.
"The Limerick Pair." *New York Clipper*, 2 January 1875, p. 316.
Loring, Frederick. "Two Song-and-Dance Men." *New York Clipper*, 22 October 1870, p. 225.
McNally, William. *McNally's Bulletin No. 11.* New York: William McNally, 1925.
Madison, James. *The Comedian,* no. 6 [1930].
———. *James Madison's Weekly Radio Service,* 21 December 1935.
———. *James Madison's Weekly Service,* no. 1 [1922].
———. *Madison's Budget,* no. 19 [1926].
———. *The Radio Humorist,* 1, no. 7 (April 1936).
———. *The Radio Humorist,* 1, no. 8 (May 1936).
———. *The Radio Humorist,* 1, no. 9 (June 1936).
"Tell Me, I Pray, Would You?" *New York Clipper*, 27 April 1875, p. 380.
"The Two Emigrants." *New York Clipper*, 24 May 1873, p. 60.
"Uncle William." *New York Clipper*, 9 January 1875.
"When You and I Were Green." *New York Clipper*, 7 September 1878, p. 188.
Wylie, Billy. Gagbook. Tony Pastor file, New York Public Library at Lincoln Center.

Miscellaneous Ephemera

ABC Biography of George Burns, [1964–65]. Mimeographed typescript. George Burns file, New York Public Library at Lincoln Center.

Burt, Sadie. Memoir of George Whiting. Unpublished typescript. New York Public Library at Lincoln Center.
"List of Original Scripts from the Tony Pastor Opera House, Accompanying the Music, Orchestrations, and Clippings From His Music Hall." New York Public Library at Lincoln Center.
Lyons, Jimmy, and Carlton, Sam. "The Rooneys." Unpublished typescript. Theatre Collection, Humanities Research Center, University of Texas at Austin.
"Pat Rooney Autobiography." Unpublished typescript. Theatre Collection, Humanities Research Center, University of Texas at Austin.
Playbill, B. F. Keith's Theatre. N.p., 13 March 1916.
Playbill, B. F. Keith's Theatre. Washington, D.C., 25 January 1925.
Playbill, Fordham Theatre. New York, December 1923. Burns and Allen file, New York Public Library at Lincoln Center.
Playbill, Morris Brothers and Trowbridge's Opera House. N.p., 13 June 1866.
Playbill, Tivoli Theatre. South Africa, 2 January 1905.
Playbill, Tony Pastor's Combination. Newark, N.J., 15 March 1865.
Playbill, Tony Pastor's Opera House. New York, 4 August 1865.
Playbill, Tony Pastor's Troupe. N.p., n.d., Tony Pastor file, New York Public Library at Lincoln Center.

Clipping Files and Scrapbooks, New York Public Library at Lincoln Center
Adelaide and Hughes, [Adelaide Dickey and J. J.]
Adelaide and Hughes, scrapbook (MWEZ, n.c. 4423)
Astaire, Fred and Adele
Barnes, T. Roy (MWEZ, n.c. 4495)
Barnes, T. Roy, scrapbook (MWEZ, n.c. 23,036)
Beane, Fanny
Bennett, Johnstone
Bennett Johnstone, Player's Collection
Bloom, Lew
Brendel, El
Bronson, Aileen
Burns, George
Burns and Allen, [George and Gracie]
Castle, Vernon and Irene
Chip and Marble, [Sam and Mary], Locke Collection (Ser. 2, NAFR+)
Clark and Bergman, [Gladys and Henry]
Cohan, Jerry
Connelly, Jane and Erwin, Locke Collection (Ser. 3, vol. 317)
Connolly, Dolly, Locke Collection (Ser. 3, vol. 317)
Cotton, Idalene
Cotton and Long, [Nick and Idalene], Locke Collection
Cressy, Will, Locke Collection
Cressy and Dayne, [Will and Blanche]
Dehaven, Carter
Delano, Jeppe
Dolan and Lenhaar, [James and Ida]
Dooley and Sales, [Jim and Corrine]
Dooley Family
Drew, Mr. and Mrs. Sidney (first wife), Locke Collection

Fielding, Maggie
Florence, William J.
Fuller, Molly, Locke Collection
Fulton, Maude
Fulton, Maude, Locke Collection (405)
Genaro, Dave
Gibson, William
Hart, Joe
Healey, John
Healey, Ted
Healey, Ted and Betty (MWEZ, n.c. 22,440)
Hines, William E.
Hite, Mabel, Locke Collection (711)
Hite, Mabel, Locke Collection (Ser. 2, NAFR+, 245)
Howard, Bert
Hyams and McIntyre, [John and Leila]
Johnson and Dean, [Charlie and Dora]
Kalisz, Armand, Locke Collection
Kalmar and Brown, [Bert and Jessie], Locke Collection
Lahr, Bert, scrapbook (MWEZ, n.c. 22530)
Lauri Family
Mason, John and Marion, Locke Collection (NAFR+, 339)
Maurice and Walton, [Maurice and Florence Walton]
Mayhew, Stella, Locke Collection (MWEZ, n.c. 23,037)
Melville, Mae, Locke Collection
Montgomery and Moore, [William and Florence]
Moore, Victor, Locke Collection
Moore and Littlefield, [Victor and Emma]
Morton, Paul
Morton, Sam and Kitty, Locke Collection
Murphy, Mark, Locke Collection
Murphy, Will H., Locke Collection
Nicholson, Paul, Locke Collection
Nobles, Milton and Dolly, Locke Collection
Norton, Angie, Locke Collection
Norton and Lee, [Ruby and Sammy], Locke Collection
Orth, Frank
Orth, Frank, Obituary file
Paige-Petrova, Locke Collection, Ser. 2
Pastor, Tony
Reynolds and Donegan, [Earl and Nellie]
Rock, William
Rooney, Pat, II
Rooney, Pat, Jr. (II)
Rooney and Bent, [Pat and Marian]
Rooney and Bent, [Pat and Marian], Locke Collection
Ross, Charles and Mabel, Locke Collection
Ryan and Lee, [Ben and Harriette] (MWEZ+, n.c. 9109.)
Ryan and Richfield, [Thomas J. and Mary], Locke Collection
Sidman, Arthur

Swain, Carrie
Suratt, Valeska, Locke Collection
Suratt, Valeska, scrapbook (MWEZ, n.c. 1906)
Ten Broeck, May
Thornton, James
Vaudeville: programmes, U.S.
Vickers, Maggie
Williams, Barney
Williams, Eva
Williams, Herbert
Wren, Martha
Yorke and King, [Chic and Rose]

Newspapers and Weeklies (news items and reviews)
Advertiser
Atlanta Constitution
Baltimore American
Baltimore Sun
Billboard
Boston Globe
Boston Herald
Boston Journal
Boston Transcript
Boston Traveller
Brooklyn Citizen
Brooklyn Eagle (*Brooklyn Daily Eagle*)
Buffalo Commercial
Buffalo Enquirer
Buffalo Times
The Cast (New York)
Chicago American
Chicago Examiner
Chicago Herald
Chicago Journal
Chicago News
Chicago Record
Chicago Record-Herald
Chicago Tribune
Cincinnati Commercial
Cincinnati Commercial Tribune
Cincinnati Enquirer
Cleveland Leader
Cleveland Morning Telegraph
Cleveland News
Cleveland Plain Dealer
Cleveland Town Topics
Cleveland World
Daily Press Knickerbocker and Albany Morning Express
Dayton News
Denver Times

Detroit Free Press
Detroit Journal
Detroit News
Duluth Herald
Erie Herald
Evening Wisconsin
Grand Rapids Press
Harper's Weekly
Hartford Courant
Illustrated American
Indianapolis Sentinel
Indianapolis Star (*Indianapolis Morning Star*)
Indianapolis Sun
Kansas City Journal
Kansas City Post
Kansas City Star
Kansas City Times
Los Angeles Daily Times
Los Angeles Examiner
Louisville Courier Journal
Louisville Herald
Louisville Times
Milwaukee News
Milwaukee Sentinel
Minneapolis Journal
Montreal Gazette
Newark Eagle
New York American
New York Clipper
New York Commercial
New York Commercial Advertiser
New York Dramatic Mirror
New York Dramatic News
New York Figaro
New York Graphic
New York Herald
New York Herald-Tribune
New York Journal (*New York Evening Journal*)
New York Journal-American
New York Mirror (*New York Daily Mirror*)
New York News (*New York Daily News*)
New York Post (*New York Evening Post*)
New York Review
New York Star
New York Sun (*New York Evening Sun*)
New York Telegraph (*New York Morning Telegraph*)
New York Times
New York Tribune
New York World
New York World-Telegram

New York World-Telegraph and Sun
Opinion
Philadelphia Inquirer
Philadelphia Ledger
Philadelphia North American
Philadelphia Record
Philadelphia Telegraph
Philadelphia Times
Philadelphia Tribune Journal
Pittsburgh Gazette
Pittsburgh Leader
Pittsburgh Post
Portland Daily Press
The Prompter (Philadelphia)
Providence News
Rochester Times
Rocky Mt. News
San Francisco Call
San Francisco Chronicle
Seattle Daily Times
South Bend Tribune
Spirit of the Times
Sporting Times and Theatrical News
St. Louis Globe Democrat
St. Paul Dispatch
Syracuse Post
Terre Haute Tribune
The Theatre: A Weekly Journal of the Stage
Times Square Daily
Toledo Blade
Toledo Times
Vancouver News
Vanity Fair
Variety
Washington Star
Winnipeg Telegram

II. Sociological Sources

Addams, Jane. "The Subtle Problems of Charity." *Atlantic Monthly,* 1899. Quoted by Gunther Barth, *City People: The Rise of Modern City Culture in Nineteenth-Century America,* p. 141. New York: Oxford University Press, 1980.

Allen, Frederick. *The Big Change: America Transforms Itself, 1900–1950.* New York: Harper and Brothers, 1952.

Anthony, Susan B., and Harper, Ida Husted. *The History of Woman Suffrage.* Vol. 4. Rochester, N.Y.: Susan B. Anthony, 1902.

Barth, Gunther. *City People: The Rise of Modern City Culture in Nineteenth-Century America.* New York: Oxford University Press, 1980.

Becker, Stephen. *Comic Art in America.* New York: Simon and Schuster, 1959.

Billigmeier, Robert Henry. *Americans from Germany: A Study in Cultural Diversity.* Minorities in American Life Series. Belmont, Calif.: Wadsworth, 1974.

Brooks, Van Wyck. *The Confident Years: 1885–1915.* New York: E. P. Dutton, 1955.

Browne, Junius Henri. *The Great Metropolis: A Mirror of New York.* Hartford, Conn.: American Publishing Co., 1869.

Buchele, Karl. *Land und Volk der Vereinigten Staaten von Nord Amerika.* Stuttgart, 1865. Quoted by Richard O'Connor, *The German-Americans: An Informal History,* pp. 113-15. Boston: Little, Brown, 1968.

Chevalier, Michael. *Society, Manners and Politics in the United States.* Boston, 1839. Quoted by Foster Rhea Dulles, *America Learns to Play: A History of Popular Recreation, 1607-1940,* p. 85. 1940. Reprint. Gloucester, Ma.: Peter Smith, 1959.

Cole, Arthur Charles. *The Irrepressible Conflict, 1850-1865.* A History of American Life, vol. 7. New York: Macmillan, 1934.

Conzen, Kathleen Neils. *Immigrant Milwaukee, 1836-1860: Accommodation and Community in a Frontier City.* Cambridge, Ma.: Harvard University Press, 1976.

Coppa, Frank, and Curran, Thomas. *The Immigrant Experience in America.* Boston: Twayne, 1976.

Dulles, Foster Rhea. *America Learns to Play: A History of Popular Recreation, 1607-1940.* Reprint. Gloucester, Ma.: Peter Smith, 1959.

Dunne, Finley Peter. "Molly Donahue, Who Lives Across the Street from Mr. Dooley." *Ladies' Home Journal,* December 1899, p. 6.

──────. "On the New Woman." In *Mr. Dooley in Peace and War,* pp. 136-140. Boston: Small and Maynard, 1899.

Durant, Will. "The Modern Woman." *Century Magazine,* 113 (February 1927), 422.

Ernst, Robert. *Immigrant Life in New York City, 1825-1863.* New York: King's Crown Press, 1949.

Evelyn, John. *The Diary of John Evelyn.* Edited by E. S. De Beer. 6 vols. Oxford: Clarendon Press, 1955.

Fass, Paula S. *The Damned and the Beautiful: American Youth in the 1920s.* New York: Oxford University Press, 1977.

Faulkner, Harold. *The Quest for Social Justice, 1898-1914.* A History of American Life, vol. 10. New York: Macmillan, 1931.

Filene, Peter. *Him/Her/Self.* New York: New American Library, 1976.

Finck, Henry. "Are Womanly Women Doomed?" *The Independent,* 53 (January 1901), 269-270.

Fish, Carl. *The Rise of the Common Man, 1830-1850.* A History of American Life, vol. 6. New York: Macmillan, 1950.

Flexnor, Eleanor. *Century of Struggle: The Woman's Rights Movement in the United States.* Revised Edition. Cambridge, Ma.: Belknap Press of Harvard University Press, 1975.

Funnell, Charles. *By the Beautiful Sea: The Rise and the High Times of that Great American Resort, Atlantic City.* New York: Knopf, 1975.

Garrison, Dee. "The Tender Technicians: The Feminization of Public Librarianship, 1876-1905." In *Clio's Consciousness Raised: New Perspectives on the History of Women,* pp. 158-78. Edited by Mary S. Hartman and Lois Banner. New York: Harper Colophon, 1974.

Gelfant, Blanche. *American City Novel.* Second edition. Norman, Okla.: University of Oklahoma Press, 1970.

Gist, Noel P., and Halbert, L. A. *Urban Society.* Fourth edition. New York: Thomas Y. Crowell, 1956.

Gordon, Michael. *American Family: Past, Present and Future.* New York: Random House, 1978.

Gorsline, Douglas. *What People Wore: A Visual History of Dress from Ancient Times to Twentieth-Century America.* New York: Viking, 1952.

Greer, Howard. "In Real Bohemia." *Theatre Magazine,* January 1920, pp. 22, 24.

Handlin, Oscar. *The Uprooted.* Second enlarged edition. New York: Little, Brown, 1973.
Hansen, Marcus Lee. *The Atlantic Migration.* Cambridge, Ma.: Harvard University Press, 1940.
Harris, Charles T. *Memories of Manhattan in the Sixties and Seventies.* New York: Derrydale Press, 1928.
Hart, James D. *The Popular Book: A History of America's Literary Taste.* New York: Oxford University Press, 1950.
Higham, John. *Strangers in the Land: Patterns of American Nativism, 1860–1920.* New York: Atheneum, 1963.
Hofstadter, Richard. *The Age of Reform: From Bryan to F.D.R.* New York: Knopf, 1968.
Horn, Maurice, editor. *The World Encyclopedia of Comics.* New York: Chelsea House, 1976.
Illustrated New York: The Metropolis of To-Day. New York: International Publishing Co., 1888.
James, Henry. *The Notebooks of Henry James.* Edited by F. O. Matthiessen and Kenneth B. Murdock. New York: Oxford University Press, 1947.
Jones, Maldwyn A. *Destination America.* New York: Holt, Rinehardt, and Winston, 1976.
Kasson, John. *Amusing the Million: Coney Island at the Turn of the Century.* New York: Hill and Wang, 1978.
Kennedy, David. *Birth Control in America: The Career of Margaret Sanger.* New Haven: Yale University Press, 1970.
Kessner, Thomas. *The Golden Door: Italian and Jewish Immigrant Mobility in New York City, 1880–1915.* New York: Oxford University Press, 1977.
Kraditor, Aileen S. *The Ideas of the Woman Suffrage Movement, 1890–1920.* 1965. Reprint. New York: Anchor Books, 1971.
The Ladies' Guide and City Directory for Shopping, Travel, Amusements, Etc. in the City of New York. New York: G. P. Putnam's Sons, 1885.
Leuchtenburg, William E. *The Perils of Prosperity, 1914–1932.* Chicago History of American Civilization Series. Chicago: University of Chicago Press, 1958.
McCabe, James Dabney, Jr. *Lights and Shadows of New York Life; or, The Sights and Sensations of the Great City.* Philadelphia: National Publishing Co., 1872.
———. *New York by Sunlight and Gaslight.* N.p.: 1882.
———. [Edward Winslow Martin]. *The Secrets of the Great City: A Work Descriptive of the Virtues and the Vices, the Mysteries, Miseries and Crimes of New York City.* Philadelphia: Jones, Brothers, and Co., 1868.
McGovern, James. "The American Woman's Pre-World War I Freedom in Manners and Morals." *Journal of American History,* 55 (September 1968), 315–333.
Marks, Harry H. *Small Change; or, Lights and Shades of New York.* New York: Standard Publishing Co., 1882.
May, Lary. *Screening Out the Past: The Birth of Mass Culture and the Motion Picture Industry.* New York: Oxford University Press, 1980.
Meyer, Donald. *The Positive Thinkers: A Study of the American Quest for Health, Wealth and Personal Power from Mary Baker Eddy to Norman Vincent Peale.* New York: Doubleday, 1965.
Mills, C. Wright. *White Collar: The American Middle Class.* New York: Oxford University Press, 1951.
More, Louise B. *Wage-Earners' Budgets: A Study of Standards and Cost of Living in New York City.* New York: Holt, 1907.
Mowry, George E., editor. *The Twenties: Fords, Flappers, and Fanatics.* Englewood Cliffs, N.J.: Prentice-Hall, 1963.

Nevins, Allan. *The Emergence of Modern America, 1865-1878*. A History of American Life, vol. 8. New York: Macmillan, 1927.

The New York Press. *The Night Side of New York: A Picture of the Great Metropolis After Nightfall*. New York: J. C. Haney and Co., 1866.

Nye, Russell. *The Unembarrassed Muse: The Popular Arts in America*. New York: Dial Press, 1970.

O'Connor, Richard. *The German-Americans: An Informal History*. Boston: Little, Brown, 1968.

O'Faolain, Julia, and Martines, Lauro, editors. *Not in God's Image*. New York: Harper and Row, 1973.

O'Neill, William L. *Everyone Was Brave: A History of Feminism in America*. Chicago: Quadrangle Books, 1969.

Pivar, David J. *Purity Crusade: Sexuality Morality and Social Control, 1868-1900*. Westport, Conn.: Greenwood Press, 1973.

Riegel, Robert. *American Women: A Story of Social Change*. Cranbury, N.J.: Fairleigh-Dickinson University Press, 1970.

Rippley, La Vern J. *The German Americans*. Boston: Twayne, 1976.

Rust, Frances. *Dance in Society*. London: Routledge and Kegan Paul, 1969.

Schaffer, Ronald. "The New York City Woman Suffrage Party, 1909-1919." *New York History*, 43 (July 1962), 268-87.

Schlesinger, Arthur Meier. *The Rise of Modern America, 1865-1951*. New York: Macmillan, 1951.

―――――. *The Rise of the City, 1878-1898*. A History of American Life, vol. 10. New York: Macmillan, 1933.

Schmitt, Peter. *Back to Nature: The Arcadian Myth in Urban America*. New York: Oxford University Press, 1969.

Shannon, William. *The American Irish*. Revised edition. New York: Macmillan, 1966.

Sinclair, Andrew. *The Better Half: The Emancipation of the American Woman*. New York: Harper Torchbooks, 1975.

―――――. *Era of Excess: A Social History of the Prohibition Movement*. New York: Harper Colophon, 1964.

Smith, Matthew Hale. *Sunshine and Shadow in New York*. Hartford, Conn.: J. B. Burr, 1869.

Smith, Matthew Hale; Williams, Henry L.; and Bayard, Ralph, editors. *Wonders of a Great City: or the Sights, Secrets and Sins of New York*. Chicago: People Publishing Co., 1887.

Sochen, June. *Herstory: A Woman's View of American History*. New York: Alfred Publishing, 1974.

Strong, Josiah. "Why the City Grows." In *The Twentieth Century City*. New York, 1898. Reprinted in *City Life, 1865-1900: Views of Urban America*, pp. 15-17. Edited by Ann Cook, Marilyn Gittell, and Herb Mack. New York: Praeger, 1973.

Sullivan, Mark. *Our Times: The United States, 1900-1925*. 6 vols. New York: Charles Scribner's Sons, 1930.

The Sun's Guide to New York. New York: R. Wayne Wilson, 1892.

Thompson, Frederic. "Amusing the Million." *Everybody's Magazine*, 19 (September 1908), pp. 378-387.

Tomsich, John. *A Genteel Endeavor: American Culture and Politics in the Gilded Age*. Stanford, Calif.: Stanford University Press, 1971.

Twain, Mark. *Mark Twain's Travels with Mr. Brown*. New York, 1940. Quoted by Bayard Still, *Mirror for Gotham: New York as Seen by Contemporaries from Dutch Days to the Present*, p. 176. New York: New York University Press, 1956.

Valentine, F. C. [Heinrich Oscar von Karlstein]. *Gotham and the Gothamites*. London: Field and Tuer, 1887.
Van Dyke, John. *The New New York*. New York: Macmillan, 1909.
Welter, Barbara. "The Feminization of American Religion, 1800–1860." In *Clio's Consciousness Raised: New Perspectives on the History of Women,* pp. 137–157. Edited by Mary S. Hartman and Lois Banner. New York: Harper Colophon, 1974.
Wiebe, Robert. *The Search for Order, 1877–1920*. New York: Hill and Wang, 1967.
Williams, Jessie Lynch. *New York Sketches*. New York: Charles Scribner's Sons, 1902.
Wittke, Carl. *The Irish in America*. 1956. Reprint. New York: Russell and Russell, 1970.
——————. *We Who Built America: The Saga of the Immigrant*. Revised edition. [Cleveland]: Case Western Reserve University, 1964.
Wolff, M. A. *Sketches of Lowly Life in a Great City*. Edited by Joseph Henius. New York: G. P. Putnam's Sons, 1899.
Wright, Mabel Osgood. *My New York*. New York: Macmillan, 1926.

Index

Adams, & Linton, 42
Adelaide & Hughes, 241
Allens, 42
Amos and Andy, 5
Anthony, Susan, B., 53
Ashcroft, and Morton, 19
Astaire, Fred, 203
Aston, Anthony, 9-10
Austin, Charles and Carrie, 25

Bara, Theda, 133
Barnum, P.T., 11, 49, 76
Barrymore, Lionel, 124, 126
Bayes, Nora, 133-35, 158
Beane, Fannie, 237
Beane, Fannie and Gilday, Charles, 42, 63, 69 71, 72
Bennett and Gardener, 42, 43
Bennett, Johnstone and Kent, S. Miller, 82
Benny, Jack, 205, 221
Berlin, Irving, 171, 190
Bernhardt, Sarah, 158
Big Broadcast of 1932, 231, 232
Black Crook, 22
Black Fawns, 22
Blaisdell, William and Levine, Clara, 83
Block and Sully, 241, 247, 248
Boshell and Mack, 47
Bowery, 1, 15, 20, 29, 30
Brice, Fanny, 158, 190
Brimmers, 55
Bruns and Monroe, 68
Bryant and Richmond, 42, 59, 72
Burgesses, 42, 55, 71
Burns, George and Allen, Gracie, 5, 6, 157, 159 173, 181, 203, 205-36, 237, 241, 247
  appeal of, 226, 228
  Big Broadcast of 1932, 231, 232
  biography, 205-6, 222, 235
  dumbell jokes, 207-12, 218, 222, 225
  early sketches, 206-7, 208
  family motif, 221

International House, 227
  joke delivery, 228-30
  material, 230-31
  radio, 234
  television, 231, 232
  two-act formula, 212-28
Burdell and Saunders, 63
Bubbles, John, 205
Butler, Robert, 14
Byrne, John and Miss Helene, 42, 60-61, 69

Campbell, Mrs. Patrick, 126
Canterbury, 14, 22
Cantor, Eddie, 190, 205, 231
Carleton, William and Bilmer, Jennie, 37
Carter and Anderson, 42
Celeste and French, 10
Charke, Charlotte, 8
Chocolate Soldier, 130
Christy Minstrels, 9
Clarence and Warner, 55
Clive, Kitty, 7
Cocoanuts, 190
Codee, Ann, 198
Cohan, George M., 64, 67, 126
Cohan, Jerry and Helen, 64-67, 69, 71, 75
Collins and Oakes, 19
Collins, James and Wren, Martha, 23-24, 25, 27, 33
Colombine and Harlequin, 7, 8, 9, 10, 20
Colonial Theatre, 76, 145
Comedie-Italienne, 7
Commedia, 7, 8
Conways, 42, 63, 71
Coote, Bert and Kingsley, Julia, 83
Craven, and Hedges, 55

Daly and Derious, 71
Daly and Devere, 84
Daly, Arnold, 126
Davis, Bette, 223
Davis, Frank and Frannie, 42, 43, 47, 61, 71

326 Index

Daytons, 42
DeHaas, Edward and Carrie, 68
Delanow, Jeppe and Fanny, 42, 49-50, 51-52, 69
Delehenty and Hengler, 19
Delmay and Archer, 63
Dietrich, Marlene, 223
Dilke and Gray, 68
Dolly of the Dailies, 153
Dolans, 84
Donovans, 84
Dooley, Gordon and Moore, Martha, 198
Dooley and Sales, 237, 247

Ellis and Moore, 42, 43, 71
Emmett, Harry and Gracie, 64
English pantomime, 7

Fairbanks, Douglas, 201
Farrell and Leland, 39, 42, 72
Fenton, Mavel, 2
Fielding, John and Maggie, 26, 28, 30-31, 42, 43, 48, 71-72
Fields, W.C., 190
Filson and Errol, 63
Florence, W.J. and Malvina Pray, 20
Follies of 1907-9, 190, 191
Forman and Meredith, 42, 63
444 Theatre, 14, 17, 38
Fox's American Theatre, 14
Foy, Eddie, 126, 158
Frenc, A.B., 10
Frank and Alford, 25
Front Street Theatre, 14, 22

Gershwin, George, 190
Girl Friend, 190
Globe, 24, 39
Gone with the Wind, 223
Grandins, 83
Grinnells, 42

Haley, Jack, 157, 158, 159-60
Hallam troupe, 10
Hallen, Fred and Hart, Enid, 41, 42, 56, 61, 136
Hallen, Fred and Fullen, Mollie, 136-37, 139
Hamlet, 2
Hamton, Walter, 126
Harper, Ida Husted, 53
Harrigan, and Giles, 90
Harris, Sam, 64
Hart, Josh and Leclaire, Laura, 18
Hazards of Helen, 153
Healey, John and Nellie, 42, 57
Healey, Ted, 196-97
Heart of Maryland, 2
Henshaw, John and Ten Broeck, May, 42, 62, 71, 72

Hines and Remington, 42, 90
HMS Pinafore, 62
Howard Athenaeum, 14
Huber and Allyne, 42, 57, 59, 60, 69
Hughes, Andy and Annie, 42, 43, 44, 71
Hughes, Nic and May, 36
Hume and Lindsay, 42

Immigrants to America, 29-31, 32, 33-34, 42-46, 85-91
The Jazz Singer, 203

Jeromes, 42
Jessel, George, 205
Jolson, Al, 201
Jones and Montague, 42, 69

Keith, B.F. and Albee, E.F., 75-78
Kemble, Fanny, 10
Keno and Welch, 77
Kern, Jerome, 190
Knight, Tom and Cottle, Charley, 19

Lacy, Dan and Mrs., 55
Lacy, Frank and Reynold, Florence, 18
Lady of Lyons, 2
Lahr, Bert, 195-96, 205
Lombardo, Guy, 231
Love, Valentine and Maskell, Nellie, 21, 27
Lowe, Hoshua, (Jolo), 3

Male two-acts, 19-20, 23, 24, 25, 35-36, 59, 77, 104
  imitations of, 24, 25, 35-36, 104
Maltese Falcon, 243
Martens, 68
Maskell Burlesque Company, Nellie, 21
Matthews and Harris, 69
Maxwells, 42, 63
McAvoy, Fred and Annie, 23, 25, 41
McAvoy, Harry and Rogers, Emma, 42, 52, 71
McCarthy and Coleman, 42, 43, 71, 72
McIntyre and Heath, 126
Merry Widow, 130
Metropolitan Theater, 29
Miller, Henry, 126
Minstrelsy, 11-12, 15, 19, 22-23, 27-28, 59
Molly Maguires, 64-65
Montpelier's Theatre Comique, 14, 24, 39, 43, 60
Morosco and Gardener, 39, 42, 43, 71
Moore and Henderson, 25, 30, 33, 37
Moore, Clara, 71
Moore, Victor, 126
Morris Brothers and Trowbridges Opera House, 15
Morris, Dan and Josie Shelby, 23, 25, 30

Morton, Sam and Kitty, 27
Murphys, 42, 43, 71

Nawns, Tom and Hattie, 85
Nelsons, 39, 42
No No Nanette, 190
Nobles, Milton and Dolly, 83, 110

Olsen and Johnson, 5
Osborne, Harry and Wentworth, Fanny, 49

Palace, The, 1, 3, 157-58, 177, 192, 193, 195, 203, 212
Parker, Lew and Pauline, 58
Pastor, Tony, 14-15, 18, 20, 22, 24, 25, 26, 30, 36, 37-38, 40, 41, 42, 46, 49, 50, 51, 57, 70, 76, 77, 137
Peaks, Eddie, 49-50
Peasley, John and Lea, 39, 42, 43, 44, 49, 71
Perils of Pauline, 153
Pirates of Penzance, 62
Plymton, Eben and Agnes, Poctor, 83
Porter, Cole, 190
Punning, 63-64, 138, 232

Quilter and Goodrich, 19

Randall, William, 9
Ray, Bill and Maggie, 36
Ray, Johnny and Emma, 146, 241, 242
Rentz's Female Minstrels, Madame, 22, 38
Redmond and Blake, 42, 43, 49
Richmond, Adah, 37
Richmond and Glenroy, 42, 237
Rinders, 47
Rivers Melodeon, Frank, 14
Roach and Castleton, 42
Rogers, Charles and Vickers, Mattie, 42, 43, 44, 61, 71-72
Rogers, Will, 190
Rooney, Pat, 191-92, 205
Ross and Fenton, 1, 2-3, 4, 5
Ross, Charles, 1-4
Russell, Lillian, 126
Ryan and Lee, 247
Ryan and Richfield, 87-89, 103

Sanford, and May, 73
Shannons and Broadway, 1, 3
Sheerans, 55
Sheridan and Mack, 35
Siegel, Emily, 25, 37
Sinclair and Favor, 84
Smiths, 42, 43
Spaulding and Rogers Floating Circus Palace, 10
Stanley and Conway, 39, 72

Stanton, Hugh and Redding, Francesca, 81
Steffens, Lincoln, 100
Stephens, W.T. and Minnie Oscar Gray, 68
Stewart, K.K. and Kimball, Jennie, 27, 37
Stoopnagle and Budd, 5
Suratt, Valeska, 128, 131-34, 154
Swain, Carrie, 58-59

Tanguay, Eva, 126
Television, 5, 234
Temple, Shirley, 223
Templeton, William, 8
Thompson and her British Blondes, Lydia, 22
Thorne and Willett, 55
Thornton, James, 126
Tissots, 68
Trimbles Varieties, 14, 37
Trollope, Frances, 10
Tucker, Sophie, 127, 157
Twain, Mark, 22

Uncle Tom's Cabin, 125

Vagabond King, 190
Vallee, Rudy, 231
Variety Magazine, 3, 85, 86, 90, 121-22, 114, 127, 128, 129, 131, 136, 138, 140, 142, 145, 148, 152, 153, 154, 158, 159, 165, 170, 174, 176, 177, 179, 183, 184, 193, 195, 199, 201, 206, 218, 227, 233, 234
Vaudeville, 1, 4, 5, 6, 7-15, 17-21, 22-25, 28-35, 36-37, 38, 39-41, 42, 49, 50, 55, 56, 57-60, 61-62, 63, 65, 68-69, 71, 72-73, 75-115, 117, 118-21, 123, 124-25, 126, 127-29, 130-31, 135, 139, 140-51, 153-54, 155-56, 158-59, 161-62, 165, 166-67, 168, 174-80, 183, 189, 191, 194, 199, 201-2, 232-33, 238-39, 240, 241-42, 243, 244-45
  acting as sketch, 61-62, 125
  American humor, 44-45
  audience, 4, 10-11, 12-13, 35, 38, 39-41, 46, 49, 63, 65, 76, 77, 78-81, 83, 84, 86, 91, 98, 99-100, 114-15, 118-21, 124-25, 127, 131, 155-56, 158-59, 191, 194, 238-39, 243
  background, 7-15, 75
  Black teams, 92-93, 94
  blackface, 36-37, 57-60, 91-93, 94, 201
  "blue" material, 200
  boy-girl interactions, 46-48, 51, 183
  confrontation of two sexes in courtship and marriage, 104-9, 114-45, 153-54, 155, 161, 166-67, 175, 180, 183, 232-33, 240, 241-42
  costume, 127-29, 155
  depicting women's changing role in America, 5, 54-55
  dialect comedy, 28-35, 69, 71, 72-73, 91, 168
  domestic matters, 55-56

"dumb" acts, 161-62, 174-80, 199, 244-45
film as competitor, 201-2
immigrant act, 84-85, 87
immigrant humor, 42-43, 44, 79
Jewish sketches, 89-90
joke routines, 140-45, 165
juvenile character sketches, 94-95, 176
legitimate stage, and, 124, 126, 127
maturation of, 1, 6, 130-31
musical comedy, 135, 189
playlets, 81-82, 83
polite sketches, 75-115
production, 117
realism, 96-98
romantic comedy routines, 49, 56
rural themes, 99-102
sentimental, non-dialect sketches, 50-52, 60, 61, 67, 104-5, 139, 140
specialization of routines, 68-69
staging, 129, 165
standards, 121, 123, 155
status, 72
themes, 74
women dancers, 17-18, 21
women's rights, 54-55, 144-51
universal humor, 48
Vidocqs, 42

Watson, Harry, and Sherman, Lizzie, 23, 25, 27, 33, 37, 43, 72
Watson, and Hutchings, Alice, 42-43
WCTU, 109, 110
Weber and Fields Company, 2, 4, 124
Wheeler, Bert, 197
White Fawns, 22
White, Frank and Lillian, 42, 59-60
Whitings, 42, 63, 71
Wild, Johnny and Stanley, Blanche, 18, 27
Williams, Barney and Maria Pray, 20, 23
Williams, Billy and Mamie, 55
Williams, Bert, 190
Winnett, Thomas and Lottie, 27, 31
Wizard of Oz, 130
Women as popular entertainers, 17-18, 21-22, 23, 25, 36-37, 58, 70-72, 82, 115, 127, 128, 131-34, 143, 148, 152-53, 173-77, 186, 198, 223, 238, 244
Womens rights movement, 4, 11-13, 53-55, 148-53, 184-86, 223, 240-41, 246
Woodson and Bennett, 42

Yates, Richard, 7

Ziegfield, 190-91